D-Day
Through German Eyes

About the Author

Having passed out from the Royal Military Academy Sandhurst, Jonathan Trigg served as an infantry officer in the Royal Anglian Regiment, completing tours in Northern Ireland and Bosnia as well as in the Gulf. After working in the City, he now has his own business training the long-term unemployed to get them into work. His books have been translated into Norwegian, Swedish, Finnish, Danish, Polish, French, Czech and Dutch editions. His title *Death on the Don: The Destruction of Germany's Allies on the Eastern Front* was nominated for the 2014 Pushkin Prize for History.

D-Day
Through German Eyes

How the Wehrmacht Lost France

JONATHAN TRIGG

AMBERLEY

Other books by the author

Hitler's Legions series
Hitler's Gauls – The History of the French Waffen-SS
Hitler's Flemish Lions – The History of the Flemish Waffen-SS
Hitler's Jihadis – The History of the Muslim Waffen-SS
Hitler's Vikings – The History of the Scandinavian Waffen-SS
Hastings 1066
Death on the Don – The Destruction of Germany's Allies on the Eastern Front 1941–44 (nominated for the Pushkin Prize for Russian history)
The Defeat of the Luftwaffe – The Eastern Front 1941–45; Strategy for Disaster
Voices of the Flemish Waffen-SS: The Last Testament of the Oostfronters
Voices of the Scandinavian Waffen-SS: The Last Testament of Hitler's Vikings

Page 1: The Atlantikwall of legend – this is one of four giant 380mm guns of the Batterie Todt in the hamlet of Haringzelle near Cap Gris Nez – all were capable of hitting the English coast. (Library of Congress)

This edition published 2020

Amberley Publishing
The Hill, Stroud
Gloucestershire, GL5 4EP

www.amberley-books.com

British Library Cataloguing in Publication Data.
A catalogue record for this book is available from the British Library.

ISBN 978 1 3981 0323 8 (paperback)
ISBN 978 1 4456 8932 6 (ebook)

1 2 3 4 5 6 7 8 9 10

Typesetting by Aura Technology and Software Services, India.
Printed in the UK.

Contents

This book is dedicated to two very special people; to John Andrzejowksi for saving my life, and to Peena for making it worth saving.

Acknowledgements

This book was originally published to coincide with the 75th anniversary of the D-Day landings and the subsequent battle for France waged that same summer. It is a truly enormous subject, encompassing the largest amphibious invasion ever undertaken, and an ensuing campaign that involved more than two million men and an unfathomable amount of equipment, supplies and machinery.

The challenge I set myself with this book was to boil this enormous clash of arms down to the view from the trenches, as it were. As ever, my editor Shaun Barrington has been nothing but supportive in this effort and I offer him my thanks for that. I would also like to pay tribute to those who have gone before me; authors such as Holger Eckhertz, Bruce Connor, Vince Milano and Richard Hargreaves, who have done incredible work to tell the story of the humble *landser*, before they are all gone. A book with a focus on witness testimony wouldn't be able to be written without witnesses, and to the veterans who have been so generous with their time and memories, particularly Rudolf von Ribbentrop, thank you.

One regret I have had in writing this book is not to have included enough about the Allied landings in southern France in August 1944 and the subsequent running battle with Johannes Blaskowitz's army group – for that I apologise, I think it is a segment of the European war which is relatively unknown, and worthy of much more time and work than has hitherto been devoted to it.

Researching and writing any book can be a solitary task, and often an obsession – and this one has proven to be no different. Endless trips to view archives, interview veterans, added to hours of telephone calls, snatched meals and a grumpy demeanour, can put a huge strain on any family, but as ever my own has exhibited a deep well of understanding and affection for which I am forever grateful; to my amazing wife Rachel and our wonderful children, Maddy, Jack, thank you.

Notes on the text

The United Kingdom contains Scots, Welsh and Northern Irish, but the Germans tended to describe everyone from our islands as *English*, so I have left it at that. The same goes for the former Soviet Union, if a veteran has used the term 'Russian', then I have kept it as such. I have tended to use the German nomenclature for their units, e.g. the 352nd Infantry Division is written as *352. ID*, short for *352. Infanterie-Division*, and German ranks are likewise; Captain is *Hauptmann*, etc.; there is a table of comparative ranks as an appendix.

Every effort has been made to cite sources and contact copyright holders. If there are any omissions I apologise and the publishers will correct on reprint. As ever in any such work there are bound to be errors; they are all my own and I ask the readers' forbearance.

Introduction

A 53-year-old Texan chain-smoker of average height, with a dodgy knee and a love of Western novels – especially those by Zane Grey, a part-time dentist-cum author – was pacing up and down the thick carpet of a large room in the Georgian splendour of Southwick House, some five miles north of Portsmouth on the English south coast. Outside, rain was lashing down onto the roof and strong winds were rattling the black-out shutters, but inside, the silence was total. Seated a few feet away from the pacing man were half a dozen of the most senior officers in the Anglo-American military, all of them bar one in full uniform, heavy with their decoration ribbons; their shoes highly polished, their trousers knife-edged. Behind them was a gaggle of aides and middle-ranking officers – standing to one side a tall, thin, lowland Scot in the blue of the British Royal Air Force, papers and charts gripped in his large, bony hands. Suddenly the pacer – popularly known to one and all as 'Ike' – stopped, looked up from the carpet to his seated audience, and said three words: 'Okay, let's go.'

Twenty-four hours later, and about eight hundred miles away as the crow flies, it was still dark in the Bavarian Alps. The air was still, the only sound that of jackboots crunching on gravel, as the bored sentries – almost all of whom were immensely tall, blond-haired and blue-eyed – did their usual rounds of the jumble of lodges, tea-houses and holiday villas. In the chalet-style house at the epicentre of the whole smorgasbord of newly built luxury buildings, all was quiet, the staff having finished clearing up the glasses and tableware from the dining room and study panelled in Swiss pine, where just a few hours before their master and some of his closest confidants had been sat round an open fire reminiscing about 'the good old days'.

One of the last to leave in the early hours had been Joseph Goebbels, a diminutive Westphalian with a pronounced limp and holder of the Third Reich's post of Minister for Propaganda. Oddly enough, the pacing smoker and the disabled propagandist were both of mixed German-Dutch heritage, but there, any similarity ended. The former was a modest man, one of the greatest military coalition commanders the world has ever seen, who would go on to become the 34th President of his country, whereas the latter was a womanising, virulent anti-Semite, who would end up foully murdering his six young children before taking his own life.

This then was how D-Day started for both sides; for the Anglo-Americans with a considered decision taken by their senior military commanders – led by the U.S. General Dwight David Eisenhower – and for the Germans with their entire leadership asleep, oblivious, and in the dark.

The German Wehrmacht had been in France for four long years by the time the ramps of the Allied landing craft came crashing down into the surf on the morning of 6 June 1944, and had somehow – in this the fifth year of the war – managed to find no fewer than fifty-nine divisions to man Hitler's fabled *Festung Europa* – 'Fortress Europe', while still fighting the Red Army in the depths of the Soviet Union and holding the Anglo-Americans at bay in central Italy. Four years in which to prepare; to build their defences, plan their response to an attack, practise their counter-moves, observe and understand their enemy – they had even had the benefit of winning the dress rehearsal at Dieppe back in 1942: and yet that summer, they failed. In less than twenty-four hours after the first Allied boots hit French soil, 24,000 British and American paratroopers were joined ashore by 132,000 of their comrades landed by sea, accompanied by a staggering 20,000 vehicles. The landings were a stunning success. The Wehrmacht suffered anywhere between four to nine thousand casualties on the day itself (the exact figure has never been accurately established), and while the Allies lost more men – about 10,000 in all, with 4,414 confirmed killed – it was still only a fraction of the official pre-assault estimates of 10,000 killed and 30,000 wounded; Private Charles East of the American 29th Division (set to hit Omaha Beach) recalled a briefing in the days before the attack, when one of his officers told the assembled infantrymen that as they were the first wave it was expected that nine out of ten of them would become casualties on the day. East remembered looking around his comrades on hearing the news and thinking to himself: 'You poor bastards.'[1] Even the British Prime Minister, Winston Churchill, so often during the war the voice of boundless optimism, said to his beloved wife Clementine the night before the landings: 'Do you realise that by the time you wake up in the morning 20,000 men may have been killed?' He didn't mean Germans.

This then was D-Day – a day and a battle of such importance, of such immensity and scale, that its story has been told and re-told innumerable times in ink and on celluloid. Across those endless pages and reels of film stride the giant figures whose genius, flaws, and decisions – both good and bad – have come to symbolise both the day itself and the ten-week campaign in France that followed; men such as Ike, 'Monty', Omar Bradley, and on the other side, Erwin Rommel the 'Desert Fox', Gerd von Rundstedt the old Prussian warhorse, and Hitler himself – von Rundstedt's despised 'Bohemian corporal'. This book is *not* their story. This book is also not a description of the brilliance of the Allied build-up to D-Day and its masterful execution.

Instead, this books roots lie, not in the sands of the five beaches themselves, but in the dunes, trenches and bunkers overlooking them, where less than ten thousand Wehrmacht soldiers woke up that fateful morning to gasp at the largest naval force ever assembled. That armada, and the roughly eight Allied divisions (including the three airborne) designated as the D-Day assault units, would be faced at first by just half as many Wehrmacht formations; the 352., 709. and 716. *Infanterie Divisions (IDs)*, and the 21. *Panzerdivision*. From a German perspective, it was the men in these formations, and the junior and middle-ranking officers who commanded them, who would determine victory or defeat on D-Day. Thereafter, the men who survived D-Day would be reinforced by several dozen other divisions, including the cream of the German Army in western Europe. It wasn't just soldiers either, the men in field-grey and *panzerwaffe*-black were joined by Luftwaffe blue, as the famed German fighter arm – the *Jagdwaffe* – sent great swathes of its vastly experienced pilot cadres to France in an attempt to break the near-total Allied domination of the skies. Even the German Navy – the *Kriegsmarine* – so often the 'third wheel' of Hitler's Wehrmacht, tried to concentrate some sort of force to land a punch on the liberators.

All to no avail. In a campaign where even Allied commanders themselves conceded German individual and tactical superiority, they were utterly defeated, and the *Westheer* (the German nickname for their army in the West) lay smashed and slaughtered in the *bocage* of Normandy and the fields and valleys around the medieval French town of Falaise; and yet on D-Day itself the Germans came close – not to decisively repulsing the landings, the Allies were too strong and well-prepared for that – but to fulfilling many of the fears of the Allied planners by disrupting and savaging the assault so badly that the whole adventure would be put in jeopardy. With that German failure, as night fell on 6 June, the entire focus of the battle then became a race to bring to bear enough men and *matériel* to defeat the enemy – what military analysts sometimes call the 'battle of the reinforcements'. On paper, the Germans had the huge resources of the Westheer on hand, and the benefit of internal land communications and supply lines to shift their forces and concentrate them against the Allies. If they could achieve the necessary mass, the Germans had a chance, albeit a slim one, but a chance nonetheless, of grinding the Allies into a sort of stalemate in northern France; and then who knows? A negotiated settlement perhaps? Extremely unlikely admittedly, but history is full of unexpected twists and turns. Away from the realms of conjecture, the priority for Nazi Germany was crystal clear: hold France. But they failed, the advantages they had were worn down by a superior Allied war machine, and then further squandered by the Germans themselves, until their defeat was simply a matter of when, and not if.

How did this happen? How did the German war machine fail so badly? A hint can perhaps be found in one historian's view of the Imperial German Army's performance in World War One: 'It displayed less a genius for war than a gift for improvisation; meeting unexpected challenges with limited resources, making the best tactically and operationally of questionable strategies and policies until the machine broke down and the men had nothing more to give.'[2] As it turned out, this would be an apt description for the same army a quarter of a century later in Normandy. The amount of paper produced about what became the Normandy campaign could cover all five landing beaches, but very little of that valuable work has been written from the German perspective, and even less from that of the men who did the fighting; not the great names, the Rommels or the von Rundstedts, but the humble German soldier – the *landser* – and the NCOs and officers who led him and shared his rations, his dangers and his fears. This story is of German failure, seen through German eyes, and primarily told by the Germans who were themselves there that fateful summer.

1

Festung Europa – 'Fortress Europe'

In the conclusion to the harrowing open scene of Steven Spielberg's 1998 D-Day film epic, *Saving Private Ryan*, two American soldiers who have survived the carnage on Omaha Beach are confronted by two enemy soldiers who clamber out of their trench, throw away their weapons, thrust their hands into the air and try to surrender. The duo are clearly terrified, and pathetically plead for their lives as the Americans bear down on them – whatever they say is to no avail, and both are shot dead in cold blood, before their killers stoop down and start rifling their pockets for mementos or anything of intelligence value – probably both. The actor and star of the film, the American everyman Tom Hanks, looks away, his face a mixture of revulsion at what the soldiers have done, and relief at having survived the slaughter on the beach.

To Western eyes – so used to the stereotype of Nazi atrocities versus Allied fair-play, that scene is shocking enough, and becomes even more so when what the executed men say before they are shot is translated into English: '*Nestřílejte. Já jsem nikoho nezabil. Já jsem Čech.*' It's not German, it's Czech, and translates as: 'Don't shoot. I haven't killed anyone. I'm Czech.'

Czech? Surely this must be one of those film errors that end up in a bloopers TV programme – nothing more than an extras casting mishap. It wasn't. Spielberg was deliberately highlighting a little-known fact, that a significant proportion of the ten thousand or so men in field-grey defending the beaches that day weren't native Germans at all; they were Russians, Poles, Georgians, Turkmen, and yes, Czechs. If he had the time and the capability, it wouldn't have been a surprise if Spielberg had gone on to show that many of the weapons those self-same 'German' defenders were using mirrored their own mixed nationalities, being Russian, Czech, and even French; the terrible irony of French tank turrets manned by Polish gunners, firing on Allied infantry, as those same men sought to begin the liberation of western Europe, is tragic indeed.

So, was this Fortress Europe? Was this how the Germans were prepared to oppose the landings the whole world knew were coming; with troops who weren't even German, armed with little but personal weapons, manning half-empty trenches, facing the best-equipped, best-trained and most heavily supported landing force in history?

Just over four years before, on 10 May 1940, a Wehrmacht fresh from its conquest of Poland, and imbued with the new doctrine of *blitzkrieg*, had befuddled the Allies by somehow getting its armour through the heavily forested Ardennes region, and then leaping over the Meuse River at Sedan to charge to the sea at Abbeville and effectively defeat the combined armies of France, Britain, Belgium and the Netherlands as a result. The 'miracle of Dunkirk' saved the majority of the British Expeditionary Force – basically the bulk of Britain's Army - but nothing could be done to save a French Army that had now been attacked by the Germans three times in seventy years. Out-thought and out-fought, the successors to the victorious *poilus* of the First World War were hammered into shards, until on 22 June a humbled French high command reluctantly signed the Second Armistice (a surrender by any other name) at Compiègne.

After a brief few months during which Berlin half-heartedly prepared its Army and Navy to launch an invasion of mainland Britain over the Channel – and its airforce was comprehensively defeated in the Battle of Britain – German eyes turned east towards the communist Soviet Union, its ideological nemesis, and remained there pretty much throughout 1941–43. Meanwhile, garrison life in occupied France settled down to the monotony of a waiting game, as the reluctant conscript and future Nobel Prize-winning author *Gefreiter* Heinrich Böll noted in a letter home to his schoolteacher wife, Annemarie: 'If just once we could come face to face with the English it would be something different from this waiting, this eternal waiting.'

The Battle of the Atlantic, the war in North Africa and the Mediterranean, all caused concern among the ranks of the German armed forces and the populace at large, but were as nothing compared to the meat-grinder in the East, where Nazi Germany was suffering roughly thirty thousand fatalities a month during 1943 alone.[1] In fact, so deadly had the eastern fighting become that the German High Command – the *Oberkommando der Wehrmacht* or OKW – calculated that in true *All Quiet on the Western Front*-style, even on an inactive sector of the Russian front where nothing worth reporting was occurring, a standard German infantry corps was losing between five to ten men killed and fifteen to twenty-five wounded *per day* to Red Army snipers, random shelling and air attack.

One consequence of this savage attrition was that Berlin sought to rest and refit divisions burnt out in the fighting in Russia by moving them wholesale to locations in safe zones far away from the Red Army. There, the survivors could recover, eat, drink, take some leave, receive fresh drafts of recruits and new equipment and prepare to head back East – and where better to do that but in '*la belle France*'? A young engineer *Oberleutnant* posted to *Grenadier-Regiment. 736 (GR. 736)* of the *716. Infanterie-Division (ID)* near Courselles in Normandy remembered:

> It was said of the troops in France that they 'lived like Gods'... And you know, when I joined the 716th ... I realised what a lucky swine I was. The food was excellent, and it was possible to buy virtually anything you wanted on the black market ... Every morning I thought of my brother in combat in Russia and I felt extremely guilty.[2]

Most of the other German soldiers likewise posted to the West were just as glad not to be serving in Russia.

> In many ways I was pleased with the posting. You see my brothers and friends had been on the Russian front, and they had terrible stories of the conditions there. Many men returned without fingers or eyelids because of frostbite. By contrast, a posting to France was renowned as a comfortable ride.[3]

It wasn't only the soldiers themselves who were often overjoyed to be sent west and not east, it was their families too: 'My family were most relieved that I was sent to France, which we imagined as a true "land of plenty".'[4]

Most German soldiers posted to France were initially only lucky enough to savour its delights for a few weeks or months at a time before shipping out back to the war, but that began to change after the Dieppe raid in the summer of 1942. On 19 August that year an amphibious force of mainly Canadian troops, backed by the British

Royal Navy and Royal Air Force, landed on the shingle beach at Dieppe in northern Normandy as a kind of 'test-run' for D-Day. In barely ten hours of fighting, over four thousand Allied soldiers, sailors and airmen were killed, wounded or taken prisoner, and controversy over the efficacy of the assault has raged ever since, despite the views of its main planner, Vice-Admiral Lord Louis Mountbatten: 'I have no doubt that the Battle of Normandy was won on the beaches of Dieppe. For every man who died in Dieppe, at least ten more must have been spared in Normandy in 1944.'

Many observers and historians – notably quite a few Canadians – have disagreed with his analysis! But what no-one disagrees about is that in the aftermath of the battle both sides sought to learn lessons from it to prepare for the 'next time', not least senior German officers such as their military supremo in the West – the *Oberbefehlshaber West* or OB West, Gerd von Rundstedt: 'Just as we are going to evaluate these experiences for the future, so is the assaulting force … perhaps even more so as it has gained the experience dearly. He will not do it like this a second time!'[5]

Thereafter, von Rundstedt harangued Hitler with unending tales of gloom regarding the state of the Westheer and of the Wehrmacht's defences as a whole, and the result – finally - was a *Führer Directive* – the written orders Hitler used to shape the Third Reich's conduct of the war. These Directives were legally binding, were to be followed to the letter and superseded any other law – in this case No. 51 of the seventy-four promulgated by Hitler in total. Issued on 3 November 1943, Hitler addressed the potential opening of a second front in the West and warned of 'consequences of staggering proportions' if the Allies should gain a foothold in Continental Europe. The directive laid the foundation for what became known to both sides as 'Fortress Europe' – for the Allies a deadly barrier that threatened the success of any landings, and for the Germans a defensive wall and infrastructure of such power that it would 'throw the enemy back into the sea'.

The overall result was envisioned to be a major strengthening of Nazi Germany's position in the West, which would enable it to defeat any Anglo-American landing. In Hitler's eyes, such a defeat would wrest the initiative away from London and Washington and give him at least a year in which to switch his forces east and finally crush the Red Army once and for all. As he declared to his cronies: 'Once defeated the enemy will never again try to invade,' and a victory would allow him to redeploy his forces to the East, to 'revolutionise the situation there... The whole outcome of the war depends on each man fighting in the West, and that means the fate of the Reich as well!'

If he could do it, the Nazi dictator would have pulled off one of the greatest and most unlikely turnarounds in military fortune in history – but there was a mountain to climb. Everything that *could* be wrong with the German military in the West in 1943 *was* wrong.

Starting at the top – there wasn't one. Gerd von Rundstedt was OB West, his second tilt at the role, and from his headquarters under a school in the Saint Germain-en-Laye *quartier* of northwestern Paris, he was ideally positioned to lead the defence of Fortress Europe against any Allied landings – except that wasn't his job – in fact it was no-one's job except perhaps Hitler himself, although as was his usual *modus operandi* the dictator preferred overlapping and confusing layers of command and control for his subordinates, whilst avoiding taking the specific responsibility himself. It was a style of leadership that would handicap Berlin's conduct of the war from its inception to its conclusion, and in many ways was a replica of the Wilhelmian-system that had contributed to Germany's defeat in the First World War.

That meant when von Rundstedt studied the wall maps and orders of battle in his headquarters, there were huge elements he could neither control, nor indeed influence much at all. Topping this list were the Luftwaffe and Kriegsmarine in the West, closely followed by the inordinately large German Army in Scandinavia, and, less controversially, Italy and the Balkans. His reach didn't even extend to all ground forces in France, Belgium and the Netherlands, as the military governorships of Paris and Brussels were independent, as were all SS and *Gestapo* operations. That left him with two Army Groups – *Heeresgruppen B* and *G* – the former in northern France under his fellow *generalfeldmarschall*, Erwin Rommel, of 'Desert Fox' fame, and the latter covering southern France under *Generaloberst* Johannes Blaskowitz. His main strike force was Panzer Group West – *Panzergruppe West* – under *General der Panzertruppe* Leo Geyr von Schweppenburg, which was jointly – yes, jointly – controlled by him and Hitler himself.

The contrast with the simplicity of the Anglo-American Supreme Headquarters Allied Expeditionary Forces (SHAEF for short) command structure, with Eisenhower at its pinnacle, is stark, and even more so when considered at an operational level. The Allies, rightly, saw the coming campaign to be one where success relied heavily on all three arms operating as one – and given the failure of Germany's *Operation Sealion* to invade Great Britain in 1940, the Third Reich should have been far more aware of the need for it. Any landing would have to be seaborne and would require substantial naval forces, those same forces would need to be protected against air attack, and last but not least, the forces landed would have to be big enough and powerful enough to defeat the opposition they met on the beaches and beyond.

So, von Rundstedt would be able to control *some* of the Army, and only the Army, and here Directive 51 had two major effects on those same troops: firstly, the German Army's infantry divisions – still the bulk of its manpower – were to be restructured, supposedly to learn the lessons of the Russian war as well as prepare more effectively for a possible landing, but in reality to increase the paper size of the Army by creating new formations, primarily to man Fortress Europe. Secondly, it began a marked shift in troop strength from East to West, including the *panzerwaffe*, Germany's rightly famed armoured branch that would provide von Rundstedt with much of his eventual combat power. There would also be a third major impact, which would be to revitalise the hitherto moribund programme of fortification building along the European Atlantic coast started back in 1941. This was not to OB West's liking; 'We Germans do not indulge in the tired Maginot spirit,' as he famously stated.

The divisional reorganisation of the infantry arm was a very big deal indeed, given that, despite the panzer myth, the vast majority of the German Army was composed of infantry foot-sloggers manning so-called *Type M1939* divisions. In fact, as late as the beginning of 1944 fully 85% of the Army still wasn't motorised.[6] That is to take nothing away from the M1939 infantry divisions. After all it had been these units, manned by well-trained and well-led volunteers and conscripts who had conquered most of Europe in 1939–40, and almost beaten the Soviets back in '41. As such, an M1939 formation was a pretty formidable beast. Each one was meant to have around 17,734 men, organised into three infantry and one artillery regiment in a tri-tiered structure; each battalion had three companies or batteries, with the infantry regiments also having three other supporting units of integral heavy and light guns, infantry cannons, anti-tank guns, mortars and reconnaissance troops. There were also battalions of assault engineers – so-called *Pioniere* – specially trained to both create their own obstacles and destroy the enemy's, along with signals, supply, military police, postal, medical and veterinary troops – the last being a very important part of the division given the Germans' massive reliance on horses. Every company had no fewer than nine horse-drawn wagons ferrying its equipment: three one-horse wagons for the machine-guns and mortars, two four-horse wagons for ammunition, one for the field-kitchen (the famed *Gulasch-kanone*), a pair of two-horse wagons for the soldiers' back-packs, and another two-horse for rations – in all no fewer than twenty-one men of every company in the Army had as their main role either driving these wagons or caring for the horses that pulled them, including feeding each horse their standard daily ration of approximately twenty pounds of oats, hay and straw, dependent on the horse's weight.[7]

The new structure – christened rather unimaginatively the *M1944-Type* – was an echo of the Army reorganisation Falkenhayn had presided over in late 1914 after the appalling casualties of the Langemarck offensives, when Imperial Germany had found itself in much the same position as its successor state; short of manpower and heralding a downsizing operation as bringing more flexibility than the previous divisional configuration, as well as increasing firepower with the addition of more machine-guns. As with much in the Third Reich in 1944, this was little more than propaganda. The reality was that the strength of each division was almost thirty-per cent lower, reduced to only 12,772 men. This was mainly achieved by disbanding the third battalion of every rifle regiment and making the artillery regiment smaller – other sub-units were slimmed down too. Even with these drastic cuts, Germany didn't have the manpower to fill the restructured divisions, so with huge reluctance the Nazi leadership had no option but to formally incorporate hated *Untermensch*[8] into their depleted ranks. This admission meant each M1944 division had 1,455 so-called eastern *Hiwis*[9] on the ration-roll, complementing 11,317 Germans. Not that this was achieved in every reorganised division before D-Day; *77. ID* for example, formed in Poland in the winter of 1943, mainly with men from the Württemberg towns and cities of Stuttgart, Ludwigsburg and Esslingen, could only muster 9,095 Germans alongside its 1,410 Hiwis, to man its sector in between the Cotentin Peninsula and Brittany in the early summer of 1944 – although many of the former were veterans, having previously been members of *355. ID*, shattered on the Russian front the previous year. But almost overnight following the restructuring, the German Army's Order of Battle (OOB) swelled dramatically, and the Westheer went from its 1943 strength of forty-six divisions to a far more potent-sounding fifty-nine.[10] This was still a very large force, comprising as it did a full twenty per cent of the Army's manpower and thirty per cent of its armour; 850,000 men and 1,552 panzers and assault-guns. The *Ostheer* (German nickname for their army in the East) was far bigger – there were no fewer than 193 German divisions facing the Red Army in the East - but the East was always the main battle zone of the European war, and Berlin positioned the majority of its forces there throughout.

However, notwithstanding that the Russian front was Berlin's top priority, the fact remains that the Germans had no fewer than four armies in France and the Benelux countries, and more troops further north in Scandinavia – eighteen divisions more in fact. Eighteen divisions in Norway and Denmark? In Norway this meant that there was one German soldier stationed there for every eight citizens (plus one German civilian administrator for every 3,700 locals – the corresponding figure in France was one for every fifteen thousand!), and that the occupying forces in peaceful Denmark were almost ten times as strong as the Kingdom's entire pre-war army. What were they there for? Was this a case of Hitlerian idiocy, or was there any reasonable basis for this seemingly inexplicable situation? Directive 51 provides part of the answer. Hitler believed that the Allies might well land in Scandinavia! Indeed, he stated in his directions to the Kriegsmarine, and indeed all three branches of the Wehrmacht, that '...it might be called upon to repulse simultaneous enemy landings in Norway and Denmark.' In a document barely the length of one side of A4 paper he mentions Norway twice and Denmark no fewer than fourteen times – it is quite simply staggering, and from a German perspective a truly criminal dispersion of fighting power. Or was it more nuanced than that?

Hitler had always seen the war through the prism of a struggle for otherwise sparse natural resources; be that food, minerals, or most important of all – oil. The Reich had some of the first, not enough of the second, and tiny amounts of the last. In Hitler's view, therefore, the war machine he needed for global conquest had to safeguard two supply lines for itself above all; iron ore from neutral Sweden and oil from Rumania's Ploiesti fields. Protecting the former had been the driver for the invasion of Norway in the first place, and when the British had followed up their abortive expedition there back in 1940 with the successful Lofoten raid in '41,[11] it was enough to give the Nazi dictator nightmares in the small hours. Correspondingly, a surprise (and it would be a big surprise to everyone, not least

Washington) Allied assault in the Balkans capable of cutting off the flow of Rumanian oil, was a threat Hitler thought he couldn't ignore – especially when Tito's growing Partisan army in Yugoslavia could provide any landing force with a ready-made welcoming party; hence the twenty-one German divisions in Greece and the Balkans. Taken at face value, it would seem that the Wehrmacht had significant forces hundreds of miles away from the anticipated main theatre of combat, albeit for some understandable reasons – what was clearly missing was accurate intelligence to enable the Nazi high command to concentrate those forces in the most likely landing areas. This, Berlin never achieved. The war waged by Nazi Germany between 1939 and 1945, despite all the myths of Teutonic efficiency, was jaw-droppingly sloppy in so very many ways, but when it came to military intelligence it surpassed itself. While the Allies diverted significant resources into every form of intelligence gathering; signals (SIGINT), communications (COMINT), and human (HUMINT), exemplified by the genius of the Bletchley Park *Ultra* programme, Moscow's masterly use of *maskirovka,* and the Allies' Operation *Fortitude* deception plans, Hitler opted to subject the Third Reich's intelligence effort to the full force of his default internal 'divide and rule' policy by allowing the SS to establish and build its own intelligence organisation to rival the Wehrmacht's existing structure – the *Abwehr.* Formed in 1920, in contradiction to the strictures laid down by the Versailles Treaty, the Berlin-headquartered Abwehr grew in size and importance over the succeeding two decades, but never managed to match the power and expertise of its peers to east and west. Its problems started at the top with its boss – *Vizeadmiral* Wilhelm Canaris. An eminently cultured man, Canaris was fluent in six languages and a keen equestrian. At first a pro-Nazi – he was one of the first senior individuals in the military to advocate that German Jews should wear the yellow Star of David on their clothes – he became convinced Germany would lose the war and delved deeply into anti-Hitlerian conspiracy. English historian Hugh Trevor-Roper described Canaris as 'more interested in anti-Nazi intrigue than in his official duties',[12] with his 'negligent rule' leading to an Abwehr that was in his estimation 'rotten with corruption, notoriously inefficient, [and] politically suspect'. Such a charge could not be levelled at its upstart challenger – Reinhard Heydrich's SS Security Service (*Sicherheitsdienst* – SD). Another outwardly cultured individual – Heydrich was an accomplished violinist, as well as a keen horseman, and he and Canaris would often ride together in

Berlin's parks – Heydrich was also nicknamed the 'Blond Beast', for his Aryan looks and his addiction to the sort of vile atrocities with which the Nazis are synonymous. The architect of the Holocaust and the commander of the *Einsatzgruppen* death squads, Heydrich wished to control all internal and external intelligence bodies in the Reich, and used the SD to try and supplant the Abwehr. In this endeavour he was helped by the Abwehr's own failings as it stumbled from one cock-up to the next, most tellingly in the East, where German intelligence gathering under Reinhard Gehlen's Enemy Armies East section (*Fremde Heere Ost* – FHO) proved woeful, seemingly forever underestimating the strength of the Red Army or failing to predict its intentions. However, the SD's own foreign intelligence arm – the *Ausland-SD* – was even more amateurish than its cousin, with both organisations overly relying on the recruitment and use of agents to carry out their tasks – many of whom turned out to be useless, or double agents, or both. The Abwehr's cack-handed attempt at industrial sabotage in the USA – Operation *Pastorius* – was a classic case in point, with all six agents discovered, arrested and executed.

It was in signals intelligence and cryptography where Berlin felt the gap most keenly, as decentralisation of effort and a lack of top-level command, control and coordination proved the Germans' undoing, as attested to by one of their own frontline signals intelligence gatherers operating in France near Lille.

> We thought the invasion would be around Calais, but the English deceived us. Again and again we heard on the airwaves that they seemed to be giving orders to start extensive troop movements towards the environs of Dover – we heard both the English and American orders ... it was very skilled because it caused us to think that that was where the invasion would come from.[13]

Eventually Hitler concurred with the American historian Robin Winks's view of the Abwehr: 'an abysmal failure, failing to forecast *Torch*, or *Husky*, or *Overlord*', and after a stormy meeting between the dictator and Canaris the organisaton was formally dissolved by *Führer* decree on 18 February 1944, and its departments taken over by Heydrich's SD – not that the Blond Beast could revel in his final victory, having died in agony two years previously from wounds sustained in an assassination attempt by two British-trained Czechoslovak agents in Prague. The change in management from Canaris to Heydrich's successor Walter Schellenberg had no discernible impact on the

German intelligence effort. FHO's counterpart in the West – *Fremde Heere West*, FHW – sent Berlin Situation Report No. 1288 on D-Day itself stating:

> While the Anglo-Saxon enemy landing on the coast of Normandy represents a large-scale operation, the forces employed comprise only a relatively small portion of the troops available. Of the 60 large formations held in southern Britain, only 10-12 divisions, including airborne troops, appear to be participating so far ... according to an Abwehr report of June 2, the forces in southern England are divided into two army groups; the 21ˢᵗ British Army Group and the 1ˢᵗ U.S. Army Group ... not a single unit of the 1ˢᵗ U.S. Army Group has so far been committed [because it didn't exist!] ... this suggests that the enemy is planning a further large scale operation in the Channel area, which one would expect to be aimed at the coastal sector in the Pas de Calais area ... the progress of the landing so far can hardly have lived up to the expectations of the enemy command as it included numerous setbacks and many abortive attempts to land.

FHW's boss – the bespectacled Alexis *Graf* von Roenne – almost certainly knew that this estimate was false or at the very least misleading, but he had turned against the Nazis a long time before, and was actively working for their downfall. A man of deep and abiding religious faith, as far as he was concerned the racism of the Nazi state was incompatible with his Christianity and it needed to be destroyed. He played no part in the 20 July plot but was caught up in the aftermath, arrested by the Gestapo and interrogated. He was sentenced to death by Roland Freisler's notorious kangaroo People's Court on 5 October 1944, and seven days later he was bound hand and foot in Berlin-Plötzensee prison, hung on a meat hook by piano wire and slowly strangled to death. On the eve of his execution he wrote to his wife: 'In a moment now I shall be going home to our Lord in complete calm and in the certainty of salvation.'

Von Roenne was undoubtedly a brave and courageous officer, but his service was a military failure, much as its counterpart was in Japan, and for pretty much the same reason; the most competent officers those two nations produced simply saw them as career dead-ends: '... the German military caste downplayed the importance of logistics and intelligence in favour of operational expertise.'[14]

It would be overly simplistic to say the opposite was true in the Anglo-American armies – especially the British Army where there has always been a cachet to being a member of a regiment with a fighting reputation – but certainly in the US Army in the Second World War at least, there was a policy of steering their best and brightest towards service in the support arms so they could properly fight the 'war of matériel' they believed, quite rightly, that they would win. Hitler, on the other hand, believed in the 'war of the man', specifically the Aryan *superman*, and that this would bring Nazi Germany ultimate victory – in this belief he was clearly delusional. Not that it was his only self-delusion, he also believed himself a devoted student of history, and would often regale (or more usually bore) his senior officers and other visitors with marathon monologues comparing his own campaign strategies and battle plans to those of some of the great commanders of history – of whom his favourite was the eighteenth-century Prussian king, Frederick II, known to posterity as Frederick the Great. The Nazi dictator saw much of the Third Reich's military accomplishments mirroring that of Frederick's Prussia, especially as the tide of war turned against the Nazis, as it often had against Frederick before his ultimate victories. However, as with so much of Hitler's world view, he only saw what he wanted to, and forgot inconvenient truths. One such was the Prussian monarch's own most oft-quoted and well-known military dictum: 'He who defends everything defends nothing.'[15] The Hohenzollern king here distilled much of what would become the most important tenet of Carl von Clausewitz's nineteenth-century military masterpiece *On War* – namely 'The talent of the strategist is to identify the decisive point and to concentrate everything on it, removing forces from secondary fronts and ignoring lesser objectives.' To paraphrase the twentieth-century British historian and military theorist Basil Liddell Hart, success in war can be boiled down to just one word: concentration. To win you must mass everything you have at one critical point, ruthlessly stripping men and resources from everywhere else to achieve the superiority needed for victory. Hitler, despite all his professed knowledge of war and the great commanders, singularly failed to learn this lesson, and for that the world can be profoundly grateful. From the remoteness of his multiple headquarters in Berlin, East Prussia or Bavaria (he hardly ever visited France during the war – back in 1940 he made a whistlestop tour of Paris in a few hours, saw the Channel coast at Cap Gris Nez and met Franco at Hendaye), the Nazi leader looked at a map of Fortress Europe, read pages of shockingly awful intelligence reports, and decided he had little choice but to defend the West against an Allied assault by spreading his available forces all over it. Thus, eighteen divisions languishing in

Norway and Denmark, occupying towns and cities where no Allied soldier would set foot until after the German capitulation in 1945. Others, such as *General der Infanterie* Kurt von der Chevallerie's *1. Armee* were stationed along the Atlantic coast facing out towards the Bay of Biscay, where storms throughout the year made it wholly unsuitable for an Allied landing approach. Nevertheless, the men of the *158., 159., 276.* and *708. IDs* found themselves garrisoning Gascony and the Basque country all the way south to the Spanish border at Biarritz. Even worse for the Germans, the *landsers* eyeing the grape harvest in Bordeaux were joined by the hard-bitten Silesian veterans of *11. Panzerdivision* under their dashing ex-Hussar and Knight's Cross winning commander, Wend von Wietersheim. It was true that three of those four infantry formations were reserve or so-called *static* units, but the *276* had a cadre of veterans from the old *38. ID* which had served with distinction during the 1943 battles on the River Dnieper, deep in Soviet Russia.

Seemingly not content with frittering away over sixty thousand men and a hundred panzers and assault guns on the Atlantic coast, Hitler and the OKW also decided that the Second Front could well be on the French rivieria, which was positively teeming with the men, guns and vehicles of no fewer than nine infantry divisions and yet another panzer division – this time the experienced and reliable *9*, its ranks filled with almost thirteen thousand men – many of them Austrians – and its sub-units sporting some 150 panzers and assault guns, including at least fifteen brand-new Mark V Panthers. Those Panthers were part of *General der Infanterie* Friedrich Wiese's Avignon-headquartered *19. Armee*. As with their neighbours in *1. Armee*, the *19* was not an OKW priority for manpower replacements and modern equipment, but a 10-divison strong German field army was nothing to be sniffed at, and although middle-aged reservists made up a large proportion of its overall establishment, it also had more than a sprinkling of combat veterans, such as in *271. ID*, formed in December 1943 from a cadre of men from the experienced *137. ID*.

Together, *1.* and *19. Armee*'s constituted *Heeresgruppe G,* responsible for Fortress Europe roughly south of the Loire River. Its commander was the East Prussian Johannes Blaskowitz. Not a member of Prussia's *junker* aristocracy (his father was a pastor), Blaskowitz mirrored his boss Gerd von Rundstedt in his slight build and desire to keep the Army out of politics, although he differed from his superior in his semi-public challenges to the brutalities of the Nazi regime, most notably when he succeeded von Rundstedt as military governor of occupied Poland in 1940 and wrote several memos to higher command detailing his concerns about SS atrocities against civilians: 'It is misguided to slaughter tens of thousands of Jews and Poles as is happening at present... The idea that one can intimidate the Polish population by terrorism and rub their noses in the dirt will certainly prove false.'

In fact, in February that year he prepared a list of no fewer than thirty-three complaints against the SS including the mass rape of Jewish women and what he described as a 'whipping orgy' in Nasielsk,[16] and passed them up the chain of command – an act that infuriated both Hitler and *Reichsführer-SS* Heinrich Himmler, and led to his sacking on 29 May.

Even the British Channel Islands contributed to German military constipation, with *Generalleutnant Graf* Rudolf von Schmettow's occupying 319. *ID* briefly becoming the Wehrmacht's largest division, with an unbelievable thirty-five thousand men on strength, as the dictator feared a pre-landing on Jersey or Guernsey as a prelude to an attack on France. After D-Day many of those same men would be shipped back to the mainland to fight and die in Normandy, but thousands more would stay in St Helier and St Peter Port until they laid down their arms and surrendered at 7.14am on 9 May 1945, having not fired a shot in anger against the Allied landings in France. The only place Hitler didn't seem to anticipate an Allied attack was over the snow-capped Pyrenees, so no divisions were stationed in its foothills, nor panzers in its passes!

This then was the fatally muddled thinking running through Directive 51, the very document that set the blueprint for all the German preparations for D-Day; eighteen separate divisions walking out in Copenhagen and Oslo, another one doing the same in Jersey, and fifteen more in southern France – thirty-four in total, with two of Germany's twenty-nine panzer formations among them. This at a time when, in northern Russia, *General der Artillerie* Herbert Loch's 18. *Armee* was battling a growing Red Army without a single panzer division in its ranks. The consequences for the Westheer of this 'defend-all' strategy were to be devastating, especially as Germany's intelligence failings led directly to their High Command selecting the wrong assault zones; not once but twice – leading to disaster on both the Eastern and soon-to-be Western fronts.

Amidst this cornucopia of major German formations spread out across the West, the most powerful was Erwin Rommel's *Heeresgruppe B*. Headquartered in the dramatic twelfth-century Château de La

Roche-Guyon in the Île-de-France region west of Paris, the 52-year-old Württemberger commanded no fewer than thirty-one divisions in northern France and Belgium. The Pas de Calais region was viewed by almost everyone on the German side as the most likely landing site for the Allies, with its hop, skip and a jump proximity to Dover, and its profusion of ports as possible logistics bases. Consequently, the larger and stronger of Rommel's two armies – *15. Armee* – held the area with an impressive eighteen divisions. Led by the tried and trusted Lorrainain Hans von Salmuth, the *15.* was first in line for just about anything and everything that came the Westheer's way; be it men or *matériel*, with its sister formation to the west, *7. Armee*, being very much the poor relation. This was mirrored in their respective commanders. Von Salmuth was an extremely experienced soldier having served on the Eastern Front since the launch of Barbarossa. He fought at Sevastopol under von Manstein, and at Voronezh in early 1943, when his Army had huge chunks bitten out of it by a vengeful Red Army. Friedrich Dollmann of *7. Armee* on the other hand hadn't seen combat since the fall of France four years earlier. In that time he had gone the way of so many officers in the comfortable West, succumbing to the earthly pleasures of the *gourmand*; fine food, excellent wine and plenty of cigars. Unable, and probably unwilling, to devote much energy to turning his designated defence sector into a bastion of Fortress Europe, he spent his time visiting museums and on sightseeing trips across Brittany and Normandy where his twelve divisions were based. It would be these divisions which would end up being the ones facing the Allied landings in early June. So what sort of shape were they in?

The cream of the crop they were not. France had long been a posting for those not deemed young or fit enough to face the rigours and savagery of the Eastern front, or equally, for men and units who had been maimed or burnt-out over there. *Gefreiter* Gustav Winter of *716. ID*, based on the coast near Colleville, was in many ways typical of the rank and file in *7. Armee*:

> I suffered very badly from frostbite during the first winter in Russia, in 1941. We had no winter clothes at that time, and in the unheated panzers the temperature could go down to minus twenty or thirty Celsius... As you can see I lost the little fingers on each of my hands ... also the tip of my nose, and my toes were damaged as well.[17]

Veterans like Winter were sprinkled thoughout *7. Armee*; the *353. ID* drew its cadre from the now-defunct *328.*, and the *77. ID* had men in its ranks from the shattered *374*, as Rainer Hartmetz explained: 'We didn't know much about the shape of the other German troops in France. Our battalion came from Russia, and that was another world.'

Hartmetz was already a *Feldwebel* – a junior NCO – at age nineteen, in the *77.*'s *Schnell* ('Quick') *Bataillon* – so-called because it was meant to be able to deploy anywhere within the divisional area at speed; and how was it meant to achieve this feat? Pedal power. Hartmetz and his comrades were issued bicycles – as were numbers of *7. Armee*'s troopers; *243. ID* had an entire regiment on them for instance, along with a second on horseback, and its third supposedly vehicle-borne, although most of its transport hadn't arrived as yet. *77.* and *243. IDs* were not field-grade frontline divisions to be sure, but they were a step-up from almost half of Dollmann's formations, which were designated as *static* or *fortress divisions* – and it would be units holding this categorisation that would do much of the fighting on the beaches.

Just as in the First World War, the German plan for the Second – as far as there was a plan – was for a series of 'short, sharp conflicts', with each one only lasting a few months, so allowing the armed services to resupply, reinforce and re-equip in between, and enable the homeland to cope without the massive disruption of converting to the kind of total war economy that transformed Britain and the Soviet Union in particular. This meant that the Wehrmacht could perform superbly – for a time – but if the conflict became a war of attrition it would begin to steadily degrade. By 1944 this was exactly the situation Germany found itself in, and it felt it most keenly in its lack of three vital elements: transport, manpower, and firepower, in that order.

With transport, the German Army of 1944 relied on the horse to almost the same degree as their forefathers had done in the First World War, and the Unification Wars prior to that. Mechanization and motorisation were viewed as essential, but aspirational, and production of the most basic form of motorised transport – the truck – was never prioritised by the Nazis, rather it was the panzer that headlined all the factory figures. Shortfalls were masked at the beginning of the war, and following that the capture of the vast vehicle parks of the French Army in particular further delayed the need for a revolution in the Wehrmacht's transport deficit. But then came the invasion of the Soviet Union, and the more or less complete destruction of the Wehrmacht's available transport pool, including the deaths of hundreds of thousands of horses in the snow and mud. German industry never caught up. Berlin then had two options for its available equipment; they could be characterised as the 'butter' or the 'fruit cordial' options – spread it out like the former, or concentrate it like the latter – Berlin went all out for the latter. Priority was given to the relatively small number of panzer, panzergrenadier and motorised divisions, affording them the luxury of wheels or tracks. The price they were expected to pay for this preferential treatment was high – they were rushed hither and thither from flashpoint to flashpoint, suffering a terrible toll in men and machines, before being replenished and made ready for the next defensive crisis or war-winning attack; *2. Panzerdivision*, for example, was reformed four times, as was *3. Panzergrenadier*, whilst *1. SS-Panzerdivision Leibstandarte Adolf Hitler* (*LSSAH* or *Leibstandarte* for short) was rebuilt no fewer than five times in as many years.

Next in line for any available transport – and that was scarce enough – were the infantry field divisions, and then, at the very bottom of the pile, came the statics, dismissively nicknamed *bodenständige* (literally 'down/rooted to earth') divisions. The intent was simple; create relatively small units from older age groups, equip them with next to no transport (incredibly the only motor vehicle some of these units had was the divisional commanders staff car) and low-levels of often obsolete heavy weaponry, and sit them on the Atlantic coast or in the Balkans to free up field units for use in the fighting in Russia. The first to be mustered back in April 1941 were the fifteen *700-series* formations, followed by an additional twelve in late September 1942. The majority of them would end up fighting in the battle of France, and two were directly responsible for defending the soon-to-be D-Day beaches; *709* and *716*.

The *716. Infanterie-Division* had been sitting in France since June 1941, a couple of months after being mobilised. Originally assigned to *15. Armee*, it moved over to *7. Armee* a year later and began its long stretch of duty amidst the lush Norman countryside. Its commander from spring 1943 was Wilhelm Richter. Richter was an '*Ostie*' from German Silesia and, unlike the majority of his men he, at least, had some combat experience having fought in the Polish, French and Russian campaigns. His division had around 8,000 men, with only two rifle regiments; *GR. 726* and *736*, instead of the more usual three, and its artillery regiment was smaller too, only having three and not four battalions of guns. For transport it had some horses and a few hundred bicycles. Over time, draftees and men wounded in Russia and sent west to convalesce bumped up its numbers, so by Christmas 1943 it reported a ration strength of 9,343 personnel of all ranks, despite the constant 'combing-out' of any men deemed to have reached the bar for service in the East – a bar that just kept on getting lower and lower, so that just five months later as spring turned to summer, Richter only had 7,771 men on roster, giving it the dubious honour of being the most-understrength division in all of Normandy. Worse still was the calibre of many of those same men; they were all either medically unfit or over the hill – the average age was thirty-one-and-a-half, with a third in their mid to late thirties, and a good number in their forties.

By comparison, the average age of the British, American and Canadian infantrymen waiting to cross the Channel was twenty-five-and-a-half – often deemed by military analysts as the optimum age for combat soldiers (modern British Army infantry units have an average age of 23–24). There are a lot of reasons why armies prefer their soldiers to be young; practically, the young can cope with the massive physical demands of combat better than their elders, but of greater import is the emotional difference between the two. In general, the young feel invulnerable and are more likely to accept the risks inherent in battle, whereas the older you are the more you not only understand – and fear - the dangers you face, but you also know you have a life to lose; a life with a spouse, children, a home, a career and so on. In simple terms, an older soldier is more likely to keep his head down when the bullets start flying.

> We tried to motivate the men by reminding them of the need to push the Alies back into the sea, and the danger to us all if they gained a foothold on the coast, and most were very positive, but a minority, who were mostly older German soldiers or Eastern troops, were quiet, and I suspected their hearts weren't in the fight.[18]

If a soldier was below thirty in a static division, it was usually because he was there on medical grounds. Martin Eineg was a private soldier in *GR. 726* stationed near La Rivière 'Although I was tall, I had a chronic lung condition which technically classed me as unfit for active service. Nevertheless, I was sent to France to man the Atlantikwall.'[19]

Eineg's comrade in the *736*, Helmut Voigt, was based a couple of miles to the east in St-Aubin: 'I was classed as medically unsuitable due to my eyesight and flat feet, so I was assigned to the 716 static division in France when I was seventeen, and I arrived there in January 1944.'[20] Medical problems were compounded by poor morale – the men simply didn't believe they would survive, let alone stop, any landing, while final victory was an impossibility to many.

> My father had told me that Germany could not possibly win and it would be like it was in the 1914–18 war, when the whole world was against us. I was even more convinced that our position was hopeless when we arrived in Colleville. There were no defences worth talking about and although there was a lot of work going on, planting obstacles and so forth on the beaches, everyone in the company knew that a good bombing would destroy everything... I felt the situation was hopeless, but when the invasion actually started I knew that it would be a battle for survival.[21]

Soldiers are simple creatures in the main, and nothing is more central to a soldiers' life than the food he eats every day. As the playwright and poet Bertolt Brecht wrote before the war in *Die Dreigroschenoper (The Threepenny Opera)*: '*Erst kommt das Fressen, dann kommt die Moral*' ('first comes food, then comes morality'). In Normandy, German rations were pretty miserable.

> On the whole morale was not good. It had a lot to do with the fact that the infantry were simply not well looked after. The food was very, very bad. At home in Germany, provisions were also pretty poor, and then there were differences between the Kriegsmarine, the Luftwaffe and then the infantry, which had the lowest possible status. We always seemed to get very bad sausage and Kommisbrot ['Army bread'], very black, horrible bread that had been stored for so long the middle of it was mildewed. When anyone in our company went home on leave we usually begged them to bring us back some bread.[22]

The Germans dealt with this the same way that soldiers have dealt with adversity and army life since time immemorial – with black humour:

> I asked Leutnant Peil, my platoon leader, about the Allies' food. There was a lot of laughing as he said, 'Boys, if you get to be POWs you'll get a lot better food over there than you ever get in the German Army.'[23]

Having said that, if there was a Norman farm close by then the age-old tradition of barter kicked in:

> The local French people were not supposed to come close to the bunkers, but in reality they would come and trade with us, offering food. They had bread, milk, cider, eggs and even fresh meat, which was otherwise unavailable to us Army lower ranks. In return we exchanged cigarettes, bootlaces and lamp oil, which the French couldn't get hold of at all... It's strange that my memory of those months before the invasion is so full of food, but that is how it was. We would say, 'Fill your belly with French ham and cider, because tomorrow you may be transferred to the East, where there is only hard biscuit and snow to eat.' Some of our bunkers were little storehouses of contraband food and liquor, and the officers would take their share when they inspected us. This would never have happened in the panzerwaffe of course, but standards were different in the *bodenständige* in France.[24]

Standards of equipment weren't the same either, with the static divisions armed with a mixture of German weapons; primarily small arms – the Kar98k rifle, MP 38 and 40 submachine-guns, MG 34 and MG 42 machine-guns – whereas the crew-served heavier weapons were more than likely to be what the men disparagingly called '*Beutewaffen*', booty-weapons, captured from the enemy earlier in the war. This was most prevalent in their artillery, and the 716. *Artillerieregiment* was typical, with eight batteries of ex-Czech 10cm howitzers, and two of former French Army 15.5cm guns. It wasn't just the guns that came from outside the borders of the Reich either, it was a lot of the soldiers too. The 716 had a number of former Italian soldiers (*Italienisches Freiwillige*), mostly in support roles, but also some ex-*bersaglieri* who had volunteered to keep fighting after Italy's surrender, and somehow found themselves in Normandy.

Away from some of the more exotic personnel, the non-Reich German troops in the occupation divisions usually fell into two distinct categories; firstly, Hiwis and so-called *Ost-Bataillone* ('East Battalions') formally on establishment, and secondly, individual soldiers officially classed by the authorities as 'racial Germans', but who were, in reality, anything but. The former would be especially important come D-Day because they made up a significant part of 7. *Armee*: one in every six soldiers in Dollmann's command was in an *Ost-bataillon*, and in 709 and 716. IDs they constituted fully one-third of the total bayonet strength, and across the Westheer there were sixty thousand of them among von Rundstedt's 850,000-strong command. Add to that the high – although impossible to verify accurately – number of *Beutedeutscher* ('booty Germans') standing in the ranks next to them, and you begin to understand just how important these men would be, come the days of battle.

For *716. ID* the *Osttruppen* were critical. Richter only had two grenadier regiments, and even these were under-strength, with railcars of his best men sent East every month whether he liked it or not. Berlin's answer was to provide him with not one, but three entire *Ost-bataillons*; *642, 439* and *441*. Or rather, it wasn't Berlin that made this dubious decision, but Adolf Hitler himself.

Rarely one to let military realities get in the way of his racist ideology and its delusions, Hitler had always regarded the great majority of the population of the Soviet Union as *Slavs* – a catch-all term he and his fellow Nazis used to denigrate the multitudinous peoples and ethnicities of Stalin's empire, and place them in the Nazis' own human racial hierarchy just above the Jews. As such, they were there to be conquered, economically exploited and starved, deprived of everything except what was required for subsistence, and effectively treated as human livestock until their time came for extermination. Clearly, there was no place in such a vision for Germany to arm them and put them in uniform; but that's exactly what they did, despite Hitler's express wishes.

> It must always remain a cast-iron principle that none but the Germans shall be allowed to bear arms. Even when it might seem expedient to summon foreign peoples to arms, one day it would prove our absolute, irretrievable undoing. Only the German must be permitted to bear arms, not the Slav, nor the Czech, nor the Cossack, nor the Ukrainian.[25]

As it happened, when the Anglo-Americans stormed ashore on D-Day they faced rifle-carrying members of all the peoples above, including Cossacks! They would meet a lot more of them as they fought their way inland.

However, despite Hitler's unequivocal opposition to the very idea of the detested Slavs serving in the Wehrmacht, the practical demands on hitherto solely German formations in Russia were so great that within just a few weeks of the invasion all manner of ex-Red Army soldiers were working with the Germans. At first it was low-level;

a German platoon would take a prisoner – invariably christen him 'Ivan' – and, instead of sending him to the rear, would get him to cut firewood, dig latrines, carry rations and so on. At first, the new man literally 'turned-coat' by being given scraps of German uniform so he wouldn't be shot accidentally, next his rations were claimed on unit strength with no indication his stomach was Russian and not German. A weapon and ammunition were claimed the same way and over time it just became normal practice. After a while, he'd become not just 'Ivan', but 'our Ivan', as one Waffen-SS soldier recalled;

> I remember we captured a Russian soldier, and he just stayed with us. He did the cooking, helped us dig shelters and did a lot of the work we didn't have time to do ourselves. One night we all fell asleep and he could've run away or done anything to us, but he didn't, he was a good guy.[26]

The question of why these men changed sides wouldn't be of much import if it wasn't for the numbers involved – which were huge – or for the fact that so many of them would face the Allies on D-Day and in the weeks that followed, where they would play a massive part in deciding if the Wehrmacht could hold on to France.

First the numbers: by September 1943 the Army's High Command OKH (the *Oberkommando des Heeres)* stated there were over half-a-million *Osttruppen* serving in the Ostheer – and everyone knew that was a major underestimate – but even so, the *official* number was still equivalent to thirty full-strength German divisions. By then, military bureaucracy had taken over and the Hiwis had transformed from more or less private, local initiatives, into becoming a regularised branch of the Army, with their own insignia, pay and ration rates, and even their own medals and service awards.[27] The majority of them served in anti-partisan and service roles in areas where Germans were few and far between. For example, in Kiev, the entire German police force for the city, its surroundings and its population of four million people, was just 120 officers and seventy interpreters. While Gustav von Bechtolsheim's 5,000-strong *707.Sicherungs-Division* (Security Divison) was responsible for maintaining order in 60,000 square kilometres of Belorussia behind *Heeresgruppe Mitte* (*Army Group Centre*).

Most Hiwis were ex-Red Army men who had either been captured or had deserted; in 1942 the monthly rate of desertion from the Red Army was 2,500, and this climbed to 6,500 by the summer of the following year.[28] The reasons men deserted were complex, but the fact remains that even after the unutterable suffering the Nazis inflicted on the peoples of the Soviet Union, significant sections of that self-same populace not only welcomed the invaders but were willing to go so far as take up arms to support them to overthrow Stalin and communism. Many were ethnic nationalists – Ukrainians, Balts, Cossacks, Chechens, Azeris, Uzbeks, Tajiks and so on – who had suffered terribly under communist rule and repression. Tsarist Russia's bread basket, Ukraine, was a case in point. It enjoyed a very brief independence after the Russian Revolution, before being taken over by the communists who then – at Stalin's instigation – imposed an unwanted land collectivization programme that led to what Ukrainians know as the *Holodomor,* or Great Famine, a near-genocidal period of enforced starvation in the early 1930s that killed anywhere between three and seven million Ukrainians. No wonder then that the advancing German soldiers were greeted at village after village in Ukraine by local girls in traditional dress bearing plates of salt, bread and vodka to welcome them. The Ukrainians weren't alone in seeing the invaders as liberators either; the countries occupied by Moscow in 1940 and forcibly incorporated as new 'Soviet Socialist Republics' – Latvia, Lithuania and Estonia – had suffered 'Red terrors' at the hands of their Soviet conquerors who had washed away their brief independence with the blood of thousands of those the Soviets viewed as class enemies: high ranking civil officials, army officers, church leaders, industrialists and members of the intelligentsia. All were arrested and executed by Moscow's all-powerful secret police, the NKVD, and were then followed by successive waves of unfortunates who were either summarily shot or deported to the living hell of the Siberian *gulags*; eleven thousand from Estonia in the first weeks of June 1941 alone, thirty-four thousand from Latvia in the first half of 1941, and tens of thousands more from Lithuania – most of those sent east never returned. The brutality of Moscow's rule was further demonstrated when the Soviets left their prisons and interrogation centres packed full of the mutilated corpses of local detainees, killed by their NKVD torturors even as they prepared to flee to the east before the advancing Germans arrived.

Many Hiwis were indeed fervent anti-communists, on ideological or nationalist grounds, but a great many others were ex-POWs who had volunteered simply to avoid starvation. The astonishing German victories of 1941 saw almost four million Soviet prisoners march dejectedly into captivity; for most of them it would mean a slow and lingering death. The German Army was neither prepared nor willing to look after so many prisoners, seeing them as nothing more than a distraction. Token efforts were made to look after them; which mostly consisted of using a rudimentary perimeter of barbed wire to section off an expanse of open steppe, herd huge numbers of men inside it, station a handful of elderly reservists and local auxiliaries around it as guards, and call it a camp. Transit Camps 131 and 220 were typical of the type; the former housed 18,000 prisoners, with a guard of ninety-two men, while the latter had over eight-and-a-half thousand prisoners and just thirty guards. Facilities were non-existent; the prisoners slept in the open, supplies of water, food and medicine were minimal, and as the sun beat down week after week that summer, disease, thirst and hunger began to ravage these oases of hell. There were eighty-one such places by the end of 1941.[29] The result, of course, was death on a massive scale. Cases of cannibalism were reported in camp after camp, and the arrival of the winter cold only increased the toll. By spring 1942 just over one million prisoners were still alive. Finally waking up to the possibility of using the prisoners as a labour pool, the Germans surveyed the survivors and found only four hundred thousand were fit to carry out any sort of work – the rest were effectively the walking dead. The shocking truth was that as many British and American POWs died in German camps during the entire war as Soviets died in the eastern camps in a single day! So, when the recruiters came around asking for volunteers, was it any wonder that many of those still able to raised their hands.

To the Ostheer's officer corps, their service was a godsend, papering over the gaps in the ranks which were fast-becoming yawning chasms as the Army suffered three-quarters of a million casualties by the end of November in that first year of the campaign, with two hundred thousand of those being fatalities. The generals knew what they were doing was strictly against Nazi racial policy, but as their formations haemorrhaged men, their rationality overcame their racism, and by Christmas 1941 pretty much one in every ten soldiers in the Ostheer were Hiwis; including in the supposedly 'super-Aryan' Waffen-SS divisions, as attested to by none other than Rudolf von Ribbentrop, son of the Third Reich's Foreign Minister, and a serving officer in the *Leibstandarte*:

Yes, we had Hiwis in the division in Russia, lots of them, everyone had them. They were fed by us and were generally loyal, and they did small auxiliary duties that we didn't have the time or troops for – they fetched and carried a lot; water, rations, ammunition and so on.

But the glaring contradiction the Hiwis presented, between the practical needs of the Wehrmacht on the one hand and the vicious racism that was the very keystone of Nazism on the other, was never resolved. So, the Germans had *General der Infanterie* Karl von Roques, the commander of all rear-area troops behind *Heeresgruppe Süd* (Army Group South), instructing his men that 'The Ukrainian region is to be viewed as the *lebensraum* of a friendly people,'[30] while at the same time Ukraine's Berlin-appointed *Gauleiter* (literally 'region leader', a Nazi Party appointment roughly equivalent to 'regional governor') Erich Koch, habitually referred to his Ukrainian subjects as 'niggers', his oft-quoted line being that whenever he met an intelligent Ukrainian he felt obliged to shoot him.[31]

The Hiwi-question came to a head in September 1943, when Hitler – having been misleadingly informed by the bureaucratic schemer and *Reichsführer-SS*, Heinrich Himmler, that Hiwi units were deserting back to the Red Army, taking their German weapons with them – announced to his stunned senior military commanders that *all* Hiwi formations were to be disbanded forthwith! For once, the senior general staff of the Wehrmacht united in opposition to Hitler's dictum,[32] arguing strongly that without the Hiwis the Russian front would collapse.

The result was a messy compromise that satisfied no-one, least of all the Hiwis themselves. A few battalions whose loyalty was considered doubtful were indeed disbanded, but a huge number – no fewer than sixty – were instead shipped to occupation duties in the Westheer over the autumn and winter of 1943/44, their places in the line taken by twenty battalions of German soldiers shipped east, hence why Wilhelm Richter had three in *716 ID*.

Of those three, the *642.* had been formed in central Russia for anti-partisan tasks by a Baltic German officer called Dolmetscher. Ninety per cent of its eight hundred members were ex-POWs, with the other 10% being German cadre personnel, including its new commander, Hauptmann Rössler. Its fellow Ost-batallions; the *439.* and the *441.*, had both been recruited from Cossack prisoners, and like the *642.* were used to tackle the ever-present partisan threat behind the front. Their German cadre personnel weren't the best of the best, but they weren't the dregs either, the *441.'s* Werner Otto Knaack being typical of the type. A 34-year-old Berliner, he had been an unemployed blacksmith before joining the army to support himself and his wife Hildegard. He took part in the *Anschluss* of neighbouring Austria, before serving in Poland, France and

Barbarossa as a truck driver in first the *218. Infanterie-Division*, and then the *293*. He participated in the failed assault on Moscow at the end of 1941, before being transferred to *Ost-Kompanie 453*, a Hiwi unit formed from Ukrainian volunteers. Absorbed into *Ost-Bataillon 441* as its *1.Kompanie* in the autumn of 1943, the Ukrainians and the now-promoted *Oberfeldwebel* Knaack went to France as part of Hitler's great Hiwi swap.

Knaack's battalion then lived up to Hitler's fears when members of its *2. Kompanie* mutinied, with forty-one men arrested in the aftermath and the company itself broken up.

None of the three *Ost-bataillons* were highly regarded by their German comrades-in-arms, but neither were they despised. *Landsers* like the *709.'s Grenadier* Heinrich Runder usually viewed them with sympathy rather than antipathy:

> ...we felt sorry for them, even though many of them were Russians ... that zone was manned by Russian units that were working for the German Army, men who had changed sides when they were captured in Russia. There was a whole company of them dotted around down there; we called it 'little Russia'.[33]

Runder's division – *709* – was in much the same position as its neighbour the *716*. As he went on to explain:

> We were a static infantry unit, which other units jokingly called 'the belly army' because of the age of our troops. This was misleading because while some were aged forty or over, others were much younger, but many of our men had been classed as physically unfit or they were considered unsuitable for service in the mobile combat divisions [Runder himself had fought in Tunisia, was wounded in the head and then transferred to the 709] There were also men in the static divisions who had previously suffered mental problems as a result of being in combat, especially on the Eastern front ... my own cousin was one such example ... he was in a dreadful battle in the east, at Kharkov, and was awarded the Knight's Cross, but despite his bravery he had a mental collapse. In the earlier part of the war such men would have been treated harshly for their symptoms, but by 1944 we were so short of manpower he was transferred to the Atlantikwall instead.

Along with the middle-aged, the unfit, the previously wounded and the *Osttruppen*, were another category of men who, although classed as Germans, were nothing of the sort and whose performance on D-Day would seriously undermine Runder and his fellow 'belly' soldiers – Albert Forster's *DVL* (*Deutsche Volksliste*) Germans. Following the end of the First World War, the resurrected state of Poland found itself with very large numbers of ethnic Germans within its borders; in the Bromberg region for example over three-quarters of the population were German. Many of these families voted with their feet and headed west over the next decade or so, so that by 1930 the percentage of Germans in Poznan had dropped from almost half to just two per cent.[34]

Then came September 1939 and the Nazi and Soviet invasions. As Berlin and Moscow sliced up a defeated Poland between them, a whole new *Gau* was created as the Reich expanded eastwards; the newborn was called *Danzig-West Prussia*, and its father was the 37-year-old Bavarian, Albert Maria Forster. Forster was a conflicted character in many ways; deeply racist and anti-Semitic, he was suspected of being a homosexual like several of his old brownshirt peers, and when faced with the racial realities of his new fiefdom he was quite prepared to flout almost every rule going in his goal of Germanising the region. In practical terms this meant that the boundaries of who was and who was not a German were elastic, and after a while ceased to exist entirely. At first, anybody who claimed 'German blood' was subjected to language tests, ancestry checks and what would be termed today as racial profiling, but after this failed to uncover the mass of ethnic Germans Forster was telling Hitler were there, the rules of the game changed so that if anyone *claimed* they were of German heritage they were taken at their word with no documentation required. When this again failed to deliver the required numbers, Forster simply made being 'German' obligatory. One of his own officials said:

> During the process of Germanising Poles on the basis of the Ethnic Register, there were many cases where whole villages or towns were compulsorily entered in the register according to fixed quotas laid down by Forster. For example, a local branch leader or mayor was instructed to enter 80% of his village as German although it was actually 80% Polish.[35]

Refusal to become Germanised became a crime and was made punishable by deportation or imprisonment.

The bureaucratic tool used to achieve the aim of a German *gau* was the so-called *DVL* policy; the *Deutsche Volksliste or* German People's List, which categorised local residents into four categories; Class 1 was at the top – *Volksdeutsche* – and was for German-speaking persons of German descent 'who had engaged themselves in favour of the Reich before 1939', such as being members of German community societies or unions. They received blue identification papers, German citizenship and could even join the Nazi Party. Class 2 was for people of 'German racial descent' – *Deutschstämmige* – who had maintained their German characteristics, such as speaking German, under Polish rule but who had 'remained passive'. Class 3 included Germans who were in mixed marriages and their children and 'indigenous persons considered as partly Polonized' – *'Eingedeutschte' or* 'voluntarily Germanised'. They got green ID papers and were essentially on probation, while Class 4 was for those who had 'actively worked in a manner hostile to Germany' – they got nothing. Nevertheless, the presumption was that *everyone* was a German deep down, no matter what. Ever keen to make Germanness attractive, Forster built in big incentives for classes 1–3. For a start, if you were Class 1–3 your property was exempt from confiscation, and you could receive better food, homes, work and goods —much of this having been stolen from Jews and other Poles.

For Forster, the results spoke for themselves; by 1942 there were 1,153,000 people from Danzig-West Prussia on the DVL; 150,000 in Class 1, 125,000 in Class 2, 8,000 in Class 4, and no fewer than 870,000 in Class 3 – officially Germans now made up over 60% of the population!

This flagrant abuse of cherished Nazi racial doctrine brought Forster into conflict with his neighbouring *Gauleiter*, Arthur Greiser, and the immensely powerful head of the SS and *Reich* Commissioner for the Strengthening of Germandom, Heinrich Himmler. The usually-feared Himmler challenged Forster on the issue, only to be completely ignored, and when Himmler appealed to Hitler as Forster's boss to intervene, the dictator shrugged it off and told Himmler to sort it out himself. In a famous and oft-repeated discussion with *SS-Obergruppenführer* Richard Hildebrandt, Forster scoffed: 'If I looked like Himmler, I wouldn't talk about race.'

However, for those Poles on the DVL it wasn't all roses, there was an enormous downside – conscription into the Wehrmacht. It would be these men – Poles and Czechs (the Germanisation process also operated in the Czech Sudetenland) conscripted into the Wehrmacht as 'ordinary Germans', who would find themselves in the two static infantry divisions in particular, and would end up facing the Allies on D-Day with not a shred of motivation to do anything but surrender on the spot. *Grenadier* Franz Gockel saw the results of the phenomenon at first-hand:

> One day while building a bunker, an *Unteroffizier* called to two men to bring him a hammer while he held up a support beam that had come loose. He yelled repeatedly, while they both stood there and stared at him dumbfounded. Then one caught on to his intentions and ran off quickly. He came back with a big smile holding the hammer up and saying to it, 'Morteck, you are a hammer.' Morteck is the Polish word for hammer.

The Normandy campaign wasn't the only time this situation reared its head; as early as December 1942, the SS itself was reporting to higher command that in Upper Silesia soldiers in German uniform were seen 'in uniform in Polish bars, conversing with Poles in Polish'. As far away as occupied Greece, partisans would be told by their German prisoners that they weren't Germans at all, but Poles. Exact numbers are impossible to come by, but Allied intelligence estimated that almost half of the *709.* and *716. IDs* were made up of ethnic Poles or ex-POWs who were unlikely to fight. As it turned out, captured Poles became such an important pool of reinforcements for the 1st Polish Armoured Division that they began to carry truckloads of spare uniforms with them so that they could simply turn captured prisoners into new comrades on the spot.[36]

GR. 726.'s Gustav Winter just got on with it:

> The static panzer I was assigned to in Normandy was an old Panzer III which had no engine or drive wheels. It was encased in concrete, literally set in a concrete box, and this box was positioned down in the ground so that the turret could operate at ground level... Because there was no power the turret was traversed by a hand wheel, and the panzer held only two men; the gunner and loader. We called it 'der Betonpanzer' ['the concrete panzer']. My assistant, my loader, was a Czech-German boy who wasn't very bright, but was very enthusiastic. We were a happy crew, just the two of us!

It would seem that Spielberg's dialogue was less a *faux pas* and more a nod to the reality of the battlefield.

Regardless of their background, it was the grenadiers of 709. and 716. IDs who stood square in the way of the planned landings; the 709 would face the Americans at Utah Beach, and the 716 would have to handle the British, French and Canadians on Gold, Sword and Juno beaches. Many German officers doubted their ability to hold the beaches if attacked, including the highly-decorated commander of 6. *Fallschirmjägerregiment – FJR. 6 – Major* Friedrich *Freiherr* von der Heydte:

> The troops for a defence against an Allied landing were not comparable with those committed in Russia. Their morale was low; the majority of the enlisted men and non-commissioned officers lacked combat experience, and the officers in the main were those who, because of a lack of qualification or on account of wounds or illness, were no longer fit for service on the Eastern front ... their weapons were from all over the world and seem to have been accumulated from all periods of the 20th century.[37]

Von der Heydte was in an ideal position to judge, given his own unit was grouped around the town of Carentan at the base of the Cotentin, and on just one two-kilometre stretch of the line even his own men were equipped with four different types of mortars hailing from four different countries; Germany, France, Italy and the Soviet Union.

The one-legged commander of the formation for which von der Heydte's men were a reserve – *General der Artillerie* Erich Marcks's *LXXXIV. Armeekorps* – and to which 709. and 716. IDs belonged, was perhaps a bit more succinct than his subordinate: 'Emplacements without guns, ammunition depots without ammunition, minefields without mines, and a large number of men in uniform with hardly a soldier among them.'

This then was *Festung Europa* in Normandy in the run-up to D-Day. Except that it wasn't – not quite. In the staff, map and briefing rooms of every major German headquarters in the West, an argument had been raging, the results of which might well decide if the Germans could hold France or not, and it was at its most bitter at the very top of the Westheer. Every soldier in France knew of it, as the *Hitlerjugend*'s Rudolf von Ribbentrop revealed:

> It had even leaked to us 'little troopers', as we called ourselves. Everyone knew that there were different views between Rommel

and Rundstedt, the Commander-in-Chief West, because Rommel wanted to have the panzer divisions on the coast, because of Allied air superiority – 'they would not get there in time' – but Rundstedt wanted to 'operate', hold them back in the hinterland and concentrate them for big offensives. In the final analysis Hitler decided it, a compromise was found, so that some panzer divisions were placed on the coast and others in the hinterland.[38]

The tank, the most important military innovation of the First World War (the aircraft already having been invented of course) – born out of the attrition of the trenches on the Western Front – was an invention that gave Great Britain a once-in-a-generation military advantage that was squandered before a politician could say 'peace dividend'. The two nations that had really seen the potential of the big, smelly metal boxes were two sides of the same coin: the Soviet Union and Nazi Germany. Stalin then washed away Moscow's expertise with the blood of Mikhail Nikolayevich Tukhachevsky and his fellow officers murdered in the Great Purges of the 1930s, but in Germany the Army Commander-in-Chief, Hans von Seeckt, and the maverick infantryman, Hans Guderian, saw in it the future of war on the Eurasian landmass and created a new branch of military service - the *panzerwaffe*.[39] Rapid evolution in the 1930s, especially after Hitler's accession to power and his decision to turn on the military expenditure taps, created the one weapon that gave Berlin the only real chance it had of winning a general European war; the *panzer division*: great mailed fists of steel, all clattering tracks and hundreds of guns belching out armour-piercing rounds and high-explosive in a torrent, as their commanders sniffed out half-gaps and weak spots to go roaring through to create confusion and terror and shatter an enemy's ability to resist. They were the very foundation of German martial might in the victory years of 1939–41, and still were in the summer of 1944. *Festung Europa* would not be held by the benighted men of the *bodenständige* divisions – that wasn't what they were created for. They were purposefully spread thin along the coastline, in the sand dunes, bluffs and hamlets; a crust of men, designed to stay put in their bunkers and trenches, holding the attackers on the beaches for a few precious hours, until they heard the metallic rattle and engine growl of the approaching panzers from over their shoulders, and the accompanying shouts and hurried feet of the grenadiers who would come to counter-attack, throw the Allies back into the sea and save the day for Germany.

2

Throw Them Back into the Sea!

> Every opponent who sets foot on French soil must be thrown back
> into the sea in the first hours. That can only be done if our panzer
> divisions are stationed right by the coast.

This was Erwin Rommel speaking to his ex-aide, and now commander
of *Panzergrenadier-Regiment 125,* Hans von Luck. Von Luck, a
veteran of Poland, France, North Africa and Russia, was destined
for Fritz Bayerlein's *Panzer-Lehr-Division,* a crack unit composed
of some of the finest instructors and demonstration troops from the
Reich's armoured warfare schools. However, a forty-nine-year-old
Lorrainian with an almost French-like penchant for fine wine, cigars
and glamorous women - and possessed of impeccable connections at
Hitler's HQ – pulled some strings and bagged him instead: 'A hearty
welcome to you von Luck... I am giving you acting command of the
regiment until the official appointment comes through.'

The speaker was *Generalleutnant* Edgar Feuchtinger. Originally an
artillery officer, Feuchtinger had won friends in high places through
his pre-war involvement in organising the military parades on the
Reichsparteitage (Reich Party Days) so beloved of the Nazis. This had
helped him gain command firstly of an infantry division, and then in
spring 1943 of one of the new *Schnell* (Fast) Divisions. The idea of
the transport-heavy *Schnelle Divisionen* (it was intended there would
be four of them in total) went hand in glove with the establishment
of the static divisions; the latter would guard the coast while the
Schnelle Divisions sat in reserve ready to intervene at a moment's
notice wherever the Allies chose to land. Feuchtinger's was christened
Schnell Division West.

The whole concept was stillborn. Germany was manufacturing more weapons than ever before, but production couldn't keep up with losses, let alone equip new divisions, so Feuchtinger's nascent unit spent four months training before the decision was taken by Berlin to drop Schnell Division West, and re-name it as *21. Panzerdivision*, a name with a short but illustrious history. First established in August 1941, the *21.* had been one of the two founding units of Rommel's famed *Afrika Korps* and covered itself in glory at Gazala, Mersa Matruh, and the capture of Tobruk. It fought the British, and latterly the Americans, for almost two years, before surrendering to those same enemies in the summer of 1943 in Tunisia. Wiped off the Wehrmacht's order of battle, its reappearance brought a touch of magic dust to the otherwise pretty dilapidated Normandy defences.

This then would be the Germans' main strike force in the event of a landing in the Seine Bay. While *709.* and *716. IDs* held off the first waves of assault troops, the *21.* would start up its engines and charge forward to victory. Alongside the *panzertruppen* would be grenadiers from another unit new to Normandy in the run up to D-Day, and one that has had a legend woven around it ever since; *352. Infanterie-Division*. Together, *352. ID* and *21.Panzer* would come closest to achieving Rommel's vision of defeating the Allies on the beaches and saving France for Germany.

Although the Wehrmacht never managed to establish a common structure for all its panzer formations, a fully manned and fully equipped German panzer division was an awesome instrument of war. Usually around 16–17,000 men strong and arranged in four major groupings – two regiments of panzergrenadiers, one of artillery, and another of panzers – with battalions of reconnaissance, anti-tank, anti-aircraft and *pioniere* troops, plus the usual support arms of signals, medical, supply and logistics. The whole division was mobile with up to two thousand trucks, seven hundred cars, the same of motorbikes, some half-tracks, plus an assortment of armoured cars and other specialist vehicles. By 1944 this establishment was little more than a pipe dream for most panzer formations, and just as the Army's infantry divisions were reorganised, so were the panzers, with the creation of the *Type 44 Panzer-Division*. Just as with their foot-slogger comrades, the stated reason for this restructuring was to adjust to new tactics and new equipment, but it also meant smaller units with fewer men, fewer panzers and fewer guns. In a quirk of fate, the only two divisions who were specifically left out of this shake-up were *Panzer-Lehr* and *21. Panzer*; the Lehr because it was actually better equipped than was laid down, and *21.* for the opposite reason – they fell well short, so short in fact that it was the only panzer division in France officially rated as 'unfit' for service in Russia. Why was *21.* in such a state, and exactly what was that state?

The core of the division was sound, built as it was of between one and two thousand North Africa veterans from the 'old' *21.*, mostly men who had been on leave or convalescing when the original divison surrendered, while pretty much all the rest were young conscripts with no combat experience. It was small, with only two battalions rather than the normal three in each of the panzer grenadier regiments (the *Panzer-Lehr* was in the same position). But what it really lacked was leadership and equipment. Instead of the nominal 179 panzers, the division's *22. Panzer-Regiment* only had 127, and none were the superlative *PzKpfw V Panther*. In fact, a full third were *Panzer Somua 35(f)*s – obsolete French tanks captured back in 1940.[1] Not only that, the regiment was commanded by a much-decorated officer of the very highest calibre, but one who also seemed to be a Jonah dogged by some of the worst military luck imaginable – *Oberst* Hermann von Oppeln-Bronikowski. On first appearance von Oppeln-Bronikowski made an impression; tall, handsome, he had all the elegant manners of the aristocratic Saxon scion he was. In his black panzer uniform, with his Knight's Cross of the Iron Cross with Oak Leaves and Swords dangling at his throat and his cigarette holder clamped between his teeth, he cut a real dash, as he had done before the war at the 1936 Berlin Olympics where he won a gold medal in the team equestrian dressage event. He had served with distinction in the First World War, becoming one of the youngest ever recipients of the Iron Cross First Class, and had continued this track record in the Second, becoming one of Germany's famed 'panzer aces' in Russia, before being given regimental command in the ill-starred *22. Panzerdivision*. Grouped together with Radu Gherghe's *1. Romanian Panzerdivision* in the *XXXXVIII. Armeekorps*, the *22.* sat in reserve behind *6. Armee* as the latter fought to conquer Stalingrad in autumn 1942. When the Red Army launched their powerful *Operation Uranus* counter-attack in mid-November, it was down to von Oppeln and his panzers to stop them and prevent Paulus and his men from being encircled in the city. In one of the strangest epsiodes of the war, the highly decorated panzer colonel failed utterly, as a collection of disasters overtook his regiment; firstly, over a third of his tanks wouldn't even start, their electric cabling having been gnawed through by hordes of mice sheltering in the same straw the crews used to protect their precious panzers from the numbing cold. Second, more were lost when they slid off the icy Russian roads, their specially-designed track sleeves having been 'lost' somewhere. Last but not least, contradictory information as to where the main Soviet assault actually was, led to the remaining panzers heading off in several different directions before being overwhelmed by the massed T-34s of the Soviet 1st Tank Corps.[2] With that failure, almost a third of a million German and allied soldiers were doomed to death or captivity in what became the Ostheer disaster at Stalingrad. The fact that eighteen months later the same middle-ranking officer was poised to play a pivotal role in another battle of vital importance to the fate of Nazi Germany must surely rank as one of the oddest coincidences of the war.

Above von Oppeln, his superior Feuchtinger was neither tainted by the bad luck that hung over the Saxon, nor afflicted with his military competence. Among a peer group of commanders that included Heinz Guderian, Hermann Hoth, Hans Hube, Hasso von Manteuffel, Georg Stumme and Wilhelm von Thoma, to name but a few, Edgar Feuchtinger does not merit a footnote. The experienced Hans von Luck described his new commander thus:

> Feuchtinger was a live and let live person. He was fond of all the good things in life, for which Paris was a natural attraction. Knowing that he had no combat experience or knowledge of panzer warfare, Feuchtinger had to delegate most things, that is, leave the execution of orders to us experienced commanders.

However, Feuchtinger did, at least, realise that his division desperately needed strengthening if it was to come up to snuff; enter stage left a slightly portly 44-year-old mechanical engineer with thinning hair and a ready smile – Major Alfred Becker – an unsung hero of the Wehrmacht.

An artillery officer by training, Becker took part in the 1940 Western campaign, crossing into Amersfoort in the Netherlands where he discovered the well-stocked – and abandoned - vehicle park of a Dutch artillery regiment. Swapping his 126 draught-horses for large-wheeled lorries, he motorised almost every gun in his regiment. In so doing he had found his true military calling. Over the next three years – and after a successful demonstration to Hitler himself in the gardens of the Reich Chancellery in Berlin – Becker created an entire organisation dedicated to recycling captured and abandoned Allied military vehicles for German use. What began as a cottage industry – turning British-built Vickers Mk.VI armoured vehicles into handily-titled *10.5cm leFH 16 Geschützwagen auf Fahrgestell Mk VI 736 (e)* self-propelled artillery – became a large-scale enterprise with no fewer than three factories, all near Paris, working full-time on the programme. The principle behind the project was simple; create large numbers of self-propelled artillery and assault guns by marrying up mainly German guns with British or French vehicle chassis, all coated in German-produced armour plating. Once the captured French vehicle parks were emptied, Becker scoured the countryside to recover abandoned vehicles from hedgerows, streams and fields all over conquered Europe. They were then taken to Paris and divided into three categories: those requiring minor repairs/refits, those requiring major repairs/refits, and those that were only good for spare parts. In total, Becker and his team produced well over two thousand vehicles for the Wehrmacht, the majority of them tracked armoured fighting units. To put that into context, only some 1,347 *Tiger Is* were ever built.

The two officers; Becker and Feuchtinger, knew each other from earlier in the war and given the latter's love of Parisian nightlife, he was often in the French capital and able to resume his friendship with his former subordinate, as well as see for himself what Becker was up to in his factories. The result was that *21. Panzerdivison* got an entire assault-gun battalion from Becker; *Panzerjäger-Abteilung 200*, as well as numerous other vehicles, making it one of the most thoroughly mechanized panzer divisions in the *panzerwaffe*. Becker was put in command of the new battalion and said of it:

The self-propelled armoured gun group was a trial unit with the purpose of obtaining a concentrated fire effect whilst in action. Each battery was furnished with six 7.5 cm guns. The front shields were 40 mm thick. Furthermore, four 10.5 cm guns were attached to each battery. These guns were constructed for direct fire, but were capable of firing indirectly. So, the 10.5 cm guns would be positioned some 500 to 1,000 metres behind the 7.5 cm anti-tank guns.

The commander of *Heeresgruppe B* extolled the virtues of the new-look division so often that it earned the nickname 'Rommel's Zirkus' from the rest of the Army. Becker didn't stop at *21. Panzer* either, he also furnished the *716.* with three companies of tank destroyers, motorised anti-tank guns and self-propelled artillery.

One of the gunners assigned to man Becker's 'armoured Frankensteins' in *21. Panzer* was Paul Breslau:

> ...all our gunners were members of the '1,000 Metre Club', meaning that they could hit a target of one metre radius at a range of 1,000 metres with nine shots out of every ten fired... It was a disgrace to lose your membership of that club.

Confident though Breslau was in the abilities of his own battalion, he had a very different view of the *709.* and *716.* grenadiers sitting in front of him on the coast.

> ...the static infantry were there to soak up any enemy attack, to slow it down and to alert us, the inland forces, of the danger. Nobody on earth expected the static divisions to defeat a serious landing... It was accepted by everyone that if there was a real invasion on that coast ... then the beach forces, the coastal forces, would probably be overrun by a focused assault. This was why a counter-attack by our mobile armoured forces was so critical to any plan to defeat an invasion.[3]

Von Luck said of the whole hybrid experiment: 'At first, we laughed at the monstrous looking assault-guns, but we soon came to know better. The assault-gun companies were trained to work closely with the grenadiers, and this was later to prove a decisive aid to our defence forces.'

The wiry Schleswiger was, however, more concerned about the division as a whole:

> The weeks went by. For a panzer division, which in the campaigns so far had been accustomed to a war of movement, the inactivity was wearisome and dangerous. Vigilance was easily relaxed, especially after enjoying some Calvados or cider, both typical drinks of the area. There was, in addition, the uncertainty as to whether the landing would take place at all in our sector.

Von Luck's own adjutant, 22-year-old *Oberleutnant* Helmut Liebeskind, agreed with his *chef* about the tedium:

> It did get on our nerves a bit, the constant orders to stand-to and then stand-down, but at least it meant there was some movement... We weren't on alert all the time, don't let anybody tell you we were ... the days passed in a fairly normal fashion, we did training exercises and were warned to have our ammunition at the ready.[4]

Despite all the problems within the division, there was still a sense of optimism in the ranks, which boded well for how it would perform come the day. The young tanker, Werner Kortenhaus, an *Obergefreiter* in *Oberleutnant* Hoffmann's *4. Kompanie*, spoke for many of his comrades:

> We thought, let them come, we'll throw them out again. We genuinely believed – and we were always being told – that we were so strong we would throw them out in no time. We were young men and in a way we burned for a little action. We had rehearsed and practised things for so long that we wanted to see some real action at last. But then we also thought there were several thousand German aircraft ready to come and give us support.[5]

Perhaps Kortenhaus should have spoken to *Leutnant* Thomas Beike about that hope, given that Beike was a fighter pilot with the unit responsible for protecting Normandy, *Jagdgeschwader 2*.

> The simple fact was that we in the fighter groups couldn't live up to the expectations that people had of us. We couldn't live up to the legend of the Luftwaffe as it had been from 1939 to about 1942 ... the command echelons of the Luftwaffe couldn't supply us with enough aircraft, spares, fuel and fresh pilots to be an effective force.[6]

Unfortunately for the Westheer, Beike's assessment of the Luftwaffe's position was spot on, with the German air arm being asked to do way too much with way too little; its hard core of Knight's Cross-bedecked aces – the so-called *Experten* – were just about holding the line in Russia, and its day and night fighter squadrons were battling bravely, but increasingly futilely, over the skies of the Reich itself against the Allied heavy bombers and their escorts, but this left next to nothing for the Westheer – Germany lost just over half of all her single-engine fighters in the month of May 1944, and with them went one in four of the entire pilot cohort – April's losses had been much the same, and June's would be even worse.[7] 'We simply did not have enough good quality, fresh pilots to replace those lost in the air ... each Luftwaffe pilot living in his château with his polished boots and so on, was under the surface a somewhat tormented individual.'

If the Wehrmacht couldn't defeat any landings from the air, could they do it at sea? Thirty years earlier it was Imperial Germany's arms race with Great Britain on the high seas that had done so much to bring on the First World War – *Kaiser* Wilhelm's plans driven by an almost maniacal desire to establish an overseas empire befitting the world power status he craved so badly for his new country. As it turned out, the heartstoppingly expensive *Kaiserliche Marine (*Imperial Navy*)* was a white elephant of quite startling proportions. Never seriously threatening the hegemony of the British Royal Navy, it spent the war fighting a number of small engagements, and the only major battle of the conflict at Jutland in 1916 was an indecisive affair at best. The rest of the time – apart from its U-boat arm – it stayed bottled up in its harbours, its 150,000+ sailors basically unemployed and itching alternately with boredom and discontent. Hugely restricted as to its composition after the Versailles Treaty, with Hitler's rise to the Chancellorship in 1933 the newly renamed *Kriegsmarine* saw its chance to once again challenge for a major role on the world stage. Under the direction of the stern and forbidding Erich Raeder, the Naval Staff authored '*Plan Z*', and submitted it to Hitler for review. It was a remarkable document, hugely ambitious, and modelled on Tirpitz's *Flottengesetze*, 'Fleet Laws', from the beginning of the century. What Plan Z proposed was nothing less than the creation – from scratch – of a fleet of around eight hundred ships, with a main force of four aircraft carriers, twelve battlecruisers and six H-Class battleships; each of which would be bigger than the *Bismarck* – at the time the largest ship in the German Navy. To man this armada the Navy would expand to a strength of 200,000. The resources required for the construction programme alone would be vast, but Raeder was clever enough to pitch Plan Z to Hitler as the way to project the Third Reich's power at a global level. He took the bait, and in September 1939 approved it, his only stipulation being that its completion date be brought forward from 1947 to 1945. The first two battleships were begun, and the hull of the first aircraft carrier – the *Graf Zeppelin* – slid down the slipway in 1938, then – years earlier than Raeder anticipated – the war started. The Navy was nowhere near its envisaged order of battle, and only 78,000 men were in service. Worse, Hitler's interest in it waned, with his focus shifting to the Luftwaffe and the Army. Nevertheless, the Kriegsmarine was assigned a leading role in one of the opening campaigns of the war, *Unternehmen Weserübung*, the invasion of Denmark and Norway, more specifically Norway. Tasked with safely landing the main assault force on the Norwegian coast, it turned into a disaster from which the Kriegsmarine never fully recovered. Firstly, the task force's flagship, the heavy cruiser *Blücher*, was sunk by artillery and torpedoes from Norwegian shore batteries in the Oscarsborg Fortress in Oslofjord. Next, no fewer than ten destroyers were lost at Narvik (half of German destroyer strength at the time), followed by two light cruisers: the *Königsberg*, bombed and sunk by Royal Navy aircraft in Bergen, and the *Karlsruhe*, sunk off the coast of Kristiansand by a British submarine. The Kriegsmarine did manage to sink some British warships during the fighting, including the aircraft carrier HMS *Glorious*, but Hitler was visibly dismayed at the scale of the losses. Raeder desperately tried to put a brave face on it, writing in his diary that summer: 'The *Führer* shows his objective: after defeat of France, reduction of the army, dismissal of all the older skilled workers. Focus of emphasis on air force and navy.' The grand admiral was fooling himself. Plan Z was shelved indefinitely, the dock workers were redeployed, and most of the hulls already-started were broken up for scrap. The Navy would get one more chance to impress Hitler by starving Great Britain out, and it would fall to Raeder's bitter rival; Karl Dönitz and his U-boats. But by the summer of 1944 the battle of the Atlantic was lost and the U-boat arm was a shadow of its former self.

What the Kriegsmarine could contribute to the upcoming fight was *Marinegruppe West* (Naval Group West) under *Vizeadmiral* Theodor Krancke. However, it was a paper tiger, as the fifty-one-year-old naval officer knew only too well: 'The few available destroyers, torpedo and speed-boats can harass an enemy landing, but they cannot effectively impede it.' This was despite France's Atlantic coast being studded with major German naval bases: Le Havre, Brest, St Nazaire and Lorient to name a few. Their berths were mostly empty, only three destroyers were tied up on the quaysides, alongside thirty-four gunboats, a few flotillas of fast S and T-boats – the so-called *Schnellboote* – and over one hundred minesweepers; now unemployed given the Allies weren't laying mines. Inside the massive reinforced concrete pens at Brest and Lorient built to house the wolfpacks, only thirty-seven U-boats sat at anchor. This was *Gruppe Landwirt* (Group Farmer), formed in March after the rest of the U-boat fleet had been evacuated to Norway away from the Allied air power that kept every German ship in its harbour during daylight hours for fear of attack. They were tasked with sinking Allied shipping when the landings occurred.

Kapitän zur See Hans-Rudolf Rösing, Dönitz's U-boat leader in the West, *Führer der Unterseeboote West,* or *FdU West* for short, was under no illusions as to how the task had changed for the crews of *Gruppe Landwirt,* as he outlined in his war diary:

> Two years ago, it was true to say that Norway had to be defended in American waters; that is, where we could sink the greatest tonnage. This precept is no longer valid. Today it is more important to sink one LST [Landing Ship Tank] in the invasion area than, say, one Liberty ship in the Atlantic.

Clearly, Rösing had no doubts as to the job ahead – although his choice of Norway as the potential invasion point yet again highlights the confusion in the Wehrmacht as to the possible site of the landings, and – just as with the Army – the Kriegsmarine responded by diverting scarce resources down the proverbial rabbit hole; in Norway's case it was thirty U-boats established as *Gruppe Mitte. FdU West* hammered home his message by driving to Brest from his headquarters in Angers in early May to impress upon his commanders just how important their role would be, as recalled by the captain of *U953, Oberleutnant zur See* Karl-Heinz Marbach: '[We were told that] once we could do no more then we should at least ram the invasion fleet, even if it were only the smallest dinghy.' Another officer present at the time remembered the reaction: 'Deadly silence gripped the room after Rösing's call, this was sheer madness, it was ludicrous to use a U-boat to accomplish what a torpedo should do.' When Rösing left to return to Angers, his captains were in despair – how had it come to this? But there was at least some potential within the navy – the Slapton Sands attack had demonstrated just how vulnerable an invasion fleet could be. In April 1944 German E-boats on a routine patrol chanced upon a practice landing off Slapton Sands in Devon. They attacked; sinking two landing craft and killing 197 sailors and 441 American soldiers.

U-boat commander Günther Hessler, echoed his boss's call – difficult to swallow as it was:

> ...of all the weapons at our disposal, the U-boat was the only one capable of destroying any considerable quantity of the enemy's invasion supplies before they had been landed; and, when balancing the amount of ammunition carried in a supply ship, or the number of tanks in an LST, against the cost in German lives and material needed to destroy these once they had been landed, there could be only one conclusion, namely, to attack the supply traffic with every available U-boat.[8]

However, resources were slim, and Theodor Krancke – while decorated and competent – was no Horatio Nelson. Morale within the Kriegsmarine wasn't high either, and twenty-one-year-old Klaus Herrig – a Naval signals corps wireless operator based at Le Havre – spoke for many:

> Some fools believed that Germany could still win the war, but I wasn't among them. I couldn't believe it by then. I think about half my comrades felt as I did. Everyone could see that we weren't invincible, as we had always been told. The outcome of the war was a dangerous thing to discuss – you could only do it with friends, or people you felt you could trust – because in every unit there was a spy or two from the political side who would be watching and listening all the time... News from home made us very concerned for our families because of all the air raids. We expected the invasion to come that summer and waited for it with mixed feelings ... if the invasion came we thought it might be the end of the war and that was what we wanted, to get the thing over and finished so we could go home. I knew I had to do my duty as a soldier, but in my innermost heart I just hoped for it to be over.[9]

Oberleutnant zur See Herbert Werner of *1. Unterseebootsflottille* (1st U-boat Flotilla), felt much the same: 'Under the concrete roof the shipyard personnel worked around the clock to have the boats repaired, equipped and fitted out ... helping to put the boats in fighting condition. We never talked about the invasion, but we thought about it incessantly – and of our deaths.'

It would be the Army then, as always Germany's most important service arm, that would have to take the lead on defeating any landing. *21. Panzerdivision* was their biggest hope of achieving that in the Seine

Bay, but von Luck and his *panzertruppen* weren't alone, Berlin had a trick up its sleeve that Allied intelligence almost missed, and come D-Day might make the difference – *352. Infanterie-Division.*

Of the five beaches the Allies would land on, the one that has dominated ink and celluloid is Omaha. It is easy to see why. All the landings were opposed, with men dying on all five, yet nowhere on 6 June came close to realising the worst fears of the Allied politicians, planners, commanders and assault troops themselves, except Omaha. To succeed in gaining the sort of lodgement on the continent that the Allies needed to prepare to liberate France, all five beaches would have to link up and form a broad front. If the Germans could throw the Allies back into the sea somewhere in the middle of the landing zone, Juno, Gold (see map, p. 313) or particularly Omaha, then there was a chance they could keep the Allied forces split, and if not defeat them at least force a major change in the plan – perhaps even cause a partial withdrawal, such as the abandonment of Utah or Sword at the western or eastern edges respectively of the assault. If – another *if* – the Westheer could then bring enough reinforcements into play quickly, then the result could be stalemate, which as far as the Allies were concerned would be the same as failure, and the Wehrmacht would have saved France for Hitler's empire.

The standard narrative of that fateful day has it that the *352. ID* that faced the American troops at Omaha was a veteran German unit recently shipped in from the Russian front; well-equipped, well-led, and with its ranks full of experienced *landsers*. Research over the last few years has shown this to be only partially accurate at best, and downright misleading at worst.

Firstly, *352. ID* was not a veteran division, filled with *alte Hasen* (old hares) as the *landsers* nicknamed their more experienced comrades, rather it had only recently been formed, and Normandy was its very first posting. Neither was it awash with the latest heavy weaponry the Reich's industries could provide. It was indeed bigger than its static neighbour the *716. ID*, being around twelve thousand-strong rather than 7–8,000, and it had more artillery, with forty-eight guns available, *but* – and it was a big but – only a fraction of the division was on Omaha on the morning of the 6th; in fact just one of its six battalions, a few light guns and another battalion attached from its eastern neighbour, the below-par *716*. Nevertheless, it would come within an ace of forcing an American withdrawal under fire that could have dramatically altered the Normandy campaign.

Back in November the previous year, when 352. *ID* was being formed, there was no way of knowing the impact the men with the winged horse emblem would have. It was created – as so many other *new* formations had been – from the remnants of units burnt out on the Russian front, in its case 268. and 321. *IDs*, both of which had suffered debilitating casualties during the Kursk fighting in the summer. To these men were added the few survivors of 546. *Grenadier-Regiment* which had been destroyed with the rest of 6. *Armee* at Stalingrad. One of the latter was *Leutnant* Hans Heinze, a former ranker wounded three times in the bloody fighting around Stalingrad's ruined tractor factory. He called 352 'a thrown-together mob ... a tossed-together heap'.[10] It's hard to disagree when you look under the skin of the division. There were only enough field officers for one per company, and only seventy-per cent of the NCO slots were filled. The private soldiers were mostly 17- and 18-year-old conscripts, who had the grand total of three weeks basic training behind them at the Schlan depot in Bohemia (now Slaný in the Czech Republic), and a full twenty per cent of them were 'Germanised' draftees, such as twenty-one-year-old *Gefreiter* Aloysius Damski.

I am a Pole. I was impressed into the German Army in February 1943. I was working in the office of a munitions factory in Blomberg when the manager called me in and said I could either go into the German forces or be declared 'politically unreliable', which almost certainly meant a concentration camp. I was only twenty-years-old and I loved life, so I chose the army. After training I was sent to Normandy to a mixed unit of Poles, Czechs, Russians and some German NCOs and officers. Most of the older men had no faith in Hitler and believed that Germany could never now win the war... We used to plant scraps of metal in fields to decoy mine detectors, wire it off and put up 'Achtung Minen' signs – most of the minefields in our area were false... I spent most of my spare time drinking, wine was very cheap, only twelve francs a pint, and my wages were equivalent to 350 francs every ten days... One day my officer called me into his office and said 'How German do you feel?' I replied, 'Well, since we are talking like this, I will tell you the truth. I was born in Poland, I was educated in Poland, both my parents are Polish and still live in Poland. How can I feel anything but Polish?'[11]

Many of Damski's fellow conscripts were physically stunted, and some borderline malnourished, growing up as they had under wartime rationing. The division duly put in a request to *Korps* headquarters for extra dairy and meat rations to feed the men up, but when this was turned down the companies improvised and began trading with the locals for meat, butter, eggs, milk and anything else they could lay their hands on. Everything else the unit needed to get itself ready for combat was in short supply; there was so little ammunition that each regiment only conducted one live firing exercise in its work-up training. There weren't even enough proper field-grey uniforms, with most of the soldiers being given olive-brown ones left over from the North African campaign – the men were told to cut off the tropical insignia and sew on a European-issue one. Hans Heinze was dismayed when, along with his immediate superior, *Hauptmann* Grimme, he went to take his first look at the *Atlantikwall*, so celebrated in Nazi newsreels:

> We reached the coast but couldn't find the Atlantikwall. We finally did come to some bunkers surrounded by barbed wire and decided to get out and look around. We went right over the wire without even tearing our trousers. Then we met a *landser* from the unit occupying the area [a member of the 716]. He had been there since 1940 and we asked him about the defences. He just said, 'If the Tommies decide to invade and disturb our peace we will roll out our gun and teach them how to be scared.' We found no cheer or solace in this remark.

Notwithstanding its weaknesses – and there were many – 352. ID had some strengths too, the most obvious being that whilst it was short of officers and NCOs, those that did stand in its ranks were almost all veterans of several years hard fighting, so there were just enough veterans to give the division a fighting chance come the landings. That well of experience started at the very top with the divisional commander, Dietrich Kraiss.

Awarded the Knight's Cross back in 1942 whilst commanding 168. *Infanterie-Division* in Russia, the fifty-four-year-old had spent pretty much the whole war in the East, and was the sort of divisional leader the Germans excelled in producing; no great strategic thinker but a tough, practical man who understood how to get the best out of his men. Kraiss's regimental commanders; *Oberstleutnants* Ernst Heyna of *GR. 914*, Meyer of *915*, and especially *Oberst* Ernst Goth of *GR. 916*, were men cast in his own image, seasoned professionals who had learnt their trade fighting the Red Army. Orthodox military man as he was, Kraiss originally organised his men for defence in depth, with only a thin screen covering the beaches. On an inspection visit, Rommel had taken exception to this arrangement and had ordered that every man and gun be moved forward to cover the beaches. Kraiss – absent for the visit itself – took umbrage, and as he knew Rommel personally, appealed to him directly. Rommel, with experience of the threat posed by Allied air power, and still smarting from von Rundstedt and Hitler's refusal to place the panzer divisions in the sand dunes, wouldn't cancel his orders completely, but instead agreed a compromise, so only Ernst Goth's men went up to the coast from their reserve positions around Saint-Lô.

The resulting movement to the coast was missed by the usually efficient Allied intelligence apparatus; they thought Kraiss's men were south of the beaches, and had no idea that some at least had gone forward and would face the landings from the very first moment. This decision *almost* cast Dietrich Kraiss as the man who frustrated D-Day.

For 18-year-old *Grenadier* Franz Gockel of *I. Bataillon/Regiment 726* of *716. ID*, it meant he and his twenty-six comrades sharing the bunkers and trenches – the *Mannschaften* – of their WN62 defensive position with thirteen new men from Goth's *II. Bataillon* – two of whom were *Gefreiters*: Heinrich 'Hein' Severloh and Peter Simeth. Simeth wasn't exactly bowled over by his new bunk-mates:

> I slept in the middle bunk, underneath me was an older man of thirty-five, already ancient to us eighteen-year-olds. Heinrich his name was, he had spent the last weeks in Bayeux at the dentist getting a set of false teeth. These didn't fit very well and each evening he placed them in a glass of water on the headboard of his bunk. There were others with us who would normally have been classed as unfit for duty, the 'Invaliden'. One eighteen-year-old had lost an eye as a child and now wore a glass one, another was hard of hearing.[12]

Not that such disabilities were confined to the 'belly' divisions. A report complied by the SS on recruitment to their own armed wing, the famously choosy Waffen-SS, openly stated that even they were accepting men 'with epilepsy, severe tuberculosis and other serious physical disabilities'.[13] As Ivar Corneliussen – a Danish Waffen-SS volunteer in the *Wiking* division – remembered, after losing an eye in the fighting on the River Dnieper in 1943, 'The doctor said it was OK that it was my left eye that I'd lost as that wasn't my shooting eye, so I could go back to my regiment once I had convalesced.'

As for Hein Severloh, he had severe health issues following the field punishment meted out to him in Russia for making 'defeatist remarks'. Now back with his unit after home leave and a very short stint on an NCOs course in Brunswick, he was assigned as orderly to *Oberleutnant* Bernhard Frerking. Frerking's role was to control the fire of the nearby 10.5cm artillery battery at Houtteville, while the defence of *WN62* itself was in the hands of *Leutnant* Edmond Bauch.

Bauch's post, *WN62* – *Widerstandnest* (resistance nest) 62 – was one of sixteen such strongpoints covering the five-mile length of what the Allied planners had designated *Omaha Beach*, and was known to the Germans as the Grandcamp sector. Numbered from 59 in the east at Sainte-Honorine-des-Pertes, to 74 in the west just beyond Vierville-sur-Mer, and manned by around eight-hundred men from five companies, these strongpoints included eight concrete bunkers with medium artillery, almost all 7.5cm calibre, a further eighteen smaller 5cm anti-tank guns, thirty-five pillboxes, eighty-five machine-guns, six mortar pits and six tank turrets embedded in concrete. The beach was bordered by escarpements and bluffs that in some places were a hundred feet high. The only viable way off the sand was via five draws – wooded ravines – that ran off the beach and through the high ground overlooking it; unsurprisingly much of the German heavy weaponry covered these routes. No two strongpoints were the same, each being designed and built to suit both the location and whatever equipment was available to defend it. Bauch and Frerking's *WN62* was the biggest and most powerful of the Omaha Beach sixteen, encompassing an area of stony ground 332 metres long by 324 metres wide. Originally housing two 7.5cm cannon, one of the guns had been moved elsewhere. The sole survivor was trained along the beach to the west and had large concrete walls on the seaward side to protect it from frontal fire. There was also a 5cm anti-tank gun and a 5cm mortar mounted in a *Tobruk*; a small type of concrete bunker, also called a *Ringstand*, plus a twin-barrelled MG 34 machine-gun on an anti-aircraft mount and two pre-war Polish machine-guns. There were two small bunkers used to house ammunition, and two larger ones which doubled up to store both ammunition and, in times of bombardment, personnel. The whole place was ringed with barbed wire, and there were even a few anti-personnel mines scattered around. Finally, in common with most strongpoints, there was a small fire-control post cum-observation bunker to keep a look-out.

The night before D-Day, Peter Simeth drew the lucky straw and got a pass to go into Treviers and visit the Variété theatre, before picking up his laundry from a local washer-woman and going to bed. Hein Severloh and Franz Gockel weren't so lucky, and spent another monotonous night rotating on the endless sentry duty roster.

> From the bunker we could hear the rhythm as the guards walked along their posts, the hobnails clicking on the ground. The password had already been given out for the evening, and our company commander was busy overseeing last-minute preparations. In our quarters we were reading and re-reading the last letters from home... In a corner two men played cards... Later on in the evening I had to go on guard again; how often this duty seemed like an eternity until you were relieved. I ran back to the bunker to get a few more hours sleep because I still had another watch to stand.

Out in the bay the largest and most powerful fleet ever assembled was steaming towards Gockel and his comrades, even as streams of transport aircraft prepared to jettison three entire divisions of paratroopers over the eastern and western edges of the chosen landing area, and waves of bombers and fighters revved their engines ready to plaster the Norman stretch of the *Atlantikwall* with hundreds of tonnes of high-explosive. This was the long-awaited landing. This was D-Day.

Over on the eastern base of the Cotentin – the peninsula, with the port of Cherbourg as its head, that juts out into the sea from western Normandy – a twenty-three-year-old *Leutnant* was carrying out yet another tour of his own *Widerstandnest*, in his case *WN5* – sometimes mistakenly referred to as '*WN104*', which overlooked the landing site designated by the Allies as *Utah Beach*. A Flensburger like von Luck, Arthur Jahnke was an officer with *GR. 919* of Karl-Wilhelm von Schlieben's hugely-understrength *709. ID*. At first sight Jahnke looked the typical belly army soldier; narrow shoulders, thick glasses and of barely medium height, you could almost see the 'unfit for service' certificate in his tunic pocket, but, tied around his neck on an old shoelace was Nazi Germany's highest award for bravery; the Knight's Cross of the Iron Cross. It was very rare indeed for such a junior officer to have earned such a medal. Jahnke and his seventy-five men of *3. Kompanie* were in an unenviable position.

Unlike the topography over to the east that favoured Franz Gockel and his comrades, there were no cliffs or high bluffs an assault force would have to negotiate to get at *WN5*. The beach, often called La Madeleine by the locals due to its proximity to the tiny hamlet of the same name, was long and flat, and the dunes behind it were low – Jahnke's strongpoint was sited near *La Grande Dune*, but the term was misleading. The Germans had tried to maximise their meagre defensive resources by clustering entrenchments and fortifications together so they could mutually support each other if attacked, so Jahnke's own position was buttressed by another four; *WNs 3, 4, 7* and *8*. While not flush with heavy weapons, Jahnke did at least have a few, including a 7.5cm anti-tank gun, two dismounted ex-armoured car 5cm pedestal guns, a First World War vintage FK-16 7.5cm field gun, various mortars and machine-guns – one of the latter fitted in an old French Renault tank turret – and most prized of all, an 8.8cm; the most effective and feared anti-tank gun of the war – in an enfilade position just to the north in StP 9. The trenches were in good shape, the men well-disciplined and alert; a consequence of Jahnke's time with them since recovering from wounds received on the Russian front. Nicknamed 'the Ivan' by his new comrades for obvious reasons, he had made himself unpopular at first by bringing a touch of rigour to his sleepy posting; firstly he banned the locals from walking through his defensive position to go fishing on the beach, and then he carried out a practice drill one night, his men shooting at an imaginary attacker. *Oberstleutnant* Keil at regimental headquarters was apoplectic, 'That Ivan has clearly gone off his rocker, he just can't wait for the show to start!'

But Jahnke had made friends in high places. On an inspection visit back in early May, Rommel himself had toured *WN5*, and on being introduced to Jahnke had asked to see his hands. Slightly baffled by the request, Jahnke had taken off his issued grey suede officers' gloves and showed Rommel his hands; all scratched and bloody from working with his men on the barbed wire. Rommel beamed: 'Well done *Leutnant*, the blood on an officers' hands from fortification work is worth every bit as much as that shed in battle.'

Never one to go overboard with praise, the Desert Fox then complained to Jahnke about the lack of obstacles on the beach itself, but Jahnke was a match for the disgruntled field marshal, explaining to him that whenever they placed them in the sand the high tide simply washed them away – Rommel let it go.

A month later, in the dark of the night, with the landings still a few hours off, Jahnke walked up and down his trenches, stopping to speak to a lone sentry manning a scissor telescope looking out to sea amidst the blackness.

'Anything out there?'

'Nothing *Herr Leutnant*. They won't come in this weather.'

There had been a storm for the last twenty-four hours and Jahnke nodded his agreement before saying good night and heading off back to his bunker to get a few hours sleep, or maybe even take a shower using the watering-can his men had rigged up for him. Before he got there the drone of hundreds of aircraft engines filled the night – they had to be Anglo-American, the Luftwaffe hadn't been seen for weeks. Uneasy, Jahnke used his field telephone to call *WN2* and speak to his friend, *Leutnant* Ritter.

'What do you think it is?'

'I have a feeling that something's up, but probably nothing that concerns us.'

'I hope you're right Arthur.'

'Of course I am. I'll come and have a tot of your cognac tomorrow just to prove I'm right.'

Jahnke knew that, given his combat experience, his fellow officers looked to him for leadership, but even so, despite his *sang froid*, he had extra rations issued to the men – it distracted them from the aircraft noise, and no infantryman turns down more food. Jahnke then went to bed but couldn't sleep. He was lying there smoking when the telephone rang. It was battalion headquarters: 'Enemy parachutists probably dropping behind your position.'

Jahnke acknowledged the alarm, slammed down the phone and shouted to *Feldwebel* Hein to get the men to stand-to. Unsure of what was happening; Hein thought it might be *résistants* saboteurs. Jahnke sent out a small patrol to scout the area behind and to the south of his position. Not long afterwards a short burst of fire was heard from the patrol area. Jahnke's men came back shepherding nineteen captured American paratroopers. The patrol commander explained to Jahnke that they had come across the paras wading waist deep in the flooded fields and had opened fire, killing several and wounding two; the rest had surrendered. Sending the wounded to be treated at his first-aid post, Jahnke questioned the remainder and then reported to battalion: 'Nineteen prisoners of the American 2nd Battalion, 506th Parachute Regiment...'

The line went dead. Jahnke checked the phone. He could only reach the two strongpoints to his immediate left and right. That did it, he knew something big was afoot, but he also knew that he and his men were now effectively isolated from the rest of their regiment. He went to check on the two wounded prisoners; an enlisted man with a bullet wound in his jaw, and a young lieutenant, only to have the latter complain loudly to him that the orderly treating them was violating the Geneva Convention by carrying a pistol. The orderly in question was *Gefreiter* Hoffmann – a Russian front veteran like Jahnke. Ever correct, Jahnke ordered Hoffmann to take off the sidearm. Having complied, Hoffmann told his boss that the two paras were very restless and the officer kept on asking him what the time was and when they would be moved inland.

In a wood a few miles away, another German medic, 22-year-old Fritz Müller, had been sent out by his commander to look for wounded paratroopers. Like Hoffmann he carried a pistol, and for the same reason, having also just come from the East. On hearing a noise he found another German soldier looting the body of an American paratrooper. Incensed, Müller shouted at him to stop, only to be told where to go. Having pulled a ring off one of the man's fingers, the looter stood up and walked away, but only got five yards before a shot rang out and he dropped dead. Confused, Müller ran over to the American's corpse only to find he wasn't dead, just badly wounded. Instinctively he began to treat him, and then after a couple of minutes Müller was hit by a cigarette that seemed to have fallen out of the sky. Soon he was being showered in cigarettes, and although he doesn't smoke he stuffed them into his pockets, planning to trade them with his comrades. He realised later that the cigarettes had been from other American paras in the trees above him, thanking him for looking after their buddy.[14]

Back at *WN5*, Arthur Jahnke had left his stone-built headquarters with its watering-can shower and cosy billet, and taken up post in his battle position; which consisted of a hole dug in the sandy soil at the end of a trench, shored up with some rough-hewn wooden planks.

Jahnke strained his eyes to see through the mist, and saw aircraft away to the north – that then turned and came straight for the tiny patch of land four hundred yards long by three hundred yards wide that was *WN5*. They were so low he saw the doors open in their bellies; bombers! Then it was just ear-splitting noise and huge concussion waves that knocked Jahnke off his feet and half-buried him. Struggling, he managed to dig himself free, but his left shoulder and arm were numb. Two of the ammunition bunkers were on fire and the anti-tank gun was wrecked. One of his soldiers, an elderly man from the Ruhr, was badly shaken; 'Everything is wrecked *Herr Leutnant*! The stores are on fire, we've got to surrender!' Jahnke didn't panic – he'd won his Knight's Cross by leading his company to capture a hill from the Soviets. Loudly proclaiming that no-one was surrendering, Jahnke ordered his men to clean up the rubble and repair the trenches. He then called *Leutnant* Ritter again:

'How is it with you?'

'Nothing much here, looks as if they were after you lot.'

Ritter was right. Moments later a flight of fighter-bombers screamed in, spraying Jahnke's position with cannon shells. The two bunkers with the 5cm guns and their crews were blown to bits.

Then the armada began to appear.

Eighteen ships started to bombard positions inland; artillery batteries, headquarters, supply and ammunition depots. Then they turned their guns on the beach-facing strongpoints. *Feldwebel* Hein shouted for permission from Jahnke to open fire on the nearest destroyer with the FK-16 – in the absence of any fire from his own artillery, Jahnke agreed – what he didn't know was that the observation post for *901. Artillerie-Regiment*, camped out in the church bell tower at Sainte-Marie-du-Mont, had been shot away, so the battery was blind, and also under air and naval attack itself. As was his reserve company; *Leutnant* Schön's *Nr. 13*, and his indirect fire support, the former Russian guns of *I/1261. Heeres-Küstenartillerie-Regiment* (HKAA – Army Coastal Artillery Regiment) outside Saint-Martin-de-Varreville, some two miles away. In desperation Jahnke ordered one of his men to get on a bicycle and pedal to the guns with instructions that they should start shelling the beach as soon as Jahnke put up two green flares.

Meanwhile, *Feldwebel* Hein and his gun crew took aim at the nearest destroyer. It was like throwing pebbles at an elephant; Hein's gun fired armour-piercing shells weighing 15lb (6.8 kg) of metal and high-explosive. One of the bombardment flotilla, the Royal Navy monitor, the *Erebus*, fired shells more than a hundred times bigger; 1,938lbs in imperial punch or 879 kilograms in metric shock and awe – and in any case, Hein's first two rounds fell short of the target. He didn't get a chance for a third: three quick salvoes from the destroyer, the first and second bracketing the gun and then the third bang on. Also hit were Jahnke's headquarters bunker, the fire control station and most of the remaining mines, detonated by the blast and concussion waves.

The naval bombardment didn't last long; less than half an hour, and then the landing craft were nearing the shore. Alongside them were what Jahnke and his men thought were mini-gunships, but were in fact one of many Allied secret weapons designed for the landings – Duplex Drive swimming tanks. The flotation skirts and extra propeller of the new weapons weren't able to cope with rough seas, but in the relatively calm waters off Utah they worked well, and only four of the original thirty-two failed to make it ashore – twenty Allied tank crew drowned with their vehicles when their LCT (Landing Craft Tank) hit a mine, as described by Admiral Morton Deyo on the *Tucaloosa*; 'Higher than her length she rises, turns slowly, stern downward and crashes back into the bay.'

The American 4th Infantry Division's 8th Regiment were the first ashore, coming under fire from Jahnke, Ritter, and their surviving troopers – but most of the Germans' heavy weaponry was gone, and the few machine-guns and mortars left weren't going to stop an assault as big as this. The first assault wave was well-trained and well-prepared, and methodically begin to eliminate the few strongpoints and bunkers of *709. ID* still holding out. Twenty minutes after the first American troops hit the beach, the Duplex Shermans arrived and the unequal battle was effectively over. Jahnke's sole remaining gun; the much-feared 88 in StP 9, had been damaged in the bombardment and managed to fire just one round – hitting a Sherman – before giving up the ghost. In desperation, the young officer turned to what he hoped was an ace up his sleeve – the *Goliath*. This box of explosives on tracks, had been designed as a remote-control vehicle that could be steered by its operator to an objective, such as a tank, and then detonated, destroying both itself and the enemy. One-shot weapons though they were, they were also pretty sensitive souls, and the air and naval bombardment had damaged both their drive and control mechanisms; a few limped out of their holding bays before breaking down, but none came close to any Shermans. Jahnke then sent up the two flares as the agreed signal to his supporting gunners – no shells came arcing overhead to smack into the Americans – his pedalling messenger lay dead in a roadside ditch less than half-a-mile away, killed by an Allied fighter.

'C' Company, 1st Battalion, 8th Infantry had *WN5* as their assault objective. With the Shermans providing direct fire support, the American infantrymen moved in to finish off Jahnke and his men. They passed a German corpse, run over by a Sherman and described by one officer as

...ironed flat like a figure in a comic book, the arms of its grey uniform at right angles to its pressed and flattened coat, black boots and the legs that were in them just as flat and thin as if they had been cut from a sheet of dirty cardboard.

Jahnke, still suffering concussion from the naval barrage, turned to his runner: 'It looks as though God and the world have forsaken us. What's happened to our airforce?'

The Russian front veteran understood the situation but hadn't won the Knight's Cross by throwing the towel in, so, he picked up his rifle and exhorted his men to carry on fighting. The Shermans lined up and fired point blank at *WN5*. One by one the trenches were smashed; first the mortar, then the ancient, half-buried Renault tank turret and its lone machine-gun manned by *Gefreiter* Friedrich; proud wearer of a pair of bottle-bottom spectacles. Somehow Friedrich survived a direct hit and scrambled clear, his leg badly torn up. Hoffmann, the now-disarmed medic, was killed. On the beach the Americans were now landing undisturbed.

Ammunition was running low among the surviving defenders, but in one of war's many cruel ironies, a US assault squad discovered a broken-down Goliath – bemused as to what it was, they threw a couple of hand-grenades at it – and missed. One intrepid soul dashed over and wedged a grenade into its forward hatch – not realising it was basically a big, unexploded bomb – the resulting blast killed him and half his buddies.

By now Jahnke was alone, still firing, but without hope: 'This then, is the end.' A Sherman fired at his position and he was again half-buried in sand and knocked unconscious. He came around to find a GI dragging him out. Even then he wouldn't give up and lunged for a rifle on the ground, only for his would-be rescuer to casually bat his arm away and say; 'Take it easy German!'

It was 8.30am. Arthur Jahnke and *WN5* had held out for two hours. The Americans began to push inland along the raised causeways above the flooded fields.

The Westheer's defensive plan relied on the counter-attack as its main weapon – it was one of the German military's dominant tactics during the war, as it had been in the First World War. As Arthur Jahnke sat disconsolately on the beach wall, separated from his few surviving men, tired and longing for a cigarette – he felt let down by his superiors and kept on asking himself the same question – where are the reinforcements, where is our counter-attack? What he didn't know – having all communication knocked out earlier – was that they had tried exactly that. The night before, *709. ID*'s divisional commander von Schlieben had gone to the general officer wargames scheduled to take place in Rennes on the morning of the 6th, and in his absence all was confusion among the German leadership – a situation not helped by the death of *Generalleutnant* Wilhelm Falley, the commander of *91. Luftlande-Infanterie-Division,* the reserve formation sitting behind *709. ID.* Falley was at the same wargames, and like von Schlieben was racing back to his unit in his staff car when he was caught up in a firefight with American paratroopers and killed. *Fallschirmjägerregiment 6* had been attached to Falley's division to strengthen it, and now, in the moment of crisis, its veteran commander Friedrich von der Heydte took charge and led his men towards the sound of the guns on the coast. In a motorcycle sidecar he reached Sainte-Marie-du-Mont, got hold of the key to the church belfry and climbed up. Looking out towards *WN5* he described what he saw:

> I had a unique picture in front of me that I will never forget. The ocean lay before me, deep blue and practically motionless. On the horizon numerous battleships lined up into an almost closed chain. Between the ships and the shore there was a brisk back-and-forth traffic of craft transferring American soldiers to the shore. The Americans were only meeting resistance from a single German bunker – which from my point of view was to the right of the ships – that was shooting at the landing soldiers.

This was Janke and his men in *WN5.* Von der Heydte could see more American soldiers marching towards him.

> Sainte-Marie-du-Mont was not occupied by German troops; by the state of his office the local commander appeared to have left in a hurry… The village lay about five kilometres from the coast, and the Americans had covered about half that distance… I met my regiment in a village called St-Côme-du-Mont and gave my first combat orders.

Those orders to *Hauptmann* Preikschat's *I. Bataillon* were clear; along with some horse-drawn guns they'd come across, Preikschat was to advance up the road to reach and occupy Sainte-Marie-du-Mont and block any further enemy advance, and, if they could, they were to then attack and relieve *WN5*. With no motor transport, no armour, and crucially, no artillery support of any significance, Preikschat led his men up the road and directly into a follow-on landing of American glider-borne troops from the 101st *Screaming Eagles*. *Leutnant* Eugen Scherer:

> Our battalion's attack progressed well at first and we rushed immediately into the paratroopers as they landed from the gliders. A gory battle developed on the disorderly ground, man against man and section against section. We took hundreds of prisoners ... and sent them to the rear because we assumed that as the regimental commander had promised us there were more German soldiers following up behind us. Unfortunately we lost time because of this fight and could no longer reach Sainte-Marie-du-Mont.

Preikschat's gun crews and their draught-horses were caught in an ambush and wiped out. With that, the German counter-attack plan to rush to the aid of Arthur Jahnke and his beleaguered men came to naught. Back at the beach a dejected Jahnke was being questioned by an American officer; 'How many guns do you have? How many men have you here?'

Jahnke refused to answer, and the officer unfolded a map showing the exact layout of *WN5* – even *Gefreiter* Friedrich's Renault tank turret was marked on it. The map was labelled '*Utah*', it was the first time Jahnke had ever seen the name. Suddenly, with an irony that wasn't lost on the young officer, German shells began to land on the beach, causing men to scatter. They were from *Oberst* Gerhard Triepel's *HKAA. 1261* over in Pernelle. 'The trajectory of the shells lay straight over my regimental command post. We were some ten to twelve miles from the target. The excitement produced in the target area by every burst was clearly visible.'

Triepel's barrage was way too little, way too late. What the fire did was fall on captured friend and foe alike, with Jahnke hit by shrapnel – a wound his American guard helped bandage. Arthur Jahnke's war was over. Having taken off his boots and socks to wade to a landing craft, he was trying to put them back on again on board a destroyer when a group of curious American sailors surrounded him on the deck and tripped him up. A not-very-amused officer bawled out his men, had them help the wounded Jahnke up, and escort him to the wardroom where he was given his first cup of real coffee in a very long time, as the American officers stared longingly at his Knight's Cross.

709. *ID*'s front on Utah had been breached in the first couple of hours of the landing, but not all along its length. To the north of *WN5* was *Grenadier* Heinrich Runder and his comrades, manning their defensive position covering an anti-tank gun and a concrete observation post overlooking the beach: 'The position was very basic in construction, being made of logs rammed into the sides of a trench in the earth. The soil was very sandy you see, and the logs were needed to hold the walls up.'

Runder had been wounded in the head in Tunisia back in '43, and wasn't looking forward to the fight he and his friends all knew was coming: 'I dreaded being in action again.Some men excel in combat, and others manage somehow to struggle through, and I was in the latter category.'

On the morning of the 6th as dawn broke, Runder caught his first sight of the landing armada:

A vast number of ships. Absolutely vast... I can tell you that my throat went dry, painfully dry, and my hands began to shake. I wasn't the only man to be affected that way, one of the very young lads began to retch as if he was going to be sick. It was the effect of pure fear...

Just as at *WN5*, Runder's position was first hit by an Allied air attack, and then by naval bombardment:

I could feel the blasts which made my ears ring and my nose bleed...I could see the large bunker behind us, which was a concrete bunker mounting an anti-tank gun. One of the rockets struck it, and simply blew the bunker to pieces. The walls and roof all flew apart, and the gun itself crashed down near our trench.

After the gunfire died down, Runder witnessed that rarity on D-Day, the appearance of a Luftwaffe aircraft that had somehow managed to get through Allied air cover: 'We saw a Luftwaffe fighter, a Messerschmitt, go over our beach very fast, and then it turned inland and just disappeared without shooting. That was the only German plane I saw that day.'

He saw plenty of Allied aircraft though, and a few hours later – once *WN5* had fallen and Jahnke was kicking his heels on the beach waiting to be taken off – Runder's position came under concerted attack from rocket-carrying American P-47 Thunderbolts:

> These rockets exploded when they landed and threw out a liquid which detonated with a very bright, red flame... There was a very strong smell of burning tar or rubber ... and one of them exploded right there at the end of my trench. The next few minutes were complete hell and chaos ... the liquid was sickening in the way it worked, it was some kind of gasoline fuel mixed with rubber or nylon or something like that. It stuck to everything like glue, to uniforms, to skin, to hair ... many of our men were completely on fire, and one by one they fell to their knees and gave up their struggle or simply fell back into the flames and disappeared from sight.[15]

Close to Runder's trench was 20-year-old *Gefreiter* Stefan Heinevez. Like Runder, Heinevez had ended up on the Cotentin after being wounded, his limp a result of the fighting on Sicily. Manning an MG 34 *Tobruk* with Sepp – a Belgian who had volunteered for the Wehrmacht, probably from the disputed border area around Eupen – Heinevez came under attack from what he believed were American paratroops.

> Sepp was sitting on the edge of the hatch looking inland with the binoculars. I asked him what he could see and he turned to me to answer, and as he did so he was shot directly through the throat... I saw the bullet emerge from the back of his neck, causing a spray of blood and tissue. He remained upright and another bullet him in the chest, causing a lot of matter to shoot out of his back, along with shreds of his uniform. He was literally shot to pieces in front of me.

Heinevez held off the Americans with his machine-gun, and was soon joined by an officer and several other men from the strongpoint-house his *Tobruk* was covering. The Germans retreated to some more defensive positions about a kilometre or so to the rear, fighting a running battle with the Americans.

> I saw several of our troops running towards me from the direction of the beach, one by one they were all hit by bullets,

knocking them down. One man was hit horribly in the head, and he lost most of his skull, another man was hit in the stomach and writhed on the ground, thrashing his legs and vomiting. Two men threw themselves down next to me, and one was immediately hit in the neck, and had his head partially severed. I fired a very long burst in an arc around the whole front of me...

Air attack from Allied fighter-bombers now became a huge threat to the young *gefreiter* and his small party, which by now included some Hiwis: 'One man – one of the Russians – was hit in the abdomen by several bullets; his body was cut in half ... the rest of us could only step over the two pieces as we ran on.'

Eventually reaching the cover of a line of concrete bunkers, Heinevez realised that safety was an illusion. The position came under sustained air attack and the strongpoint he was in was hit by the same rockets that created so much havoc for Runder and his comrades. The destruction was awful to behold:

One rocket hit our blockhouse on the wall outside the gun aperture, and the explosion was completely blinding... I saw fragments of burning material pour in through the aperture ... these fragments expanded and burned ... this fire simply would not go out, it covered the gun crew and sank into their ammunition pile. There was complete panic and disorder... The men near the gun were consumed in these white flames, uniforms peeled off in scorched pieces, and their bare skin was set alight by the fire... Someone threw open the steel door of the bunker, and I hurled myself at it... I made the mistake of looking back into the bunker... I can tell you that the interior was a vision of hell, an obscene sight that remains with me even now.

Germany's *landsers* hadn't earned a fearsome reputation for nothing though, and no sooner was Heinevez outside the burning bunker than he armed himself with a submachine-gun and joined a comrade cradling a *panzerschreck*, the German version of the American bazooka. Taking up position amidst smashed vehicles and shattered concrete, the two men opened fire on an approaching tank:

The *panzerschreck* man said to me; 'It's a Sherman, we can finish him,' and before I could answer he fired... The explosion wasn't large, but I saw many fragments of metal burst off the hull immediately, and the tracks stopped moving... I heard crackling noises which sounded as if it was burning.

Not content with his first success, after Heinevez reloaded him the *panzerschreck* gunner took on another Sherman, which he disabled but did not destroy.

This was an incredible success for us, to have hit two tanks with two shots, and I remember feeling a sensation of great pride in this achievement ... but the second tank fired on us with high-explosive... The *panzerschreck* man was hit by shrapnel in the shoulder and neck and began bleeding heavily. He threw away his weapon and took a grenade from his boot, handing it to me ... he told me we should blow ourselves up rather than be captured. He was either very fanatical, or mentally unbalanced.

It seemed like the game was well and truly up for Heinevez and his kamikaze comrade, when 'there was the noise of another tank from the south, from the direction of our lines. I believed our panzer reinforcements were arriving at the last possible moment to assist us and defend the bunker line, as the Feldwebel had promised us in the bunker.'

The unknown *Feldwebel* had confirmed to Heinevez and the other soldiers in the bunker what the German plan of action all along the coast was intended to be: 'Reinforcements were coming up from the south and east, and we only had to hold the bunker for a few hours before our panzers would arrive to push the attackers back to the beach and into the sea.'

But the plan didn't work. 'All that arrived was a single, solitary StuG III gun.'[16] That was the story of the Wehrmacht's D-Day – summed up in ten words.

The Germans were playing a poor hand badly, but they still had two picture cards left; Franz Gockel, Hein Severloh and their comrades of *352. ID*, and the crews of *21. Panzer* – could they make the difference?

As landing craft packed full of American assault troops motored towards Omaha, *Unteroffizier* Henrik Naube of *916. Grenadier-Regiment* – based in a *Widerstandnest* on the western edge of the landing site at Vierville-sur-Mer – was thankful to have survived the bombing and shelling that had killed many of his comrades: 'One man tried to run ... he was caught by an absolute storm of shrapnel, and his torso was ripped across and broken open... His body produced a lot of steam in the cool air, which filled the trench for a while.'

As the barrage lifted, Naube prepared to fight back.

> I lifted the MG 42 back up and re-sited it in the firing slit. I remembered my father had told me many times that he had done this himself as a machine-gunner at the battle of the Somme back in the first war; he and his comrades hid deep in their dugouts with their guns and then raced to fix their guns back in place before the British attacked – now here I was doing the same thing.[17]

At the other – eastern – edge of Omaha, Franz Gockel and Hein Severloh were doing much the same in WN62. It was just after 6am.

> We were just defending ourselves, we wanted to survive. They were not our enemy ... we didn't know them and we had no option to say yes or no to what was happening – I just remember thinking they had more ships than we had men.

Gockel settled down behind his MG 42 and waited, as did Severloh in his foxhole overlooking the beach. At first, the young *gefreiter* thought his opponents were the British, and only realised they were American when he saw the bright, white painted letters 'US' on the bows of the incoming landing craft before the ramps dropped and the attack began.

> They jumped into the cold water up to their shoulders and chests. Some disappeared under the water for a moment and, half-swimming, half-wading, they began to move slowly onto the beach in front of our strongpoint. At that moment there was complete silence in the bay, not one shot was fired. We had strict orders to wait until the GIs were only about 400m from the edge of the beach and were wading in water up to their knees... Once the Americans had firm ground under their feet they waded in two long lines, one after the other, through the water, with the left hand firmly on the pack of the man in front. Everything was so calm, so organised, that you had the impression that they were merely carrying out an exercise ... we were well aware that the GIs below us were being led like lambs to the slaughter.

Henrik Naube thought the same as Hein Severloh:

> It was orderly, very orderly. The craft were stopping at a point
> where the water was about chest or neck height, and the men were
> running down the ramps and jumping into the water, holding their
> guns above their heads... In most cases the men tried to advance one
> behind the other, with each man holding the backpack of the man in
> front. It was as if they were conducting a drill or an exercise.

Except it wasn't. Severloh heard his commander, *Oberleutnant*
Frerking, mutter 'Poor swine,' before he gave the order '*Los!*' and
the German defenders opened fire. Another machine-gunner, Franz
Rachmann, recalled the moment: 'This was the first time I had shot
at living men, and with my machine-gun I fire, I fire, I fire! For each
American I see fall there came ten hundred others!'

One of Rachmann's comrades manning a 5cm gun recalled the
initial fighting the same way: 'We watched the landing craft under
the direct fire of our guns and could see precisely what happened
to the Americans, it was terrible.'

Severloh went on:

> I could clearly see the water shoot up where my machine-gun
> bullets hit. When the small fountains approached the GIs they threw
> themselves down. After just a few minutes panic broke out among
> the Americans. All of them lay in the cold, calm water, some tried to
> get to the nearest beach obstacles.

What Severloh was doing in the east was being mirrored by Naube
over in the west.

> The Americans were about four hundred metres away from us. I did
> not sight on them individually at first, but I began firing and swept
> the gun from left to right along the beach. This knocked down the
> first few men in each line; the MG 42 was so powerful that the
> bullets would often pass through a human body and hit whatever
> was behind it. So many of these men were hit by a bullet which
> had already passed through a man in front, or even two men. .The
> Americans began to run, wade or stagger forwards, trying to get out
> of the water and onto the sand itself. They still moved quite slowly,
> and because of that and the close range they were easy targets to hit.

Also at the eastern end of the beach was *Obergrenadier* Karl Wegner, one of the youngsters who had done their three-week basic training before being posted into *352. ID*, in his case to *GR. 914* where he was trained as an MG 42 gunner.

> ...I pulled the trigger up tight. The MG roared, sending hot lead into the men running along the beach. I saw some go down, I knew I had hit them. Others dived for whatever cover was out there. The bullets ripped up and down the sand. This 19-year-old lad from Hanover had just cut down several men. My mind rationalised it; this was war. Even so it left a sour taste in my mouth. But now was not the time to think of right or wrong, only survival... After the first few moments had passed my mind became automated. I would fire as I had been trained to do, in short bursts 15 to 20 cms above the ground. When the gun jammed I would clear it quickly because every second counted... We knew where to shoot... When I pulled back the bolt for what seemed to be the thousandth time, I paused for a good look down the beach. I saw *Amis* [*landser* slang for American soldiers] lying everywhere. Some were dead, and others quite alive... What I saw convinced me that, for the moment, it was worse down there than it was for us where we were, although we had taken – and were still getting – a pounding.

Unlike at Utah where Arthur Jahnke and his few men were decimated by the bombardment and then outgunned by the American Duplex Shermans, at Omaha enough German automatic and heavy weapons had survived to stall the landings. Machine-gunners like Hein Severloh kept up the pressure:

> The landing craft were now coming on in waves, a great swarm in an irregular formation. There was a break and then the next wave came. As the boats approached I concentrated on the ramps. As soon as they came down for the GIs to jump out I began to fire ... the GIs tried to find cover behind the beach obstacles which still towered above the waves, or behind the corpses of their fallen comrades which were washing up and down ... until the next wave I fired at everything which moved in the water and on the beach.

A few metres away Franz Gockel watched in awe as the Americans were slaughtered.

The troops from the first landing craft made the first steps in close formation, but broke apart under the first burst from our dependable MG 42... The beach became strewn with dead, wounded and shelter-seeking soldiers. The waves of attackers broke against our defences.

It was the same story at the other end of the beach in front of Henrik Naube.

> ...the shallow part of the sea immediately in front of us was full of bodies, probably at least a hundred bodies ... the tide was starting to come in, and these bodies were rolling and swaying with the movement of the water... I began to feel pity for these troops because they kept arriving in landing craft. The craft would deposit them in the shallows and they would walk towards us through the water in the same way as the first set of troops. We fired at them in the same way, causing the same deaths and injuries.

After two hours of fighting, the defences at Omaha were still holding; clustered together in strongpoints, the slit trenches, eight concrete bunkers, thirty-five pillboxes, six mortar pits and eighty-five machine-gun nests were doing the job they were designed for – holding the majority of the enemy on the beach. Some American troops had somehow managed to get off the sandy killing field; determined and lucky men under courageous and equally lucky junior leaders, but most were still lying on the sand and shingle trying desperately to stay alive as withering German machine-gun fire searched for them amidst the obstacles and the already dead and dying. For the first and only time that day, the Allies seriously considered withdrawing from a beach they had landed on – and the defenders could see it! Franz Gockel saw the American naval transports out at sea turn about, and closer into shore it seemed to Henrik Naube that he and his comrades were doing just enough to carry the day:

> ...one of the landing craft came close to the shallows, and whoever was in charge of it seemed to hesitate. The craft slowed and steered carefully ... as if selecting a place to land, but it did not make a final approach. It turned away, making a manoeuvre as if it was trying to turn around and leave the scene... But as this craft turned away it presented its flank to our 88mm guns, and it was shot immediately below the waterline ... the craft began to capsize

rapidly as the water flooded in... I saw that whole landing craft go up in flames within seconds and sink very quickly. I thought; 'If many more try to turn away like that, there won't be enough Americans to replace the dead ones on the beach, and so we will win this dreadful fight.'

This particular landing craft was almost certainly LC92, and it was actually a mine that did the initial damage before an 88 finished her off. Minutes earlier her sister landing craft; LC91 had been set on fire by another 88 strike – she would burn in the water for eighteen hours.

The mixed bag of defenders in *WN62* – Severloh, Wegner and Naube were all 352, but Gockel and most of the rest were from the *716's I Bataillon* detached to Kraiss's division – settled into a grim routine.

Now came the second wave of landing boats and another wet walk for the *Amis*. We defended our bunkers very well, but with every casualty we weakened as more and more *kameraden* were killed or wounded... Some of the *Amis* had reached the seawall and thought they had reached safety from our fire, but this was short-lived. Our mortars had waited for this moment and now laid down a terrible shelling on top of them, showering them with splinters and rocks, and inflicting heavy casualties on those men who had sought shelter there.

Naube was getting into his stride, just as Gockel was:

I aimed more selectively, to make the ammunition last as long as possible. I fired short bursts at small groups of men and hit them that way... The only time we stopped firing was when the gun barrel began to overheat, and the mechanism showed signs of misfiring. We didn't want to run the risk of the gun breaking down, so we rested it to let it cool. We took up our rifles and used them instead, aiming at the Americans coming out of the water.

Hein Severloh was in the same position as his comrades: 'I sometimes used my rifle, since I could fire aimed shots at individual soldiers and at the same time give my machine-gun a chance to cool down.'

In fact, Severloh claimed to have fired no fewer than four hundred rounds from two rifles that day, and a staggering 13,500 through his MG 42; that's an ammo weight of over 560 kilograms – or more than five newborn African elephants. Little wonder he later acquired the soubriquet 'The beast of Omaha'. An NCO, unknown to Severloh by name, was ferrying him ammunition from a nearby underground store, but with a cyclical rate of fire of over 1,200 rounds per minute that had earned the MG 42 the nickname *Hitlersäge* or Hitler's buzz-saw, it wouldn't be too long before the defenders began to run out of bullets. As a veteran *Feldwebel* from 352. *ID* had put it to an inspecting officer just a couple of days previously: 'Herr Major, we have enough ammunition to stop the first, second, third, fourth, and maybe even fifth wave of Tommies. But after that they're going to kick the door in on top of us, and then all will be lost.'[18]

With the beach defences holding – just – the Germans now had to swing into action with the second part of Rommel's strategy to push the Americans back into the sea: counter-attack into the surf. If the Omaha landing could be repulsed, then Collins's U.S. VII Corps would be isolated on Utah, and Montgomery and Eisenhower would have to face the extremely unpalatable reality of a split landing. The Germans had a problem, however: who was going to counter-attack?

In the west, von Schlieben's 709. *ID* was spread all over the Cotentin, the 91. *Luftlande-Infanterie-Division* was leaderless after Falley had been killed in action, and while von der Heydte's paras were indeed counter-attacking towards Utah, they simply weren't strong enough to make the difference; and crucially all these formations had one overwhelming deficiency – no motorised transport. So their ability to move swiftly towards the oncoming Americans, and then concentrate to launch an attack was effectively nil. The problem was doubled when it came to massing for an assault by those same units towards Severloh, Gockel and their remaining comrades still holding out on Omaha – the distances were too great to be covered on foot in the few hours available before the ammunition was spent, and the mass on the beach became too overwhelming to be held any longer.

Sitting in his headquarters at Littry a few miles from the beaches, Dietrich Kraiss knew he had only two options: Feuchtinger's 21. *Panzer* far away to the east, or his own reserve – *Oberstleutnant* Meyer's *Kampfgruppe Meyer* (a *Kampfgruppe* or *KG* – in English 'battlegroup', was an ad hoc grouping of different units brought together to carry out a set task and was often called after its commander). Kraiss had positioned his division in an orthodox inverted triangle formation, with two of his three regiments forward near the beaches themselves; Ernst Heyna's *GR. 914* spread out to the west of Vierville-sur-Mer towards Carentan, Ernst Goth's *GR. 916* from Vierville east towards Arromanches-les-Bains, and in reserve around Saint-Lô, *KG Meyer*, comprising all of *GR. 915*, and *352. Fusilier-Bataillon*. He also had some armour tucked away; *352. Panzerjäger Abteilung* with fourteen *Marders* and ten *StuG III Ausf. G* assault guns.

As would have been expected from an experienced divisional commander like Kraiss, his imperative was to hold his own line with his own men – and in any case, *21. Panzer* was in some disarray, as failings in German command initially held it static in its laagers, before sending it east of the River Orne on a wild-goose chase to hunt down British paras, before finally deciding the main threat was on the beaches and re-directing it once more.

Given the total muddle *21. Panzer* had gotten into, it was clear Kraiss couldn't rely on help from that quarter, so it was to *KG Meyer* that he turned. As Feuchtinger's panzers began to drive hither and thither around Caen and the Orne, *352's* commander found himself on the horns of a military dilemma. *Major* Paul Block, his divisional IIa (Adjutant), had received a message from *Hauptmann* Richard Roth, the German officer commanding one of *716. IDs Ostbataillon*'s; Werner Knaack and the Cossacks of *441 Ost-Bataillon*. Roth's headquarters were at Crépon, northeast of Bayeux, with his four rifle companies manning *WNs 35* through to *40*, spread out around a coastal artillery battery and some of the *716's* own guns at Ver-sur-Mer. His report sent shock waves reverberating around Kraiss's HQ. Roth stated that the men of his *1. Kompanie*, based in the tiny hamlet of Vaux and covering towards strongpoint *WN33a*, were in action against waves of assault craft and were on the verge of being overrun. Simultaneously, his *4. Kompanie* had fought off an enemy advance from what was Gold Beach towards Asnelles, but a larger Allied force with armoured support was now heading for Meuvaines where his *3. Kompanie* was dug in, and given his lack of heavy weapons and manpower he considered it unlikely they could hold. If Meuvaines fell, then the D65 main road would belong to the enemy and he could drive straight to Crépon and east to Bayeux and, more importantly, to Caen. When asked by Block why he hadn't reported this to his own divisional headquarters, the young battalion leader explained that he had no contact with his division – and neither did Kraiss. The *Generalleutnant* was a very worried man. Further reports only confirmed his fears: Allied bombardment knocked out the Cossacks' only heavy weapon – a 7.5cm anti-tank gun – enabling 'C' Company, the Canadian Scottish Regiment, to capture the remains of *WN33a*, as described by the unit diary:

'C' Company, commanded by Major D.G. Crofton, landed at about 0750 hours and came under machine-gun and mortar fire as they raced across the 75–100 yards of beach. They found their targeted pillbox already demolished by the naval bombardment. They moved onto their second objective, the Château Vaux. The Scottish stormed the château and tossed several hand-grenades inside. A group of dispirited Germans quickly surrendered. [These were almost certainly men of Roth's 1. Kompanie.]

Lieutenant Schjelderup's platoon, followed by company headquarters, pressed forward along the centre, up the road to Vaux and then through the tree-filled gulley towards the open fields beyond. Then the platoon attacked three machine-gun posts, one after another. It was grim going, but not a man faltered. The platoon took about fifteen prisoners, one of whom led the assault troops through a heavily-mined area in the gulley. Once through the minefield, the platoon started out across the fields in extended formation, moving through the tall grain towards the gap between Ste.Croix-sur-Mer and Banville. The other platoons came up on the flanks, closing up on either side of company headquarters towards the tip of the woods.

One of the prisoners was the Berliner, *Oberfeldwebel* Werner Knaack – his war was now over.

As the reports mounted up, so did Kraiss's worries. It looked as if Richter's *716. ID* on his right was disintegrating, which would leave his flank open to be turned by an advancing enemy that could then wheel west and roll up his entire line – he had to secure his flank. But if he sent *KG Meyer* to shore up his right-wing, then his reserve would be committed and he would have nothing left to attack towards Omaha, relieve his beleaguered men there and throw the reeling Americans back into the sea.

This then was the moment of decision for the only German infantry division which was toe-to-toe with the Allied assault troops *and* capable of landing a major blow on them that day; should Kraiss's reserve attack north to relieve Goth's *GR. 916* on Omaha and try to finish the job by pushing the Americans back into the sea, or should it veer northeast towards Gold and Juno and seal off his vulnerable flank? The former choice was hugely risky; the men would be advancing into the teeth of naval bombardment and air attack, and any success could be momentary, as they might then be outflanked on their right and annihilated by the day's end. The latter choice carried far less risk and would safeguard *352. ID*, at least for now. Once protected on his right, then Kraiss could once again turn north and launch a counter towards Omaha – this was the sound military option, the one any sane, competent officer wouldn't hesitate to take – but from a German perspective, it was also, without a shred of doubt, the wrong one. A commander with a greater appetite for risk, such as Rommel himself, might very well have taken the gamble, struck north and potentially thrown the entire Allied plan into disarray, but Dietrich Kraiss, for all his solid professionalism, undoubted bravery and devotion to duty, was no Desert Fox. In one of the least recognised episodes of that fateful day, a 54-year-old German divisional commander from Baden-Württemberg, now almost wholly forgotten by posterity, decided to stick and not twist, and chose the safer, orthodox option. *KG Meyer*, with half of Kraiss's armour, would counter-attack towards Gold and Juno, secure Crépon and form a blocking position that would protect his right flank and – hopefully – re-establish communications with *716. ID*. Ernst Goth's *GR. 916* and its attached *716.* battalion would have to rely on their own resources and initiative for now; Franz Gockel, Hein Severloh, Henrik Naube and Karl Wegner were on their own. (See map, p. 314.) To be fair to Kraiss, communication with the strongpoints covering Omaha was patchy and not always accurate. For example, at 1012hrs the command post at *WN62* had radioed its headquarters with a message: '*WN60* is holding, *WN62* is firing with one machine-gun, but the situation is critical. The rest of the 1st and 4th companies are counter-attacking.' The only part of that report that was true was the critical nature of *WN62*'s situation. Elsewhere on Omaha, the few defenders were getting fewer. In Karl Wegner's bunker, his gun commander *Obergefreiter* Lang had already been wounded by shrapnel when he heard the sounds of movement at the pillbox entrance to the rear:

> He moved back with his pistol drawn. We feared the *Amis* had gained our rear and were going to finish us off... Then we heard cries of '*Nicht schiessen! Ich bin Deutscher!*' Lang peered out and pulled someone back in with him. Like us he was a young grenadier, but he was bruised and bloody about the face with a

deep gash on his right leg... He said that in his strongpoint most of the men were *volksdeutsche*, Alsatians and Poles. Things went well until the *Amis* fired directly on them, most then refused to fight and demanded their commander surrender the position. The commander, an *Obergefreiter*, became infuriated and threatened to execute anyone who didn't fight. From behind, one of them fired a shot and killed him, and since the grenadier – Helmuth – was now the only 'German' left in the bunker he was disarmed and beaten up... Lang became very angry at this story. He took Helmuth to the entrance and ordered him to show him where his former position was – it was about 100 metres off to the left. No firing was coming from it. Lang picked up the field telephone receiver only to throw it down in a fit of rage; the line was dead. He picked up several grenades, and we understood then what he intended to do. My friend Willi began to say something but was cut short by Lang with the order; *'Deckungsfeuer!'* (Covering fire!)... We watched as Lang made his way to the bunker. Shrapnel and bullets were flying everywhere, but he made it. We saw him throw in the grenades and throw himself to the ground. Explosions followed, levelling the place. When the dust settled Lang got up and ran back towards us. Fate was not with him this time. Fire from one of the landing craft cut him in two. We were horrified, he was the first person we knew who had been killed, and he had died right in front of us – he wouldn't be the last.

...The mood was grim after Lang's death. The fighting went on and we could see smoke belching from one of our strongpoints, while others had fallen silent. We had no way to contact those that still resisted ... we felt quite alone. We kept up our fire at the *Amis* on the beach, but only to keep them away from us... My thinking was simple, 'don't shoot at me and I won't shoot at you.'

GR. 916's Ernst Goth was a decorated, experienced officer, with a reputation for calm, effective command. Realising he had to hold the line until division could send him some sort of help, he planned his own counter. The aim was to attack towards the beach with *Hauptmann* Grimme's *II. Bataillon*, securing the village of Colleville in the middle of his line, and relieving those strongpoints still fighting. The battalion was still relatively strong, having 6. *Kompanie* and the remains of 7. *Kompanie* under *Leutnant* Heller, 8 under *Leutnant* Berty and 5 under *Oberleutnant* Hahn. To increase the impact of the assault, it was ordered to begin at the same time as *KG Meyer's* thrust to the east, so as to try and convince the Allies that they faced a much wider attack than they actually did. But little was going right for the grey-haired *Oberst* that day, and he was becoming the proverbial Dutch boy at the failing dyke – and fast running out of fingers. It seemed every time he was ready to go, a report would come in of another gap in the line that needed to be plugged, and men and time would be lost doing just that. *Gefreiter* Joseph Häger was manning a machine-gun north of Coleville:

> I kept firing for several hours at everything that moved in front of me, I think I fired about two thousand rounds, I don't know how many men I killed or wounded. At about 11 o'clock we were forced to withdraw, and with *Obergefreiter* Huf I helped cover the retreat to Colleville. At one point I suddenly ran out of ammunition and shouted to Huf who was lying right beside me; 'Where's the ammo? Where's the ammo?' I turned around and as I did so Huf toppled over. He had been shot through the head, a tiny trickle of blood was coming out of a small hole in his forehead... I got into Colleville where I found the remainder of my company. There were less than twenty men from the original one hundred and twenty who had been there that morning. I hoped that some of them were cut-off and would join up with us later, but they never did. We lost one hundred dead in the first few hours of the invasion.

The clock was ticking, the original noon H-hour soon slipped by, and by two in the afternoon not only had Goth's hail-Mary counter-attack still not materialised, but Grimme had lost Hahn and Berty, the latter killed, the former badly wounded, as they strove to hold the Americans, even as Colonel George A. Taylor was famously telling his men lying under the German guns on Omaha: 'There are two kinds of people who are staying on this beach: those who are dead and those who are going to die. Now let's get the hell out of here.'

For Henrik Naube and Karl Wegner, over on the western edge of the beach near Vierville, the ceaseless American pressure and lack of any sort of relieving force were body-blows.

> My loader was hit in the back of the neck by mortar splinters, and he had to withdraw from the gun position... A replacement loader

took over, bringing with him a new pair of ammunition boxes...
I then saw flashes and gunfire for the first time on top of the cliffs
on the other side of the ravine that we were close to. This was a
terrible moment because it suggested that the Americans on the
beach had somehow climbed up and and broken through... I could
see hand-to-hand fighting ... with our troops and Americans so
close that I couldn't fire onto them. The ferocity of that fighting
astonished me. Men were lunging at each other with fixed bayonets,
with their rifle butts and even with entrenching tools and shovels...
Some men were in flames, and other men were shooting or stabbing
them as they staggered around on fire... I was hit and wounded at
this point, by shrapnel from a tank round ... the machine-gun was
blown out of my hands all together. I was stunned, and I slumped
down into the bottom of the trench to try and get the gun back, but
it was damaged and couldn't be used... My new loader was killed
outright when a splinter came in and pierced him through the ribs.
It was a large piece of metal, the size of a knife, and it stuck out
from his torso as he lay dead beside me. In my mind I accepted I was
going to die.

For Karl Wegner – now the senior soldier in his bunker – options were
running out as the pre-landing warnings of the anonymous *Feldwebel*
began to come to fruition.

I finished up a belt of ammunition and waited for Willi to load
another one into the gun. He pushed through the starter tab and
I noticed it was only a 50-round belt. Normally the belts were
linked together for about 200 rounds. I told him to get some
more as this wouldn't last long, and he simply said there wasn't
anymore to get. I looked at him in disbelief, then realised we were
standing in a pile of empty ammunition boxes, belts and spent
shell casings. All that was left of 15,000 rounds. The two of them
looked at me, and I can still see their faces silently asking me,
'What should we do now?'

Things were no better to the east for Hein Severloh, Franz Gockel,
and the other twenty-nine men in *WN62*: 'Time seemed to go very
quickly, I can only remember looking at my watch once, and then the
ammunition began to run out. The depot at Houtteville was empty,

there was nothing left. We only had about 50 rounds left for the machine-gun.'

Severloh had even fired off belts of phosphorescent tracer rounds designed for nighttime – and which gave away his position – but somehow, he was still alive. As for Gockel, his machine-gun had been smashed and put out of action the same as Naube's, and so he was down to firing single shots with his rifle and a pistol. 'Enemy troops had driven into and around our bunker and our ammunition was low.'

Failure was now simply a matter of logistical maths. The companies fighting on the beaches could only hold if they had enough ammunition to keep up a heavy, suppressing fire on the American assault troops – and they were running out of bullets. Their only hope was Grimme's counter-attack, which, if it succeeded, would bring them ammo, reinforcements, and help in clearing up the penetrations of small numbers of Americans who had managed to fight their way off the beaches.

One of Grimme's grenadiers was Martin Eichenseer, and he understood all too well the ammunition nightmare:

> ...added to our already cumbersome field gear were vast quantities of ammunition... I was loaded down like a pack-mule with about seven belts, at two hundred rounds a belt, of MG ammo around my neck, twenty egg grenades stuffed in my pockets and another twenty stick grenades, which I tucked into my belt, boot tops and pack. With my rifle slung on my back and a five-hundred round ammo can in each hand, I headed off to the fighting. I was positive that if just one bullet struck me they would have to sweep up what was left in a dust pan.

But Grimme's attack was too weak and had stalled, and the divisional reserve, which could have made all the difference, had met disaster.

KG Meyer, at first, had had significant success, sweeping forward and rudely shoving back the British spearheads, who were dumbfounded to be facing German armour so early into the landing. It didn't last. The British steadied, and under heavy air and naval bombardment, Meyer's thrust was stopped dead in its tracks. Unable to make any headway, he radioed Kraiss for permission to strike back west and link up with Goth. Realising his mistake, although not the enormity of it, Kraiss agreed, only for Meyer's retreat – for that is what it was – to be turned into a shambles as the reinvigorated British attacked the Germans as they fell back. Withdrawal in contact is renowned as the most difficult phase of combat for any unit to undertake, and Meyer's *kampfgruppe* did not handle it well: firstly, *Fusilier-Bataillon 352* was smashed into shards, then their headquarters was overrun. Among the bodies were not only their commander, but *Panzerjäger Abteilung 352*'s too. Minutes later, *Oberst* Meyer himself, desperately trying to stitch his *KG* back together, was also killed. It was left to his Adjutant, as the senior surviving officer, to shepherd the survivors back. Kraiss's plan had misfired, and misfired disastrously.

The impact on Omaha for the Germans was more or less immediate; the chance to throw the Americans back into the sea was gone for good. Now all that was left for the men of *352.* and *716. IDs* who had fought so hard against such massive odds, was escape – as Hein Severloh and Franz Gockel understood only too well:

> We had to retreat. As we made our way back, *Oberfeldwebel* Pieh was hit by rifle fire... As we made our way through the communications trench another man in our group was killed by a shot through the head. Pieh, though hit again, still managed to crawl to the rear with us. A short time later I was hit. A bullet shattered my left hand [three of Gockel's fingers were left hanging on by the tendons]. A *kamerad* bandaged it and said 'Gockel, you should be glad, that's a good *heimatschuss* [wound bad enough to get the man home, a blighty,or million-dollar wound]. I don't know how the rest of us are going to get home.'

With all his ammo gone, Severloh found himself and a few other comrades crouched in a trench with *Oberleutnant* Frerking. Frerking gave the order to abandon *WN62*. They all shook hands and then dashed out of cover. Jumping from one shell crater to the next, Severloh somehow managed to reach the opposite side of the rise and threw himself into a shallow depression. Another grenadier, a radioman, fell beside him, panting heavily, his chest heaving with the effort – no-one else made it. Frerking and all the others were killed.

Karl Wegner had come to the same conclusion as Gockel and Severloh:

> First we put all the rounds we had in our pouches into belts for the MG. For the rifles we left what was already in there; five rounds... The final count was 64 rounds, a number I'll never

forget. We put them all in one belt... Rummaging through the mess, Helmuth also found two grenades, an added benefit... We all crouched in the entry way, I took a deep breath and nodded to them. Both grenades flew out at the same time, the explosions followed. I sprang through the doorway... When I got out into the open the bullets were flying all about. With some luck I made it to a slit trench a few metres away... I had just landed in the bottom when my kameraden toppled in on me... Both looked as scared as I felt.

The trio kept on moving, dodging from one trench to the next, until

...a cascade of rifle fire landed around us. I saw Willi's helmet fly off and his body snapped back. I jumped over Helmuth and crawled to him. He was not even scratched. When we picked up his helmet we saw that a round had gone through the rear skirt, knocking it off his head. Naturally he did have one massive headache!

All along Omaha it was the same story; one strongpoint radioed in: 'Direct all gunfire onto the beach, every shell a certain hit. We are getting out.'

Joseph Häger, along with his best friend, Ferdinand Klug, were still fighting north of Colleville, but were nearing the limit of their endurance:

We held our position in the trenches for more than an hour. It was the most terrible time in my life. We were continually shelled and under fire from snipers. One of our *panzerschrecks* hit an enemy tank, we saw the flap opening and a soldier was half-way out when there was another explosion and it burst into flames with the soldier still hanging from the turret. I said to Ferdie; 'I hope we have a better death than that, I'd rather have a bullet.' We were ordered into a bunker... It was already full of wounded men, there were about thirty of them lying on straw, absolutely terrified and crying out the whole time. There was hardly any air inside, and a man in the observation hatch shouted that the enemy were starting to pile up earth against the ventilators... The company commander told us to breathe together; 'Breathe in when I say IN, and out when I say OUT.' The battalion commander was firing a machine-gun through a small aperture by the door... Finally the company commander said to the battalion commander; 'Sir, we can't carry on. The wounded are suffocating.' He replied; 'We'll fight our way out if we have to. Count the weapons and get the men ready to go.'

The battalion commander's defiance was not shared by his men:

At that point there was almost a mutiny, and some men started pulling the bolts out of their rifles... Just then the man in the observation hatch shouted; 'My God, they're bringing up a flame-thrower!' We heard the 'woof' of the flame-thrower but the flames couldn't get through the staggered sections of the ventilation shaft, although it turned red hot before our eyes. Now there was near panic ... eventually we took a dirty white sheet from one of the wounded and with the help of a broomstick pushed it through the observation hatch... We dropped our weapons and made for the door... Suddenly the battalion commander asked the radio operator if he'd made contact with the regiment. The operator shook his head. The battalion commander went very white, stepped back and dropped his machine-gun... We were made to lie down on the grass at the end of the trench, and take off our equipment, boots and tunics. I said to Ferdie. 'It's all over for us now.'

Joseph Häger and Ferdinand Klug had survived Omaha.

'Our position was hit again by shells or mortar rounds,' recalled Henrik Naube, 'that is the last thing I remember of the fighting ... many pieces of concrete were tumbling around, and some of them fell on top of me. After that I don't remember anything else until I came around to find myself lying on my back, with my ears ringing painfully...I turned my head, which was extremely painful to do, and saw that I was lying among the debris of our *Widerstandnest.*' Naube survived – to his great surprise. Having seen with his own eyes the carnage he and his comrades had inflicted on the American assault troops, he fully expected to be shot out of hand: 'When I thought about the beach, the piles of bodies down there... I thought the enemy would kill us regardless of the Geneva Convention or anything like that. Would we have shown them any mercy if the roles were reversed, if we were the attackers?'

The Wehrmacht's chance at Omaha was gone, thrown away by a commander making the *right* decision in the *wrong* situation. But the Westheer still had one card to play on 6 June – *21*.

Panzerdivision and its Olympic gold medal-winning, Knight's Cross-wearing panzer commander – Hermann Leopold August von Oppeln-Bronikowski.

It was on the British and Canadian landing sector – from west to east, Gold, Juno and Sword beaches – that the German 'defensive crust and counter-attack' strategy to defeat the Allies would be played out in its purest form, and it was here that jubilant young German *panzergrenadiers* would find themselves washing their boots once more in the Channel, before having to swallow the bitter pill of retreat.

Given he had been forced to lend Franz Gockel and the rest of his battalion to Kraiss's *352. ID*, Wilhelm Richter had been left with relatively few choices as to how he positioned the remainder of his understrength *716. Infanterie-Division* in the run-up to D-Day. With only five battalions to play with, he opted to put three forward in *Widerstandnests* and strongpoints overlooking the beaches, with one sitting to the rear as his reserve, and the last over on his left, linking up with *352. ID*. There was little defence in depth, but so short of men was he that he had to man the coastline with one of his two assigned *Ost-bataillons*; the Russian and Cossack 642. Although regarded by some as fit only for labouring tasks rather than combat, 642 sat astride the Orne River in the villages of Amfreville, Hermanville-sur-Mer and Merville-Franceville-Plage. What this meant on the ground was that nineteen miles of beaches were defended by just twelve companies of mainly middle-aged or convalescing German grenadiers, with each company expected to cover well over a mile. In an attempt to give Richter at least a bit more punch, *Korps* command had allocated him eight additional artillery batteries to complement his own twelve; a not insignificant eighty-three guns in total. But, robbing Peter to pay Paul, *Korps* then insisted that Richter *lend* four of those batteries to Kraiss. To further complicate matters, Richter's now-sixty-seven guns were a total hodge-podge, with many being captured Czech, French or Polish, and almost all of them were positioned in unroofed earthen bunkers or in open gun pits in farmers' fields – easy meat for Allied naval guns and air strikes.

With so few resources at its disposal, *716. ID* was a thin crust indeed, but it did have *21. Panzer* and its 120-odd panzers and assault guns just behind it – surely, they could upset Allied plans on D-Day and deliver on Rommel's counter-attack approach? What actually happened to *21. Panzer* on D-Day was the classic 'order, counter-order, disorder' scenario that should be taught at every officer training staff college in the world as an object lesson in how not to conduct a successful operation.

Who was actually in charge? The wartime Wehrmacht had a reputation for clarity of command that, in Normandy, was often thoroughly undeserved. A more-or-less one-nation army had somehow conspired to produce a spaghetti junction of responsibilities among different headquarters and commands that stretched all the way back from the waves on the beaches to Adolf Hitler himself, whereas the polyglot Allied forces were the very model of unified command and control – unsurprising perhaps, given that the Allied powers were truly exceptional at building partnership and co-operation at every level, while the Axis were dreadful at it. What this boiled down to in practice on D-Day itself was that even as the Allied assault troops were clambering down into their landing craft off the beaches, the man giving the orders to the closest German armoured formation was not Edgar Feuchtinger, or commander *Panzergruppe West*, Leo Geyr von Schweppenburg, nor was it *Heeresgruppe B's* Erwin Rommel, or even OB West, it was in fact the entirely unremarkable figure of Wilhelm Richter, a parishioner of Hirschberg, Silesia.

To be fair, Richter was a perfectly presentable member of the German officer class. He had fought in the First World War, as well as in Poland and the West, and, latterly, Russia. Although a veteran of long standing, he had not distinguished himself in any major way during those years, as can be discerned from the fact his first divisional command was not a first-line formation, but the poor, unloved, 'belly' *716. ID.* None of the commentaries of the time talk of him as an imposing or charismatic figure, or of him having any great tactical or operational expertise – and he definitely had no experience of commanding armoured troops – and yet he was the man that Berlin had decided, entirely by default, would have operational control of *21. Panzer* in Normandy during those first, crucial hours of the landings. And in those early hours of D-Day Wilhelm Richter thought he knew exactly what the greatest threat was; the as yet unknown number of British paratroopers armed with little more than rifles, Sten guns and PIATs, and with only as much ammo as they could carry, landing east of the River Orne. So, at 0120hrs Richter ordered *21. Panzer* to send its nearest sub-units to cross over to the eastern bank of the Orne and sweep them up. Just forty minutes later he upped the ante and ordered the entire division to head east and destroy the paras. The commander of the division's *II. Bataillon*, *Major* Vierzig, had been on the move with his men during the night to take part in a planned divisional exercise, and remembered the orders:

> Towards 0100 I had moved my battalion into the scheduled exercise area six miles east of Falaise. Over Caen and the coast the sky was red with the glow of fires. We heard the ceaseless detonations of the Allied aerial bombardment, but this didn't strike us as unusual since such attacks had become quite a regular feature... Towards 0220 a motorcycle dispatch rider arrived from headquarters; order from Regiment: 'The battalion will immediately return to its stations and stand by for action.'

Vierzig's peer commanding *I. Bataillon* was *Major* Wilhelm von Gottberg, based in the tiny village of Fresné-la-Mère, southeast of Falaise: 'By 2.30am all our panzers had their engines running and we were ready to go. We were burning to fight... But no orders came, we couldn't understand it. I was furious, and I kept imagining that while we were waiting the Allies would be busy occupying all the strategic hills.'

One of von Gottberg's men was baby-faced Werner Kortenhaus in *Oberleutnant* Hoffmann's *4. Kompanie*:

> I joined *22. Panzer-Regiment* of *21. Panzerdivision* of the German Army in 1943, when I was eighteen years old. The regiment was divided into eight companies; each company had seventeen panzers, and in each panzer were five soldiers. As a wireless operator, I made sure communications worked inside our panzer and that we could communicate with the other panzers. We were all young – we weren't generals or anything, and when D-Day happened I had just turned nineteen... I joined the Army straight from school, so I didn't have a family of my own at the time. My parents and grandparents were living in Solingen, near Cologne, where I was born, and where I still live today. My family didn't generally know where I was, as we young lads were rather lazy and didn't write home very often. Also, I had very bad handwriting and anyway, we weren't allowed to say where we were stationed. On 6 June 1944 we were camped near Caen... We weren't right at the front, where the infantry were, we were kept slightly back, to see where the landing would take place... by 2am we were ready to move ... waiting for the order to march,

but nobody gave it. We stood around our panzer and simply waited. The driver switched on the motor to warm-up the engine, thinking we would be driving off at any moment, and then he switched it off. After an hour he switched it on again, and then off again. We kept asking ourselves, why doesn't the order come through? We didn't really know what was happening, all we knew was that we were on standby and ready to fight.

It seemed all ranks of *21. Panzer* were waiting to be told what to do, but Richter had already given the order, as confirmed by his own headquarters log; so why weren't they moving?

In truth, some of them were. *Major* Zippe's *II. Bataillon* of *Oberstleutnant* Josef Rauch's *Panzer-Grenadier-Regiment 192* was on the march, heading southeast from its billets to the east bank of the Orne. One of Zippe's companies was billeted in the tiny commune of Périers-sur-le-Dan, with its beautiful eleventh-century church. The roar of departing motors signalled to the couple of hundred residents that they were once more alone – something the Germans would come to regret later in the day.

Another of Zippe's companies, *Oberleutnant* Braatz's *8* was based to the southwest, and included the battalion's *panzerjäger* platoon, commanded by a veteran of North Africa, the Austrian *Oberleutnant* Hans Höller.

I was quartered in a private house in Cairon, a village about eight miles northwest of Caen and about the same distance from the coast ... the alarm was sounded at 2.00am on 6 June ... we were equipped with French transport, armoured Renault half-tracks fitted with mortars [some of Alfred Becker's creations]. Our vehicles were loaded in the shortest possible time with munitions and were soon ready to go... Under cover of darkness, and with enemy aircraft roaring overhead, we reached our point of engagement, Bénouville, without any trouble... Our command was initially rather indecisive, and whether or not the order to attack came from regiment or battalion I cannot say. We were able to storm Bénouville and occupy half the town, but we weren't able to take the exit road to the coast, and this remained out of our hands the whole day.

The reason Höller and his men couldn't retake the whole of the town was simple; the British were continually receiving reinforcements and the Germans weren't, as attested by Höller himself:

> The mass of enemy paratroopers fought doggedly and received continuous reinforcements from the coastal area. We had to watch, with great bitterness, the endlessly growing numbers against us, knowing we would receive no support. The most we could do was hold the position and try to interrupt the advance.

21. Panzer's armour wasn't getting into the fight, as *Major* Vierzig of *II. Bataillon* knew only too well: 'From 0400 onwards the battalion stood by, ready to move and ready for action. But nothing happened... We waited.'

What was the hold-up? The controversial post-war German revisionist historian and writer, Paul Carrell, wrote in '*Sie Kommen!*', his account of the Normandy campaign from the German standpoint, that the delay in the panzers responding to Richter's command was down to Feuchtinger's own concern that either *7. Armee* or the OKW itself should confirm any such order, given *21. Panzer* was the sole armoured reserve in the immediate area. After the war ended, Feuchtinger himself seemed to confirm this assertion:

> Since I had been told that I was to make no move until I heard from Rommel's headquarters, I could do nothing immediately but warn my men to be ready. I waited patiently all that night for some instructions, but not a single order from a higher formation was received by me. Realising that my armoured division was closest to the scene of operations, I finally decided, at 6.30 in the morning, that I had to take some action.[19]

Is that truly what happened? Other post-war accounts have only further muddied the waters, with talk of Feuchtinger's 'arms-length' style of command of his division, and his well-known love of the Paris highlife contributing to the failure of command during those critical hours. Was Feuchtinger on his way to the French capital for a night of pleasure when the alarm sounded and was then forced to race back, losing precious hours? Or was he actually in Paris with his South American mistress – as Samuel W. Mitcham Jr. asserts in his book – cavorting in a 'sleazy Parisian nightclub'. Von Luck, as one of his own regimental commanders, confirmed that he had seen a letter written by Rommel's Chief of Staff at the time, Hans Speidel, that said; 'I called Feuchtinger between 1.00h. and 2.00h. on 6.6.44, but couldn't get him. It wasn't until the morning of 6 June that my first general staff officer got through to him.' In addition, von Luck said that *Hauptmann* Eberhard Wagemann, a staff officer serving with the division at the time who would go on to general-rank in the post-war *Bundeswehr*, told him he had informed Feuchtinger of the Allied airborne landings between two and three o'clock in the morning while the latter was *in Paris* (author's italics), and that the general had then arrived back at his headquarters some *four hours later*. Given this testimony and the general confusion of the time, it would seem that none of these scenarios as to Feuchtinger's whereabouts can be ruled out. Whatever the reason, the panzers and their crews sat idling in woods and town squares across the area during those crucial small hours. For the officers and men involved the frustration was palpable, including the 25-year-old commander of von Gottberg's *1. Kompanie*, *Hauptmann* Herr:

> I was the commanding officer of one of those unfortunate panzer units which was expecting the invasion in the environs of Blocqueville near Falaise. I was stationed in the château at Couliboeuf. I was catapulted out of bed by the alarm at about two or three in the morning... I assumed that the regimental commander was using these circumstances to instigate an exercise for us... I withdrew at about 6.30am without receiving orders, the high command was unable to make any decisions. They simply did not know if the invasion would occur east or west of the Orne at that point.

By then the massive Allied naval bombardment plastering the whole of Richter's frontlines should have made it abundantly clear to any senior German commander where the gravest danger lay – the beaches west of the Orne - but apparently not to the headquarters of *7. Armee* itself, where the decision was made to send the routine daily 0645hrs report to OB West describing the tonnes of high-explosive ploughing up the bunkers, trenches and strongpoints of *709, 716* and *352. IDs* in the following manner: 'Purpose of naval bombardment not yet apparent. It appears to be a covering action in conjunction with attacks to be made at other points later.'

Again, to be fair to 7. *Armee*, one of the major advantages of sea-power is that it can move – and quickly – so a fleet bombarding the Normandy beaches one day can then steam east and start bombarding the Pas de Calais on the next, but where that might be fairly easy for a few dozen capital ships and their escorts, for the armada the German observers were seeing in the Seine Bay, it would amount to an operation of such elaborateness as to stretch the bounds of credulity. Whatever the merits of the decision-making at the time, the hitherto missing-in-action Edgar Feuchtinger now made up his mind and, finally, the panzers got their orders: 'I ordered my panzers to attack the English 6th Airborne Division which had entrenched itself in a bridgehead over the Orne, as to me this constituted the most immediate threat to the German position.'

In confirming Richter's orders from over four hours previously, Feuchtinger had jumped, and jumped completely the wrong way.

Towards 0600 an orderly officer I had sent to Regiment came back with the news that the Allied invasion had begun... At last, towards 0900, the battalion received orders in writing to move off at once towards the northeast. The order said; 'Air-landed enemy troops east of the Orne to be wiped out.'

Major Wilhelm von Gottberg's *I. Bataillon* received the exact same order as Vierzig's *II. Bataillon* had:

...at last at 7.15 we got orders to move and to assemble at Chicheboville Wood [a few miles southeast of Caen near Tilly-la-Campagne]. I ordered my seventy-three panzers to get under way ... we got to Chicheboville Wood and by noon we had passed Caen.

Werner Kortenhaus was quartered in the hamlet of Epaney, near Jort:

It wasn't until 0800 that morning, after we had been standing around for nearly six hours, that we finally got the order to march north to Caen. We were amazed that we had had to wait so long – we were ready by 0200 and would rather have left under the cover of darkness.

By now, Hans Höller's *panzerjäger* platoon, and indeed the rest of *Oberleutnant* Braatz's *8. Kompanie*, was deeply embroiled in fighting the paras east of the Orne, as *Major* Vierzig and the rest of their panzer comrades drove through the darkness to reach them:

> I sent dispatch riders to the companies, and the long column got going… During the move we were lucky. At first there were no *jabo* [slang for Allied fighter-bomber, short for Jagdbomber] attacks, and we approached the area of the airborne landings without having suffered any losses.

At last, Höller's reinforcements would arrive – only they didn't.

War, perhaps more than any other field of human endeavour, is one that demands absolute focus and ruthless prioritization to be prosecuted successfully – especially if your side doesn't have an overwhelming advantage in resources – and while destroying the airborne landings east of the Orne would have been a victory for the Germans, it would have had an empty one. To be fair to Richter, the paras were, at the time he first gave his orders, the only enemy troops he was aware of, but even so, his decision to send von Oppeln-Bronikowski's panzers against lightly-armed paratroopers can be seen most charitably as misguided, and at worst as a mistake far worse than Dietrich Kraiss's erroneous lunge with *KG Meyer* towards Crépon later that same day. Armoured troops were (and still are) an airborne soldiers' worst nightmare – as Arnhem was to prove a few months later – but in this instance, Richter's orders look more like a *'we must do something'* scenario rather than sound military logic; which Kraiss at least had on his side.

As for Feuchtinger's incompetence there are no such caveats. Either he was absent – *in flagrante* – during some of the most important hours for the Wehrmacht during the war, or he simply sat on his hands waiting to be told what to do by someone else; and then when he finally decided to act he sent an entire panzer division on a fool's errand at the exact same time that almost four divisions' worth of well-equipped, superbly-trained and heavily-supported assault troops were jumping off their landing craft and ripping into Richter's completely outmatched battalions on the beaches.

Those self-same beleaguered defenders were waiting for – and fully expecting – a counter-attack by their own forces; why? Why was there such an emphasis on the counter-attack in Wehrmacht philosophy? If there wasn't, then von Schlieben's failure at Utah, Kraiss's at Omaha, and any issues with von Oppeln-Bronikowski on Sword and Juno, would be judgements on their reactions and not about doctrine; but the counter-attack as an operation of war was central to German military thinking. Ever since the events of D-Day, much has been made by historians of the fundamental difference in strategy between von Rundstedt's plan to wait until the Westheer had built up enough strength to land a decisive blow, versus Rommel's advocacy of holding the Allies on the beaches and countering immediately to throw them back into the surf. True, these approaches are markedly different, but one could argue the biggest difference between them is of timing, and not of action; both rely on victory to be won by counter-attacks and, big or small, any such strike relies on three fundamentals: speed of reaction, massing of forces, and co-ordination in the assault. As *21. Panzer's* Paul Breslau said; 'counter-attack is the surest form of defence – that was the thinking of the Wehrmacht, and it was very true.'

Had the Germans now missed the boat, were they too late? Was the chance for a successful counter-attack to reach the sea gone? Well, not completely, not yet. At last, some semblance of sanity seeped into their higher command when *LXXXIV Korps* itself finally intervened, countermanded Feuchtinger's orders, and sent the panzers back west towards the beaches; to their commanders' annoyance:

> Hardly had I made this decision [to attack the paras east of the Orne] when I received my first intimation that a higher command did still exist... I was ordered to stop the move of my panzers against the Allied airborne troops and turn west to aid the forces protecting Caen.

Piqued he may have been, but there can be no doubt that abandoning the attack on the paras and turning the panzers around was the right thing to do. By now though, it was noon, the sun was burning off the morning cloud cover, Caen was in flames from Allied bombing, and the dreaded *jabos* were everywhere.

Over near Omaha, Kraiss's reserve – *KG Meyer* – were almost all on bicycles or on foot, making any counter-attack they made painfully slow, but *21. Panzer* was one of the most highly-mechanized formations in the Wehrmacht (thanks in no small part to Alfred Becker of course) and that meant there was still a chance to snatch a measure of victory even as the landing craft bearing more troops, equipment and supplies kept bowling in to Sword, Juno and Gold – but everything hinged on getting back over the Orne to the western bank, getting through Caen, and co-ordinating a proper counter-attack between the panzers and their grenadiers – and that was easier said than done.

> I myself [*Oberleutnant* Herr] having pushed so close to the coastline … could see, like an appalling swarm of grasshoppers, the flotilla of ships lying off the coast, and to my dismay low-flying aircraft, whose whistling I could hear passing over my panzers. The platoon leader of *No. 2* platoon, *Leutnant* Döll, had made an advance on foot with his infantry and had retrieved about thirty English soldiers from a bomb crater… Going through Caen presented some problems, there was a bridge, the last one intact over the Orne, which was being ceaselessly attacked by *jabos*… I was able to get all my panzers over the bridge without a single loss. I can't remember the exact interval but basically once each aircraft dropped its bomb it pulled up in order to allow the next one to make a run and that gave us the time to send one panzer over at a time.

The prize was worth it though. If the Germans could combine von Oppeln-Bronikowski's panzers with Rauch's grenadiers as soon as possible, and send them forward to drive to the sea in between the Canadians on Juno and the British 3rd Infantry Division on Sword, then they could rush troops forward, turn left and right and roll up the British beachhead from the flanks; the initiative would then be with Berlin and not London or Washington, and American flags on Utah and Omaha would fly alone.

Von Oppeln-Bronikowski was at the rear of his own column. Having led his regiment out to go chasing paras, when ordered to literally do an about-face he had turned his own panzer around and become tail-end Charlie. All roads led to Caen, even as the Allied bombers pulverised it, and, correctly surmising that the streets through the city centre would be choked with debris, he ordered the panzers to go through the industrial suburb of Colombelles in the city's northeastern outskirts; a good decision, but one that ate up precious time the Germans didn't have. For the 45-year-old veteran *Oberst* there was a measure of light relief as he slowly wound his way through the rubble-strewn streets of Duke William's still-burning capital. He spied three clearly-drunk German soldiers tottering down the road loudly singing '*Deutschland über alles*' – what else could he do but laugh.[20] Perhaps he remembered back to 11 May when Rommel had come to his own headquarters in

Falaise at seven in the morning on a surprise inspection, and he himself was nowhere to be found, being out enjoying himself with his brother officers at some celebration or other. When he finally turned up half an hour later, he muttered, 'What a disaster,' but Rommel, a very light drinker himself, surprisingly let it go. Or perhaps the Desert Fox was giving some leeway to an officer who had a reputation for sharing his men's discomfort on exercise by sleeping under his panzer with his crew rather than getting cushy officers' accommodation, and one who had a personal tally of over fifty enemy tank kills on the Russian front. Whatever, the switch through Caen in full daylight had a price; six panzers were lost to *jabo* attacks. For *21. Panzer*, they would be the first of many.

Not that everything was going the Anglo-Canadians way either. The Allies were on a timetable; one designed to land as many men and as much *matériel* on the beaches as possible to blunt any German counter-attack, and then push inland to take their biggest D-Day objective – the city of Caen. Determined to try and stop them was a 34-year-old German officer with dark, thinning hair and a rather serious demeanour – Heinrich Hoffmann. Hoffmann was a man with a reputation. His brother officers had a saying about him; 'When Hoffmann gets to a place, things start happening.' D-Day was to prove that saying true – he was a Kriegsmarine *Korvettenkapitän*, and he was about to throw a torpedo-shaped spanner in the Allied works off the Anglo-Canadian beaches.

The night before D-Day Hoffmann had spoken to his wife back home in Marburg. She was apprehensive about the landings that everyone knew had to come at some point, and he had told her that everything was quiet and she had no need to worry. A few hours later, Hoffmann's bland reassurance was proven entirely false when his namesake – *Konteadmiral* Karl Hoffmann, Chief-of-Staff for *Marinegruppenkommando West* – walked into his situation room in the Place de la Concorde in Paris in his dressing-gown, to be told by his radar officer, *Leutnant* von Willisen, 'Large numbers of blips on the screens, I think the invasion is here. This can only be the invasion fleet.' Hoffmann agreed: 'Signal *OB West*, and the *Führer*'s HQ, the invasion is on. Alert all naval forces and bases.'

Back in Le Havre, the more junior Hoffmann was woken from his bed by the alert, and in no time at all was aboard his ship - the *T28* – heading out to sea followed by the only other sea-worthy members of his usual flotilla of five small, fast torpedo-boats; the *Jaguar* and the *Möwe*. Racing into the darkness at twenty-five knots, the three boats were left alone by the fleets of Allied aircraft passing overhead every few minutes. Then, at about half-past five that morning they approached what Hoffmann thought was a fog bank, only to see a lone aircraft appear out of it – it was actually an enormous smokescreen. Hoffmann had seen an Allied fleet in the Channel before – two years before, at Dieppe to be precise, and he had attacked it then – he would do the same now. Carving through the smoke, the three ships suddenly hit clear water and sky, and in front of them loomed a sight to chill their blood. One of Hoffmann's *Matrosen* (the naval equivalent of the *landser*), Heinrich Frömke, summed up all their thoughts: 'It's impossible, there can't be that many ships in the world!' Hoffmann didn't hesitate; '*Toni Dora Six!*' *Jaguar* and *Möwe* followed suit and eighteen torpedoes were in the water heading towards the targets. Great skill enabled the battleships HMS *Warspite* and *Ramillies* to evade the killer fish, but the Norwegian destroyer; HNoMS *Svenner*, wasn't so lucky. On her bridge the captain, Lieutenant-Commander Tore Holthe, and his British liaison officer, Lieutenant Desmond Lloyd, could only watch helplessly as the torpedoes hit them amidships. The resulting explosion lifted the 111-metre long, 1,740 ton destroyer out of the water, before she split in two and sank, taking thirty-three of her crew with her.[21] Hoffmann and his comrades turned and ran for the smoke as fast as their engines could carry them. Arriving back at Le Havre, Hoffmann downed a cocktail of his own devising, Napoleon brandy mixed with Grand Marnier, before reporting to his boss, *Konteadmiral* Hermann von Bredow. Chainsmoking captured English woodbines, Hoffmann and the admiral used binoculars to try and count the Allied ships they could see in the Bay of the Seine from the vantage point of their Le Havre base – they stopped after reaching two hundred. Von Bredow said to his subordinate: 'It's a miracle you're here Hoffmann, we were all convinced that none of you would ever make it back once we'd seen that!'

The torpedo boat skipper wasn't finished yet though, and as night fell he went out again with his three-ship flotilla, determined to cause the Allies more grief. This time, Hoffmann used the enormity of Allied resources against them. Heading out into the Channel, he motored towards the English coast before swinging around and blending into the stream of Allied ships heading to Normandy – the darkness shielding them from discovery. Approaching the main fleet Hoffmann didn't push his luck. The flotilla shot off their torpedoes and heard three big detonations that, according to Hoffmann, lit up the night sky 'as if it was day'. Thinking they were under air attack, the Allies sent up a wall of fire into the sky, allowing Hoffmann and his comrades to quietly disappear into the darkness and head home unscathed. A grateful Hitler would award Hoffmann the Knight's Cross for his courage. Tremendously brave and audacious as Hoffmann's actions were, they had no measurable impact on the Anglo-Canadian landings.

While Hoffmann and his mini-flotilla couldn't do much to help *21. Panzer*'s gathering counter-attack, the still-fighting *716. ID* could – and did. Two years previously the Nazis' paramilitary construction arm – the *Organisation Todt,* or *OT* – had begun work on *Widerstandnest 17* just to the south of the hamlet of Colleville-sur-Orne (now renamed Colleville-Montgomery in honour of the British commander). Eventually the 24-hectare complex would include eighteen bunkers including two H608-type command post bunkers with armoured observation cupolas, and an H605 bunker for the guns with which it was never equipped. However, since it was on relatively high ground, it did control the nearby artillery of *WN16*. The site was sophisticated by *Atlantikwall* standards, with mechanical ventilation systems, medical facilities, ammunition and food storage bunkers, and trenches connecting it all together – even the telephone lines were buried at least two metres below ground to protect them from bombardment. Although lacking heavy weaponry, it was protected by machine-guns in Tobruk pits, minefields and barbed wire. As the biggest strongpoint in the area, it was selected as the headquarters of *Oberst* Ludwig Krug's *Grenadier-Regiment 736*, and garrisoned by 150 officers and men. Overlooking Sword as it did, come the morning of D-Day, Krug had been directing fire down onto the beach for as long as he could call it in from guns that were being rapidly silenced. Coming for him was Lieutenant-Colonel Richard E. Goodwin's 1st Battalion, the Suffolk Regiment, which had landed on Sword at around 0830hrs before heading inland to start seizing its assigned objectives; the first of which was *WN19*, guarded by *Nr. 3 Kompanie* of *Ostbataillon 642*. The Suffolks made short work of it and moved on to their next target – *WN16* and its artillery, known to the British by the codename '*Morris*'. Capturing Morris took longer than expected, and it wasn't until around midday that Goodwin's men finally approached their third and most important assignment, *WN17*, or objective *Hillman*.[22] Supported by tanks, artillery and a machine-gun platoon from 2nd Battalion, the Middlesex Regiment, a path was cleared through the mines by

Royal Engineers to allow Captain Geoff Ryley's 'A' Company to begin the assault. At first all went well, and the men from Ipswich and Aldeburgh began to fight their way through the trenches, only to see their attack stall when Captain Ryley was killed by German machine-gun fire. Next, Shermans were brought up onto the site, firing directly at the German cupolas, but the rounds just bounced off. The stubborn defence of Krug's grenadiers was achieving exactly what *21. Panzer's* counter-attack needed; fixing the British troops in place.

Even as a stymied *KG Meyer* was retreating from its abortive thrust towards Crépon a few miles to the west, the Germans had, by some minor miracle, managed to get an anvil into position at *WN17* – what they needed now was a hammer – and said *21. Panzer* hammer was at last getting through Caen and beginning to form up to its north.

Back on Sword Beach there was confusion and disorder as men and machinery came ashore and piled up. The timetable was going by the board, but with effective resistance on the beach annihilated, the disembarking troops could shake themselves out in relative peace before heading inland. The key British formation that would meet *21. Panzer's* counter-attack – although it didn't know it when it landed that morning of course – was Brigadier K. P. Smith's 185th Infantry Brigade, supported by elements of the 27th Armoured Brigade. Smith would not be a success in his appointment, and would be replaced at the beginning of July, his biggest flaw being a lack of drive, and on 6 June that was a serious flaw indeed, as whether he knew it or not his brigade was in a race to reach the key high ground in the area; the Périers ridge. This ridge – often called the Périers rise – was no mountain range for sure. In fact, its two highest points were marked as 'Point 55' and 'Point 61' on the maps issued to Allied troops to indicate their spot height in metres above sea level. The ridge ran roughly northwest–southeast from Plumetot, through Périers-sur-le-Dan – only that same morning the billet of one of Josef Rauch's panzer-grenadier companies from *Major* Zippe's *I. Bataillon* – to Beuville, and although the slopes on both its sides were gentle, they were excellent killing grounds with open vistas seemingly made for tank cannon and anti-tank guns. The Germans were well aware of the ridge's importance; Ludwig Krug's *WN17* was sited on it, and it was the 'hills' that Wilhelm von Gottberg had fretted about earlier in the day. Von Gottberg would be one of several German Cassandras that afternoon.

Leading the British advance were the infantrymen of Lieutenant-Colonel F. J. Maurice's 2nd Battalion King's Shropshire Light Infantry, accompanied by two Sherman squadrons of Lieutenant-Colonel Jim Eadie's Staffordshire Yeomanry (Queen's Own Royal Regiment) and some self-propelled guns of 7 Field Regiment, Royal Artillery. They had advanced four miles from the beach and were still full of vim as they moved up the ridge around three in the afternoon.

Unbeknown to them, the leading elements of 21. *Panzer* were fast approaching from the other side. First to arrive at the base of the ridge below Biéville were Herr's 1. *Kompanie* and battalion headquarters, closely followed by the combined 2. and 3. *Kompanien*, commanded by von Gottberg. They spread out to the west of Herr's line as the panzers drew themselves up ready to start their attack. Slotting in still further to von Gottberg's left were the armoured cars and half-tracks of *Hauptmann* Rätzer's *I. Batallion, Panzer-Grenadier-Regiment 192*. Josef Rauch was with Rätzer, determined to lead his men from the front, and he would soon be joined by none other than the *Korps* commander himself. General Erich Marcks – whose fifty-third birthday it was that day – went forward from his headquarters despite the risk from *jabos*. The one-legged Marcks found von Oppeln-Bronikowski briefing his officers – Feuchtinger was nowhere to be seen – and tried to impress on the veteran Saxon just how vital an operation this was: 'Whether the invasion is defeated or not depends on you, if you don't succeed in throwing the British into the sea we shall have lost the war.'

Von Oppeln-Bronikowski remembered his shock at hearing Marcks statement: 'Victory or defeat – the war itself – depends on me and my sixty panzers, just my sixty!'[23] Nevertheless, the panzer ace was a decorated, professional soldier, so he straightened his back and told his general; 'I shall attack immediately.' Satisfied, Marcks hobbled off to join Rauch's grenadiers.

The die was cast, this was it. The last chance the Germans had to finish D-Day with some sort of win; break through the British, reach the sea, and the initiative would lie with them. Fail, and the Allies would have successfully established a beachhead that could prove decisive for the campaign, and for the battle for France. It was now just after four in the afternoon, and three companies of German panzers (Hoffmann's 4, with Werner Kortenhaus amongst them, had been detached by Marcks's order to stay east of the Orne with von Luck's panzergrenadiers), a handful of armoured cars and a single battalion of grenadiers faced three squadrons of Shermans – the Staffords third squadron had just arrived – some 6- and 17-pounder anti-tank guns, and a battalion of British infantry. The Germans had been hoping they would be met at the ridge by *Hauptmann* von Lyncker's dozen guns from *Panzerjäger-Abteilung 200*, but of them there was no sign – Richter had moved them earlier in the day to reinforce his embattled division and hadn't informed 21. *Panzer* – neither was there any sign of the sixty-odd panzers of Vierzig's *II. Bataillon*, struggling as they still were to get through Caen.

With no artillery support, or cover from von Lyncker's absent 88mms, von Oppeln-Bronikowski personally led the attack up the ridge with Herr's twenty-five panzers of *1. Kompanie* and *Stab* (headquarters staff). The attack did not begin well, as *Hauptmann* Herr testified:

> It was late afternoon by now and we came upon a stationary column of Sherman tanks, at about 5–600m distance... I gave the order to attack, to drive round these tanks to get better firing positions, as the range of my Panzer IV wasn't good enough. The decision was, however, taken out of my hands as the other side opened fire. The 'skirts' over the tracks of the panzer, that were to protect us from mines etc, just swirled up and literally flew through the air round us.

The German Mark IVs were at a serious disadvantage. Their long-barrelled 7.5cm main guns were tried and tested tank-killers, but they were advancing in the open against British tanks in hull-down positions with consequently low silhouettes, and anti-tank guns with profiles that made them next to invisible to their opponents. As one panzer crewman recalled: 'The first Mark IV was blazing before a single German panzer had the chance to fire a shot.'

As Werner Kortenhaus's history of his own *21. Panzerdivison* said of von Oppeln-Bronikowski's attack:

> At first these panzers received no opposition, then, as they moved up the hill, the English opened heavy defensive fire from both tanks and anti-tank guns. Their position was tactically well-chosen and their fire both heavy and accurate... The remainder moved forward, firing at where the enemy were thought to be; but the English weapons were well concealed and within a few minutes, we had lost six panzers.

Herr himself was lucky to survive the British fire:

> I personally had always been afraid of burning to death in the cockpit
> of my panzer, so I lengthened the lead of my neck microphone so
> I could sit behind the turret. It wasn't a sensible thing to do but I'd
> had such appalling experiences when I had had to extract the bodies
> of comrades from burnt-out panzers and put them in coffins that
> were as little as three-quarters of a metre long ... so when my panzer
> received a hit the shrapnel struck me, I fell to the ground and had
> to feel around my knees with my hands to check that I still had legs,
> blood was pouring out of me. *Oberst* von Oppeln-Bronikowski, in
> despair, asked me what to do, and I replied that if he didn't know
> then how on earth was I to?[24]

Von Oppeln-Bronikowski was little better off than Herr, as his own
Mark IV was hit and put out of action. Meanwhile, sweeping round
to the left of the ridge were Wilhelm von Gottberg and his thirty-five
panzers, as they charged towards Point 61 and its road junction, the
highest point of the whole Périers feature and a position only about
a hundred metres from the anvil of Krug's regimental headquarters at
WN17. 'The position was the same. The fire of the English, from their
outstandingly well-sited defensive positions, was murderous.'

Major von Gottberg was of the same mind as his own unit record:
'Just as I feared, the Allies had occupied all the strategic positions.
Ten of my panzers were knocked out even before they were within
firing range.' The German narrative continues: 'Within a brief space
of time, the armoured regiment of *21. Panzerdivision* had lost a
total of sixteen panzers, a decisive defeat, from which, especially in
morale, it never recovered.'

Von Oppeln-Bronikowski called off the counter-attack. His
regiment had been soundly beaten, and a quarter of his *I. Bataillon*
lay burning on the ridge, their crews either dead, wounded or
running for their lives. On the other side, from the British beaches,
the BBC reporter Alan Melville was recording a dispatch in readiness
to send it back across the Channel for broadcast: 'I can still see the
signs of a typical panzer battle being raged on the slightly raised
ground ahead of me.'[25]

What Melville couldn't see – hidden as they were by the lie of the
land – were Rätzer's panzer-grenadiers, accompanied by Rauch and
Marcks, as they drove north and felt their way forward along sunken
roads, farm tracks and half-forgotten lanes. There was no way the

whole battalion would have remained undetected in a countryside that was starting to fill with roaming Allied soldiers, so the battalion's sub-units began to spread out, with companies and platoons finding their own way. Then, somehow, elements of the battalion suddenly found themselves driving into the environs of the seaside towns of Lion-sur-Mer and Luc-sur-Mer, to the complete astonishment of a few shocked British soldiers and the remnants of *III. Batallion* of Krug's *GR. 736*, who were still holding a handful of coastal positions to the west of Caen. (See map, p. 314.) One can only imagine the relief the belly soldiers felt upon seeing the panzergrenadiers arrive, after hours of fighting against impossible numbers, with ammunition and hope running very low.

They'd done it though! Against the odds *21. Panzer* had reached the sea. Alas for them, without any panzers, as von Gottberg back with the surviving tanks explained: 'We had to give up, we dug in around a farmhouse at Lébisey' (now swallowed up by Caen, Lébisey is effectively a northern suburb of the city).

1. Kompanie's Oberleutnant Herr was less sanguine than his commander:

> I am not able to describe exactly how things then went, but after we disengaged ourselves from the enemy and re-grouped in a rearguard position I wanted to re-position *Leutnant* Lehman's panzer with whom I was in radio contact, and which was about fifteen metres from my own panzer. I wanted him to move backwards a bit further, when I got the strict command: 'No panzer moves even a centimetre.' Barely ten minutes later, his panzer received a direct hit; in fact, right when I was in the middle of a radio conversation with him. The *Panzer IV* has a 7cm-thick glass observation window in the turret that gives one a 360-degree view. The shell must have directly hit this spot as the black forage cap that Lehman always wore was hurled out and landed on my panzer in the shock waves of the explosion. I looked over and saw that the whole turret had been blow away – it was an appalling sight. I was so furious that I jumped out of my panzer, ran to my commander and reported that; 'I have just sacrificed another panzer on direct orders.' It was a dreadful situation.

Their regimental commander was even more down-hearted than either Herr or von Gottberg; 'Caen and the whole area could have been taken in a few hours. Instead, German officers with twenty to thirty men apiece, were marching back from the front, retreating towards Caen.' He was even heard to say aloud: 'The war is lost.' He then gave his last order of the day; 'Panzers to be dug in. Position must be held.'

Nevertheless, some of Rauch's grenadiers were standing on the sand with the Channel lapping at their feet. Marcks himself hadn't made it through, but no matter; now it was time to reinforce success and push reinforcements forward. By now it was past seven in the evening and getting dark, which suited the Germans as it took the Allied *jabos* out of the equation, as well as impairing their naval guns' ability to fire other than by map references – directly observed fire was out of the question until dawn the next morning. The Germans still had significant portions of *21. Panzer* that hadn't been committed to the beachhead battle yet; for example *Major* Waldow's entire *Panzer-Aufklärungs-Abteilung 21* (panzer reconnaissance battalion 21), which had been involved to the east of the Orne, as reported by *Leutnant* Rupprecht Grzimek:

> At dawn a liaison officer whom we had sent to von Luck reported that not only had an airborne division landed east of the Orne, but the enemy had brought up a vast armada off the coast and was preparing a landing from the sea. Heavy naval guns now joined in the landing operations. The weak units on the coast were apparently already involved in fierce fighting... By making full use of cover we reached the area just west of Troarn in the early afternoon more or less without interference.

Also uncommitted were Rauch's own *II. Bataillon*, and von Luck's regiment to the east of the Orne – along with *Oberleutnant* Hoffmann's *4. Kompanie* of panzers, and a very eager Werner Kortenhaus:

> We had the feeling that now things were really getting going. At one point during that day we saw the town of Caen in the distance, and over it a thick cloud, from bomb attacks – and I thought, 'my God, this is war.' Later we spotted English parachutists to our right in a cornfield, but we didn't pay them any attention as that was not part of our orders. They looked over at us and we at them, but we drove on. It was then clear that this was the beginning of an invasion. We had been training for many months, so to some extent we felt that it was good that things were finally starting. But we had no real idea of what war really was – we only learned

that later. We were young lads, we'd been taught how to work the panzers, and we wanted to experience things. But then in the afternoon we had our first fatality – we were attacked from the air and took cover under the panzers, but one of us wasn't quick enough and was killed. That was a shock for me. We were so young and naïve.

Hans Höller was as frustrated as Kortenhaus, though for different reasons: 'We went to the *Château* de Bénouville, and a woman tried to block our way, but we stormed in anyway and went to the top floor where we could get a very good view of the bridge and the coast, but we found that the *château* was being used as a maternity hospital for local women, so we left it so it wouldn't be fired upon, even though it was perfect for an observation post and for our weapons.'

Then the saga took another dramatic twist. 'No-one who saw it will ever forget it,' said Kortenhaus. 'Suddenly, the hollow roaring of countless aeroplanes, and then we saw them, hundreds of them, towing great gliders, filling the sky.' Hans Höller and his men saw them too: 'An uncanny silence seemed to descend upon everything and everyone, we all looked up, and there they were just above us. Noiselessly, those giant wooden boxes sailed in over our heads to land, whereupon men and equipment came pouring out of them.' For Höller's platoon it was a turkey shoot; 'We lay on our backs and fired, and fired, and fired into those gliders, until we couldn't work the bolts of our rifles anymore. Our 2cm flak troop shot some down and damaged many more, but against such masses, it seemed to make little difference.' For Werner Kortenhaus and his comrades of *4. Kompanie*, it seemed as if their moment had finally come:

It was a unique opportunity, but there was a wait before the order came crackling in my earphones: 'Panzers advance.' And then the air was alive with calls of: 'Eagle to all, Eagle to all, come in, please!' Engines roared into life, flaps clanged shut, and we rolled in cautious tempo and attack formation towards Herouvillette. But before we had even fired a shot, darkness had fallen over the rolling panzer formations, and then warning lights shot up – we were attacking positions held by our own *panzer-grenadiers*! Baffled, the men shook their heads. Obviously, an advance into empty space. And that was all that we, a strong panzer company, achieved on this decisive day.

What the Germans were seeing was the British 6th Airborne Division in action, and specifically its airlanding brigade with heavier weaponry than their parachute oppos, and with ammunition and supplies for those that came before; and it coincided perfectly with the arrival at Bénouville of the 185th Brigade's 2nd Battalion, Royal Warwickshires, commanded by Lieutenant-Colonel H. Herdon. Höller and his men were now facing tanks as well as lightly armed paras:

> We could see an enemy tank stopped outside a house; the tank officer was talking to the inhabitants. Our right-hand gunner was unable to crank down the barrel of his anti-tank gun low enough to fire, and we couldn't risk starting the engine because of the noise. We decided to push the vehicle over the edge of the incline so that it could get a shot, and after several dramatic moments we managed to do so without being noticed. The suspense was dramatic, then Gefreiter Wleck cranked the gun handles frantically, depressed the barrel, targeted his objective, and fired. Meanwhile, the English commander had gotten out of his turret, and walked up to the house to talk to the occupants; obviously, he hoped they would tell him where we were. The end of the tank was instantaneous. As our first shell hit, the petrol and ammunition exploded with such violence that the house beside the tank collapsed in ruins. Clearly, the English still hadn't a clue as to where we were; they fired wildly, at extreme range, and in all directions, and under cover of the uproar, we were able to start up and get away.

For a very rattled Edgar Feuchtinger, the glider landing was the final straw. Convinced it was a lightning Allied response to Rauch's success in reaching the sea, and that major parts of his division were threatened with being cut off, he immediately abandoned any plans he might have had to reinforce his subordinate – although, as ever, he was keen to lay the blame elsewhere: 'I now expected that some reinforcements would be forthcoming to help me hold my position, but nothing came.'

Feuchtinger then crowned his *dies horribilis* by unilaterally deciding to tell Rauch to pull his men back from the coast: 'Another Allied parachute landing on both sides of the Orne, together with a sharp attack by English tanks, forced me to give up my hold on the coast. I retired to take up a line just north of Caen. By the end of that first day my division had lost almost 25 per cent of its panzers.'[26]

Apparently Marcks – back from his foray into the field with the same panzergrenadiers – strongly objected to Feuchtinger's decision, but then why didn't he overrule his incompetent panzer general? That question will forever remain unanswered, and it must have been asked by the officers and men of *I. Bataillon* of *192. Panzer-Grenadier-Regiment* as they mounted their waiting vehicles, set off through the darkness back to their lines in the south, and looked back at the inky blackness of the Channel – it would be the last time any of them ever saw it while carrying a weapon – just the latest in a long line of *maybes* for the Germans on D-Day. Rommel's plan to frustrate the landings had been clear; a relatively thin crust of infantry – mainly static divisions – were to man the *Atlantikwall* defences and hold the attackers on, or close to, the beaches. Reinforcements, mostly mobile, would then immediately swing into action, counter-attack, and throw the Allies back into the sea. As a strategy it was risky, but given the overall lack of resources at the Westheer's disposal, it was no worse than any other plan. The key for its success was a trade-off; the Germans would swap size of force for speed of response. That meant frontline commanders buying into the principle that it was more important to get men counter-attacking onto the beaches as quickly as possible, rather than waiting for additional troops coming up from the rear. Better one grenadier on the sand than a whole division five miles from the surf, was effectively Rommel's mantra for success. But the Germans didn't achieve this; why? The standard narrative for the Nazi failure on D-Day is that for a variety of reasons their highest levels of leadership failed, and failed utterly: because many of their divisional, *Korps* and Army commanders were absent, many at the planned war games in Rennes, or in Rommel's case at home in Germany for his wife's birthday; and because others such as Geyr von Schweppenburg and von Rundstedt himself were curiously silent for most of the day, all the way up to Hitler, whose own staff refused to wake him fearing their master's wrath. All this is true of course, but what is overlooked amidst this litany of blunders is that German mid-ranking leadership, especially at regimental and divisional level, also failed to do what it had ostensibly been trained to do, and that is to think at least one level up and deliver on their higher commander's intent; von der Heydte's paras over in the west at Utah had no chance of achieving Rommel's goal, operating as they were without adequate motorised transport, and with the *709.*'s beach defences being overrun so quickly. But at Omaha the

Germans had an opportunity at least to hold the Americans, if not force them to evacuate the beach under fire – Dietrich Kraiss had chosen to send *KG Meyer* northeast instead, to shore up a flank that in the end didn't much matter. Further east, at the Anglo-Canadian beaches, *21. Panzer* had the best chance of all, to sweep forward and drive a wedge between Juno and Sword – indeed Josef Rauch and some of his grenadiers did exactly that – but the hugely experienced von Oppeln-Bronikowski's counter-stroke had been mangled and, inexplicably, he had failed to press it home. His inept divisional commander had then put the last nail into the Germans' D-Day coffin by losing his nerve and pulling Rauch back from the sea. As a German account said: 'The one and only chance on D-Day had been lost. Never again was there to be such an opportunity.' Wilhelm von Gottberg was of the same mind: 'I am still convinced that if we had been given orders to attack during the early hours of the invasion we would have succeeded in throwing the enemy back into the sea. But there was nothing I could do but curse the short-sightedness of my own high command.'

With the hammer repulsed, what now of the anvil? Richter's *716. ID* had been in the eye of the storm all day and was visibly wilting. Created, manned and equipped to do nothing more than delay an attacker for a few hours and hold its bunkers until the planned counter-attacks came swinging in, it had been faced by an Anglo-Canadian landing force that outmatched it in every conceivable way. The result was Armageddon for its 8,000 men. As its distraught commander told von Oppeln-Bronikowski in a moment of self-pity: 'My troops are lost, my whole division is finished.' Of the four German and two *Ostbataillone* of *716. ID* defending the beaches, only one was still at anything like its pre-dawn strength, the rest had been cut to ribbons; however, his pathetic lament wasn't entirely accurate. His four strongpoints grouped around the high ground of the Périers ridge, codenamed by the British planners as *Sole* (WN14),[27] *Morris* (WN16), *Daimler* (WN12) and *Hillman*, had indeed come under sustained assault from well-briefed Allied troops who knew exactly where they were and had practised how they were going to capture them. WN14 and 16 had been taken as planned, although not on time. WN12, with its four gun casemates, had been a tougher nut to crack, holding out until 6pm, even as Rauch's men approached the sea to the west. As for WN17 (*Hillman*), the Suffolks were struggling. The

East Anglian's sister regiment in the brigade tried to bypass it and make a dash for Caen, but German machine-guns poured fire into the Norfolks and slowed their advance. In an attempt to use brute force to overwhelm the defenders, Shermans from 'A' Squadron the Staffordshire Yeomanry, and 'C' Squadron of the 13th/18th Royal Hussars, drove onto the very top of the strongpoint and fired down into it, gun barrels depressed spraying shell and shot, but with the vast majority of the enemy underground, the effects were minimal. Now seriously behind their own schedule, the British called on additional support, with two batteries from the 33rd and 76th Field Regiments, Royal Artillery, bringing down a barrage onto the very top of the position, but again, with little discernible effect. British Royal Engineers of the 246th Field Company were up next, working their way through the underground galleries and chambers with the Suffolks, using explosive charges to try and blast the defenders out, but as they laboriously worked their way forward it became obvious that the complex was far larger than they had been told to expect. Nonetheless, the continual pressure took its toll on the Germans, and not long after 8pm that evening the British reported that most of *WN17* was in their hands – which wasn't true, although the Suffolks didn't know that at the time.

Four hours later, at midnight, a telephone rang at Wilhelm Richter's headquarters bunker near Caen. His staff looked at the phone in surprise, they'd barely received a call all day, most of the lines having been cut by the Allied bombardments. An operator passed the receiver to the divisional Operational Chief of Staff (*Ia, Gerneralstabsoffizier*) *Major* Bachus.[28] Bachus asked who it was, then handed the phone to his boss; '*Oberst Krug, Herr General.*'

Richter took the receiver and heard Krug's voice down the line: 'Herr General, the enemy are on top of my bunker. They are demanding my surrender. I have no means to fight them, nor any contact with any of my units. What shall I do?' *Generalleutnant* Wilhelm Richter, who a few hours earlier had informed 7. *Armee* that the landing had been pushed back into the sea, but who had then realised that not only was that not true but five of his six battalions were now little more than fragments, could only say to his subordinate: 'I cannot give you any further orders. You may now act on your own initiative. *Auf Wiedersehen.*'

Just under seven hours later, at 0645hrs on 7 June, Ludwig Krug had made up his mind. His batman gave his jackboots a final polish, picked up two suitcases containing the *Oberst*'s personal items and, followed by three of his officers and seventy men from the original garrison of one hundred and fifty, Krug appeared on the surface of *WN17* and surrendered to a suitably astonished battalion of Suffolks, who had been sitting on the strongpoint all night, completely unaware of what was beneath their feet. After relieving Krug of his briefcase, some of the British infantrymen went down into the bowels of the bunker complex so recently vacated by the men of *GR. 736*. To their delight they found something that Ludwig Krug couldn't carry away – his personal champagne store.[29] It probably didn't soften the blow of losing two officers and five men killed, along with twenty-four wounded, to capture the place.

D-Day was over – the Wehrmacht had been comprehensively beaten on Rommel's 'longest day'. The strategy of relying on a series of fortifications intended to span a distance of hundreds of miles, with forces that could realistically defend only a fraction of that, was exposed as the immense folly it was; seventeen million cubic yards of concrete and one and a half million tons of iron couldn't compensate for divisional defensive sectors in northern France averaging anywhere from 50 miles to a ridiculous 93 miles in length. In Nazi propaganda the *Atlantikwall* was almost always characterized by the colossus of the four-gun Todt battery at Cap Gris-Nez in the Pas de Calais; a lone eagle-eyed German sentry standing next to one of its gigantic 15-inch ship-killing guns and the mountains of concrete encasing it – Google the *Atlantikwall* and this often appears. In reality, much of the defences were hastily-built earth bunkers, their trench walls timber-clad, with captured French tank turrets sporting obsolete Czech machine-guns. Any 'wall' as a military obstacle had been rendered fallible with the coming of gunpowder, and *Festung Europa*'s wall was no exception. As the semi-mythical founder of the famed Spartan martial system is supposed to have said: 'The strongest walls are built of men.' Von Rundstedt, no Lycurgus, but a vastly experienced officer, said of the wall:

> The strength of the defences was absurdly overrated, the Atlantikwall was an illusion, conjured up by propaganda to deceive the German people as well as the Allies... It was nonsense to describe it as a 'wall', Hitler himself never came to visit it and see it for what it really was.[30]

Or to quote another experienced and even more famous general: 'Fixed fortifications are a monument to the stupidity of man.' (Patton.)

By D-Day, most of the men manning that piece of 'propaganda' – and indeed a full quarter of the entire Army – were in their mid-30s or older, not, perhaps what Lycurgus had in mind. It was a point their opponents appreciated, men like the US Army Ranger Carl Weast, who landed on Omaha: 'If we'd have been confronted with first-class German troops they'd have just tore our ass up, fortunately we were up against some of the lousiest troops in the German Army. These guys didn't want to fight, none of them did, and we were fortunate in that. Otherwise…'[31] After landing, a dumbstruck Weast had been standing guard over his headquarters when about thirty-five German soldiers appeared on the road coming towards him; the men were in a column of twos, with their wounded piled into an old buggy pulled by some of their comrades. 'We put them in an orchard, put one man guarding them and tried to interrogate them. Hell, there were no Germans there! They were all Hungarians, Romanians, Russians, anything but Germans. I think there was one German, an NCO. He'd been on the Eastern front, was middle-aged and looked like he wanted to do anything but fight a war, believe me.'[32]

The Ranger was not alone in his view of the opposition the landings had faced, but it was by no means a universal view. Private Francis Williams of the British 6th Battalion, the Green Howards, had landed on Gold Beach and fought the men of *716. ID*. His best mate, Bill 'Rufty' Hill, was killed on the beach, whereupon Williams – who had already won the Military Medal for bravery earlier in the war – charged the enemy machine-gun position responsible, killed two of its defenders and took the other six prisoner. As he escorted them back down to the beach, he noticed 'one of them had a sort of band around the bottom of his sleeve, and on it were the words *Afrika Korps*. I said to him, "You Rommel's man?", he said "*Ja*" and I pointed to my Africa Star and said "Me Eighth Army," it was a bit like *Tarzan and Jane*. I shook his hand and went back to what was left of my platoon.'

One of Weast's countrymen also saw a different side to the German defenders as he tried to interrogate a captured member of the hard-fighting *352. ID*, who, sitting on the bloody sand of Omaha, refused to give anything other than his name, rank and number – as per the Geneva Convention. The American interrogator became increasingly angry at his prisoner's defiance, and, in frustration, fired his carbine into the sand between the man's legs. The German pointed to his crotch and said; '*Nicht hier,*' then pointed to his head – '*hier*'. The American gave up.[33] Over on Sword, Lord Lovat's commandos weren't getting much out of two of their prisoners either, until they realised neither could speak German as one was Russian and the other a Pole; switching to French proved to be the answer.

***

In 1522 the Ottoman Sultan Suleiman the Magnificent, the greatest of his line, headed out to sea in four hundred ships to try and conquer Rhodes and eject its Christian rulers, with an army of 180,000 men; this gargantuan venture is dwarfed by the sheer immensity of what the Allies amassed off the shores of Normandy that June. Now, even as the beach-side interrogations went on, the flow ashore of men, equipment and supplies continued unabated from the holds and decks of the armada's 6,939 vessels, which included 1,213 warships and 5,726 transport craft, merchantmen and ancillaries, from no fewer than eight different navies – although three-quarters were British. According to the official British record, joining the 15,500 Americans and 7,900 Britons who landed from the air, were 75,215 British and Canadians, and 57,500 Americans who arrived by sea on D-Day itself. With them were more than 20,000 vehicles of all types, as the most mechanized army in history came ashore to find itself facing one that still relied on a form of transport Lycurgus would have recognised – the horse.

Martin Eineg was a youthful eighteen-year-old ex-Hitler Youth member, who had been posted to an anti-aircraft battery in Bavaria before being sent west to the belly *716. ID* because of a chronic lung condition that had him classed as 'medically unfit'. Captured on the morning of D-Day he was corralled with other prisoners waiting to be transported off the beach.

> The beach was completely full of transports, including many vehicles we had not seen before and we did not even know how to describe … one thing in particular struck many of us as amazing; all along the beach there were no horses! We found it astonishing. This huge army had brought with it not one single horse or pack-mule! All their transport was mechanized … every German unit had its stables and veterinary officer, and here were these English without that need at all. For us, this symbolised the Allies capabilities.[34]

Eineg wasn't the only *landser* who was swiftly learning this would be a new type of war. Over in the American sector another POW was thinking the exact same thing:

> If that had been a German army, even in 1944, there would have been a lot of horses and wagons there, in the supply element, because of the lack of fuel and trucks. In fact, one of the other captured men with me stupidly asked one of the American guards: 'But where are your horses?' the American just laughed at this and gave him a cigarette.[35]

Hein Severloh remembered seeing a horse-drawn cart being used by his comrades to carry the wounded on D-Day, and Karl-Heinz Voss – also of *352. ID* – who was acting as a dispatch rider that day, found himself detailed to speed with all haste to divisional headquarters at Littry with a captured copy of the whole plan of attack for the U.S. V Corps; 'My *Hauptmann* told me that the plans were to get to divisional headquarters in Littry as fast as possible, and I was to turn them over to no-one except *Major* Block or *Oberstleutnant* Ziegelmann. I left the door of the command post and *mounted my horse*.'[36]

Back in June 1941, almost exactly four years earlier, the Wehrmacht had invaded the Soviet Union with almost three-and-a-half million men. With them were 3,400 panzers and other armoured vehicles, 7,200 artillery pieces and 2,800 aircraft. The men, their equipment and supplies were carried by 600,000 trucks, cars and transports, and over *one million horses*, who, when the Russian mud and snow swallowed up the trucks, ended up doing most of the heavy lifting for the whole campaign. Four years on and German industry hadn't managed to make them redundant, in fact with fuel at an increasing premium, the horse was becoming even more important for the Wehrmacht as it regressed into an almost Bismarck-era organisation; the Normandy campaign and the battle for France would partly be about the truck versus the horse.

***

The Germans had two crumbs of comfort from D-Day: Carentan at the western end of the beachhead, and Caen at the eastern – neither had been taken as the Allies had planned. A glance at any map would tell you why they – and especially Caen – were so important; just about every road of any size in the region went in and out of the two.

To occupy them was to be able to use that road network to break out of Normandy and into the rest of northern France – without them the Allies would be stymied. The Germans needed to deny them to the Allies to deny them the rest of France. This next stage of the fighting would be a race as to which side could pour reinforcements of men and equipment into the battlefront the quicker; the battle for France wasn't won or lost quite yet. The campaign would now enter a second phase, more deadly than the first, although for many it had been deadly enough already:

> On the morning of 6th June we saw the full might of the English and Americans. At sea, close inshore, the fleet was drawn up, limitless ships small and great as if for a parade, a grandiose spectacle. No-one who did not see it could have believed it. The whistling of the shells and shattering explosions around us create the worst kind of music. Our unit has suffered terribly – you and the children will be glad I survived.[37]

So wrote a German *landser* to his wife back home. The unposted letter was found on his corpse.

3

Hold the Line!

Wilhelm Richter's headquarters bunker was just to the north of Caen, dug deep into the side of a sandpit for protection against barrage and air attack. Far from spacious at the best of times, it was jam-packed with officers, staff and wounded soldiers when Richter took Ludwig Krug's despairing telephone call on the night of D-Day. As well as his own men, Edgar Feuchtinger had somehow fetched up there, although to what useful purpose is almost anyone's guess, and also there, dismayed at what they were hearing from a general of the German Army, stood two officers; one in field-grey and the other in a camouflage battle-smock. The former – Fritz Witt – reported to Richter with the following admonition: 'I have been on my way to you for eight hours. I lay a good four hours in roadside ditches because of air attacks. The division's marching columns are suffering serious losses in men and material.'

The other man was instantly recognisable to everyone in the bunker, and indeed to probably every living German. This was Kurt Meyer, known to one and all by his nickname – *Panzermeyer*. The illegitimate son of a coal miner, Meyer was now the 33-year-old commander of an entire panzergrenadier regiment. His earlier exploits had earned him the Knight's Cross he wore at his neck, and the adoration of his young troopers, as well as that of the folks back home. In many ways he was the epitome of what Hitler intended the Waffen-SS to be; 'racially pure', recklessly brave, totally ruthless towards the enemy and those considered as 'getting in the way' – namely civilians – scornful of any weakness, determined to win, and shorn of the class-bias that still predominated in the regular army. Having spent the war so far in the *Leibstandarte*, he was now a senior officer in a division which would have its baptism of fire in Normandy, and which would, in so many ways, come to symbolise the German campaign – *12. SS-Panzerdivision 'Hitlerjugend'* – the *'HJ'*.

Missing from this tableau in Richter's headquarters bunker was one other general officer, whose formation, just like its Waffen-SS stable-mate the *Hitlerjugend*, would come to be forever associated with the Westheer's ultimately disastrous struggle to hold France; Fritz Bayerlein from the Army's *Panzer-Lehr-Division*.

Both formations had been recently raised, both had been established, manned and equipped to be 'best in breed', and both were fêted as the finest formations the Third Reich could produce in this fifth year of the war; but they were very different animals.

The *Panzer-Lehr*, much like the *Grossdeutschland*, was a premier Army formation to its trigger fingertips. Formed in December the previous year, there was barely a new recruit in its ranks, with the vast majority of its members being transferred in from the training and demonstration units of the *panzerwaffe*'s two *Panzertruppenschulen* (Armoured Troops Schools) in Munster and Wünsdorf. As you would expect, the officers and men posted to act as instructors and demo troops for the favoured arm of the German Army were no laggards. All were experienced combat veterans with service records encompassing Poland, the Western campaign, the Balkans, Russia (of course) and North Africa. In the Schools they had passed on their extensive knowledge to the students, demonstrated tactics in the different phases of war, and allowed the students to practise those tactics themselves using 'live' troops in a training environment. However, although this work was immensely valuable for the long-term effectiveness and professionalism of the *panzerwaffe*, the Wehrmacht was so desperately short of experienced soldiers it just couldn't afford to overlook these extremely capable manpower pools. So, in one of a multitude of decisions the leadership of the Reich made based on short-termism and good old-fashioned desperation, the *panzertruppenschulen* were stripped of swathes of their instructors and personnel, who were sent to the Nancy/Verdun area in northeastern France and transformed into a fighting division. Given their prior experience, the men didn't need much work-up training, their time was instead spent on familiarising themselves with their new comrades and with their new equipment, and what a lot of equipment there was! The quartermasters didn't stint when it came to the *Panzer-Lehr*, in fact, so lavish was its equipment table that it officially became the best kitted-out division in the Wehrmacht. Alongside its eighty-nine Panthers and ninety-nine *PzKpfw IVs* were eleven *PzKpfw IIIs*, ten *StuG IIIs*, eight *Tiger Is*, plus thirty-one *Jagdpanzer IV* assault-guns in its *panzerjäger* battalion.[1] By any measure this meant the *Lehr* had unprecedented punch, and its other major components were treated in the same manner. Every single one of its *panzergrenadiers* moved by armoured vehicle, such as the ubiquitous *Sd.Kfz. 251* half-track (there would be an astonishing 612 of them in the division by D-Day – double the number in a normal panzer unit), instead of by truck as was the case in every other Army panzer division, where only the first grenadier battalion was so equipped; something that made a huge difference to infantrymen moving around battlefields riven by shot and shell. It wasn't just the *Lehr*'s infantry either; the division's engineers and reconnaissance troops were the same, with the latter also having a company of the new *Sd.Kfz 234/2 Puma* armoured cars.

To whom would Berlin bequeath this magnificent martial gift? The choice fell on a tough 45-year-old Bavarian who had served under Heinz Guderian in Russia, and then under Rommel in the *Afrika Korps* – *Generalleutnant* Fritz Bayerlein. A no-nonsense soldier, Bayerlein had recently commanded 3. *Panzerdivision*, leading it in a successful break-out from Kirovograd in Ukraine, and as such, his professional credentials were not in doubt, however, not all was rosy in the *Panzer-Lehr* garden. Just like 21. *Panzer*, the *Lehr* only had four battalions of panzergrenadiers, and not six like most other armoured divisions. This meant that in a battle of attrition it would burn out pretty quickly, as casualties mounted amongst its bayonet strength; and therein lay its biggest problem – what type of battle was it actually designed to fight? A mechanized force like the *Lehr*, with its array of armour, mobile infantry, and experienced rank and file, was tailor-made to lead the charge in the great, sweeping land battles that characterised so much of the fighting on the Russian front. There, on the seemingly endless steppes where air attack was minimal, it could carry out the war of space and manoeuvre it could excel at, but instead it was assigned to Normandy – an area less than a seventh of the size of what would become the *Operation Bagration* battlesite in Belorussia that same summer,[2] and so claustrophobic and confined by its own terrain that it was discounted by the OKW planners as a probable landing site for the armour-heavy Allies. These then were the cracks in the *Panzer-Lehr's* façade into which the Allies would pour the acid that would eventually destroy it.

While the *Lehr* was adjudged an élite formation on account of the accumulated experience of its bemedalled personnel and its huge armoured inventory, the *HJ* was also viewed as special, but for altogether different reasons.

It wasn't its weaponry which marked it out, although it included some ninety-six *PzKpfw IVs* and seventy-nine Panthers (but not a single *Jagdpanzer IV* as they still hadn't arrived), nor was it its overall strength, which by D-Day stood at 20,540 – admittedly far above the *Lehr's* 14,699. Rather it was who made up the roster, or the bulk of it anyway. Formed in 1943, the *HJ* was, as was standard practice in both the Army and Waffen-SS at that time of the war, assigned a cadre – a *stammeinheit* – from an experienced division, in its case the famed *1. SS-Panzerdivision 'Leibstandarte SS Adolf Hitler'* – Hitler's own bodyguard. About two thousand *LSSAH* men were transferred, where they took up most of the leadership and staff appointments at company level and above, all the way to the divisonal commander himself, *SS-Brigadeführer* Fritz Witt. The son of a salesman, Witt was an early member of the SS, joining the Bodyguard in mid-March 1933 as one of its original 117-members, before having an exemplary career during the early years of the war. Witt was a tall, powerfully built man, who led from the front and had an often informal, almost paternal relationship with his men, despite his own youth – he was only just thirty-five when he took command – which was useful, because the *HJ* was specifically raised from the young men of Germany who were born in the second half of 1926. That meant that they were almost all just eighteen – all sixteen thousand and more of them – and not just any entries in the 1926 births register, preference was given to young men who were members of the *Hitlerjugend* (Hitler Youth) organisation. Although preference was not really an issue since the *Gesetz über die Hitlerjugend* (Hitler Youth Law) came into effect in March 1939. This was a legal obligation which conscripted all German youths into the *Hitlerjugend* (girls went into their own version) — even if their parents objected. In fact, parents who refused to allow their children to join were subject to investigation by the authorities. Needless to say, from then on, Germany's teenagers joined the Hitler Youth, and by 1940 it had eight million members. All militaries throughout the ages have recruited from the young, war is a young man's game after all, and if you walk around any barracks in the world and expect to see masses of soldiers in their thirties and forties then you will be disappointed; but what made the *HJ* so different was not that it had eighteen year-olds in it, but that it was *formed* from eighteen-year-olds, and this was something special, even in Nazi Germany. Every infantry unit in modern armies has teenagers in its ranks, but they're a minority, not so in the *HJ*. Ever since Gottlob Berger (or Artur Axmann)[3] first came up with the idea, the division was intended as a symbol of what Nazi youth could achieve on the battlefield, even if some of its own officers and members didn't pay this much heed:

> Basically, they were boys between the ages of seventeen and eighteen who were prepared to fight for their fatherland, as was customary at the time – nothing else. We knew from the start that we would be at a disadvantage on the battlefield, from 1942 on we began, somewhat self-mockingly, to speak of the 'poor man's war', which we were waging, given the enemy's superiority, and which was especially applicable to the fighting in Normandy.[4]

This was Rudolf *Rudi* von Ribbentrop – a highly decorated officer of the *LSSAH* and son of the Third Reich's Foreign Minister, Joachim von Ribbentrop. Like Fritz Witt he had been transferred to the newly-established *HJ* as a member of its cadre after winning the Knight's Cross in Russia during the spring fighting at Kharkov. Hanging around his neck, the medal 'cured his throat-ache' as the saying went. Despite his privileged position and poster-boy image, von Ribbentrop was a realist about Nazi Germany's situation: 'In the winter of 1941/42, when I was in a military hospital near Berlin [he would be wounded five times in all during the war], I suddenly realised that my mother no longer believed there would be a satisfactory end to the war.... Looking grey and worn-out she had not denied it ... the silence had been the first hint.'

Von Ribbentrop's doubts about final victory mirrored the lack of conviction among some of the rank and file. The *HJ* has often been characterized as a hotbed of blind obedience, with brainwashed teenagers gladly going to their deaths among Normandy's *bocage*, but that view needs to be challenged with the reality of its short-lived history. One young weapons mechanic in the division, Rudi Schmierer, fought in Normandy, and then took part in the retreat to Belgium. At the border, the car he and a comrade were driving broke down. While waiting for help, the other soldier said he had had enough and was going to head home to Hamburg. After he had left, Rudi dumped his rifle into a hollow tree, stole some civilian clothes from a nearby farm and began the long walk home to his native Austria.[5] There weren't many Schmierers in the *HJ* though. It was an all-volunteer formation, and so many youths came forward that two thousand of them were sent instead to backfill the ranks of the *LSSAH*. This fervour to join up has often been cited as evidence of fanaticism among the volunteers, something ex-members such as Rudi von Ribbentrop are keen to refute:

> My soldiers were not fanatics. The term 'fanatics' probably comes more from the respective war propaganda! My soldiers were young men who fought very well and many of them fell in the fighting, but they don't deserve the negative term of 'fanatics' and that attitude did not appertain to them.

Despite this assertion, it was clear that the *HJ* was more than 'just another division'. It was intended from the start to be a living embodiment of Nazi superiority, a manifestation of the exceptionalist philosophy that Germany was increasingly clinging to as the key to turning the tide of the war and bringing final victory. This philosophy was fundamental to Nazi ideology, and in German military thinking it was expressed in the widely held belief that man for man the Germans were better than their opponents, something some of those same opponents, such as the British Chief of the Imperial General Staff, Sir Alan Brooke, on occasion seemed to concur with: 'There is no doubt that the Germans are the most wonderful soldiers.' At the beginning of the war this belief system was coupled with more advanced German weaponry, as well as superior tactics and doctrine – the *blitzkrieg* in the West in 1940 being the apogee of this entire approach – but by 1944 these advantages were largely negated, especially by the overwhelming mass of Anglo-American and Soviet equipment, and their respective learning curves on the battlefield. So, in response, the Germans increasingly fell back on an erroneous belief that they would win in the end because of their innate superiority as human beings; men would overcome machines. Nazi propaganda fed into this falsehood, the newsreels constantly highlighting stories of individuals who had overcome the odds to win a victory on one front or another. It is hard to know how much the ordinary *landser* bought into this myth, but what is indisputable is that in their diaries and letters a recurring theme is of them knowing they will be up against an enemy with overwhelming material superiority, but who weren't their equal as men. *SS-Schütze* Jochen Leykauff of the *HJ* wrote: 'Our first action lay ahead, we were looking forward to it. The Allies planned to take apart the "baby milk division" as they called us, but we were not afraid.' Leykauff's compatriot in another newly raised Waffen-SS formation; *Hauptscharführer* Helmut Gunther of the 17. *SS-Panzergrenadier-Division 'Götz von Berlichingen'* thought along the same lines: 'In Russia we had fought men against men. We knew that in Normandy it would be men against machines... We still felt an absolute sense of loyalty.'[6]

Hitler himself was of the same view, as he expressed to his entourage on 6 June as he stood in his dressing gown in the Berghof: 'The news couldn't be better. As long as they were in Britain we couldn't get at them. Now we have them where we can get at them.'

Illogical and hopelessly naïve as this was, the *HJ* in particular earned a reputation in Normandy for almost superhuman feats of endurance and courage, and a large part of that achievement can be laid at the feet of the teenagers who made up its ranks:

> We knew that we were quick, agile and confident. We trusted our officers and NCOs, who had been hardened in battle. We had known them since the beginning of training. During combat training, with live ammunition, we had enjoyed seeing them in the mud together with us, with steel helmet and submachine-gun.[7]

Not that all of the new recruits reflected so positively on their training; 'In the Waffen-SS you couldn't do anything if an *Unterführer* hit you during training. The purpose of the training is to make you just as they are; it's pure sadism.' However, comments like this are rare, and must be seen in context – this testimony was given by a captured *HJ* soldier during interrogation, where, perhaps, he was keen to distance himself from his division. Nevertheless, it was true that the training had been tough and also unorthodox, given the lack of time the unit had to reach operational readiness.

> During their training, square-bashing was frowned upon. March-pasts and similar exercises were not practised. Everything focused on training for battle and this took place under the most realistic battle conditions possible. Physical toughening was achieved through sport; route marches were disapproved of as being unnecessary

and harmful. General von Geyr Schweppenburg stimulated the development of progressive training in marksmanship. This took place exclusively in the countryside, target exercises in barracks ceased completely.[8]

Whatever their respective merits and faults, *Lehr* and the *HJ* would be critical in the Normandy campaign given that they possessed more than a quarter of the Westheer's entire armour complement of 1,552 panzers on D-Day. On that day both divisions were on standby, Fritz Witt having reported to OB West five days previously that the HJ was 'ready for offensive actions'. Consequently, the *HJ* moved up to Caen on the 6th itself, but the *Lehr* didn't move until the following day, and when it did it came in for a rude shock, as Bayerlein himself recalled:

> By noon on the 7th my men were already calling the main road from Vire to le Bény Bocage the '*Jabo-Rennstrecke*' ['the fighter-bomber racecourse']. Every vehicle was covered in tree branches, and moved along hedgerows and the fringes of woods ...

Serious or not, the Wehrmacht's need was clear – move troops up to seal off the beachhead and stop any Allied break-out. Keeping the British out of Caen was central to achieving that goal, so both the *Lehr* and the *HJ* were committed to that sector of the new front. The following phase of what was now the Westheer's Normandy campaign should have been just as clear: rush in divisions from elsewhere to win the inevitable 'battle of the reinforcements', and build up an operational reserve big enough to launch a co-ordinated, planned counter-attack that would drive the Allies back into the Channel. As one German para officer near Utah said; 'Every day is crucial...in fact every hour – the enemy is bringing his reinforcements ashore. Only by destroying the landing craft, the enemy fleet involved in the whole operation, can we destroy the enemy's supplies and give ourselves a chance to drive him back into the sea.'

The counter-attack would need to be dominated by armour – it had to be an unstoppable mailed fist, battering and bludgeoning its way to the sea – so the Westheer's panzer formations; including the *Panzer-Lehr* and *HJ*, needed to be put back into reserve as quickly as possible to husband their strength, and their place taken by the infantry whose main role in war is to take and hold ground. The *landsers* would then dig in, hold the line, and fix the Allies in position until the counter-stroke was ready to be launched – simple.

It wasn't of course. The confusion, weak leadership and poor intelligence that had bedevilled the Westheer in the run-up to D-Day continued in its aftermath. Even with the Allies ashore, the all-too-familiar argument between Rommel and von Rundstedt and their competing visions as to how to defeat the landing continued unabated. Rommel:

> If the enemy gets his foot in, he'll put every anti-tank gun and tank he can into the bridgehead and let us beat our heads against it, as he did at Medenine {Tunisia, 6 March 1943]. To break through such a front you have to attack slowly and methodically under cover of massed artillery, but we, of course, thanks to the Allied air forces, will have nothing here on time.

OB West's view was expressed by Guderian:

> Our opinion was that it all depended on our making ready adequate reserves of panzer and panzergrenadier divisions; these must be stationed far enough inland from the so-called *Atlantikwall,* so they could be switched easily to the main invasion front once it had been recognised

The two men were at loggerheads, with any chance of agreement being remote to say the least. Rommel; almost frenetically energetic, a master of mobile, armoured warfare, whose experience in North Africa had taught him the threats posed by Allied air and firepower, against von Rundstedt; a member of Prussia's old *Junker* nobility – the *Uradel* – servants of the monarchy since the time of Frederick the Great, endowed with no titles and little wealth, but possessed of a distinguished lineage dating back to the twelfth century. Rommel preferred to lead from the front, seeing the battlefield with his own eyes, making snap decisions based on what was happening on the ground, and driving his men on remorselessly. Von Rundstedt's style was different. He was most comfortable in his headquarters, analysing reports from subordinates, making balanced judgements based on sound military practice, and following the battle on wall-maps. The two men couldn't seem to be more different, however they were more alike than they perhaps wished to believe.

First and foremost, both had tasted success; in Poland, France in 1940, in *Barbarossa* for von Rundstedt, and in the desert for Rommel. Both men were also disillusioned, to a degree, with Hitler and the Nazis. The *Führer* had sacked von Rundstedt in Russia in 1941, and Rommel felt he and his men had been hung out to dry in the African campaign. Each had been approached for support by the coterie of plotters who would attempt to assassinate the Nazi dictator in July, but turned them down; in von Rundstedt's case apparently with the comment; 'Why always me? Let Manstein and Kluge do it.'[9] They were both creatures of habit – Rommel might well drive over three hundred kilometres a day in his staff car, hurrying from one unit to the next, inspecting everything in his path, but he was pretty much always back at his *château*-headquarters at La Roche Guyon every evening for dinner with his staff, followed by a stroll round the battlements before making himself comfortable on a bench specially positioned by his chief naval advisor, Friedrich Ruge. The two men would look across the Seine, over the shrubs Ruge had had cut back so as not to obscure his boss's view, as he regaled him with summaries of the novel *Gone With The Wind*. Von Rundstedt preferred to stay in his headquarters most days, rarely rising before ten and never working beyond eight in the evening. He would often be found reading the trashy detective novels he was so enamoured of, dining with his staff *a la* Rommel, and indulging himself with the cigars and cognac that were slowly killing him. His son, *Major* Hans-Gerd von Rundstedt, wrote to his mother Bila referring to his father's 'somewhat plentiful nicotine and alcohol consumption'. The historian Chester Wilmot said of him; 'The truth was that Rundstedt had lost his grip. He was old and tired and his once active brain was gradually becoming addled, for he had great difficulty in sleeping without the soporific aid of alcohol.' One of von Rundstedt's senior panzer commanders described him thus:

An elderly man and a soldier of thorough training with adequate experience in practical warfare, but without an understanding of a three-dimensional war involving the combined operations of the Army, Kriegsmarine and Luftwaffe. He was a gentleman and had the personal confidence and respect of his subordinate commanders and his troops. His authority was limited and quite handicapped. His chief of staff [*General der Infanterie* Günther Blumentritt] was not a suitable complement, either as to capability or character.

This would seem a harsh judgement indeed for a man who would have served his country for no fewer than fifty-two years by the time he retired. It would also seem to disregard the clarity of von Rundstedt's judgement following D-Day when he argued either for a timely withdrawal to a new defensive line to the north, or a political solution to the war. Frankly, the two field marshals' argument as to how to defeat the landings was moot, given the role Adolf Hitler would come to play in the campaign.

The European war can be seen through a multitude of prisms, one of which is the reversal in the decision-making process at the highest levels of command of the two giant totalitarian states that dominated the conflict, Stalin's Soviet Union and Hitler's Third Reich. The Nazi dictator's belief in his own strategic genius meant he was always getting involved in decisions, from the very beginning of the war, which should have been properly left to his military commanders, the stop order to the *panzerwaffe* in front of Dunkirk that allowed the British to rescue the core of their army being a classic example. But, by and large, it was the professionals of the German General Staff that called the shots – once policy had been decided of course. However, this arrangement broke down in the winter of 1941/42 with the disastrous *Operation Typhoon* defeat in front of Moscow. This battle, which buried the German Army of 1940/41 under Russian snow, was also notable for the clash between the majority of Hitler's generals on the one hand and the dictator on the other – and the latter won, proceeding to carry out a wholesale cull of senior officers (including von Rundstedt) culminating months later in the removal of Franz Halder as *OKH* chief of staff. From then on, it was Hitler who dictated all military decisions, sometimes down to minutiae, relying on incompetent yes-men such as the once-respected former artillery officer Wilhelm Keitel, memorably described by his peer, Ewald von Kleist, as 'a stupid follower of Hitler'. Keitel was sneered at by pretty much every other senior commander in the Wehrmacht as a spineless toady – even acquiring the derogatory nickname of '*Lakeitel*', a pun on his surname (in German '*Lakai*' means '*lackey*'). His comment on practically any matter was 'The *Führer* is right!'

Conversely, it was Stalin who began the war making all the important calls for the Red Army – a situation that led directly to the gargantuan losses of the summer and autumn of 1941. From then on, the balance started to swing the other way, until Red Army generals like Zhukov, Koniev and Rokossovsky were firmly in the military driving seat – although at no time did Stalin remove himself from the equation and give the generals free rein; the Georgian supremo always had the last word!

As for the Anglo-Americans, they demonstrated that democracies often have an uncanny knack of finding a system that binds politicians and generals together in a common endeavour and leaves enough room for all their egos; Eisenhower's SHAEF and its relations with Washington and London – despite being extremely difficult on occasion – are an exemplar of clear command and control in the most complex of circumstances.

By contrast, the senior German command structure in the West was a masterclass in dysfunction, inter-service rivalry, inefficiency and confusion. The upshot was that senior military decision making often resembled the worst machinations of imperial courts throughout history, and was incredibly wearing on those involved. An exhausted von Rundstedt told Gerhard Engel, one of Hitler's adjutants, that he was 'too old and had had enough'. As the German commanders tried to make sense of their labyrinthine hierarchy, they were further handicapped by the continuing misjudgements of their intelligence services. The Allied deception plan; Operation Fortitude, continued to work to perfection, fuelling *Fremde Heere West's* mistaken assumption that 'the enemy is planning a further large-scale operation in the Channel area, which one would expect to be aimed at the coastal sector in the Pas de Calais area,' even after the Normandy landings, hamstringing the German response from the get-go. As with several other major decisions, in this aspect of the campaign the Germans were prisoners of their own experience. They simply couldn't believe that the Anglo-Americans would be able to land and then re-supply a significant force without securing a major port – hence why the *Atlantikwall* defences were clustered around them. A German officer based near Calais expressed a common view: 'We certainly didn't think it was possible to land large numbers of tanks, trucks, and so on directly from the sea onto a beach. We thought the Allies would assault the seafront sector of a port city, as they had tried to do at Dieppe in 1942.'[10] German intelligence had failed to understand the Allies' capabilities, or to discover the genius of the artificial Mulberry harbours that were so valuable during the first few weeks of the campaign. The proof of all this was in the pudding: by 11 June the Allies had put ashore 326,547 troops, 54,186 vehicles and 104,428 tons of supplies. This was an incredible achievement, given that every man, every gun, every gallon of fuel, bullet and tin of bully-beef had to be shipped across the sea. The Germans could transport everything they needed by rail or road, and 'out-reinforce' the Allies, however, their own intelligence and command failings meant severe delays in the movement of those all-important infantry divisions to Normandy.

A perfect example was *Generalleutnant* Hans Schmidt's *275. ID*, part of *7. Armee* and based north of Nantes. Formed in December 1943 from elderly reservists and some Russian front veterans from the disbanded *223. ID*, it had three grenadier regiments, an artillery regiment, an anti-tank battalion, and all the usual sub-units of a standard division of *landsers*. It received orders on D-Day to move up to Normandy with all haste; some of it did at least. The actual order was to detach two infantry battalions, the fusilier battalion, one of the artillery battalions and a single company of engineers, and send them north. The rest of the division – the bulk of it – was to stay where it was, twiddling its thumbs. The trains carrying the selected men left for Normandy early on the morning of 7 June. The lead train reached Avranches – on the outskirts of the battle zone – at 2pm that afternoon, whereupon it was attacked by *jabos* and destroyed. The following train was also attacked and seriously damaged, suffering heavy casualties. The survivors were ordered off and told to start making their way to the front on foot, a distance of roughly sixty miles. With the track ahead now unusable, the remaining trains were re-routed to another line, which was then promptly attacked, resulting in no fewer than nineteen line breaks. Unable to move forward, the *landsers* sat waiting on their stalled trains for twenty-four hours. The officials of the *Reichsbahn* then made another attempt to get them to Normandy, this time detouring via Fougères on the Brittany–Normandy border, but that line was then attacked and cut. The backlog was now twelve-trains long, and with no other choice, the troops climbed down from their carriages and began the trek north on foot. It was now the morning of 9 June. It had taken them two days and two nights to travel less than thirty miles. It would be another three days before they reached the battlefield, footsore, tired and already learning to keep a look-out for the dreaded *jabos*. The rest of the division didn't follow until over a full month later.

Regardless of the mismanagement that would plague them throughout the campaign, the *landsers* on the frontline were making do as best they could do on D+1, when reinforcements should have been flooding towards them. Ernst Goth's *GR. 916* even counter-attacked and reached the sea to relieve the beleaguered defenders of *WN76* at Pointe et Raz de la Percée. Falling back to the main battle line with their rescuers, the strongpoint's young company commander reported to Goth on his experiences of being cut-off, but his reception was not what he expected:

> *Oberst* Goth was not pleased with me at all. In fact, he was furious that I had not been there to be used in the last attack ... he yelled at me that I couldn't fight and should be shot. I think he was going to shoot me on the spot, but without warning the *Amis* attacked the command bunker. I turned and faced him saying 'Let me go back to my men and I will show you how well I can fight.' He nodded and sent me off. At first I was demoralised by the event but then realised he was only giving me a shove in the right direction.[11]

Not that Goth was content to just sit in his headquarters and shout at his subordinates. Like so many German officers of the time he was a hands-on leader of men. A few days later he went forward in his personal *kubelwagen* with his driver to try and get a clearer picture of what was going on up the line. Soon after heading off, they came upon some American troops. Unseen, they pulled in, and the two men went forward. They found about forty GIs digging into a poor position. Ordering his driver to go back to headquarters and bring forward every man who could carry a rifle, Goth himself worked his way round to the rear of the Americans and settled in to wait. On hearing his men begin to arrive some time later, he opened fire on the surprised Americans with his machine-pistol, pinning them down. His reinforcements then attacked, and the GIs fell back in confusion. Ernst Goth was placed on the *Ehrenblatt des deutschen Heeres* (Honour Roll of the German Army)[12] as a result of his actions that day.

Gratified as Goth was at the award, he would have been even happier had his superiors been able to tell him that help was on its way in the form of a wave of reinforcements – but they couldn't, as they weren't. What should have been a flood of troops was in reality a trickle, and instead of *Korps* and divisions, came regiments and battalions instead. What that meant for frontline units such as Ernst Goth's *GR.*

916 was that it was continuously holding over four miles of front with a thousand men at most. Typical of this approach was *Schnelle-Brigade 30* – commanded by the splendidly named *Oberstleutnant* Theodor *Freiherr* von und zu Aufseß, scion of a noble family that had furnished Bamberg with more than a few of its Prince-Bishops down the centuries. The unit was mainly composed of reservists and convalescents, many of them, like their own *Oberstleutnant*, Bavarians hailing from the famed *gebirgsjäger* mountain corps, and now fighting in the fields and orchards of Normandy. Designated a *Schnelle-Brigade*, indicating its mobility and ability to pack a punch, its only heavy equipment consisted of five obselete Czech 4.7cm anti-tank guns mounted on ex-French Army R35 tank chassis, with the infantry mounted on bicycles. It was drip-fed into Ernst Goth's *GR. 916*, and joined elements of no fewer than thirty different formations and services, including unemployed sailors, construction workers and labour battalion men. These 'pressed-men' were distributed out amongst Goth's companies to at least give them a chance of learning to survive from his veterans, but their losses were huge nevertheless, as they had little chance to learn the techniques and habits that might keep them alive.

It wasn't as if the Westheer didn't have men; in addition to 7. *Armee* in Normandy, there were three others in the rest of France and the Low Countries. *General der Infanterie* Kurt von der Chevallerie's Bordeaux-headquartered *1. Armee* was the weakest on paper, comprising four infantry divisions, of which three were reserve or belly formations; *158., 159.* and *708. IDs*, with only one, Kurt Badinski's *276. ID*, being anything like frontline-calibre. Von der Chevallerie's ace in the hole though, were his mobile formations; the veteran *11. Panzer* and newly-raised *17. SS-Panzergrenadier-Division* 'Götz von Berlichingen'. With no sign of an additional Allied landing in the stormy Bay of Biscay, these formations could have been sent north *en masse*, but instead, only the *Götz von Berlichingen* was despatched straight after D-Day, with *276. ID* following twelve days later. The only other *1. Armee* formation that went to Normandy was the *708. Infanterie-Division*, whose two regiments of poor-quality *Landesschützen* personnel arrived just in time to be annihilated at Falaise. Wend von Wietersheim's *11. Panzer* got its marching orders, but to go east, not north, where it became *19. Armee*'s sole mobile reserve. As for *19. Armee* and its ten divisions, the experienced Austrians of *Generalleutnant* Erwin

Jollasse's 9. *Panzer* were sent to Normandy with the infantrymen of the static 338. *ID*, but only in early August. Preceeding them, although not by much, went 271. and 272. *IDs* – both in mid-July. The only division ordered north in invasion month was the under-strength 277. *ID*.

Nevertheless, the tardiness in drawing on 1. and 19. *Armees* was as nothing compared to the situation with the largest (and closest) formation the Westheer possessed; Hans von Salmuth's 15. *Armee*. Centred in the Pas de Calais where Berlin expected the main Allied landings to come, von Salmuth's army was a behemoth. Bigger than 1. and 19. *Armees* combined, its fifteen infantry divisions and three Luftwaffe field divisions were by no means all up to strength, or of high quality – 48. *ID* for example included a high proportion of 'Germanised' Poles, whose loyalty was dubious at best. But it also included a few veteran formations like 331. *ID*, whose Austrian grenadiers had two years experience in Russia under their belts, and several others, including 84. and 85. *IDs*, who had a hardcore of eastern front veterans. If the mass of 15. *Armee* was ordered to move to Normandy then the initiative could shift to the Westheer. Instead, the Allies deception plan continued to work its magic, and only Erich Diester's two-regiment 346. *ID* belly division went to help 7. *Armee* in the days after D-Day – and only then because it was based at Le Havre and so almost within gunshot of the beaches. The rest of 15. *Armee* didn't move an inch. Finally, in late June, Berlin begrudgingly detached another three infantry divisions to the Normandy fighting, by which time 346. *ID's* grenadier companies were down to fifty men apiece, with half a dozen anti-tank guns their sole remaining heavy weaponry. By the end of that same month the other side had poured in over 850,000 men, 148,000 vehicles, and 570,000 tons of supplies, and twelve days later the one millionth Allied soldier stepped ashore in Normandy.

It wouldn't be until the end of July that the remaining divisions of 15. *Armee* were released for combat, by which time the vital role they could, and should, have played in shoring up the Normandy front and paving the way for the decisive counter-attack, had been squandered.

With Berlin's eyes still on the Pas de Calais, the task of holding the landings was left to 7. *Armee* and its uninspiring commander, Friedrich Dollmann. Originally eleven divisions-strong on D-Day, four were already engaged by the day's end, meaning Dollmann only had seven others to push into the battle, of which four were static or 'near-static'[13] divisions, with next to no transport and few heavy weapons. To make matters worse for Dollmann, it was obvious that the Allies had two very different objectives: Caen in the Anglo-Canadian sector, and Saint-Lô in the American. Thirty-three miles apart as the crow flies, the two cities were literally at opposite ends of the beachhead, which negated 7. *Armee's* ability to concentrate its limited forces on a single area. With no massive reinforcement wave appearing, an overbearing Berlin, and a run-of-the-mill commander, 7. *Armee* simply drip-fed units forward to achieve nothing further than to try and hold the line. Dollmann had few options available to him for sure, but adopting this approach was a recipe for a slow death, as he would be unable to build up armoured reserves, while suffering terrible casualties amongst his precious panzergrenadier battalions in particular, as they did the job of the infantry and dug-in amidst the fields and cow-byres.

The results were predictable. Relatively quickly, the campaign became one of attrition – exactly the sort of battle the Westheer needed to avoid given their relative dearth of men, machines and supplies, with the Germans forced into continual improvisations to plug gaps as they appeared. Account after account from Germans who fought there, speak of the constant cobbling together of remnants of units to seal a breach in the line by retaking a wood or a small hill, or to throw back yet another threatening Allied advance, such as on 16 June when the Americans captured Hill 108 and the village of Les Buteaux, not far north of Saint-Lô. Peter Simeth was on patrol in the area:

We had reached the destroyed village and started to work our way through it. Immediately we began to take fire. We made for the cover of a roadside ditch, but it was soon apparent that we couldn't stay there either. We dashed towards a damaged house, only to find the *Amis* already in residence. Then we saw the tanks. The *Oberfeldwebel* ordered us to fall back as fast as we could go. It was strange that the *Amis* didn't follow us.

In an action typical of the time, Ernst Goth's own command post came under attack, as *GR. 916* withdrew marginally south to avoid possible destruction. Goth desperately needed help, so Kraiss sent him a *kampfgruppe* to help cover the move – it was led by a paymaster, and consisted of clerks, cooks, bakers and a handful of previously wounded grenadiers returning from hospital treatment – all in all the

'*KG*' was just thirty men armed with nothing more than rifles, pistols and a few hand-grenades.[14] The real surprise was that it worked. Stop-gap measures were exactly that. What the Westheer needed could be summed up in six words: *air, sea, land forces – more of*. The question was would they get them.

4

Planes, Ships and Rolling Stock

Less than a month after France sued for peace in 1940, on the sun-drenched 19th of July, Adolf Hitler summoned twelve generals of the Army and Luftwaffe to the magnificence of the famous Kroll Opera House in Berlin, and in a ceremony designed to echo the grandeur of Napoleon's triumphs, the dictator made a speech about a possible peace proposal with Great Britain, and then bestowed the coveted rank of *Generalfeldmarschall* (field-marshal) on all of them.[1] This was an important moment in the Third Reich's progression towards world war; symbolically, it was the latest in a very long line of acts of defiance against the Versailles Treaty and the Weimar Republic – both of which had banned the rank – and it further bound the Wehrmacht, as Germany's most powerful institution, to the Nazis and to Hitler personally. It is a fact that professional soldiers love promotions and awards, and the acquisition of both has always been a prime motivator of military men (and women) through the ages. Other, more venal, rewards were perhaps also on the assembled officers' minds too, with each qualifying in their new position for an annual payment of 36,000 *Reichsmarks* (approximately £194,000 today), as well as becoming exempt from income tax – both for life. Just as with Napoleon's marshals more than a century earlier, so the *Führer*'s new caesars would dominate the early years of the war, with men like Rundstedt, Bock, Leeb, Reichenau and List commanding armies and army groups as they stormed across the Balkans and into the Soviet Union.[2]

Standing to Hitler's immediate right in the official photograph of the three Luftwaffe men among the twelve was a tall figure, immaculate in his pressed uniform, polished jack-boots gleaming, his new and ornately decorated marshal's baton held firmly in his right hand. This was Hugo Sperrle.

Sperrle had commanded the German *Condor Legion* in Spain during the Civil War, and then *Luftflotte 3* (Air Fleet 3) for the invasion of France. His success was rewarded not only with his promotion, but by being left in command of the Luftwaffe in France and the Low Countries for the next four years. It's fair to say he turned this position to his personal advantage. The first thing he did was to install himself in a sumptuous apartment in the magnificent *Palais de Luxembourg* in Paris, not far from his boss Hermann Göring's own suite of rooms in the same building – the latter using them during his trips to loot art and antiques from the French capital. Sperrle then indulged himself completely; losing so much at the gaming tables that Hitler had to gift him 50,000 *Reichsmarks* to try and pay off his debts – typically, when Hitler then rang Sperrle at the Palais, an aide had to tell him that the *Feldmarschall* wasn't in residence, having decamped to the upmarket resort of Biarritz on the Atlantic coast 'for a much-needed holiday'. While there, Sperrle continued his quest to try and eat every gourmet delicacy France had to offer, piling on the pounds as he did so, and raising eyebrows even among a Nazi hierarchy steeped in corruption and venality. Albert Speer, after a visit to Paris where he met Sperrle, said of him; 'The *Feldmarschall*'s craving for luxury and public display ran a close second to that of his superior, Göring; he was also his match in corpulence.' A view shared by the Propaganda Minister, Joseph Goebbels, in his diary: '*Feldmarschall* Sperrle ... was not equal to his tasks. Like all Luftwaffe generals he has withdrawn to a castle and is there leading a sybaritic life. Air warfare against England probably doesn't interest him much more than, say, an excellent luncheon or dinner. The *Führer* wants to recall him.' But he didn't.

With Berlin sitting on its hands, Sperrle continued on his merry way, now sporting a monocle in his right eye – he thought it made him look aristocratic – and exercising the rabid misogyny he was renowned for, screaming in rage if any military telephone operator he spoke to was a woman, and throwing the phone down in anger. The Luftwaffe *Generalleutnant* Hermann Plocher recalled a walk round an airbase in France with Sperrle – whom he knew well – when the latter spied a woman in military fatigues enter a mess-hall; 'Do I see correctly? Is that a woman going into the mess-hall where our heroes eat?' Plocher replied it was, and that she was in fact a German agent who had just returned from a very dangerous mission behind enemy lines. Sperrle spluttered, visibly deflating, and replied; 'I know. That's what I mean. She should be dining in the generals' mess.'[3] Unsurprisingly, under Sperrle's watch, *Luftflotte 3* deteriorated from being one of the finest military instruments in the Wehrmacht's armoury into a paper tiger. A deal of that decay can be laid at Berlin's feet, and particularly Luftwaffe high command, which, under Göring's 'absentee landlordism', saw Germany's air arm inexorably slide towards irrelevance and defeat. Not that Göring alone was culpable. The service's own long-serving chief-of-staff, Hans Jeschonnek, when presented with a plan to exponentially increase fighter production to 360 aircraft per month in 1943 to combat growing Anglo-American air power said, 'I do not know what I should do with more than 360 fighters!' In truth, Sperrle and his *luftflotte* were the victims of what was loosely known as the 'Milch system' – named after its architect Erhard Milch – that built the Luftwaffe into a force capable of fighting a succession of small campaigns with long rest periods in-between – this, after all was what Berlin anticipated. As such, large-scale investment in aircraft production, pilot training, repair facilities and the stockpiling of spare parts was deliberately disregarded. This approach conspicuously failed in the Battle of Britain, and meant that by 1943 the Luftwaffe was only capable of securing air superiority for short periods over limited sectors of the vast Russian front against the Soviet Union's often indifferent VVS ('*Voyenno-Vozdushnye Sily*' – 'Military Air Forces'). The system's biggest failing, though, was in not training the mass of pilots Germany would need to face the combined Anglo-American airforces. There were enough eager young Germans willing to join up, but recruiting and training new pilots wasn't seen as a priority, so much so that one young volunteer recounted how on turning up to his local recruitment office in the summer of 1941, he was turned away due to a 'lack of vacancies', and redirected to the paratroops instead. With a relative trickle of replacements coming through, training was shortened and hurried, with new pilots often reaching their *staffeln* (squadrons) without ever having fired their aircraft's guns before. The results were disastrous – by D-Day almost half of all German aircraft losses were due to accidents rather than enemy action – and those losses were huge, especially in the skies above the Reich itself against the Allied 'heavies' and their fighter escorts. The figures speak for themselves. In the month of February 1944, *Luftflotte Reich* wrote off a third of its entire single-engine fighter force, along with 18 per cent of its fliers, this climbed to over half its available fighters in March and one in five of their pilots. The 15 March entry

in the war diary of *Jagdgeschwader Udet's III. Gruppe* was typical of
the time: twenty aircraft were launched to attack the Allied bomber
fleet; two pilots were killed and their aircraft destroyed, two pilots
were shot down but parachuted to safety, and two crash-landed – a
total of two pilots dead and six aircraft lost – almost a third of the
whole force. The arrival in Europe of the American P-51 Mustang
in particular was decimating the *Jagdwaffe*; not that Göring was
prepared to listen to the new reality, as communicated by his own
Inspector General of Fighters, the highly-decorated Adolf Galland,
when he reported to Hitler on the appearance of Mustangs over
Germany itself.

'What's the idea of telling the *Führer* that American fighters have
penetrated into the territory of the Reich? That's nonsense Galland,
what gives you these fantasies?'

'Those are the facts *Herr Reichsmarschall*. American fighters have
been shot down over Aachen, there is no doubt about it!'

'That is simply not true Galland, it's impossible.'

'You might go and check it yourself, the downed planes are there
at Aachen.'

'What must have happened is that they were shot down much
further to the west. They could have glided quite a distance further
before they crashed.'

Galland's sarcasm was palpable – 'Glided to the east sir?'

The USAAF shot down 3,706 German aircraft in daylight operations
over the Reich during 1944. Galland responded by stripping pilots
from every other branch of the Luftwaffe to try and replenish
Luftflotte Reich:

> The strained manpower situation in units operating in defence of
> the Reich urgently demands the further bringing up of experienced
> flying personnel from other arms of the service; in particular for the
> maintenance of fighter power, tried pilots of the ground-attack and
> bomber units, especially officers suitable as formation leaders, will
> now also have to be drawn on.

As early as 1943 only forty per cent of the Luftwaffe was on the
Russian front, the most important theatre by far for the Nazi
war effort. This meant that the Wehrmacht's war-critical summer
offensive – *Unternehmen Zitadelle* to destroy the Kursk salient – was
only supported by some two thousand aircraft, not enough to affect
the result. Even though the failed assault lasted just two weeks and

overall losses were low at 159 aircraft, by its end the air force was exhausted, with fuel, ammunition, spare parts and serviceability played out.

A year later, the Luftwaffe's strategy to combat the anticipated Anglo-American landings in France was ready; christened the *Drohende Gefahr West* plan ('Threatening Danger West') The concept was simple – keep a thin screen forward, while dispersing the rest of *Luftflotte 3* far enough away from the coast to protect it from Allied attack, and then, once the landings had been made, to switch all available forces rapidly from every other front – including Russia and the *Heimat* ('homeland') – to support the Army. This was the genesis of what became popularly known to the officers and men of the Westheer as the '1,000 fighters' promise; that the moment the long-awaited second front opened, an enormous armada of the mighty Luftwaffe would descend from the heavens and wreak havoc among the Allies, providing an umbrella over the Army's grenadiers and panzers, while driving the British and American *jabos* from the sky, and helping the Kriegsmarine turn the Channel into the graveyard of the Allied fleet. Göring himself said privately: 'The moment the British try and invade France to establish a second front, I will not leave a single fighter aircraft defending the Reich. Every single fighter which is air-worthy will be sent forward, and the Reich itself will not have an aircraft to its name – come hell or high water.'

Consequently, *Luftflotte 3* was seen by Berlin in a similar fashion to the doomed divisions of the belly army – there to hold the enemy long enough for the reinforcements of élite units to arrive and achieve victory. As it was, Sperrle's belly 'army' was 820 aircraft, not an inconsequential figure – but, as with the Italian *Valle* scandal back in 1939 – not all was as it seemed.[4] Of those 820 aircraft on the rolls, only half were single-engined fighters (another eighty were specialist night-fighters), dragooned in two *Jagdgeschwader*; *JG 2 Richthofen*, and the 'Abbeville Boys' of *JG 26 Schlageter*.[5] Serviceability in the frontline squadrons was poor and only around 170 were combat-ready on any given day. With so few fighters airworthy, the Luftwaffe's 'eyes-and-ears' needed to be at their very best, to allow the two *jagdgeschwader* to concentrate their firepower at the most vulnerable point. This meant the Germans' long-range *Wassermann* and *Mammut* ground radar sites[6] and their reconnaissance squadrons – but both were in dire straits. The Allies concentrated on the radar locations, identifying ninety-two, and attacking all of them. By D-Day seventy-six were destroyed, and the rest were badly damaged. In desperation, the fighters of both *JG 2* and 26 went up day after day to try and protect them but were faced with overwhelming odds. In April, 102 of them were shot down, and in May it was even worse with 119 aircraft blown out of the sky; *JG 26* alone lost 106 fliers in the five months up to May, with *Luftflotte 3* losing a quarter of its fighter pilots killed every month. As for the 116 aircraft in the reconnaissance wings, only half were serviceable at any time, and even those were of little use, as Hubert Meyer of the *HJ* discovered when he visited one of their bases prior to D-Day:

> We went to Evreux to visit the Luftwaffe squadron that performed reconnaissance flights over England, and asked them how much they knew, and could they judge how far advanced the Allied plans were. The air commodore [probably Major Hans Wolff of FAGr 123] told me that he had been unable to penetrate airborne defences over England for weeks because of the fighters and flak ... that was all the information we needed, to know that it was going to be soon.[7]

Germany's answer to its lack of fighters was to ratchet up anti-aircraft defence, with the number of guns in *Luftflotte 3* almost doubling in twelve months to a staggering 10,481 by D-Day[8] Some of these would prove a very nasty thorn in the side of the British a few weeks later – although not in the air. Perhaps Nazi high command hadn't heard the joke doing the rounds among Berliners at the time, about the army deserter whose punishment was to be tied up and fired at by the city's entire air defence force – he was found dead a week later, of starvation.

Perhaps Sperrle couldn't have significantly changed the scales in *Luftflotte 3*'s favour in the summer of '44, but it's also fair to say he didn't try very hard either. An energetic and committed officer could have done a great deal to strengthen his hand, such as preparing proper base facilities for the '1,000 fighters', instead of which the designated airfield network in northern France was rudimentary at best. One of the Germans' own reports into their readiness stated that

> ...the airfields which had long been earmarked for the emergency day-fighter *geschwader* from the Reich in the event of an invasion ... were completely inadequate. In almost every case no headquarter

building had been constructed and dispersal points had not been organised. There was a complete lack of splinter screens, trenches, dug-outs, shelters, teleprinting and wireless installations, and of ammunition and fuel depots.

Major Ewald Janssen's *Schlachtgeschwader 4*, a ground-attack wing flying Fw 190s, was based at Clastres-St Quentin in the Aisne *département*, covering 15. *Armee* in the Pas de Calais, when it got the call to send its *III. Gruppe* to Normandy. Gerhard Weyert led his thirty-four aircraft south of Paris before looping back to their new home at Laval in Maine, just south of Normandy. On the way they were jumped by American fighters and lost four pilots killed and another injured. When they landed at Laval they were shocked to find the lack of preparation. 'There were no refuelling vehicles, no bomb-loading trolleys, no personnel to assist, and above all no airfield defence.' Regardless, they attacked the beaches that same afternoon, but with very little success. The next morning they went up again; four waves of six aircraft each. Flying fast and low, the Focke-Wulfs hopped from treeline to hedgerow, forever looking up to try and avoid the Allied fighters prowling above – the Mustangs saw them anyway. Cumbersome and slow, with their underslung bomb-racks full, the German fighter-bombers had no choice but to jettison their payloads and scatter home. Three of the waves were forced to turn back, and only one got through to hit the beaches – it wasn't nearly enough. Back at base the unit diarist wrote in despair: 'Despite favourable weather we achieved little ... successful operations are impossible without effective fighter co-operation.'

The next day more of the same, with three attacks launched and repulsed. By now the unit diary was openly critical of higher command as the pilots believed that; 'orders were being issued only by people who had no idea of the situation or the strength of the enemy defences.'

Within a fortnight Weyert and his men were forced to relocate south to Avord in the Loire valley, and then Conches a week later. Bled white in the fighting, they were withdrawn to Jakobstadt (present-day Jekabpils) in southern Latvia at the beginning of July.

Another Luftwaffe unit sent to France as part of the *Drohende Gefahr West* were the 'defence of the Reich' fighters of *Jagdgeschwader 1 'Oesau'*. Within hours of receiving the order, *Oberleutnant* Eder led thirty-two fighters west and headed for Essay in Normandy. *En route* they heard that their original destination had been bombed so diverted to Le Mans. On changing course, they were bounced by Mustangs and *Leutnant* Johann Brünnler was shot down and killed. Flying on, the remainder landed safely, and were soon joined by other *staffeln* until there were a hundred of them on the ground and ready to go. Mistakenly deployed on ground-attack missons – for which the high-altitude anti-bomber pilots had no training – they launched multiple missions over the next few days. One of their number was *Oberfeldwebel* Herbert Kaiser, a veteran senior NCO with nine victories against the Allies in North Africa, and a further forty in Russia, before being transferred to homeland defence. Despite his experience, he was shaken by what he found in Normandy:

> If the missions we had undertaken as fighters in the defence of the Reich until then had been tough and tested our nerves, the missions on the invasion front were giving us an insight into hell. I will never forget our first mission ... skimming over the landing beaches at Caen. The surface of the sea was saturated with hundreds of boats of all sizes, while the sky was filled with bomber formations going to attack our front, accompanied by countless fighters. Lost in the middle of all that, a handful of Messerschmitts – us!

A night-time raid on *JG 1*'s airbase on 9 June destroyed seven aircraft and damaged another five. Following another raid six days later which smashed an additional pair of fighters, the decision was made to move the *geschwader* to its original – and now repaired – destination of Essay. However, during the relocation, they were attacked near Alençon by the Mustangs of the American 354th Fighter Wing. The Germans downed two of the Mustangs but lost five aircraft, with three pilots and a hitch-hiking mechanic killed. Landing at Essay, they were bombed the same day by B-24 Liberators and the airfield was made unusable.

Now more resembling hapless refugees than a veteran fighter wing, the survivors transferred to a new base at Semallé, south-east of Alençon – whereupon they came under attack again – this time from strafing Mustangs that shot up fifteen fighters on the ground. Another eleven non-operational aircraft awaiting repairs were also destroyed. In the ten weeks that *JG 1* was in Normandy before it was sent back to Germany to rest and refit, it lost 106 aircraft, with twenty-seven pilots killed, three captured and two seriously wounded.

***

Back in Paris, indolent, indulgent, and increasingly irrelevant, Hugo Sperrle left most day-to-day matters to his subordinates, only occasionally bothering himself with questions military, such as his missives on how to tackle growing French resistance activity, which became known as the 'Sperrle Ordinances', recommending *résistants* be met with 'extreme severity and the most ruthless methods'. On hearing of the D-Day landings, the bejowled *Generalfeldmarschall* roused himself from his *escargots* and issued the following order:

> Men of Luftflotte 3! The enemy has launched the long-anticipated invasion. Long have we waited for this moment, long have we prepared ourselves, both inwardly and on the field of battle, by untiring, unending toil. Our task now is to defeat the enemy. I know that each one of you, true to his oath to the colours, will carry out his duties. Great things will be asked of you and you will show the bravest fighting valour.

As a hollow piece of bombast, this proclamation has few equals.

Leutnant Wolfgang Fischer of the *Richthofen* took off first thing on the morning of 6 June with eleven other Fw 190s to attack the British landings on Gold. Arriving over the beaches he saw the Allied naval armada for the first time:

> Poor Germany! An armada larger than I could ever have imagined... such a concentration of firepower was impossible... We took a conscious risk to continue our attack. Having fired our rockets, we attacked landing ships, then the shore. As far as I know, one of my rockets hit the bow of a troop transporter, probably a Victory-class ship.

Fischer barely escaped with his life. Over Sword it was much the same, a scene immortalised in the film *The Longest Day*, when the Luftwaffe ace, Josef 'Pips' Priller of *JG 26* –played by Heinz Reincke – took off from his base at Lille-Nord and strafed the beach with his *Rottenhund* (Luftwaffe term for a wingman) *Unteroffizier* Heinz Wodarczyk, on what Priller only half-jokingly calls a 'suicide mission'. *Gefreiter* Hammel of *21. Panzer's* recce battalion didn't see Priller's sortie, but did witness one of the few German fighter flights that day: 'As we moved forward to the northeast we saw, towards midday, two Messerschmitt fighters flying north low over the Orne, they were the only German aircraft we saw that day.'

Only thirty-six German aircraft were recorded in total that day over the Anglo-Canadian beaches, with the Allies shooting down seven of them. The *Jagdflieger* fared even worse over the American landing sites, with twenty-four downed and seven limping home damaged – accidents wrecked another sixteen.

This shouldn't have been a surprise to anyone, given the David and Goliath mismatch between the two opposing forces. As far back as 1942 Great Britain alone was producing more aircraft than the Reich, but it was the entrance into the war of the United States that totally transformed the balance of power in the air. American industrial and human capacity was such that it could support large aerial forces in the UK, the Mediterranean and the Pacific, while also supplying the Soviets, *and* building up a significant invasion-ready pool. The scale was breathtaking; on the American mainland, General 'Hap' Arnold was training no fewer than 30,000 pilots a year from 1941 onwards, and each one amassed more flying hours than a German novice could ever hope to achieve, before being seated in an excellent, modern machine, well-serviced, with limitless aviation fuel and spare parts. The German fighter ace, Günther Rall, sent west from Russia to face the Allies, viewed his American counterparts with envy:

> ...almost everything is different from the Eastern front, with one exception, that here too we are faced by sheer weight of numbers. But these numbers are now made up of pilots who have years of meticulous training in the American homeland behind them, and who have only been declared operational after four hundred hours of flying. They are fresh, aggressive, well-schooled in tactics and are flying superior equipment.

Rall's final point was one shared by his comrade, twenty-two-year-old Ernst Schröder of *JG 101*: 'I thought the Bf 109G was a '*scheissbock*' (shit-bucket), and it was a crime it was manufactured until 1945.' Extremely difficult to fly – particularly to take-off and land – the 109 *Gustav* had been primarily designed to survive in the skies over the Reich battling the Anglo-American heavies. For new *Jagdwaffe* pilots like *Oberfähnrich* Hans-Ulrich Flade, sent to the front with barely sixty hours of flying time under his belt, the arrival at his *staffel* was very deflating: 'The frontline units were desperately short of experienced and capable fighter pilots.' In contrast to Allied policy, Nazi Germany didn't prioritise aircraft production or new pilot training; as seen first-hand by the Armaments Minister Albert Speer when he visited the major Junkers aircraft plant in Dessau and met with the firms General Manager, Dr Heinrich Koppenberg:

> ...he took me into a locked room and showed me a graph comparing American bomber production for the next few years with our own. I asked him what our leaders had to say about these depressing figures, and he replied; 'That's just it, they won't believe it,' whereupon he broke into uncontrollable tears.

Speer's partner in aviation – Erhard Milch – had the same foreboding when he discussed ramping up production with the Luftwaffe supremo: '*Herr Reichsmarschall,* your total demand is for 360 new fighter aircraft per month. I fail to understand. If you were to say 3,600 fighters, then I would be bound to state that against America and Britain combined even 3,600 are too few! We must produce more.'

By D-Day the imbalance between the capabilities of the two opposing sides had become absurd. Against Sperrle's 170 combat-ready fighters the Allies could field 4,029, with *Luftflotte 3*'s 100 sorties on landing day met by 14,674 Allied ones. So complete was Allied domination of the Normandy airspace, that by 1020am – barely four hours after the landings began – the hydrogen-filled barrage balloons anchored into position above the beaches to protect against Luftwaffe attack were cut loose to float away, as the Luftwaffe threat failed to materialise, and it was clear to the naval commanders that the balloons were actually acting as aiming markers for German artillery based inland.

For the *landsers*, the realisation that the sky above them now belonged to the Allies and not the Luftwaffe, was a massive blow. Helmut Liebeskind – von Luck's adjutant – spoke for many of his comrades:

> Above all we were bitterly disappointed by the total non-participation of the Luftwaffe. We had always worked so well together, and the fact that it had now dropped out of sight so completely we found incomprehensible. If we had had the support of the Luftwaffe things would have been different.

Ernst Düring, a *Hauptmann* in Kraiss's *352. ID*, commented bitterly on the lack of German airpower when he espied the Allied naval armada: 'Hundreds of ships stretched out for a breadth of three to four miles. They were lying out there like a flock of sheep and I couldn't understand why the Luftwaffe didn't strike.'

Hauptmann Hans Groos of *JG 26* explained what happened to his own fighter wing that day when he and his fellow pilots flew to their forward base at Le Mans just before it was attacked by roving Allied *jabos*:

> The situation in Le Mans was indescribable. A fighter *Gruppe* which had just arrived from Germany – come to set up shop there – were caught on the ground, and only four of the twenty-five aircraft of the *Gruppe* that set off were fit to fly again. The others had been destroyed shortly after landing. On the edge of the airfield, many Ju 52s which had provided the technical means of transporting the *Gruppe*, were reduced to charred wrecks.

Even worse for a flier like Groos, was when he found himself truck-borne and on the receiving end of the kind of ground-attack he and his comrades were meant to be meting out, rather than suffering:

> On a long road, completely exposed, we passed a convoy of approximately twenty-five trucks transporting rockets destined for our artillery. Before our eyes this convoy was attacked by four Mustangs which, in roughly seven passes, tore them to shreds. A quarter of an hour later, there were only three or four vehicles intact, all the others were on fire at one-hundred-metre intervals.

What then of the '1,000 fighters' promise? Was it just another of Göring's falsehoods, pronounced with huge fanfare and then ever so quickly forgotten? Rommel thought so, as he explained to his old *Afrika Korps* subordinate, von Luck '[We can defeat the landings] if enough fighters are in the air which can be thrown against the powerful Allied air forces... I don't believe in the "1,000 fighters" Göring means to send here.'

Rommel's rationale was simple and undeniable – 'Göring has let us down before in Africa, and at Stalingrad.' However, the Desert Fox was wrong, and the vainglorious head of the Luftwaffe was true to his word. *Drohende Gefahr West* was initiated and fighters from every other front began moving to Normandy – three hundred came from Russia in less than a week, and no fewer than fifteen separate *geschwader* from *Luftflotte Reich*, crippling the oh-so-carefully built *Reichsverteidigung* (Defence of the Reich) organisation, and clearing the skies over the Reich for the bomber streams. The rest of occupied France was stripped too, and if there had been any fighters left on the Italian front they would have gone as well. One of the pilots sent to Normandy was Alfred Wagner:

> We were stationed at Biarritz close to the Spanish border. We were awakened early in the morning and told we were going to be transferred north straight away. We were transported on lorries because we didn't have enough planes to fly there. On the way we were attacked continuously by English fighter planes… On arrival we were quartered in a château, quite a comfortable place. There was a landing strip nearby and it was from there that we flew our missions.

The Luftwaffe was living up to its pledge, but not according to their Army comrades, like Hans von Luck: 'There were about 130 Messerschmitt fighters available in France, of the transfer to France of the "1,000 fighters" promised by Göring, there was no sign. They were needed, as always, for the defence of the Reich.'

When von Luck and his men did see the Luftwaffe, their suspicions seemed to be confirmed.

> On 8 June, to our surprise a few Messerschmitts suddenly appeared. They were at once involved in an air battle. An RAF fighter was shot down over the British lines, the men all raised their arms in jubilation, were the promised '1,000 fighters' about to turn up after all? But a Messerschmitt was also shot down. The pilot was able to save himself by parachute and landed near the reconnaisancce battalion. He was brought to me, swearing and waving his arms about, 'What are we supposed to do with a couple of fighters against this superiority? Where the hell are the 1,000 fighters?' We didn't know either.

Thus was born the belief among so many German Army veterans of the Normandy campaign that whilst they fought so stubbornly to contain the landings, their comrades in Luftwaffe blue sat on their hands. In fact, nothing could have been further from the truth. Hundreds of pilots descended on Normandy and took off day after day to try and pierce the Allied air umbrella over the beaches and help the *landsers*.

On one mission an American Thunderbolt appeared in front of my snout, as they say. He tipped himself away to the right so that I could see the pilot quite clearly. He was black! A black American! We looked at one another, I pressed the trigger, there was an explosion and he was gone. But I never forgot him. We had been eye to eye, opposite one another and that left a deep impression on me.

Alfred Wagner's success was short-lived, as he and his comrades were constantly being met by an impenetrable wall of Allied fighters that regularly outnumbered them twenty-to-one and more.

We'd been told that the Luftwaffe had a superiority in numbers of ten to one. The prospects looked good, especially after I'd shot down seven of those ten, but it was a lie. When I was shot down myself we were being attacked by three or four Allied planes at one time – so much for Luftwaffe superiority! I was hit from behind and saw flashes sparking from part of my wings. The wings were shredded. I felt a stab in my right foot. It must have been an explosive shell, and my foot was shredded too. My plane started to burn, and I had to get out. I ejected the cockpit hatch, but couldn't push myself out properly because my right foot was useless. I managed to push myself out with my arms, but as I did so my right arm struck the bodywork and the bone broke.... The air battles in France took place quite close to the ground and my parachute had only just enough time to open... Lying on the ground I shouted for help like a madman and a French farmer came over and asked '*Allemand soldat?*' And all I could say was '*oui, toute suite, hôpital!*' He replied '*doucement, doucement*' (softly, softly) and disappeared.

A short time later a second Frenchman appeared, spoke to Wagner, and then also vanished, only to reappear with a German military policeman who mistakenly thought Wagner was British and proceeded to shoot him while he was lying injured on the ground! Shocked, Wagner screamed at the man in German, whereupon he was finally given help. Incredibly, Alfred Wagner survived, but lost his right leg below the knee, one of his toes, and the middle bone of his left foot – he never flew again.[9]

Wolfgang Fischer was another *jagdflieger* who found himself on the wrong end of the air battle, just a day after his raid on Gold:

Pieces of shrapnel tore into the fuselage and engine cowling. I knew instinctively that this was it, and half expected to see my life flash before my eyes... Hauling the stick back into my stomach, I pointed the nose of the Focke-Wulf skywards. I needed to gain altitude, not only to escape the tracer being hosed up at me but also to give myself sufficient height to bale out... We had flown a wide arc out to sea before mounting our attack and now, fortunately, a stiff offshore breeze was carrying me towards the coastline... I found myself reflecting on my present predicament descending helplessly towards the Normandy invasion beaches.[10]

Wagner and Fischer were just two of the 594 German airmen shot down in the fortnight after D-Day. But they kept on going up, flying 9,471 fighter sorties by the end of the month. In the same period their opponents flew an astonishing 163,403. Victims of the failures of their own high command, arriving *geschwader* were '*ausgeblutet*' – bled out – within days. Allied air superiority was so marked that their fighters could range far and wide into the French hinterland, pouncing on the *Jagdwaffe's* makeshift airfields, destroying 350 aircraft on the ground by month's-end, and hunting them down miles away from the battlefield, ensuring that their Army *kameraden* never saw their sacrifice. One such encounter occurred over Argentan on 10 June, when the American 78th Fighter Group bounced a flight of German fighters. The dogfight lasted almost thirty minutes – a very long time for an aerial combat - and by the end the honours were about even with the Americans losing ten of their P-47s shot down, to the German's seven destroyed and four damaged. The difference was that the Allies could replace their losses in the blink of an eye – the *Jagdwaffe* simply could not. Without the numbers to meet the Allies on a level playing field as it were, the Germans – as usual – put their faith in quality over quantity, in men over machines. As one of the Luftwaffe's own internal reports concluded; 'Our pilots must attempt to counterbalance this obvious disadvantage by greater enthusiasm and courage.'

As a doctrine for success this was pathetic; the reality was that high command bet the house on the *Experten* of the Russian front and the *Heimat*. From the beginning of the century, German military aviation had been in thrall to the primacy of the 'fighter ace' – the 'Experten' as they became known. Manfred von Richthofen, the Red Baron, epitomised the type, and it reached its ultimate expression in the Nazi Luftwaffe where a pilot's kill tally was everything. From the moment a *jagdflieger* joined his *staffel* he was examined for his ability to be a lead flyer, and if viewed as such was given every opportunity to 'increase his score' with almost unlimited tours of frontline duty, complete freedom of action and wingmen specifically tasked with protecting him whilst he shot the enemy out of the sky – and shoot them out of the sky the *Experten* did. The top scoring RAF ace of the war – the splendidly named South African, Marmaduke Thomas St John 'Pat' Pattle – claimed over forty kills (the exact number is disputed), while Francis Gabreski's twenty-eight was the highest achieved by an American in Europe – compare that to Erich *Bubi* Hartmann's astonishing 352. Hartmann was by no means alone, with dozens of *Experten* climbing over the 100-kill mark. The noted Swedish war historian and Luftwaffe expert, Christer Bergström, described them as 'men who were absolute masters of aerial combat, virtual flying war machines'. It is hard to disagree. But with half of all German fighter pilots being novices in the summer of '44, essentially it was down to Rall (272 victories on the Russian front) and his comrades-in-arms to achieve the impossible. They tried … and failed. Rall described how the Americans in particular were 'sweeping German airspace clean from tree-top height up to an altitude of 11,000 metres.' Rall himself was swept from the sky, losing his left thumb, an injury that effectively ended his war.

The *Experten* arrived by the dozen in France, their Bf 109 and Fw 190 aircraft bedecked in kill markings, their uniforms encrusted with the medals and awards earned in three years of battle. Most of them died there: Karl-Heinz Weber – 136 kills, Friedrich Wachowiak – 86, Eugen-Ludwig Zweigart – 69, Herbert Huppertz – 68, Karl Kempf – 65, August Mors – 60, Siegfried Sinsch – 54, and, perhaps most famously within the *Jagdwaffe* ranks; Emil *Bully* Lang – 173 victories, and still the record holder for a single day's tally, a remarkable seventeen kills over Kiev back in November '43. Those who survived the charnel house over northern France were still capable of hurting the Allies, using all their experience and cunning to outmatch their opponents. Theodor Weissenberger was one such. The slick-haired, sometime-racing driver was a 175-kill veteran in *Jagdgeschwader 5* when sent to Normandy. He claimed another twenty-five victories in a few days, including five P-47s on 7 June, two more the next day, another three on June 12, and then three RAF Typhoons and an American Mustang a month later. He was one of the lucky ones – from D-Day up to the end of August, a heavily-reinforced *Luftflotte 3* lost 2,127 aircraft in combat – that's more than double the entire airfleet on the day of the landings. But even before the end of June it was reporting that 'fighter operations [are] now only conditionally possible. Effective reconnaissance and fighter operations entirely ruled out for the invasion area. Thirty Anglo-American airfields constructed and operational in the bridgehead.'[11] Despite Rommel and von Luck's doubts, Hermann Göring had, for once, lived up to his promise – it just wasn't enough.

Once the landings began, Karl Dönitz – just like Sperrle – issued a clarion call to his men and sent orders to attack the Allied fleet immediately. Inside the U-boat pen at Brest, Herbert Werner was astonished to see some eight hundred sailors burst into song on hearing the news. 'They were eager to sail against the enemy, even if it meant sailing straight to their deaths.' Werner's grim assessment was right. His own boat, *U415*, was an old Type VIIC, the so-called 'underprivileged' as he christened them in his post-war memoir, *Iron Coffins*, that had 'already outlived too many patrols'. With envious eyes he looked at the new *Elektroboote* fitted with a *Schnorchel* that allowed them to recharge their batteries while remaining submerged – *Gruppe Landwirt* only had eight. The orders were clear though, all the U-boats were to put to sea at once and attack the Allied fleet, and to reach them as quickly as possible they were to 'remain on the surface and race unprotected towards the southern English coast at a time when the sky was black with thousands of aircraft and the sea swarmed with hundreds of destroyers and corvettes.' Werner's thoughts on the mission were unsurprising: 'The Tommies must have thought we had lost our minds.' Under cover of darkness seventeen U-boats of *Gruppe Landwirt* left Brest harbour and headed for the armada. The first Allied air attack came in just after 0100hrs the next morning as Werner witnessed: 'Tracer spurted in various directions, then the sound of gunfire hit our ears. Fountains reached into the air. A spectacular firework display erupted, engulfing U-boats and aircraft.'

A second attack came in before two and its arrival was captured in *U415's* log: '0145 – Next astern attacked by aircraft. I open fire with her. Aircraft shot down by U256. Radar audible on all bearings, strength 3 to 4. 0220 – Radar no longer audible to starboard, so assume aircraft on run-in. Sunderland approaches from green 40. I open fire.' The flak guns on the German submarines poured fire into the sky, desperately trying to keep the Allied Sunderland flying boats and Liberator bombers at bay: 'Four giant water columns leaped skywards behind a riddled aircraft as it tried to escape our fire, then some shells from our 3.7cm gun hit the plane broadside. It exploded in mid-air, then plunged into the sea.'

The log continues:

> The Sunderland's bombs have brought my diesels to a standstill. The boat rises high in the water and settles by the stern, so that water enters the conning-tower hatch. Order 'clear lower deck, clear away rubber dinghy.' Radio out of action so can't report... Boat remains afloat... Rudder jammed to starboard.

Werner vividly recounted the event in his memoir:

> Four savage eruptions heaved *U415* out of the water and threw our men flat on the deck plates. Then she fell back and the four collapsing geysers showered us with tons of water and sent cascades through the hatch. *U415* lay crippled, bleeding oil from a ruptured tank, slowly coming to a full stop – a target to be finished off with ease.

Werner was wrong though – sinking *U415* wasn't easy, despite her damage. Twice more she was attacked and twice she survived, even as the crew raced to get her back underway. Several hours later Werner's chief engineer gave him the news – they were good to go. 'Quickly the men climbed up the bridge and dropped one by one through the round opening into their iron coffin... I watched the deck gradually sink below the surface, and as the water crept up to the bridge I slammed the lid shut. Seconds later the floods engulfed the boat.'

Despite the U-boats' success in downing several of the attacking aircraft, the assaults had done the job; one *Schnorchel* and five *non-Schnorchel* boats – including *U256* and *U413* – had no choice but to turn around and limp for home. One of them, Dietrich Sachse's *U413*, would finally be sunk on 20 August, only one crewman would survive. As for Werner, he struggled back to Brest for repairs, but *U415* never went to sea again; it hit a mine in Brest harbour on 14 July and sank on Bastille Day.

The U-boats kept up their semi-suicidal attacks in the days after D-Day, the officers and men exhibiting courage of a kind that is difficult to appreciate unless one has experienced the terror of being under attack while in a large cigar-case beneath the waves – *U984*'s log provides a flavour of what these submariners endured during the twenty-four hours it was hunted by a surface group dropping depth charges off the Britanny coast 7–8 June.

2000. Six miles west of Ushant. Although enemy radar is still audible, I decide to schnorchel a little to ventilate the boat. We have now been submerged for nearly 42 hours without a change of air, and for the last twelve hours breathing conditions have been extraordinarily bad. The men have literally been gasping for breath. A certain amount of relief has been obtained by breathing through potash cartridges, with the aid of escape apparatus mouthpieces.

2212. I am now close to the coast, my batteries completely exhausted, so decide to return to Brest.

U984 recharged its batteries and replenished its torpedo bays in port, and headed out once more – on 20 August it was lost with all hands in the Bay of Biscay.

U763 also came under sustained attack in the Channel on 7 July, and while *Kapitänleutnant* Ernst Cordes tried to remain as neutral as possible in his log, it's obvious just how atrocious an experience it was for the crew:

1645. South of Isle of Wight. Bottomed again in 55 metres. Enemy still has contact. I shall wait here until night. Depth charges are now fewer and further between. Thirty-four detonated in our near vicinity between 1600 and 2000. Despite the addition of oxygen and the use of potash catridges, the air has become perceptibly fouler... The crew are becoming exhausted. It is nearly thirty hours since the boat was last ventilated. The first cases of vomiting occur... During the thirty hours of the pursuit, 252 depth charges were counted in the near vicinity, sixty-one at medium range and fifty-one at long range.

Cordes's fellow captain, Richard Becker, had a similarly dreadful voyage on 20 June as his *U218* tried to lay mines off Land's End:

0400. Bomb or depth charge concussion has apparently fractured a tappet level on the port diesel ... owing to insufficient exhaust pressure the safety valve lifts and the exhaust gases escape into the boat, filling all compartments and necessitating the wearing of escape apparatus.

0503. Naxos gives three separate warnings ... dived to eighty metres.

1200. Several men suddenly taken ill during the forenoon. By noon two-thirds of the crew are suffering from severe head and

stomach aches, nausea and retching, and are no longer fit for duty…
There are several cases of fainting through over-exertion and carbon
monoxide poisoning.

1230. Rise to periscope depth in an attempt to ventilate with the
port diesel.

1240. Port diesel starts … safety valve lifts again, filling the boat
with exhaust fumes … further cases of poisoning.

1250 State of the crew continues to deteriorate.

1400. Surfaced to change the air in the boat. I cannot wait until
dusk.

1406. Dived… Milk is issued to counteract the effects of the
poisoning. Six men, in a state of collapse, given injections of lobelyn
sympatol to stimulate the heart action.[12]

From D-Day to the end of August, the Kriegsmarine claimed to have
sunk thirty-two ships and landing craft, and damaged another eight;
British records admit to seven damaged and twenty-one sent to the
bottom, including the Royal Navy frigate HMS *Blackwood* – sunk by
Hanskurt von Bremen's *U764* after the latter's arrival from Bergen,
Norway – and the infantry landing ship the *Maid of Orleans*, destroyed
as it headed back to England on 28 June. Tragic as all these attacks
were for the men who were killed or wounded as a result, they were
pinpricks for an Allied fleet numbering thousands of vessels. The cost to
the Germans was disproportionately high; twenty U-boats were lost in
the same period, including Hans Märtens's *U243*, sunk by a Sunderland
on what was the submarine's first mission, Georg Uhl's *U269*, sunk by
a RN frigate southeast of Torquay, Heinz Geissler's *U390*, which sank
the British anti-submarine trawler HMS *Ganilly* and damaged the *Sea
Porpoise* off Utah Beach before being sunk herself in a British depth
charge sweep, and Klaus Hartmann's *U441*, which survived the 'sortie
from Brest' that almost destroyed Herbert Werner's *U415* – only to be
lost three weeks later with all hands. *Gruppe Landwirt* had failed.

Finally, in mid-September, *FdU West* admitted defeat and stopped
the slaughter – although he tried to put a positive spin on the failure.

15.9.44. Our U-boat effort in the Channel is thereby terminated, the
old fighting spirit of the U-boat arm has again magnificently stood
the test. A comprehensive survey of operations shows that, contrary
to our initial misgivings and the doubts that assailed us… We were
right in employing the U-boats… The results achieved were good and
losses tolerable, though heavy.

Perhaps the U-boats *Matrosen* would have disagreed.

While Dönitz was sending his U-boats out into the Channel, Krancke tried to concentrate his surface forces for an offensive against the Allies. First, he ordered the three ships of *Zerstörer-Flottille 8* (8th Destroyer Flotilla); *Z24*, *Z32* and *ZH1* – the latter formerly the Dutch destroyer *Gerard Callenburgh* – to sail north to Brest from their base at Bordeaux in the Gironde estuary. Attacked by a Beaufighter from RAF Coastal Command en route, *Z32* was damaged but able to continue and reach port. Extra anti-aircraft guns were hurriedly bolted onto every available stanchion and deck-plate, and the destroyers were joined by *T24* – the only surviving torpedo boat from *Torpedobootsflottille 4*. On 8 June, a day after they arrived in harbour, all four vessels put to sea. Their commander, Theodor von Bechtolsheim aboard *Z32*, had clear orders: reach Cherbourg, and then attack the Allied fleet off the Normandy beaches.

Krancke's hope was that von Bechtolsheim would attack from Cherbourg in the west, and Hoffmann would do likewise from Le Havre in the east. To beef Hoffmann's force up, Krancke sent *Leutnant sur See* Johannsen's *Torpedobootsflottille 9* from Cherbourg to Le Havre – miraculously, it arrived unscathed.

The Allies weren't playing by Krancke's rules though, and after being tipped off by an Ultra intercept about von Bechtolsheim's move, Captain Basil Jones and the eight British, Canadian and Polish destroyers of the 10th Destroyer Flotilla sailed to intercept. At 0100hrs on 9 June, about thirty miles east-northeast of the tiny Breton island of Île de Batz, the two flotillas detected each other and opened fire. Trafalgar it wasn't, but in what became known as the battle of Ushant (it was also called the battle of Brittany), the outnumbered Germans came off worse. *ZH1* – hit by a torpedo which blew off her bow – was scuttled by her captain Klaus Barckow, while von Bechtolsheim's *Z32* took a pounding and was driven ashore on the island and wrecked. *Z24* and *T24* only managed to escape by hiding on the other side of a British minefield. As for the Allies; Jones's flagship, HMS *Tartar*, was slightly damaged, but not a single Allied seaman was killed or wounded in the engagement – the Germans lost thirty-nine men killed.

With the Cherbourg assault force sunk, wrecked or scuttling back to Brest, it was down to Hoffmann and his Le Havre-based torpedo boats. The risks were dreadful, but night after night they went out and tried to pierce the defensive screen around the fleet, or attack the eighteen convoys per day sailing back and forth between the southern English coast and Normandy. On 10 June they got lucky and torpedoed SS *Brackenfield* as it was steaming towards Juno Beach. When SS *Dungrange* turned to help its fellow cargo ship, it was torpedoed too – both ships sank quickly. Numerous LCTs and LSTs also fell victim to the German predators, until the Allies decided enough was enough, and on the night of 14 June a large force of RAF Lancaster bombers flattened Le Havre port and most of the town. Civilian casualties were high, but the raid effectively ended the naval threat, with the *Möwe*, *Falke* and *Jaguar* all sunk at anchor, and only *T28* surviving the night.[13]

After the bombing of Le Havre and the failure of the U-boat attacks, the Kriegsmarine was left with only one option, and that was to work with the Luftwaffe to lay mines to try and stem the flow of shipping across the Channel. The Germans used a newly developed mine – the Oyster pressure mine – which was set off by the trough of a ship's bow wave and was undetectable at the time. By D+10 about two thousand of them had been laid and ships were starting to go down. Then the Allies got lucky, and one was found intact on the shore by Sub-Lieutenant Young of the Royal Navy Volunteer Reserve. Shipped back to England, it was studied and counter-measures deployed; all shipping was ordered to cut speed to a bare minimum in the invasion area to reduce the bow wave and the resulting drop in pressure prevented detonation of the new mines. A heavy swell also caused five hundred of them to explode harmlessly. Thereafter Allied shipping wasn't seriously threatened.[14]

By 16 June the Allies had lost sixty-four ships in the Channel; five to the Luftwaffe, and the rest to mines and the Kriegsmarine – hardly a game-changer given the size of the Allied fleet – and in return, Rösing's U-boats and Krancke's *Marinegruppe West* had both been decimated. Yet again, bravery alone had been proven to be no match for the overwhelming might of the Allies. Helmut Schmöckel, the commander of *U802* based in Lorient, was clear what his priority was from now on: 'I had a fine crew, a happy crew, I knew I could trust them, the "happy times" when U-boats scored many victories were long gone… Now the main thing was to survive.'[15]

Perhaps Rösing and Krancke should have heeded the words of *Generalfeldmarschall* Erwin Rommel: 'Courage which goes against military expediency is stupidity, or, if it is insisted upon by a commander, irresponsibility.'

With the Luftwaffe being shot out of the sky miles from the battle-front and the Kriegsmarine more or less extirpated, it was down to the Army to contain the beachhead. To do that it needed men, equipment, ammunition and the whole kit and caboodle of a modern fighting force. The fastest and most timely method the German Army knew to deliver what was necessary to where it was needed had been the same since the army itself had been founded – the railway. Indeed, so important were the railways to the German war machine that some historians argue that it was railway timetables and not government policy that dictated the timing of the First World War. True or not, a quarter of a century later, the Germans were as reliant as ever on the train for the mass movement of men and supplies, especially given their dearth of motor transport; and the Allies knew it.

Back in March, Winston Churchill authorised test raids by RAF Bomber Command on the rail marshalling yards in six French and Belgian towns; Amiens, Lougeau, Le Mans, Trappes, Aulnoye, Kortrijk (Courtrai) and Laon, to see if a large-scale air campaign against the railway system was feasible, given current bombing accuracy. The results were better than expected. However, the man in charge of the UK's heavy bomber fleet – Arthur 'Bomber' Harris – was no fan of the idea, believing as he did that Bomber Command was a strategic weapon, and that if used properly – i.e. to flatten Germany's cities – it would end the war by itself. He set out his objections in a series of memoranda:

> Nor is the bomber force suitable for cutting railway communications at definite points. Indeed, in western Germany, France and the Low Countries, owing to the multiplication of roads and railways and the impossibility of maintaining the requisite action in the prevailing weather conditions, such a policy is probably impracticable with any type of bomber force.

In the same memo, Harris rubbished the idea of using heavy bombers against the *Atlantikwall*. This was despite a meeting he had had in early '44 with one of his group captains, Solomon Zuckerman:

> He (Harris) had only one question to put, he said, and he wanted a straight answer 'yes or no' – nothing more. 'Could heavy bombers be used to bomb coastal defences?' I paused a second, and then said, 'yes'. It was clearly not the answer he wanted, and no further word on the matter was spoken.

The reason Harris was asking Zuckerman was that he wasn't just any group captain, he was in fact a scientist who specialised in the new field of operational research, particularly the actual impact of bombing on targets. 'Solly', as he was known, went on to work with the designated Commander-in-Chief Allied Air Forces for the invasion of Europe – the RAF's Sir Trafford Leigh-Mallory – to devise the 'Transportation Plan', or 'Zuckerman's Folly' to its critics. The plan's main aim was to 'paralyse the railways from western Germany to the assault area to such an extent that major reinforcement by rail would be virtually impossible'.

Zuckerman's insight, learned in the Italian campaign, was not simply to drop vast tonnages of ordinance on the lines themselves as they meandered through the countryside, but to go after the locomotives and the marshalling yards that serviced them. No locomotives meant no trains. The plan won approval, and the raids began, Bomber Command attacking at night, and the United States Eighth Air Force during the day, supplemented by the *jabos* of the Allied Tactical Air Forces. Eighty targets were hit in all, the majority by the British, with the 28,000 tons of bombs dropped in May reducing overall rail traffic to half its January level, and the 52,000 tons in June almost shutting down the network completely. No fewer than five hundred locomotives were destroyed or damaged by fighter-bomber attacks in the run up to D-Day, and even the hitherto 'indestructible' Saumur railway tunnel was caved in by the very first use of 'Dambuster' Wallis's 12,000lb Tallboy 'earthquake' bomb on the night of 8 June. In a German report dated 3 June 1944 it seems they were beginning to think the damage could never be made good:

> ...the systematic destruction that has been carried out since March of all important junctions of the entire network ... has most seriously crippled the whole transport system... It is only by exerting the greatest efforts that purely military traffic and goods essential to the war effort ... can be kept moving... The Reichsbahn authorities are seriously considering whether it is not useless to attempt further repair work.

Another *Reichsluftfahrtministerium* (*RLM* – Reich Air Ministry) report from the 13th of the same month confirmed that the raids

> ...have caused the breakdown of all main lines; the coast defences have been cut off from the supply bases in the interior ... producing a situation which threatens to have serious consequences ... large-scale strategic movement of German troops by rail is practically

impossible at the present time and must remain so while attacks are maintained at their present intensity.

The effect on German mobility was devastating. Trucks – arguably the most underrated piece of military kit in the twentieth century – already in short supply, were no longer available to manoeuvre men and weapons quickly around the battlefield, but were instead diverted to logistics duties behind the lines, where they proved easy meat for the *jabos*. The reinforcements that should have been hurried to the front in box-cars were now crawling forward at walking pace.

Take the example of two Brittany-based divisions; Karl Sprang's 266. and Paul Mahlmann's 353. *ID*s. Both had been established with a cadre of Russian front veterans, and then backfilled with almost two thousand *Osttruppen* each. When the call came to head to Normandy, Sprang, a Stalingrad survivor, formed a *kampfgruppe* composed of his best men and dispatched them northeast on 10 June. Four days later, Paul Mahlmann led his entire division out. With the railways out of action and the *jabos* overhead, both units were forced to travel on foot, and then only at night.

It took them more than a fortnight to get to Normandy, having advanced to the sound of the guns at a pace slower than a typical American Civil War march eighty years earlier. By contrast, a UK-based Allied infantry division could reach the Normandy front in less than two days.

The effect on the *landsers*' morale of this lack of mobility was profound, especially for the veterans who had only known the Eastern front, as one Waffen-SS *Unterscharführer* from 10. *SS-Panzerdivision* '*Frundsberg*' described after a journey that took him from Russia across Europe into eastern France, whereupon he faced a wearying slog of several hundred kilometres via back-roads to reach the concentration area in Normandy:

We are now 30km behind the front line after a nightmare journey across France which has taken a fortnight under the most frightening of conditions on account of enemy planes… I have hardly slept at all and have forgotten how many times the enemy has strafed us. We have suffered many casualties in men and vehicles, but our Luftwaffe has not ventured to put in an appearance. There was nothing like this in Russia.

Not all *Frundsberg* men were as lucky as this NCO. One contingent from the division, in transit from Russia in late June, was on a train in the sidings at the Vaires-sur-Marne marshalling yards on the eastern outskirts of Paris when RAF Bomber Command attacked. In the maelstrom of explosions, several bombs fell on the train itself, others hit several adjacent railcars carrying a cargo of mines. The resulting explosions near enough wiped out the *SS* men.

Fritz Bayerlein of the *Panzer-Lehr*, having endured Allied air power in North Africa, knew the *Ostfronters* were in for a shock: 'Our friends from the east cannot imagine what they're in for here.'

By the end of August, the Allied fleet had landed no fewer than 2,052,299 men, 438,471 vehicles, and 3,098,259 tons of supplies in Normandy – the Wehrmacht was losing the *Materialschlacht* (*matériel* war) so despised by the gentlemen of the German General Staff – and with it, the campaign – and France.

5

The Battle for Caen

The United States of America is a great country, and without it, Great Britain could not have liberated western Europe and then helped the Soviet Union defeat Nazi Germany. Having said that, it is also true to say that since the end of the war, an impression has been created in certain quarters that it was the US which did the lion's share of the heavy lifting – particularly on D-Day and thereafter – and here, Hollywood especially must shoulder some responsibility for what is a misconception not borne out by the facts and figures. The earlier-mentioned film *Saving Private Ryan* is a classic example, with not a Tommy or Canuck in sight at any time, and just one very brief – and derogatory – mention of Montgomery ('He's overrated!') as the *leitmotif* for what is portrayed pretty much as an American-only operation.

The reality was different. Three-quarters of the fleet in the Channel – and more than half the aircraft flying overhead – were British, and it was the British and Canadian armies who made up more than half the 'boots on the ground' on the day itself – no disrespect to the French and other nationalities who went ashore too. Simultaneously, Great Britain was fighting Imperial Japan in Asia[1] and the Indian and Pacific oceans, the Third Reich in Italy and the Kriegsmarine's U-boats worldwide. However, this was the high-water mark of British strength in Europe. Almost five years of war had emptied the barrel, and the divisions which landed on 6 June and in subsequent weeks were the last hurrah before American military power began to tell. Britain was running out of men.

Canada – long one of Britain's most faithful allies – was in the same predicament, albeit for different reasons. The Canadian Prime

Minister Mackenzie King, ever mindful of the deep divisions created in his society by conscription during the First World War, determined that Ottawa's policy in this new conflict would be non-compulsion; only volunteers would serve overseas. Completely understandable as this was in a political sense, militarily it doomed Harry Crerar's First Canadian Army to chronic under-manning. By the beginning of July the British and Canadians had just five divisions left in the UK to be sent to France (four infantry and the 4th Canadian Armoured). In contrast, the US had nine divisions sitting in England waiting to be shipped across the Channel, plus Alex Patch's entire Seventh Army being readied to invade the south of France. Back on the US mainland the depots were still in full swing processing more men every day – and so replete were the ranks that the powers-that-be could afford to reject as unsuitable one-third of all candidates.

On D-Day this 'changing of the guard' was in the future; Britain was still the senior partner in the coalition, and so it was the British Army that was assigned ostensibly the most important objective on landing day – the liberation of the city of Caen. One look at a map and ten minutes viewing from a drone would suffice to understand just why Caen was so vital; it was Normandy's biggest city and its historic capital, but more importantly it was, and is, the hub of the entire regional road network. Those roads run east–west and all-points south, and they are set in rolling, open countryside, with none of the patchwork quilt of tiny fields, sunken lanes and battlement-like hedgerows of the infamous *bocage* country further west. Possession of the city and its environs would allow the Allies to unleash the full power of their mechanised forces and drive for Paris and the borders of the Reich itself.

It is less than nine miles from the surf on Sword Beach to the city centre as the crow flies, and the British were confident of reaching and seizing it in a few hours. They did not. Ludwig Krug's stubborn defence of *WN17*, and *21. Panzer's* counter-attack on the afternoon of the 6th were just enough to stall the British advance. Nevertheless, the British were confident that a renewed push on the 7th would see them liberate Caen. For their part, the Germans were just as confident that the 7th would be their day, with Kurt Meyer studying the situation map in Richter's headquarters and remarking to Feuchtinger: 'Little fish! We'll throw them back into the sea in the morning!'

Neither would be right – and after more than a month, both would be exhausted and awash with blood. What happened in the interim was a slogfest that reminded some of its older participants of the fighting in France almost thirty years before. The mostly inexperienced Anglo-Canadians stumbled forward, employing ever greater amounts of firepower to try and bludgeon their way through a defence made stubborn by some of the toughest divisions the Germans could field: *2. Panzerdivision*, *21. Panzerdivision*, *Panzer-Lehr*, and no fewer than five of the seven Waffen-SS armoured divisions mustered during the war; the *Leibstandarte, Das Reich, Hohenstaufen, Frundsberg* and last but not least, the *HJ*.

This was not the *bocage* fighting of Normandy legend. The battle for Caen was characterised by large, set-piece Allied attacks, supported by massive artillery and air support. Those assaults were generally met by defenders stunned by weight of high-explosive, but somehow doing just enough to hold on. Those same defenders would then surge forward in the counter-attacks that were embedded in Germany military doctrine – only to be blown away by Allied guns; little territory would be won or lost, and the ground would be littered with the dead and smashed and burning vehicles. Both sides would then brush themselves down and prepare for the next round, but all the time the German ranks were being thinned by the attrition that was the Westheer's death-knell, as Allied air supremacy choked off their reinforcements and resupply.

That scenario was still some way off though on the morning of 7 June, when the 9th Canadian Infantry Brigade resumed its advance just to the west of Caen itself. Unbeknown to the infantry and their supporting Stuart and Sherman tanks, Meyer had during the preceding night positioned two battalions of his *SS-Panzergrenadierregiment 25* around the villages of Epron and St Contest, along with fifty panzers of *SS-Obersturmbannführer* Max Wünsche's *SS-Panzerregiment 12* – no mean feat given what they faced on the march, as graphically attested to by Meyer himself:

We are hunted relentlessly, but cannot afford to take cover, the march must go on! A string of Spitfires is attacking the last platoon of 15th Company... The platoon is driving down a sunken road, evasion is impossible. A grenadier is lying in the road, a jet of blood shooting from his throat, an artery has been shot through. He dies in our arms. The ammunition in an amphibious vehicle explodes with a loud bang, the blast shoots flames high into the sky, and the vehicle is torn to pieces. In a couple of minutes the rubble is pushed aside, there is no stopping – on, always on!

One of Meyer's own teenage grenadiers, *SS-Sturmmann* Helmuth Pock, also remembered that nightmare journey:

> The number of our vehicles knocked out by the enemy keeps growing … they are sitting where they were hit, burnt-out. Grenades are scattered about with shells and all types of munitions, and amongst them are dead soldiers. The march … becomes more and more dangerous, the pastures and fields are ploughed with bomb craters.

Now though, the bloodshed seemed worth it. An entire Allied brigade was advancing through the fields and orchards to the west of Caen, right under the guns of Meyer's SS troopers – and they had no idea of what was about to happen:

> An enemy panzer is pushing through the orchards of St Contest, now it stops. The commander opens the hatch and surveys the terrain. Is he blind? Hasn't he realised that he is only two hundred metres from the II Bataillon's grenadiers and that the barrels of our anti-tank guns are aimed at him? He calmly lights a cigarette and blinks at its smoke. Not a single shot is fired. The battalion maintains excellent fire discipline… Enemy panzers are rolling towards Authie from Buron, my God, what an opportunity, the panzers are driving right across II Bataillon's front! I give orders to all battalions, the artillery and the panzers, 'Don't shoot, open fire on my order only!'… The enemy commander seems to only see [Carpiquet] airfield, it is directly in front of him … he doesn't seem to realise that his destruction awaits him beyond the reverse slope… Wünsche quietly transmits the enemy panzer movements… I give the signal to attack to Wünsche and can just hear his order – '*Achtung panzer – marsche!*' The enemy panzer at the head smokes and I watch the crew bailing out. More enemy panzers are torn to pieces with loud explosions… III Bataillon's grenadiers are very determined … the enemy has now been struck deep in the flank.

Understandably, Meyer was jubilant, and with the Canadians falling back in confusion, he went onto the offensive. But with what would become a terrible routine for the Germans, they were met by determined defence and massed artillery fire, to which the SS men had no answer, and left Meyer himself dumbfounded: 'I have never experienced such concentrated artillery fire before; inevitably I think of Verdun.'

Again, one of Meyer's own grenadiers echoed his boss's words – *SS-Sturmmann* Karl Vasold: 'Critically-wounded panzer comrades were coming to the rear, they had lost hands and suffered severe burns.' Rudi von Ribbentrop lamented the lack of air cover, but unlike so many of his comrades, didn't blame the Luftwaffe:

My comrades and I experienced that the Luftwaffe was actually no longer existent and had no chance against Allied superiority – there were just too many of them and our Luftwaffe comrades too few. I saw this for myself when I counter-attacked with my own company – which comprised about fifteen Panthers at the time – against Allied armoured forces that had advanced to the outskirts of Caen. Anyway, out of the sky came about fifteen or twenty Allied planes – I think they were American Lightnings, but I'm not absolutely positive – they attacked us and bombarded us but we were very lucky and I didn't lose a single panzer, but even so, it was a terrible experience.

Von Ribbentrop knew what he was talking about, having been wounded in a *jabo* attack as he was driving back from a company exercise in his staff car just before D-Day:

Suddenly bursts of machine-gun fire flew about our ears – my driver's and mine. I turned around and saw an enemy plane about fifty metres behind us shooting all its guns. Instinctively I put my head between my knees – this is what saved my life – and shouted to my driver; 'Stop! *Jabo*!' Then I was hit in the shoulder-blades and realised I was paralysed, and what is more that blood was spurting out of an exit wound in my neck near the carotid artery. I managed to roll out of the vehicle, and called out to my driver; 'Pull me into the ditch, he's coming back!' He managed to drag me into the ditch as the *jabo* attacked twice more and tried to get our vehicle to burst into flames. It was most impressive, as the rounds from his guns missed my head by a hair's breadth and clattered against the paving. I was now lying on my back, the carotid presumably hit – I thought it was the end! I wasn't even in shock though – perhaps after being wounded a number of times [this was von Ribbentrop's fourth wound in action] it doesn't occur. My driver, who was very upset, was trying to press a gauze dressing onto my throat, which wasn't of much use. I waited to pass out from blood loss, and asked my driver to say my farewells to the company and to tell my mother exactly what happened to me – it was all over. Except it wasn't! A short while later I felt a pricking in my right big toe, as when a foot had 'gone to sleep' and then woken up again. Sensation and mobility returned. I was able to stand up and go back to the car. I told the driver to try the engine, which he did, and lo and behold it started! The *Kubelwagen* was extremely difficult to set light to you see!

Taken to a nearby Luftwaffe hospital, he was treated and told he was very lucky to be alive; a milimetre to the left and the bullet would have hit the spine from behind and the carotid from in front and nothing would have gotten him to the operating table in time. 'As we would have said in my Westphalian homeland – "the dear Lord cares for the stupid!"'

Slated for transfer back to Germany for further treatment, von Ribbentrop instead absented himself from hospital and went to rejoin his unit; 'I wanted for all the world to stay with my company. I had trained them and led them from day one, and was very attached to them – they were my boys and I wasn't going to leave them in the lurch to face the invasion alone if I could help it. So I drove after my company, which led to me being reported as a "deserter" by the senior doctor!'

The upshot of the *HJ*'s fight at St Contest was that the Canadian advance to Caen was hurled back. Meyer could be well pleased with his men – they'd come through their first action, but seventy-three had been killed, mostly by Allied artillery fire, and three hundred in total had become casualties –ten per cent of his regiment's complement. Many more 'successes' like that and it would cease to exist. *Leutnant* Rudolf Schaaf – an army artilleryman – saw for himself the way Meyer's men handled themselves: 'The SS showed that they believed that thus far everybody had been fighting like milkmaids.' Schaaf – twice wounded in Russia, the second leaving him with a pronounced limp that rendered him unfit for further active duty in the East – was not a little affronted by that opinion, given he had been in the eye of the storm in strongpoint *WN12* at Ouistreham on D-Day with the *4/ AR.1716* and its four ex-French Army 15.5cm guns. However, he saw the surviving *HJ* troopers return that evening; filthy, dog-tired and deflated: 'It was a very sad chapter for them.' One of their own officers wrote in his diary; 'I could have screamed with rage and grief.'

As for Meyer himself, he was shocked to be told by no lesser a personage than Geyr von Schweppenburg that 'the war can only be won now through political means.'

The *HJ*'s post-action treatment of eleven Canadian prisoners-of-war was a terrible crime. Soldiers of the North Novia Scotia Highlanders and the 27th Armoured Regiment the Sherbrooke Fusiliers; the men had fought bravely but were forced to surrender as the tide of battle turned against them that afternoon. The *HJ* lined them up outside Meyer's headquarters at the ruined *L'Abbaye d'Ardenne* and shot them in the back of the head.[2] To the eternal shame of both Meyer and his division, they would not be the last to be murdered.

Having failed to liberate Caen on D-Day, or the days immediately following, the British and Canadians opted for 'deliberate attack'; a military term denoting significant planning and preparation, all-arms co-ordination, and supporting fire from artillery, naval and air assets – lightning-quick this would not be. However, with the German lines still not solid, and their units only arriving at the front in dribs and drabs, there was a good chance of success for Operation Perch when it was launched on 10 June. A classic pincer movement, Montgomery's plan was to send strong forces to the east and west of Caen, find gaps in the defence and take the city from the rear or from the flanks – whatever worked. The greater part of two entire Corps went into the attack, with the *Panzer-Lehr* and *21. Panzerdivision* in the firing line.

21. Panzer of course, had been in action since the landings began, and had launched a counter-attack of its own just the day before. Hans von Luck had given the orders personally: 'We assemble before dawn, before the enemy air force can intervene or their navy be effective. The motorcycle escorts of the reconnaissance battalion and the grenadiers of *II Bataillon* will lead, followed by *I Bataillon*, supported by the panzers of *Nr.4 Kompanie*, as well as Becker's SPW's.'

One of those motorcyclists was Gefreiter Hammel: "With support from the panzers and SP guns we soon forced our way into Escoville. The remaining civilian population had gathered by the church, we found a few children running around ... and took them to the church.'

Yet again, a promising start to a German attack came up short for lack of numbers – one company of panzers was never going to be enough to do real damage, as Werner Kortenhaus and *4 Kompanie* found to their cost:

That day was for us one of the hardest actions ever. We assembled with about ten panzers under the trees of the avenue south of

Escoville. We drove with closed ports, one after the other... We intended to switch to broad wedge formation for the attack, with the grenadiers behind and alongside us. Then everything happened very quickly; *Panzer 432* was hit and lost a track. Thirty seconds later *Panzer 400* was hit and our company commander, *Leutnant* Hoffmann, was staring in horror at the bloody mess that had been his leg, while *Panzer 401* exploded, blowing open the hatches and literally flinging the crew out. We had seen three panzers, including our commanders, destroyed in a few seconds... On my panzer [a MK IV with a short-barrelled 7.5cm gun] the turret jammed, so that I could only shoot into the hedges with my machine-gun. The fire became more intense, so that on orders from *Major* von Luck we had to withdraw, as did the grenadiers... The other drivers began hurriedly to reverse, under cover of a hail of fire from their turret-guns and machine-guns. Terrified, they watched the exploding mushrooms of earth and smoke shoot up around them, and saw too late the dead and wounded grenadiers lying around the road of retreat; some had been squashed by the panzers. Perhaps six minutes had passed... The enemy artillery fire continued unabated. Some thirty or forty grenadiers must have been killed by it... We realised that we could no longer drive the British back into the sea.

21. *Panzer* was fast becoming an experienced formation, and now it would be *Panzer-Lehr*'s turn for its baptism of fire. Despite its lack of direct action so far, the *Lehr* had arrived in the line already shaken and bloody. Ordered to move in daylight the one hundred miles from its assembly areas in the south to the front, its commander Bayerlein had protested: 'My request for a delay until twilight was refused, we moved as ordered and immediately came under air attack. I lost twenty to thirty vehicles by nightfall.'

Helmut Ritgen, one of Beyerlein's panzer commanders, wrote in his memoirs:

Even today memories of this march still evoke nightmares for those who took part... The division's columns had hardly gotten underway when they were spotted by enemy reconnaisance aircraft and attacked shortly afterwards by *jabos* with rockets and bombs. They flew in clear skies, spotted the columns, attacked, then called on other *jabos* to replace them. Soon mushroom clouds of black smoke rose from vehicles on fire ... the advance was slowed by every attack... The speed of advance was slowed even further still by bombs dropped on roads, towns and bridges.

Having refuelled and rested-up for a few hours in a forest near Alençon that same night, Bayerlein was ordered to keep going; 'at daylight (morning of the 7th) General Dollman...gave me a direct order to proceed and there was nothing else to do...It was terrible.'

Neither Ritgen, nor Bayerlein's adjutant – Alexander Hartdegen – liked what they saw:

The further north we drove the more we could see the *jabos* had been busy; here were the results of their work – burning vehicle wrecks on the side of the road spewing black smoke. At times, men would suddenly appear through the smoke as if through fog... Dozens of wrecked vehicles, now no more than steel skeletons, lay by the roadside burning and smouldering. The sector from Caumont to Villers-Bocage was a road of death; burnt-out trucks, bombed field-kitchens and gun tractors ... with dead bodies strewn alongside.

In Bayerlein's own words, the division had suffered the journey from hell to reach the still-forming front: 'By the end of the day [the 7th] I had lost forty fuel-bowsers and ninety other trucks. Five of my panzers were knocked out as well as eighty-four half-tracks, prime-movers and self-propelled guns. These were serious losses for a division not yet in action.'[3]

But that was the fate of every division moving to Normandy – constant air attacks were a given. The *Lehr* should have been tough as teak – but it wasn't. From its inception, self-doubt dogged it, eating into its very heart, and that of its commander, Fritz Bayerlein. Only forty-five that summer, *Alte Fritz*, as his adoring soldiers called him as a nod to the Prussian legend, was tired; so very, very tired. His war had begun with the invasion of Poland back in autumn 1939, and had never really stopped since then. He'd contracted hepatitis and muscular rheumatism in Africa, and that same campaign had ground him down – as it had so many of Rommel's officers – and it showed, his deep-set eyes and care-worn features made him look ten years older. By the summer of '44 he was disillusioned with the Nazi leadership and doubting the prospects for victory in the West. In France his own *Ia* (chief operations officer) Kurt Kauffmann was damning: 'He was a very good soldier, but he was worn out. In Normandy he showed himself nervous and weak.'[4]

He was not the driving force a division like *Lehr* needed. As was so often the case, a leader's malaise was reflected in his subordinates – men like Helmut Ritgen: '[Our] Flak was limited to some light anti-aircraft guns and our own machine-guns. But our fire was too little, hits on target were few and we rarely destroyed an aircraft. A lot of us thought; "what use is it if we down a few aircraft among this mass of *jabos*?"'

Ritgen's logic may seem sound, but in Russia, from the very first day of invasion, the Red Army had promulgated the policy that whenever a German aircraft was seen in the air its own ground troops should fire every weapon they had at it regardless, be it heavy machine-gun down to rifles and pistols – their intention being to raise the morale of their men, which it undoubtedly did; but it also had the surprising effect of downing significant numbers of those self-same aircraft and killing an awful lot of German aircrew. Would such a policy have cleared the skies above Bayerlein's boys – no – but might it have lifted their spirits and perhaps made some pilots fly a bit more circumspectly? To be fair to the division, its officers and men were plunged headlong into a type of battle they weren't geared up for. Even so, one can't help but feel that the *Lehr* could have done with a bit of Red Army logic that summer.

As it was, Perch got an early gift when Ultra decrypts identified a major German command and control centre in the gathering dusk of 10 June. Additional intercepted radio traffic marked out a small *château* and its adjacent orchard on the outskirts of the village of La Caine. In no time at all an RAF air-controller vectored in no fewer than forty Typhoon fighter-bombers. Sentries raised the alarm but their warning shouts were already too late. Screaming in at over three hundred miles an hour, the pilots dropped their payloads before raking the ground with cannon and machine-gun fire. Before the dust had time to settle, a follow-on wave of seventy-one B25 Mitchells emptied their bomb-bays on the site as well. Radio trucks, staff cars and supply wagons went up in flames, and in a few short minutes Geyr von Schweppenburg's newly-established *Panzergruppe West* headquarters was obliterated. Von Schweppenburg himself was wounded and his chief of staff and operations team killed. The Westheer's entire armoured fleet was effectively leaderless as the tall, urbane general retired to Paris for two weeks of treatment and recuperation.

Events on the ground weren't going quite so smoothly for the British though. Hans von Luck's attack on the 9th might have foundered, but *21. Panzer* was proving a hard nut to crack in defence, and the

51st Highland Division's pincer assault to the east of Caen made little headway, being called off on the 12th. One grenadier caught up in the fighting was the teenaged dispatch rider – *Gefreiter* Walter Hermes – serving in Josef Rauch's regiment. Back on D-Day he had found the time to write a letter home 'My dear parents, the British have landed...I'm well and healthy, don't worry about me, I'm sure I'll see you soon. We'll soon throw these British back into the sea.' He had then taken a nap. His luck didn't hold for long.

> We were retreating towards Caen. As we were assembling in a little village, I can't remember the name, we were suddenly ambushed. I remember the company commander shouting 'Fix bayonets! Close combat, we're surrounded!' Suddenly there was an explosion and the motorcyclist standing next to me was hit in the stomach and died instantly. I was knocked off my feet, but wasn't hurt. I had never seen anyone die before and I was suddenly very scared.

Minutes later, he was caught up in another firefight:

> One of us didn't make it. I heard him grunt and give a deep sigh as he got to the ditch and I tried to pull him in but couldn't get hold of him. As I reached forward to get a better grip, to my horror my hand went straight into his wound. I could feel his blood and his body still quivering, it was like grabbing death itself. I was sick and petrified. [Then it was over.] A British captain and five soldiers came out with their guns aimed at us, we dropped our weapons and threw up our hands and I said to one of the men with me 'Thank God we aren't going to die.' I began to think about my family and I remembered the letter I had written... I didn't feel too bad about being captured and I was thankful to be alive.

As for the *Lehr*'s baptism, it came under heavy attack at the village of Tilly-sur-Seulles and its vital road junction. In fighting that became hand-to-hand, both sides suffered severe casualties, but the Germans held, despite the Allies savaging the new division with a hitherto unseen weight of fire the aftermath of which was described to Hubert Meyer by an *HJ* NCO eyewitness: 'The enemy had virtually cut to pieces units of the *Panzer-Lehr* division with heavy weapons. SPWs and other equipment had been ripped apart, and next to them, on the ground – and even hanging in the trees – were body parts of dead comrades. A terrible silence covered all.'

While Bayerlein's men held, Dietrich Kraiss's *352. ID* did not. Having suffered twelve hundred casualties on D-Day alone, the division had carried on fighting doggedly for every inch of ground, its resilience exemplified by Ernst Goth and his *GR. 916*. One of its young company commanders who had done sterling service was ordered to report to Goth's château HQ to receive his next orders. His reception was not what he expected.

> I entered the room and informed the Oberst of my presence. He looked at me and snapped me into the proper stance of attention – I was shocked. He looked at me and dressed me down. He roared at me that a German officer is always clean and presentable when he reports to a superior, regardless of the situation. With every word yelled I felt more and more the dirt and sweat which covered my body. He was even more angry at my beard, which was not intentional. I just hadn't had the time to shave. Goth ordered me to remove myself and report back in ten minutes as a proper German officer.

Chastened, he left, brushed down his uniform, found a blunt razor and scraped off several days' growth, cutting his face repeatedly in the process. Exactly ten minutes later he reported again with rivulets of blood running down his face onto his hastily brushed tunic – Goth smiled in approval and gave him his new orders.[5]

But the cracks were beginning to show. Supplies weren't getting through as the *jabos* pounced on any movement during the day – and that included ammunition of course, so the *landsers* had to improvise, as Karl Wegner soon realised when he was only given a thousand rounds of mixed tracer and ball for his MG 42 – not exactly an excess when you consider its rate of fire was between 1,200–1,500 rounds per minute! Feared and detested by the Allied soldiers, it wasn't universally liked in the German ranks either, as from their point of view its ammo-hunger was a major disadvantage. One SS trooper, Andreas Fleischer, was scathing about it; 'An MG 42 machine-gun squad was usually eight men strong – the gunner, the loader and then six others whose main job was to do nothing else but fetch ammunition for it – just one touch on the trigger and that was it, fifty rounds gone, it was dreadful!'[6] Unsurprisingly, Wegner asked for more, and was handed another five hundred rounds of training ammunition tipped with wood. Angry, he protested loudly to the *Feldwebel* in charge, who gave the grenadier short shrift: 'Now listen up! The *Amis* are not like the Ivans because they value lives. So, if you need to retreat, save the live rounds and fire a belt or two of this stuff at them, because they will take cover and give you time to get away. I know this because we've been doing it already.'[7] The NCO's logic was sound, but when American soldiers found captured German machine-gunners with wood-tipped rounds they sometimes thought it was a dastardly act of the 'Hun', akin to using dumdum bullets, and those prisoners rarely found their way back to the rear. Given what the MG 42 could do to advancing Allied soldiers, it is perhaps no surprise. David Holbrook, a young troop commander with the British East Yorkshire Yeomanry described the experience: 'There was a colossal hail of fire coming over the top of the wall. The Germans had these fast-firing machine-guns called spandaus and they were literally ripping an orchard to pieces, you've never heard anything like it, you suddenly find yourself enveloped in a sort of hail of tracer wondering what the hell was happening.'

For the Germans, it wasn't just resupply that was breaking down either – it was the men themselves. By 9 June, Goth's entire *II Bataillon* had just three officers left alive; *Hauptmann* Grimme the CO, and two *Leutnants* – Heller and Heinze. Heller now commanded the remnants of 6, 7 and 8 *Kompanies*, while Heinze still led 5. All three men were Russian front veterans, but weren't immune to the stresses and strains of this new battlefield. Heinze remembered an incident after a particularly terrible Allied bombardment.

> They hit us with all they had, literally driving us into the ground. After this bombardment I went to find *Leutnant* Heller. The ground was torn apart and I found him with his men in a dug-out. He was crying. He wasn't ashamed of his tears because he was crying for his men who'd been killed. This much-decorated soldier had been in the French campaign of 1940 and in Russia. He said to me; 'If they would only fight us man to man we would have a chance, we can't fight their planes and bombs.' I knew he was right.

In the absence of the air cover they so desperately needed, Heinze, Heller and the rest were adapting to the new way of making war. 'Our tactics were simple when attacked by infantry. We would hold with the aid of the hedgerows. If we saw the *Amis* withdraw we then did so ourselves because in moments *jabos* and *Arifeuer* (*landser* slang for artillery fire) would pound our foxholes. Then their infantry would take over our old line, thinking we were destroyed. Afterwards they would advance casually and we would hit them from the next hedgerow. We lost ground... It was all we could do.'

They lost men too. Hans Heinze was particularly affected by the death of one of his senior NCOs, *Stabsfeldwebel* Nielen. 'This loss affected me greatly, he had been like a father to me.' Heinze also lost his battalion commander. Grimme was missing believed killed in an Allied barrage, and into his shoes stepped a *Hauptmann* Loges from *I Bataillon*, an ex-school teacher who was not cut from the same cloth as his predecessor:

> *Hauptmann* Loges was not able to deal with his new command. Most of the time he stayed in his bunker, and only rarely ventured outside. Once, a piece of shrapnel came through the bunker's roof and landed right between his feet. Instead of being happy at his good fortune he just broke down, it was just too much for him to take. For an officer his outburst was disgraceful. After this he became even more of a recluse.

Heller and Heinze responded by ignoring him and leading the battalion themselves.

To try and fill the gaps in the ranks, the division absorbed anybody and everybody wearing any sort of German uniform who was within its constantly shifting unit boundaries. Karl Wegner, now no longer a callow youth but a veteran of *GR. 914,* saw for himself what that meant when his machine-gun team were allocated some pretty dubious *Reichsarbeitsdienst* 'volunteers'. The RAD, Reich Labour Service, was a state organisation with a compulsory six-month service period for males prior to their military service.

> These men – actually most were boys of sixteen – were the survivors of a RAD detachment. Many had no weapons... The Leutnant said, 'Kalb, these three are assigned to you, get them some weapons and divide out what you have for ammunition.' Kalb saluted and the officer left... He then turned and began to give orders to the three of them... All of a sudden we heard Kalb and the older RAD man arguing. This fellow was yelling that he was ... a grade higher than Kalb and so he demanded to be treated with the proper respect at all times. Kalb grabbed him with both hands and threw him into the ditch... He was told to pick up several cans of ammunition and do as he was told or Kalb would put a bullet in his brain. Kalb told Willi and me that if this guy caused any trouble we should shoot him in the ass

and leave him for the *Amis*. He was never a problem because the very next day he was caught out on the road by the *jabos* and cut down.

As Heinze's description details, Kraiss's men weren't just fighting the British but also the Americans in the hedgerows as they provided the link between the panzers of the *Lehr* and the *HJ* west of Caen and the German paras battling to try and hold Saint-Lô in the east. It would have been a titanic task for an up-to-strength unit, and was simply beyond the resources of the battered grenadiers. *352. ID* lacked ammunition and artillery support, the paucity of vehicles meant they had no option but to travel everywhere on foot, the men were dog-tired and hungry, and there weren't nearly enough of them, as Martin Eichenseer of *GR. 916* acknowledged:

> We had fought as hard as we could, but were no match for the force the *Amis* could throw at us. We contested every metre of ground, mostly because it was a matter of survival for us. I sometimes wonder why we fought like that since by then most of us – even if we didn't say it – knew the war was lost ... but since our youth, the willingness to fight for the Fatherland was branded on our souls. We did have some fanatics, but they were soon silenced by the harsh realities we encountered... In the final analysis our own survival drove us on. Every engagement we survived was a victory for the individual, no matter what ground was won or lost. And now I was alone with two other men from another company, with very little ammunition, cut off, and not sure what to do. We crept like cats from place to place, hoping to find our lines or ... other Germans with a leader among them. Stray shots, bad luck, or the will of God, I'll never know, but by nightfall the other two were dead and I was alone. I found a place on the top of a rather high hedgerow, curled up with my machine-gun and waited for something to happen. I fell fast asleep.

Something had to give, and in the end the inevitable happened; the line was just too long, and contact with the *Lehr* was lost. Suddenly, a gap of several miles appeared in the German front line near the road junction at Caumont-l'Éventé. The British XXX Corps, having pulled back from its assault at Tilly, probed further south, searching for a weak spot, and found it at a small town whose name has almost become a byword for the Normandy campaign: Villers-Bocage.

Home to around a thousand people, the town sits amidst high ground near the Odon River, more or less astride what was then the main road between Caen and Rennes away to the southwest; the *Route Nationale 175*. There was no garrison in the town, and the only Germans for miles were *I.SS-Panzerkorps*' one and only reserve – a single battalion of panzers. Spread out over the countryside, number 2 company had been detailed to cover the town. It was meant to have twelve panzers but only six were operational and in position, the rest having either broken down or been damaged on the hundred-mile road march to the front they had been forced into enduring from their assembly area at Beauvais, northwest of Paris. No tanks were good at covering long distances by road, and the fifty-seven tonne *Panzerkampfwagen VI Tiger* was especially poor at that particular task. It was Tigers nevertheless which lay in wait at Villers-Bocage on 13 June, and not just any Tigers, but vehicles from *Schwere SS-Panzerabteilung 101* (101st Heavy SS Panzer Battalion*)*.

Enormously expensive and time-consuming to manufacture, the Germans only built 1,347 of what was arguably the most famous panzer of them all. To try and maximise their impact most were grouped into special heavy battalions and then attached to different divisions for as long as high command deemed necessary, although a few favoured divisions such as the *SS-Totenkopf* and the Army's *Grossdeutschland* had their own.

Just as the panzers themselves at Villers-Bocage weren't run of the mill, neither was their company commander *SS-Obersturmführer* Michael Wittmann. Standing five feet nine inches tall, the 30-year-old Bavarian was not the blond-haired *Aryan* of the posters, but a poster-boy he was, nonetheless. Having joined the Waffen-SS before the war, he found himself in the *Leibstandarte* serving in a *StuG III* crew, and it was there, in an armoured vehicle, that he found his true calling. Faced by what seemed like a limitless gallery of targets in Russia, he succeeded at the two things all the great panzer aces needed to achieve; he survived, and he killed tanks – lots of them. By the time Hitler presented him with the Oakleaves (the *Eichenlauben*) to his Knight's Cross on 2 February 1944, his tally stood at a staggering 117, and he was lauded by Goebbels' propaganda machine like some sort of movie star. He now had a different crew from the one he fought with in Russia – apart from one, *SS-Unterscharführer* Balthasar 'Bobby' Woll. Woll, now a Tiger commander and fellow Knight's Cross winner in his own right, had been Wittmann's best man when he married his fiancée Hildegard back in March, and when his Tiger had to be left behind for repairs, Wittmann had snapped his old comrade up and kept him. Now, on the morning of 13 June these two men would play a leading role in an engagement that has become as famous as it is controversial.

Advancing into the town was the spearhead of the British 7th Armoured Division, the renowned 'Desert Rats', specifically the Sherman and Cromwell tanks of the 4th County of London Yeomanry (Sharpshooters), a few artillery pieces of the Royal Horse Artillery and a company-plus of 1st Battalion the Rifle Brigade with numerous half-tracks, bren-gun carriers and other support vehicles. The plan was clear; secure the town and the nearby high ground, and enable the rest of the division to pass through and slam headlong into the exposed flank of *Panzer-Lehr*. The German front would then be rolled up, and Caen would fall from the west. Interviewed for Nazi newsreels after the ensuing fight, Wittmann took up the story:

> The decision was a very, very difficult one. Never before had I been so impressed by the strength of the enemy as I was by those tanks rolling by; but I knew it absolutely had to be and I decided to strike out into the enemy... I had no time to assemble my company; instead I had to act quickly, as I had to assume that the enemy had already spotted me and would destroy me where I stood. I set off with one panzer and passed the order to the others not to retreat a single step but to hold their ground.

Wittmann also admitted that Bobby Woll stiffened his resolve when he said to his commander; 'Look at them. They're acting as if they've won the war already.' That made his mind up, he told him; 'Well, we're going to prove them wrong,' and he attacked.

> I drove up the column and surprised the English as much as they had surprised me! They never left the road, they were so surprised that they took to flight, not with their vehicles, instead they jumped out and I shot up the vehicles as I drove by... I drove toward the rear half of the column, knocking out every tank that came towards me as I went. The enemy was thrown into total confusion.

In those twenty or so minutes, Wittmann and his Tiger basically ended Operation Perch. Using a combination of his panzers superlative

88mm main gun, the almost-impenetrability of its frontal armour, the terrain, and his experience; Wittmann cannoned and machine-gunned his way through Lieutenant-Colonel Arthur, the Viscount Cranley's column, until hits to his Tiger forced him to abandon it. By then the damage was done; wrecked and burning British tanks, half-tracks and gun carriages lay everywhere. Rolf Möbius, one of Wittmann's fellow Tiger officers, and commander of *1 Kompanie*, entered the town just after the fight: 'The left side of the road was one big pile of wreckage, which was obscured by smoke from burning vehicles. To the right, in the direction of Caen, we discovered two Cromwell tanks. They began to turn around, but we were able to destroy them both. Terrified Englishmen were running everywhere.' Wittmann was hailed as a hero by the Nazi propaganda machine and promoted to *SS-Hauptsturmführer*.

For the Allies, the defeat at Villers-Bocage was a setback, and proof – if any was needed – that the Westheer was still a force to be reckoned with. In the eyes of many Germans, Wittmann's feat was something altogether greater – a sure sign that victory was still possible against the mass of enemy *matériel*, as long as they kept the faith. In Normandy, and during the whole French campaign, this belief that men could defeat machines was kept alive by the officers and men of the Waffen-SS. Walter Kruger, an *HJ* signals officer, said of his own troopers, 'They had received a proper training in the Hitler Youth, they had a sense of order, of discipline, and they knew how to sing!'[8] This wasn't a case of lions led by donkeys, most of the SS rank-and-file knew what to expect at the front and accepted it as the price they had to pay to win, as one SS trooper explained: 'We thought of the Americans as children. But we knew that their air forces would be a terrible problem. We were not frightened of their men, but of their material.' This wasn't based on some sort of 'SS-only' fanaticism. By the summer of '44 the old entry standards for the Waffen-SS had long been ditched, and not just for the rash of newly raised formations, but for the 'old' divisions too, including the successor to the very first armed SS-*Verfügungstruppe* unit, the *2. SS-Panzerdivision 'Das Reich'*.

After its latest bloodletting in Russia it had been sent to France, ostensibly to rest and refit, but in truth to be completely rebuilt from the ground up, so savage were its losses. There were just enough veteran officers and NCOs to provide it with a hard core, what it needed was men to fill the ranks. In years gone by its *Deutschland* and *Der Führer* regiments would have had their pick of the litter, but not now. Onto the rolls came a rag-tag assortment of recruits, including the 17-year-old Elimar Schneider, who survived the war and penned a book about his experiences entitled *SS-Beutedeutscher* – 'SS-Booty German' – under the pseudonym *Sadi Schneid*. Schneider was an Alsatian, cursed to be born in one of mainland Europe's disputed border regions. Annexed back into the Reich after France's defeat in 1940, Alsace-Lorraine was treated like any other *Gau* in Hitler's state, and German Alsatians were liable for military service like everybody else. Coincidentally a number of the Westheer's senior commanders in France were from Lorraine's capital, Metz, including *15. Armee's* Hans Salmuth and *21. Panzer's* Edgar Feuchtinger. On 25 August 1942, under pressure to up recruitment, the obligation for military service was extended to all French citizens in the region, an action that according to official government figures led to the drafting of no fewer than 130,000 ethnic Frenchmen into the Wehrmacht – over 42,000 of whom would end up either missing or killed in action before the war's end. One such hapless conscript was the bespectacled Marius Meyer, drafted into the German Army on 16 April 1943, less than three years after being discharged from the French Army following the 1940 surrender. Aware that the families of draft dodgers risked deportation, Meyer left his wife and daughter and reported for duty. Sent east to Küstrin in Germany (now Kostrzyn nad Odrą in western Poland), he 'manufactured' an injury to try and get excused from service, but the examining doctor refused to help and sent him off to his unit regardless, as he described in a letter to his grandson:

> I arrived safe and sound. In Strasbourg we had to wait a long time because of an air-raid alert, while outside there was heavy bombing. From what I heard afterwards it resulted in a lot of victims and homeless; and this right in the middle of the day. I am here in treatment, not intensive, lighter duty and I must get some X-rays next Thursday… Today I was summoned by the Court Officer because of a communication from the hospital stating that I was at fault for arriving one day late… It is now up to you to clarify the story for me to avoid a punishment.[9]

The Alsatians weren't universally welcomed into the Wehrmacht, especially in the Waffen-SS where the willing-volunteer principle was still seen by many old hands as sacrosanct. One of *Das Reich's* officers was not a fan: 'It was a terrible mistake to send men from Alsace to fight in the West when they had such strong links with

France; the effects were not only military, there was a rapid increase in crimes committed by men that required severe punishment.' As always in human societies, and military societies are no different, name-calling was common, with Alsatian recruits routinely called '*Franzenköpfe*' – 'French heads', and worse, as one newly-minted *Reich* grenadier – Gustav - soon found out: 'For some reason the Germans thought the Czechs made better soldiers than the Alsatians, and they promoted them first. The Army was the same, you'd meet Army troops who'd say "Oh no, it's the Alsatians! Thank God the Waffen-SS has got them and not us!" They called us *"faule Hunde* – lazy dogs!"' But the Army did get them too, as one of Franz Gockel's comrades in *716. ID* discovered:

> After coming back from a patrol we were turning our weapons back into the armourer. A new man from Alsace handed over a loaded flare pstol. The armourer told him to unload it, but the Alsatian misunderstood and pulled the trigger. The flare shot out, hitting the armourer in the chest. It was a serious wound, but the man survived.[10]

Another Alsatian, Gustav Guschtie's route into SS uniform wasn't exactly the stuff of the propaganda posters. 'I'm from Mulhouse in France... It was the main city in the Alsace region, which was French at the time; the Germans came in 1940 but it didn't matter much because this type of thing happened every so often in the region – one day we were German, the next we were French.' Gustav's *laissez-faire* attitude to the German presence ended when he discovered his wife sleeping with a German officer. He confronted him and beat him up pretty badly. Arrested, he was tried, found guilty and sent to prison in January 1943. Sitting in his cell, the door opened to admit a Waffen-SS officer who was visiting the jail on an inspection tour. 'He looked at me and smiled, I was 180cm tall, blond-haired, blue eyes and pretty muscular, he said to me "do you want to get out of here?" the next thing I knew I was in Czechoslovakia being trained.'[11] Gustav's story didn't end well. Badly wounded in Russia, he managed to survive the war and return home, only to discover his son had died from a lung infection whilst he was away, and that his unfaithful wife had disappeared – he never saw her again.

As for the teenaged Elimar Schneider, he was no fervent 'Siegfried' either. Volunteering for the Waffen-SS wasn't even his idea, it was his mother's. She was a devotee of the *Führer*, who had had Elimar's father sent to a Nazi internment camp by denouncing him as an Alsatian autonomist. Elimar's elder brother had been convicted of black-marketeering but had avoided prison by volunteering for the armed SS, while another brother – possibly in an attempt to balance the scales – became a *résistant*. As for young Elimar, his mother badgered him to follow his elder brother into service, and at the tender age of seventeen he duly did, arriving in Bordeaux in February 1944 for training as a member of *Das Reich*'s reconnaisance battalion. Still naïve about military life, he complained of toothache and was sent to the unit dentist. He then appeared on parade minus one of his front teeth, to the evident mirth of his veteran SS NCO instructor. Within a few weeks of joining the division, this young man, caught between two countries at war, his family split between them, found himself standing with the rest of his company in front of their senior NCO – *SS-Hauptscharführer* Kurz – after returning from a nightime sweep against the local *maquis*, listening intently to his words of advice:

> Boys, if the *Amis* land one day they won't be throwing potatoes, and I'm going to need all of you. That's why I keep emphasising to you that I don't need dead heroes but live ones. Remember everything I've taught you in training. A fraction of a second's carelessness at the front and it'll do for you. Again, I urge you – trust me. If you do what I do, you've got a chance of coming out of it. Always obey my hand and my eye, and you'll thank yourselves later. I'll guarantee to do everything I can to keep your skins in one piece. Can I count on you?
> *JAWOHL HAUPTSCHARFÜHRER! SIEG HEIL! SIEG HEIL! SIEG HEIL!*

This was what the Waffen-SS was able to achieve with so many of its members. It didn't make them instant heroes though. A short while later – on the journey north to Normandy – Schneider and his comrades came under fire from local *résistants*, and cowered behind their half-track, only for Kurz to appear and physically shove them out of cover to return fire; 'We won't win the war with soldiers who hide behind their vehicle at the first shot!'[12]

With the failure of Perch, the Anglo-Canadians began preparations for the next offensive that they hoped would liberate Caen. In the meantime, the front settled down somewhat, although for the Germans there seemed precious little respite, as von Luck testified as he launched another counter-attack: 'We moved shortly before dawn after heavy and concentrated fire by our rocket-launchers. We took our opponents – elements of a Canadian division – by surprise, and they gave up the village at once.'

Alfred Becker was pleased with what he saw of the initial fighting: 'From advanced positions the commander of the battery was able to direct the action of every gun from his scout vehicle by means of wireless transmission. The fire effect was very high grade, mainly because wireless sets of the latest design were available. These sets enabled us to escape enemy targeting by using very low frequency and relaying through many tanks.' This good fortune didn't last long however, as von Luck recounts:

> Then began the heaviest naval bombardment we had experienced so far. We could see the firing of the battleships, cruisers and destroyers. The shells, of all calibres up to 38cm, came whistling over like heavy trucks, to burst and rip vast craters in our lines. British *jabos* swooped down on us unhindered; a veritable inferno broke over our heads… The Canadians came back and after hand-to-hand fighting with heavy losses on both sides, forced us to give up the village again.

The dispatch rider, *Gefreiter* Hammel, was tired: 'The barrage of fire was the worst we had suffered so far. When we pulled back to the village of Cuverville … another heavy barrage of fire rained down on that village too. Was there absolutely nowhere left where a man could get a breather and some sleep?'[13]

Von Luck noted that the British and Canadians were laying minefields, which led him to believe that – for now at least – they weren't going to attack again. Over to the west of Caen, the *HJ* suffered a bodyblow when their divisional commander Fritz Witt was killed in a British naval bombardment of his temporary HQ at Venoix. Just as with von Schweppenburg, Allied signals intelligence and target location proved the panzer man's undoing. When the first shells landed Witt and his staff ran from the house to take cover in the slit trenches dug in the back garden for that very purpose, but the 36-year-old was too slow, and a lump of shrapnel sliced through his face, killing him instantly. Witt's brother had been killed in Greece with the *Leibstandarte* back in 1941.

Into his jackboots stepped Kurt Meyer – becoming officially the youngest divisional commander in the Wehrmacht – and as Rudi von Ribbentrop said, 'Kurt Meyer – *Panzermeyer* – as everyone knew him, was without doubt one of the most outstandingly talented commanders I ever served with or under, only Jochen Peiper was better in my opinion, and even then not by much.' He would need to be if the *HJ* was to survive.

In the days following Perch, von Rundstedt and Rommel met Adolf Hitler at *Wolfsschlucht II* (Wolf's Ravine II – one of the twenty headquarters around Europe Hitler had built) near the tiny hamlet of Neuville-sur-Margival in France's Aisne *département*. Still three hundred miles from the front, Hitler showed no interest whatsoever in either seeing the fighting for himself, or the men who were doing that fighting. Instead, he contented himself with haranguing his generals with his usual mix of pseudo-history and anticipation of victory. But in a rare display of unity and resolve, OB West and the commander *Heeresgruppe B*, refused to be brow-beaten and tried to explain to their *Führer* the reality of what was happening on the ground;

> The troops, *SS* and Army alike, are fighting with the utmost courage, but the balance of strength tips more heavily against us every day… Movements by day are stopped by the enemy, he bombs whatever and wherever he likes… In some cases we cannot speak of divisions, only of *kampfgruppen*.[14]

Von Rundstedt then outlined a radical alternative to the Germans' slow death in Normandy:

1. The *Westheer* to conduct a timely withdrawal from Normandy to a prepared defensive line on the Somme river,

2. France south of the Loire and Rhône rivers to be abandoned and 1. and *19. Armee*'s sent north to the new line, and

3. Von Salmuth's *15. Armee* to leave its positions in the Pas de Calais and move immediately to join *7. Armee* and cover its withdrawal back to the Somme.

If Hitler accepted the plan then von Rundstedt said he *might* – just might – be able to contain the Allies, hold them in northern France, and foil an advance that would take the Anglo-Americans to the very borders of Germany itself. Rommel forestalled his leader's inevitable question by saying that such a course of action would then give Hitler the opportunity to conclude a 'political settlement' – code for a negotiated peace – with the Allies.

This was the moment. Having been unable to stop the landings and throw the Allies back into the sea, two of the most respected officers in the Wehrmacht had appraised their leader of the military situation and recommended an approach that could, possibly, avoid disaster for the Westheer. Both *generalfeldmarschalle* stood silently on the bare concrete of the underground conference room, hands clasped tightly behind their backs, their eyes boring into their leader as he sat on a stool in the middle of the floor. There were no other chairs, no tables, no map-boards.

For what seemed an age the Nazi dictator didn't say a word, then with a shake of his head and hand he dismissed it. Giving up half of France was 'politically impossible'. In any case now that Germany's much-heralded wonder weapons had arrived (the very first V1 flying bomb had hit London three days earlier) the tide would surely turn. He insisted that all the Westheer had to do was hold on a little while longer, and to help them do that reinforcements were on the way – most importantly the *II. SS-Panzerkorps* and its component *9.* and *10. SS-Panzer-Divisions*.

The meeting broke up. Von Rundstedt returned to his Paris headquarters gloomier than ever, whereas, astonishingly, Rommel was suddenly a picture of optimism, writing to his wife: 'I'm looking forward to the future with much less anxiety than a week ago.' But then the Desert Fox always seemed to see-saw in his moods, and could not see through Hitler's façade to the abyss he was plunging Germany into.

Back in Normandy, on the day of this momentous conference, the Allies made another attempt to capture Tilly-sur-Seulles. Discovering a stretch of the line that was held by a single company of the *HJ*, a huge artillery barrage was laid down, with no fewer than three thousand shells fired prior to the ground attack going on. Four days into his new role as divisional commander, Kurt Meyer went forward to see for himself what was happening; 'The trees are uprooted and flung into the defenders' lines, and waves of tanks follow the barrage, they fire round after round into the wood.' Faced with overwhelming odds, his young grenadiers fell back but somehow didn't break. 'The division's front is stable, but losses have reached critical proportions, wounded lie behind an earthen wall waiting for transport. Dead comrades are buried in the orchard. Thick ground mist cloaks the destruction.' Tilly finally fell two days later.

Hitler may have been unwilling to grasp the nettle in Normandy, but at least he was as good as his word on the SS panzers. Straight – although not fresh – from Russia, came the *9. SS-Panzer-Division 'Hohenstaufen'* and its ever-present stablemate *10. SS-Panzer-Division*

'*Frundsberg*'. Both raised in 1943, their cadres consisted of veterans drawn from the existing Waffen-SS field formations, but the volunteers needed to fill the ranks weren't forthcoming, so, in a move that shocked many of the old diehards, conscription was used to flesh out the regiments; no fewer than 14,000 of the first tranche of 27,000 men. These weren't just any conscripts either, they were 17- and 18-year-old ethnic Germans – *volksdeutsche* – from the ancient German expatriate communities in the Balkans and southeast Europe; Transylvanian Saxons, Bessarabian Germans, Banat Swabians, and a dozen other groupings from centuries-old German settlements. These young men were in SS uniform, arriving in France and meeting their new enemy for the first time. Two of them were the *Frundsberg*'s Egon Schulze, and the *Hohenstaufen*'s Ewald Krassmann.

> As soon as the invasion of Normandy began, my division was transferred from Russia to Normandy... We went straight into battle against British units... As I had learned a little English in secondary school, I was ordered to establish a prisoner collection centre with a couple of comrades in a village immediately behind the front, near Hill 188, which was being fought over... When we had sorted things out the prisoners were brought in. They were young guys like us, very confused, but glad that for them the war was over... The British stayed with us for two or three days and then they were transferred further to the rear, to be replaced by fresh prisoners... I always took a couple of prisoners with me when I was searching for food during the quiet spells... There were still cows running around in the meadows surrounding the village, though they had all been injured by artillery shells. We slaughtered one. One of the prisoners was a cook and he prepared a wonderful roast for us all. As we sat down to eat, enemy artillery opened up and our house took a direct hit, which badly wounded the cook. Fortunately, transport arrived that evening to take the prsioners away and he got medical treatment.

This, perhaps, was not what Allied soldiers expected from the feared SS, as noted by Ewald Krassmann:

> The fighting was very severe, with many losses on both sides. Once, for a period of two days, we had a captured Canadian pilot with us in the radio wagon. We treated him as one of us, sharing the same rations, comforts and dangers. As he could speak some German, we got on with him quite well. Eventually we were able to hand him

over to a prisoner-of-war collection centre. Just before he left us, he turned to us and said he was glad not to have been taken prisoner by the SS! Whereupon we showed him the SS runes on our collars. His face went bright red and then very pale. He had been amongst his most-feared adversaries and not realised it.[15]

The new divisions were meant to be used in a planned German offensive to drive north and retake Bayeux, splitting the Anglo-Canadians in the east from the Americans in the west. However, this move was scuppered by the launch of the next British attempt on Caen; Operation Epsom. Launched on 26 June, the intention was to carry out a *blitzkrieg*-style attack west of the city and outflank the defenders. It turned out to be a costly slog with over four thousand Allied casualties, and only slightly fewer German, as the newly arrived SS units joined with the *HJ* and clashed head-on with the advancing British near Grainville-sur-Odon. A panzer loader in one of the *Hohenstaufen*'s Panthers remembered the fighting:

Under SS-*Hauptscharführer* Holte, my platoon of *II Bataillon, 9. SS-Panzer-Regiment*, drove into an attack in the area of Grainville, and fought with British tanks that were all around us. In the course of the fighting our Panther took a direct hit on the hull machine-gun ball mount. The phosphorous shell penetrated the armour and our panzer was immediately in flames. Holte yelled, 'Bail out!' He, the gunner and myself, made it out of the turret, but the radio-operator, Gödtke, and the driver, Appel, were badly wounded and couldn't get out. From the outside we tried to open their hatches, but to no avail. The heat was unbearable, and then the ammunition inside the panzer exploded. We ran back thirty metres, threw ourselves into a shell crater and had to watch as our panzer burned out. It was a coffin for Appel and Gödtke, and we could do nothing to help them.[16]

An *HJ* mortarman, Wilhelm Fecht, was in the thick of it all; 'Our mortar battery had thirty-six tubes, and with these we always gave the enemy a thorough hammering. After every second salvo we had to change our position so that the enemy couldn't pinpoint our position... Sometimes the enemy artillery could pinpoint our position to within a couple of metres if you used your radio.'[17]

After four bloody days the offensive was called off, and both sides took another breath. The German defenders had once again stubbornly resisted, only giving up ground when forced to do so, and then constantly counter-attacking, only to be met by heavy naval and artillery fire that rained down high-explosive and shrapnel on their heads, causing horrendous casualties. Poor weather prevented the British from using as much air power as they wished, but even so, for the *Frundsberg* staff officer, Ewald Klapdor, it was a rude shock:

> The air action is just unbelievable. Above all, it's very one-sided. Formations of silvery four-engined bombers form a continuous stream, an image of untamed might... What a change in conditions from the Eastern front! Here the scene is different, there is effectively no German aerial support any more. In the invasion area there's only one air-force – that of the western Allies.

A week passed, during which the British and Canadians made preparations for another new offensive – their third in four weeks. This one was christened Operation Charnwood, and was designed as a straight-up frontal assault on Caen itself from the Anglo-Canadian lines directly north of the city. Infantry and tanks would advance behind a creeping artillery barrage, and overhead would be clouds of aircraft ready to strike anything foolish enough to move – so far so usual. The big difference this time would be that the city itself was going to be heavily bombed right at the start. It was hoped this would knock out the defenders.

The new offensive chimed with a changing of the guard amongst the senior German command. First to go was von Rundstedt as OB West. Infuriated at OKW countermanding one of his orders, he phoned *Lakeitel* and left him in no doubt as to his fury at what he rightly saw as muddle-headed interference by men hundreds of miles from the fighting trying to micro-manage the battle. Legend has it that when Keitel bleated; 'What shall we do? What shall we do?' von Rundstedt replied; *'Macht Schluss mit dem Krieg, ihr Idioten!* 'End the war, you idiots!' Although according to Rundstedt's chief-of-staff, Günther Blumentritt, who claimed he was present during the famous exchange, his boss omitted *'ihr Idioten'*. A shocked Keitel scampered off and reported what von Rundstedt had said. Hitler relieved him of command on the spot, and appointed Hans Günther von Kluge in his stead – it would change precious little at the front, and as for the old Prussian warhorse, the war wasn't finished with him quite yet.

Von Schweppenburg followed his superior out the door, sacked by Hitler who was obviously in one of his 'clear-out' moods. *General der Panzertruppe* Heinrich Eberbach was his replacement. Badly wounded in Russia, Eberbach was hugely experienced, highly decorated and destined to fail as gravely as his predecessor. In the skies above Caen the Allied heavy-bomber raid went ahead with the *Frundsberg*'s Ewald Klapdor watching:

> The city is nothing more than a mushroom cloud rising into the sky. The most important city in Normandy after Rouen; Caen, city of William the Conqueror, is destroyed. He left there in 1066 to conquer England. Today English bombers wiped out his city.

For the *21. Panzer*'s Edmund Brinke – caught underneath the bombs – there was no musing on history: 'One moment I had one foot on the armoured car to scramble up inside, the next I was lying in a pool of blood and debris against the wall of the nearest building. When I struggled up I saw the terrible sights of bodies among the wreckage, the remains of our vehicles, and half a German body over one of them... Only one of my comrades survived with me.'

The burden of the subsequent fighting fell on the *HJ*, who were remorselessly driven back by their attackers and forced to abandon their headquarters at the *L'Abbaye d'Ardenne*, as vividly recounted by panzergrenadier Erhard Kinscher:

> During the late afternoon of 8 July I received an order to take an MG 42 and, together with *SS-Sturmmann* Hampel and a runner from 13. Kompanie, to cover the withdrawal of the regiment. I hung a belt of three hundred rounds around my neck, and fitted another belt of one hundred rounds into the breech... To get a good field of fire for the MG 42 I went through the northwest door of the Abbey, which was already coming under enemy artillery fire. In front of me I could see a low wall, beyond it was a meadow surrounded by a hedge... I wanted to check what was behind the hedge, so I crossed the wall and set off across the meadow. Halfway across I came under heavy fire and I heard Hampel shout; 'Erhard, come back, come back!' I fired off the whole belt of ammunition towards the hedge and sprinted back, zig-zagging, and leapt over the wall and out of sight of the enemy... What we saw took our breath away, there were so many enemy tanks and infantry... The smoke of battle cleared and we could see that the enemy had taken Ardenne... Then, as *SS-Untersturmführer* Kneip

looked though a hole in the wall in the direction of Cussy, a burst of fire from a submachine-gun took him in the chest. Through this small gap in the wall he had been hit by seven bullets! My comrade Hampel dragged him back under cover. To try and see where the shots had come from, I carefully went through the door and towards the wall. As I did so an enemy soldier appeared. I stood there with my MG 42 levelled directly at his stomach but he passed by without seeing me. After a long wait, Hampel and I made our way around the wall and back to where Kneip lay. He gave each of us his hand, and then quietly died. We lay there for some time, but little or nothing stirred. Whenever I saw any suspicious movements I let off a burst of fire and it soon stopped. In the first light of dawn ... we withdrew... For my part in covering the withdrawal from the Ardenne Abbey I was awarded the Iron Cross Second Class.'[18]

Charnwood was an attritional battle, and while not exactly a stunning success it did eject the *HJ* from the city. What had been intended as a swift advance to liberate the city on D-Day, seize the neighbouring airfield at Carpiquet and turn Caen's road network into the launch pad for a break-out into open country and a march to Paris, had become a meat-grinder for men and machines. Given what they were up against, many Germans – of whom Rudi von Ribbentrop was one – were surprised that they held out so long;

After the Allies quickly succeeded in forming strong bridgeheads from which they could fully exploit their material superiority – we were involved in desperate defensive battles. I myself, with my company, was assigned to try and hold back British and Canadian armoured forces on the outskirts of Caen. We had no Luftwaffe or artillery support, and it was only ever going to be a matter of time before we were defeated and pushed back by the enemy. We had no choice but to abandon Caen despite the bravery of our men, and our casualties were huge.[19]

The gunner, Heinz Trautmann, saw at first hand what the defenders had been reduced to: 'Every day our reserves grow less. Boys of seventeen are in the line, and grey old men, grandfathers. The *Heimat* is sucked dry, there is nothing more to give.'

Back in the UK, frustration at the lack of success was building among the senior political and military leadership, and the public. Montgomery – acutely aware of the latter, and under threat from the former – decided on yet another offensive, *Goodwood,* which would be co-ordinated with a simultaneous assault by the Canadians – *Atlantic.* Nothing would be left to chance, and *Goodwood* would be the sort of set-piece attack the field-marshal was comfortable with and had previously conducted well. But *Goodwood* was no *Supercharge.* When Montgomery launched the latter at El Alamein it not only pierced the Italo-German line, it shattered their mobile forces and sent them reeling back in headlong flight – what Montgomery would have given for that result in Normandy. As it was, after the offensive ended, Monty sought to downplay what he'd hoped to achieve with it, but there seems little doubt that he intended it to be Normandy's El Alamein.

One man who would play no part in the upcoming story was *Generalleutnant* Wilhelm Richter. The commander of *716. ID* was worn out, as was his unit. Shattered on D-Day, survivors and stragglers had trickled back in over the following days as the division had stayed in the line alongside *21. Panzer* and fought to hold the Anglo-Canadians. Ten days after the landings began, more than half the division had been wiped off the roll. Even its *Ostbataillone* were gone; the Cossacks of *441.* hadn't given up after their battles on the 6th, fighting with tenacity and determination and giving the lie to the oft-repeated view that all the *Osttruppen* let their German comrades-in-arms down – by 22 June only two hundred men were left in the battalion. A few days later, it was officially declared destroyed and was disbanded. Some of the few steppe riders who survived found themselves amongst the twenty thousand *Osttruppen* and *Hiwis* in Allied POW cages at the time. As for *441's* sister battalion, the *439,* it continued to serve with Kraiss's *352. ID,* and was credited with 'fighting hard' in official reports of the time, especially during the battle for Carentan. It would escape Normandy only to be wiped out in the fighting in the Colmar Pocket eight months later.

By the beginning of July, Richter reported to *7. Armee,* 'My division had been defeated and badly beaten up in Normandy.' Removed from frontline duty on the 10th, it was redeployed to southern France to rest and refit and took up coastal security positions around Salses-Perpignan-Elne, close to the Spanish border. Richter went with it, but not for long. In September he was posted to occupied Norway to take command of a Luftwaffe ground unit, and there he sat out the rest of the war without hearing another shot fired in anger.

Much criticism has been laid at the door of the *716. ID* and the other static divisions in the wake of the D-Day landings, but their failure to repulse the assaults should be balanced with what they achieved; on Juno for example, the men of *716. ID* inflicted almost a thousand casualties on the Canadian 3rd Infantry Division. With over twenty-one thousand men in total coming ashore on day one this would seem pretty small beer, except when you appreciate that the vast majority of the overall losses occurred in the first hour, with the first and second waves suffering a casualty rate of almost one man in two.[20] Short of men, with next to no air or naval cover, no armour or transport, and supported by a hotch-potch of obsolete mainly booty artillery, the belly army had done all that could be reasonably expected of it.

Another actor who had done all that could be expected of him, and a lot more besides, was *Oberst* Ernst Goth of *Grenadier-Regiment 916*. A tough professional who had led his men in an exemplary fashion and won Honour Roll status for his personal bravery, Goth was mentally and physically burnt-out. At times he had had elements of twenty different units under his command, as stragglers and reinforcements were scooped up and pushed into the line to try and hold the enemy – it had never been enough, and he and his regiment had been remorselessly driven back. On 14 July – the same day Herbert Werner's *U415* was sunk in Brest harbour – he collapsed from exhaustion in his command post and was evacuated to a field hospital. *Oberstleutnant* von und zu Aufseß of *Schnelle-Brigade 30*, took over command.

Ernst Goth's loss was a blow for the defenders, but his departure from the battle wasn't felt as widely as that of the man who exited just three days later – Erwin Rommel. The commander of *Heeresgruppe B* had breakfasted on fried eggs and brandy with Sepp Dietrich at his *I. SS-Panzerkorps* headquarters at St-Pierre-sur-Dives. Heading back in his staff car, he was on the main road, three miles north of Vimoutiers, when two Canadian Spitfires spotted him and attacked. Rommel's driver, *Oberfeldwebel* Daniel, took evasive action but a 20mm cannon shell shattered his left arm and shoulder, killing him instantly and causing the car to swerve into a tree stump and flip over into a ditch. Rommel was flung onto the road and suffered three skull fractures, a shattered cheekbone, a damaged left eye and a mass of facial and scalp lacerations that bled profusely. His injuries were so bad he wasn't expected to live. That was the end of the Desert Fox's role in the battle for France. Von Kluge – already OB West – also now assumed command of the army group.

Four days later, *Goodwood* was launched, alongside the Canadian *Atlantic* operation. As was now the norm, it was preceded by a massive artillery barrage – this time from no fewer than seven hundred and twenty guns – and accompanied by the naval bombardment that the German defenders had especially come to fear and loathe; in this case from two cruisers; *Enterprise* and *Mauritius*, and the 15-inch guns of HMS *Roberts*, a Royal Navy monitor capable of throwing a shell weighing 1,938 pounds out to a distance of over thirty kilometres.[21] What made the softening-up process different this time was that Montgomery had managed to sweet-talk the Americans – and strong-arm Arthur Harris – into diverting medium and heavy bombers into a direct support operation; two thousand and seventy-seven of them to be exact. The morning of the 18th was clear and bright, without a breath of wind – it was set to be a beautiful, warm day in Normandy. But not for the Germans of the 16. *Luftwaffen-Feld-Division* or *21. Panzer*. One of the latter's crewmen described the scene:

> The men got into the panzers and closed the hatches, or crawled underneath for protection. We saw little dots detach themselves from the planes [there were 1,056 Lancasters and Halifaxes in the first wave alone], so many of them that we thought they were leaflets, we could hardly believe they could all be bombs. Then began the most terrifying hours of our lives. It was a bomb carpet, regularly ploughing up the ground. Among the thunder of the explosions we could hear the wounded scream and the insane howling of men who had been driven mad.[22]

As the last bombs fell, the artillery started up. Twenty minutes later a second wave of bombers – this time American B-26 Marauders – flew over and released almost six hundred tons of explosives to add to the 4,900 already dropped. A third and final wave of American aircraft added yet more; 1,360 tons. Cowering underneath it all, Werner Kortenhaus reported seeing the remaining panzers of his company literally bounced into the air by the blasts, their gun sights and optics wrecked, engines befouled, air filters and exhausts blocked with dirt. The crews had to resort to digging them out from under mounds of earth by hand. Even then, only nine of *Panzer-Regiment 22*'s Mark

IVs were in any fit state to resist the ensuing British onslaught. It was far worse for the infantry of course, as the *landsers* didn't have the benefit of armour-plate to protect them. One of *I. Bataillon Panzer-Grenadier-Regiment 125's* company commanders – *Leutnant* Gerhard Bandomir – said, 'The initiative of each of us withered. We just sat and waited to die, unable to do anything. It was a hot and sunny day in Normandy. However for all of us it was a most dismal and depressing day, we were powerless to do anything.'

Advancing British infantry picked up dazed survivors from the *16. Luftwaffe*, but had to leave them sitting down by the roadside for a while before they were physically able to stand up and walk back in a straight line to the POW cages. To the Tommies it finally looked like they had the Germans beaten. A swift advance out of the Orne valley and up onto the tactically vital high ground of the Bourguébus ridge seemed imminent, and then all manner of possibilities would be opened up – a push down the *Nationale 13* to Lisieux, or perhaps even a bold dash south on the *158* to Falaise? Constant German defensive improvisation seemed to have run its course. At the headquarters of *Panzer-Grenadier-Regiment 125,* Hans von Luck was just returning from a three-day furlough in Paris with his fiancée Dagmar.

> Shortly after nine I arrived at my command post and was looking forward to a Normandy breakfast... The commander of *I. Bataillon* greeted me briefly... I sensed that something wasn't right... Then came the report that almost took my breath away – 'Since five o'clock this morning the British have been bombing our sector ... the firing stopped barely half an hour ago.'

Von Luck immediately asked for reports from his sub-units; 'How are things with your *I. Bataillon,* any news?'

'Not yet, we've no radio contact.'

'How about the Tigers and our own panzer battalion?'

'No radio contact.'

'And *II. Bataillon*? Major Becker's assault guns? Has division been told?'

It was obvious to von Luck that his deputy had lost control – he relieved him and sacked him a few days later. Almost five years of combat experience kicked in; von Luck issued orders to inform division of the situation, ask for reinforcements, and he then jumped aboard a command panzer and headed down the main road towards Caen. He reached the village of Cagny astride the *Nationale 13* and saw with horror that a large force of British tanks were already south of it. Where his *I. Bataillon* was meant to be was a field of bomb craters with enemy tanks crawling forward. '"My God," I thought, "the bombing and artillery barrage has destroyed the battalion."' His next thought was for the Tigers, where were they? Aware of the village's tactical importance, the Germans had garrisoned it with one of their deadliest sub-units; *3. Kompanie* of Rolf Fromme's *schwere Panzerabteilung 503*. The company commander was a twenty-one year-old Baltic German aristocrat and panzer ace; *Leutnant* Richard Wilfred Harry Erich *Freiherr* von Rosen.[23] When the bombers came over, von Rosen had taken cover under his Tiger;

> It was Hell and I am still astonished that I ever survived it. I was unconscious for a while after a bomb had exploded just in front of my panzer, almost burying me alive... The bombardment of 18 July was the worst we had ever experienced in the war. Although we were in foxholes under our panzers we took a lot of casualties ... some of the fifty-seven-ton machines lay upside down in bomb craters thirty feet across. They had been spun through the air like playing cards. Two of my men committed suicide; they weren't up to the psychological effect. Of my Tigers, only one was operational. All of them had been covered in dirt and earth, the guns disadjusted, the engine cooling systems were out of action.

Another of von Rosen's men was 'driven insane from the effects of the bombs'. With their ears still ringing the survivors began to take stock. Incredibly, only fifteen of von Rosen's one hundred men were dead, but their behemoths weren't so lucky; all were damaged, three looked like write-offs, and one was lying on its turret. Von Luck knew none of this – all he did know was that British armour was advancing unhindered and had to be stopped in any way possible. Leaving Cagny to return to his headquarters, he saw near the church a battery of four German 8.8cm anti-aircraft guns with their barrels pointing at the sky.

What happened next has become as much part of the legend of the Normandy campaign as Wittmann's action at Villers-Bocage or Hein Severloh's on Omaha, and although it has been questioned by some historians – as they all have – there seems little doubt as to the thrust of the story, even if some of the details may perhaps have been exaggerated over time. The next lines are from von Luck's own memoir:

> What are the guns doing here? I didn't see them on the way here. Under a tree I called a halt, bailed out, and ran to the battery. A young Luftwaffe *hauptmann* came up to me; '*Herr Major*, can you tell me what's going on?'
>
> 'My God, what are you doing here? Have you any idea what's happening over there to the left of you?'
>
> 'I belong to an air-defence ring to protect the factories and city of Caen against air raids. At the moment I'm waiting for the next air attack.'
>
> 'Man', I replied as calmly as I could, 'you've already been bypassed by enemy armour. North of here it's absolutely swarming with tanks. Move your four guns into position on the northern edge of Cagny at once and engage them. Don't worry about the ones that are already going south, hit the enemy from the flank, and you'll force the advance to halt.'
>
> His reply came just as calmly; '*Herr Major*, my concern is enemy aircraft, fighting tanks is your job. I'm Luftwaffe.' He was about to turn away… I went up to him, drew my pistol, levelled it at him and said; 'Either you're a dead man, or you can earn yourself a medal.'

Unsurprisingly, the Luftwaffe *hauptmann* opted for the latter. Von Luck showed him where he wanted him to go and gave him his orders.

> 'Here, place your guns in this apple orchard. The corn over there is so high that you will be well protected and still have a field of fire over it. Shoot every tank you see. I'll see if I can send you a platoon of grenadiers to guard against surprise attack. Should the situation become critical, destroy your guns and withdraw to the south. I hope our Tigers will soon be able to mount a counter-attack from the right. With them we should be able to beat the enemy attack back, especially as it's not accompanied by infantry as far as I can tell. Understood?'

Von Luck then drove back to his command post, where Alfred Becker was waiting for him. 'One of my batteries has been completely knocked out by bombs, two batteries on the left flank are intact and will support the grenadiers of *I. Bataillon* who have gone into action against the British infantry. The other two batteries will be going into action at any minute on the right flank, where Major Kurz, without first waiting for orders, has set up a defensive front with his *II. Bataillon*.'

Helmut Liebeskind then returned from division, and von Luck heard from his adjutant that he would soon receive *Hauptmann* Brandt's reconnaissance battalion as reinforcements, and that elements of the *HJ* and *LSSAH* were on their way too. Manfred Thorn, a panzer crewman with the latter, approached the battle:

> I found myself on the way to Tilly-la-Campagne, in one of the twenty-five panzers that had left Bully-sur-L'Orne in the early hours of the morning. I was driving panzer number 734, and at nineteen years of age was considered one of the 'old men' of the unit. We moved into a totally evacuated village with no idea of what was to come. All the houses were intact, and the area was surrounded by lush green fields and meadows. Our platoon came to a halt in an orchard on the east side of the village, with our panzers facing northeast towards Bourguébus. I picked a spot for our panzer near to a house and camouflaged it well. The sounds of battle were still some way off, but every now and then a stray shell would come whistling into the village and make us run for cover.[24]

The SS were still some way off on the morning of the offensive, so it was down to von Luck's press-ganged 88s to do the heavy lifting. That would start with the Scots of the Fife and Forfar Yeomanry, as their regimental history relates: 'The first tank to be hit was Major Nicholl's. A moment later, Captain Miller's was destroyed...The land laid waste by the bombers seemed like a piece of devastated territory which could scarcely conceal a living thing...Yet suddenly there came evidence that the enemy was there and very aggressive too.' Twelve tanks were lost in the first few salvoes. The 23rd Hussars, following the Scots, came to a juddering halt as smoke-blackened and wounded crewmen came running back from the cornfields. Meanwhile, Werner Kortenhaus and the nine surviving Mark IVs of *Panzer-Regiment 22.* tried to counter-attack into the oncoming Hussars, but outnumbered from the start, eight of their number were soon burning.

Von Luck, going forward – again – saw for himself the impact of his hasty defence:

> The 8.8cm cannons were firing one salvo after another. One could see the shots flying through the corn like torpedoes. The men on the guns were proud of their first engagement as a *panzerjäger* unit. All four guns were intact and had not been attacked. In the extensive cornfields to the north of the village stood at least forty British tanks, on fire or shot-up. I saw how the tanks that had already crossed the main road were slowly rolling back. Becker's assault-guns had also joined the battle. From the right flank they shot-up any tank that tried to bypass the village.

The tanks Becker's guns were hitting were from 3rd Royal Tank Regiment (3 RTR), which had been tasked with bypassing all resistance and taking the ridge – come what may. Bill Close, a major at the time in 3 RTR, later told von Luck what it was like from his side: 'Suddenly, when we had got to about a thousand metres from the villages on the ridge, we came under concentrated fire from eighty-eights. Within seconds about fifteen of our tanks were stationary and on fire. All attempts to turn aside to left or right failed. By late afternoon I only had a few tanks left.'

Back with von Rosen's Tigers, it had been a race against time. The crews knew that once the bombardment was over the attack would be coming their way; orders were given, repairs were made, and somehow, six of the heavies were made battleworthy. It would be the British Guards armour who would face von Rosen's men now – the most successful Tiger-equipped panzer battalion of the war, with a kill ratio of one to 6.75 in their favour. Bill Close saw their impact in the battle:

> We'd warned the Guards Armoured Division coming after us about Cagny. In spite of that, they pushed on and within seconds lost about twenty tanks there. We could see how the leading regiment tried to avoid the fire from Cagny, but in so doing several tanks were knocked out, this time from woodland in the east. The attack came to a standstill. We were so glad ... to escape the fire of your damned eighty-eights.

The Guards tanks joined the seventeen hundred in total that were destroyed by the 503rd in its short existence. Goodwood continued until 20 July, but for all intents and purposes it died that day at Cagny and on the slopes of the Bourguébus ridge.

The repercussions for both sides were profound. It seemed at first that it was the British who came off worse; suffering more than four thousand casualties and losing upwards of four hundred tanks for a few square miles of relatively unimportant real estate. Montgomery, the operation's author and overall commander – already under pressure from his critics – had suffered a major self-inflicted wound. He had pre-emptively announced to the media that the offensive was 'winning everywhere', when it patently wasn't, and that was all his enemies needed to skewer him. With precious few friends to come to his defence; his vinegary personality, lack of charm and brittle over-confidence saw to that – he lost crucial support from Eisenhower, and even Churchill, and with it, control of the campaign. But what Goodwood showed – more than the frayed edges of one man's ego – was the true state of the British in France by late July. After seven weeks of constant fighting against a determined and skilful enemy, the army it had taken Britain two or more years to build was showing visible signs of wear and tear, as von Luck recognised:

> Monty took the field with all three tank divisions, supported by infantry and artillery. While the Guards Division operated very cautiously for lack of experience, we discovered to our surprise that the 7th Armoured Division was doing the same... It was 'over-experienced' and for that reason operated with extreme caution.

The veteran panzer officer had not only witnessed the result, but had, partly, diagnosed the cause. At its heart was a complex set of often overlapping factors proving that while all armies may be created equal, they are not all the same, and some of the differences between the British and German armies – and to an extent the Americans as well – were fundamental as to why the Westheer held out in Normandy for so long. And why it lost France in the end.

As a nation, Great Britain has always had an ambiguous relationship with its army. The soldiery may be drawn from the populace at large, but it seldom reflects it. The only time it truly does act as a mirror to its own people is during times of universal conscription – outside of that it is a self-selecting professional body cut off from the civilian population. Occasionally, one or two 'pick-up truck wars', as Antony Beevor memorably christened so many of the conflicts Britain gets involved in, breaks through the public consciousness, but any upswell of support tends to recede as quickly as it appears – Rudyard Kipling's poem *Tommy* is as relevant today as it was when it was first penned.

The detachment with which the British populace view their army has meant in practice that a military career is not generally seen as one to be pursued; a career in the professions in the UK usually means medicine, the law, or finance, and this is where so many of the best and brightest go – not so in Germany in the early twentieth century. Since its creation as a nation state in 1871, to wear a uniform was to have status; among your family, your friends and society at large. In Great Britain, being an army officer is often viewed with polite bafflement.

As it happens, the United States had much the same issue, and got round it by proclaiming that it had 'the best paid soldiers in the world', in fact, so good was the GI's remuneration – and at an average per rank of three times that of their British or German counterparts it really was that good - that whilst the troops sat in the UK waiting for D-Day arrangements were made to pay the men twice a month rather than just once, so it wouldn't seem to the rationed Brits that their American allies were so much better off. PFC Vernon W. Tart understood the situation: 'Being GIs we were richer than Croesus; there were few restaurants in town but we were advised not to use them but to go to our Quonset hut for meals as food was in short supply in England, but being lazy GIs we'd always go to a restaurant if we were downtown.'[25] Whitehall in contrast has a long and inglorious history of mealy-mouthed penny-pinching when it comes to the services.

As for the high status of the profession of arms in Germany, this didn't arise by chance, but was a deliberate policy instituted by Otto von Bismarck. The Iron Chancellor was striving to bind the multitude of mini-kingdoms, principalities and petty dukedoms together after the Franco-Prussian War, and he understood that common institutions were key to achieving the goal of a properly unified country; that meant in particular the Wilhemine monarchy and the armed forces, specifically the Army. As in the UK, the army was structured on a local basis, with formations raised from a single town or region – this gave those same units a powerful sense of cohesion. The difference was size; in the British Army a local regiment will consist most often of a single battalion of six hundred men, whereas the Germans would recruit a division of twelve thousand from the same locality – an attritional battle such as Normandy quickly debilitated the former, while the latter was better able to absorb casualties and still maintain its effectiveness.

The selection and allocation of recruits also played its part in German frontline superiority in Normandy. The Americans, and to a lesser extent the British, channelled the better educated and higher-grade recruits towards technical services, the Signals, Engineers and so on, and in the case of the Americans the logistics' services especially. In Germany there was little kudos to be found in the technical branches, the best recuits went to the teeth-arms: the infantry, artillery and above all armour – the famed *panzerwaffe*. The exceptions to these rules, on both sides, were the élites. With the Allies this meant in particular their airborne forces; the men of the First Allied Airborne Army were selected and trained to be the very best – but they comprised a mere four divisions - whereas the Germans raised seventeen divisions of paras and specialist mountaineers, and that's before you get to the Waffen-SS and the ten or so of its divisions that could claim premier status. This resulted in the Anglo-Americans best and most aggressive combat soldiers placed in lightly armed parachute units mainly held in reserve for hopefully-decisive operations, whilst the Germans put theirs in units that were up close and personal at the front, and it was at the front that the difference between the four (including the Canadian) armies was at its most exposed.

Life on the frontline, 'in the field'– and in Normandy it was literally in the field – is wearing and debilitating for a human being. Everything is hard; daily tasks that take little effort or time in civilian life become complex and demanding. For the new British Normandy divisions, built from a mix of volunteers and conscripts – with no previous military training – it was extremely tough. Through no fault of their own, the majority of men who filled the ranks found military life extremely difficult to adjust to. There were exceptions of course, but more often than not officers and men viewed their service as something to be endured so they could return home and pick up their lives where they left off. In combination, these circumstances adversely affected performance in combat. Max Hastings, the war reporter and author – and no stranger to roughing it – said of Normandy: 'The living conditions of infantry in the frontline resembled those of Flanders thirty years earlier. British boots and serge battledress were notoriously prone to damp. Sodden canvas web equipment stiffened. Mould and rust became endemic ... Men were always tired, because even when there was no great battle to fight, the simplest everyday tasks – cooking, finding a tolerable place to sleep, wash, defecate – became major challenges on the battlefield.' The battalion war diary of the Canadian Toronto Scottish described it thus: 'Living conditions at the front are not cosy. Water and soil make mud. Mud sticks to everything ... matches and cigarettes are unusable.'

It sounds obvious to say it, but casualties significantly worsened the situation. However, while that is indeed a truism, it would seem from the evidence they had a disproportionate impact on the battle-worthiness of Allied versus German formations in the line. For example, by 6 August 7. *Armee* had suffered a colossal 144,261 casualties of all types, and had only received 19,914 replacements, yet it was still combat-effective despite having a shortfall of well over a hundred thousand men. By contrast, a month earlier the Americans had suffered 37,034 casualties, and the British 24,698, with an infusion of new blood of 79,000[26] – more than making up for losses – and yet it was the British units in particular which were showing signs of fatigue – why? The answer to that conundrum is complex. Partly it was the numbers themselves. The Third Reich had access to more bodies than Britain – it was also the nature of the different societies, with Nazi Germany being a militarised state, not a parliamentary democracy. Another element can be found in the training of both armies, and the penalties each imposed for infractions of discipline. But as good a place to start as any is the distinctly different attitudes to casualties that pertained in the Wehrmacht in comparison with the British Army. Neither side *liked* losses of course, but the Germans tended to view them in terms of the impact those losses had on combat performance, whereas loss of life or limb was very much seen as an evil in itself by the British. That attitude started at the top; Alan Brooke, the professional head of the British Army, was, like pretty much all senior officers at the time, a veteran of the First World War, and specifically the Western Front, and it was that blood-drenched conflict that had seared itself onto the consciousness of Britain and its armed forces. Brooke was known to prefer victory through *matériel*, 'pitiless industry' as it was termed by senior officers, and as Brooke himself called it, 'the results of Passchendaele without its cost in blood' – he even avoided using the word *attrition* if he could. The Germans too had paid the blood-price of the First World War, but had not come away with quite the same view; their lesson learned on minimising losses wasn't based on material superiority, but rather a doctrine that emphasised the primacy of attack and counter-attack, and the importance of individual soldiers and junior commanders using their initiative – much to the surprise of the likes of Lieutenant Roy Dixon of the South Staffs Yeomanry: 'The great story used to be that the Germans wouldn't fight unless there was somebody there to give them orders, we soon realised that this was nonsense.'[27] The stereotype of the German automaton shouting '*Zu Befehl*!' as he and his unthinking comrades marched to death and glory was shown to be the myth it was. Rather, while it was not quite the opposite, an argument could be made for a certain lack of initiative in the British ranks, as a report written back in 1943 by the Army's own Director of Military Training at Fifteenth Army Group in Italy, stated:

> Our tactical methods are thorough and methodical, but slow and cumbersome. In consequence our troops fight well in defence and our set-piece attacks are usually successful, but it is not unfair to say that through lack of enterprise in exploitation, we seldom reap the full benefit of them. We are too flank-concious, we over-insure administratively, we are by nature too apprehensive of failure and our training makes us more so.

The German view was a little more brutal: 'The British soldier is a little slow-witted. The NCO is for the most part very good. Junior officers are full of theoretical knowledge, but in practice are generally clumsy ... not really trained to be independent.'[28]

That last point on junior commanders is key. They are the ones who ultimately implement the battle-plans of senior officers, and of political leaders – they are at the sharp end. German small-unit leadership training emphasised speed of decision-making and a strong preference for action, with detailed planning seen as a luxury. Not so in the British Army. Take the basis of all British operational procedure; the issuing of orders to one's men (and women) about a specific task to be undertaken, be it an ambush, a deliberate attack or whatever. The focus is on the preparation of said orders and the incorporation of a vast array of possible scenarios. Focus is put on the ground; the terrain over which the troops will move and fight, the mission itself, what is it, what does it imply as primary and secondary tasks, and so on – the list of what is involved is lengthy, and a good set of orders will take a commander several hours of uninterrupted time to prepare and then give. As troops gain experience, this timescale is shortened, but it is still significant. In Normandy, where a British junior infantry leader had a 70 per cent probability of being killed or wounded before the war ended, no sooner had they become experienced then they became a casualty, and their replacement had to start all over again from a lower starting point as training time for new officers became shorter and shorter as the casualty lists grew. The results can be read in unit diaries, performance reports and letters galore from the campaign: a lack of cooperation between tanks and infantry, poor small-unit leadership, a paucity of aggression in combat units, over-reliance on artillery and air-power, over-caution in attack.

The fact that the Wehrmacht relied more on the human over the machine, was not just down to a conscious choice either, it was one of necessity – the Germans had bodies, but comparatively little in the way of hardware. There were two main reasons for this; the German population was a mark higher than Britain's, with eighty million souls within the Reich's 1939 borders, and another ten million ethnic Germans who constituted Europe's so-called 'German problem' with 3.5m in Czechoslovakia, 1.2m in Poland, over 800,000 in Romania, three-quarters of a million in Yugoslavia and so on. The second reason was the Nazis' exploitation of POWs and foreign labour, much of the latter forced, including straightforward kidnapping and deportation, particularly from the occupied territories of the Soviet Union. By D-Day this expat workforce numbered over 7.5 million (two million POWs and around 5.5 million civilians) and comprised a fifth of the Reich's labour force, enabling the German government to conscript a far higher proportion of its adult male population into the armed services; 6.5 million into the Army, 1.5 million into the Luftwaffe, 810,000 into the Kriegsmarine, and 600,000 into the Waffen-SS by 1944. Those recruits were then put through a spartan training regime that conditioned them for the privations of the front. Horst, an *HJ* trooper and eighteen-year-old graduate of the NAPOLA Adolf Hitler School system,[29] explained the morning routine for himself and his group of seventy-five new recruits: '6am reveille, two men were selected to go get coffee and the morning ration of bread and jam and bring it back to the barracks...then at lunch we were given bean soup, three boiled potatoes and a piece of bread.'[30] In the US Army in particular this would be viewed as a punishment regime, not basic training.

The recruits would then find themselves not as in the British Army in a 600-man regiment, but in a 10,000-man division – and that is where a German soldier had his home, in his division. This was important, as a division's size meant casualties didn't impact the unit as much as it would in a smaller regiment. This is 'big unit theory', and it has positives as well as negatives. The British system is well suited to the colonial policing role its army fulfilled for so many years, giving regiments the sort of iron-hard cohesion that made last-stands such a speciality of British arms; think Isandlwana, Rorke's Drift and Gundamuk. The German system was that if a soldiers' own unit was destroyed, he could be swiftly incorporated into another and remain combat-worthy – this was the startingly effective *kampfgruppe* system. If, however, a grenadier was unable to deal with the horror around him and tried to escape it through flight, then the Wehrmacht was quite prepared to wield a savage stick, as the *Leibstandarte* veteran, Erwin Bartmann, recalled from when he was an instructor: 'The execution of *fahnenfluchtingen* (deserters) was a weekly routine that took place on Fridays in front of a sandy hillock. To see at close range the atomised blood and guts blast out of the condemned soldier's back as bullets shot through his body must have shocked the recruits.'[31] In the First World War the German Army executed forty-eight men for desertion; during the Second the figure was thirty thousand. Little wonder then perhaps that the BBC's Robin Duff wondered at the discipline of German snipers in Normandy: 'There they sit ... they chain themselves to the tree, so that they won't fall out if they're wounded, and cover themselves with a sort of camouflaged apron, and then wait for men who are alone.' Again, little wonder perhaps, that some Allied servicemen became indifferent to their enemy's suffering, as the British medic, James Byrom, saw at first-hand when he took a badly wounded teenaged German soldier into a field hospital, only to have the attending doctors simply ignore him and his charge. When Byrom made a fuss and insisted they look at the lad, they 'showed not the slightest flicker of interest'.[32] The teenager died as Byrom watched.

It seemed to some that as the British manpower barrel was being scraped – with the consequent impact on military performance in the attritional fighting for Caen – the Germans had pulled another rabbit out of the hat, and proved, once more, the innate toughness of the *landser* and the military system to which he belonged. And yet. The Westheer had lost half the men the Allies had in *Goodwood*, and less than a third of the tanks, but whereas the conveyor belt from the beaches soon replaced British tank losses, barely a man or machine was arriving on the other side of the line to make good the gaps torn in the German lines. Heinrich Eberbach reported on the condition of one of the line divisions: 'The day's losses were very heavy. Of what was 16. *Luftwaffe-Field-Division* there is effectively just the staff and some rear services left.' Those men left in the line were increasingly hungry, their uniforms filthy and patched, their ammunition pouches half-empty, as the *Frundsberg*'s Ewald Klapdor noted: 'Important supplies no longer reach the front. There's no peace, even at night. The roads are lit up from the sky with floodlights and flares. For the first time the enemy has succeeded in paralysing the supplies for the frontline across hundreds of kilometres.'[33] Of the 2,300 tons of food, fuel and ammunition required on a daily basis to keep 7. *Armee* functioning, just four hundred tons was getting through.[34]

Neither was it entirely true that German morale was still rock-steady, or that attrition wasn't having a major impact even among the supposed élite, as *Das Reich*'s *SS-Sturmbannführer* Otto Weidinger knew only too well: 'With the increasing bombing attacks on German towns, and the heavy civilian losses, the morale of the troops is badly affected. Every day soldiers receive news of the destruction of their homes, the tragic death of wives and children. They return from leave depressed...The years of fighting bolshevism in Russia have also affected the men's nerves.'

The old Nazi Party beerhouse brawler and now commander of *I. SS-Panzerkorps,* Sepp Dietrich, had already told Rommel before *Goodwood*: 'I am being bled white and getting nowhere. We need another eight to ten divisions in a day or two, or we're finished.' Kurt Meyer – never one to admit publicly any sort of weakness or doubt in final victory, wrote in his diary: 'We know we are approaching a catastrophe.'

The struggle for Caen was protracted and bloody. The goal of trying to secure the city on D-Day itself was over-ambitious to say the least, but the resilience of the German defence was difficult to foresee. Ever since the campaign there has been debate among historians – and many veterans – as to how much credit for the eventual American break-out should go to Montgomery and his achievement in drawing the lion's share of German military might to the far east of the Allied lodgement around Caen, so leaving the west so vulnerable. That the Germans viewed the eastern side of the battle area as the more important is evident; for example, the allocation of Waffen-SS divisions was, throughout the war, always a good indicator of where Berlin thought the greatest threat lay. The fact that of the six Waffen-SS divisions in Normandy, only one was in the west facing the Americans speaks volumes. The seemingly endless bashing at Caen meant that there were no fewer than 645 panzers and ninety-two infantry battalions facing the Anglo-Canadians at the end of July, and just 190 panzers and sixty infantry battalions fighting it out with the Americans.

The fighting for Caen – ultimately successful – was also, probably, the moment the baton of military leadership finally changed hands from Great Britain to the United States in terms of where real military power lay in the alliance. From now on it would be the Americans who would dominate operations in the campaign, but first it would cost them in blood and treasure to earn that right. They would pay the price at Saint-Lô, and in the *bocage*.

6

The Battle for Saint-Lô

The US Army Ranger, Carl Weast, said 'A veteran infantryman is a terrified infantryman.'[1] He knew what he was talking about. After surviving D-Day, Weast and his comrades found themselves fighting through exactly the sort of terrain that the Germans had dismissed as wholly unsuitable for military operations – the *bocage* of *Basse Normandie* (Lower Normandy).

This ancient patchwork quilt of tiny fields and orchards, hemmed in by narrow sunken lanes and man-made hedgerows atop earthen embankments that resembled medieval ramparts, was a defenders' dream, and an attackers' nightmare. Generations of Normandy smallholders had jealously guarded their precious few acres with hawthorn and ivy entanglements, buttressed with centuries of rock and stone that the land had ceaselessly thrown up. Much of it is gone now; cleared for tarmac roads and efficient agriculture, but some shards of it still survive – as do similar pockets across the water in forgotten corners of Cornwall, or in the Irish border counties of Armagh and Tyrone. This would be the battleground.

Over in the east; the fight was for Caen, fields and farms dotted with an occasional hill that needed to be taken; not so the west. Here it was about the *bocage* and getting through it to seize the initiative and achieve the goal of all goals for the Anglo-Americans – the break-out. Once they were out of the claustrophobia of the lodgement, their mechanised power could run riot and tear the increasingly horsedrawn Westheer to ruins. Before that nirvana, the Americans first had to liberate Carentan, the gateway to the Cotentin peninsula, then the peninsula itself and its all-important city of Cherbourg – the nearest major port for the Allies – and finally Saint-Lô. With the latter in American hands there would be room in the landing area for the Allies to begin to manoeuvre and open a path to Brittany and beyond. This was Germany versus the United States; the new world against a terrible flag-bearer of the old – it would become an epic.

The forces which would fight it out in this little patch of France couldn't have been more different. Carl Weast's army was the most modern, mechanized force on the planet, with a list of advantages that seemed to run on and on. They were better paid and better educated – half the American enlisted men were high-school graduates and ten per cent had been to college. Man for man they were taller, fitter and heavier than the Germans, as the para Eugen Griesser noted: 'The Americans were mostly young lads, around twenty years old, big and strong guys, they wore combat uniforms in which they carried around half a store's worth of kit; canned rations, chewing gum, chocolate, spare ammo, explosives and even pictures of naked girls!' They were better supplied and sustained – an American GI tucked into a box of K-rations every day, and while they were constantly lambasted as lacking in flavour, texture or variety, they provided a fighting man with a well balanced diet and all the calories, vitamins and nutrients he needed. His opposite number had no such luxury, relying on the company horse-drawn *Gulasch-kanon*, and if that failed, as it often did, having to fall back on 'canned meat that was blue, so we called it "Old Man"',[2] his breadbag and whatever he could scrounge or steal from local farms and fields, as one *Das Reich* grenadier remembered:

> Our rations were monotonous and we hadn't eaten meat for some time... Our *Spiess* [senior company NCO responsible for supply] hit on a plan and lay in wait near a burned-out vehicle, the victim of a previous air attack and still mistaken for a target by Allied pilots. The *Spiess* waited, pistol in hand, for the next *jabo* attack, and when the Allied plane came in with cannons and machine-guns firing, he went into a nearby field and shot a cow. He then went to the farmer and bought the dead beast from him – the farmer blamed the Americans of course and was only too glad to sell the carcass... We were only too pleased to eat meat again ... a good *Spiess* can organise anything.[3]

It wasn't just rations either, all American supply levels were three times higher per division than for the Germans; that's three times the amount of ammunition, fuel, spare parts, clothing – everything.

On the whole – despite present-day enthusiasts championing items of German equipment like the *MG 42* and the *Nebelwerfer* – American kit was usually better, and they had an awful lot more of it. Their standard-issue firearm, the M1 Garand rifle, was semi-automatic with an 8-round magazine that allowed a trained soldier to fire forty to fifty aimed shots a minute, while the German *Kar98k* was based on a bolt-action pre-World War One design that restricted a man to half his opponent's rate of fire. The *landsers* didn't like their grenades either, as the *fallschirmjäger* Richard Onderka pointed out:

> Our grenades, both the 'stick' and 'egg' versions, were so ineffective we called them 'cocoa tins'. They really were made from tin, and we used to joke that you would need to put a grenade in an *Amis'* pocket to cause him any harm. Allied grenades were much more dangerous than ours because they had cast-iron jackets.[4]

Even American combat clothing was superior, as *352. ID*s Karl Wegner found to his horror:

> When I was inducted I was issued the new pattern of uniform. It was quite different from that of my older brother [Wegner's brother was serving in the Waffen-SS in Russia]. I wasn't allergic to wool, but this stuff really made me itch. I thought of how proud my brother looked in his smartly cut uniform; mine was quite dull looking … then one day while we were out on quite a long route march the sky just opened and the rain fell without mercy. Wet to the bone, we sloshed back to our barracks and up to our rooms to change for evening mess. To my complete astonishment as I unfastened my buttons they came right off the tunic still attached to the patches of wool to which they were sewn… I wondered how we could win the war if our uniforms melted in the rain.[5]

What the Germans had though, was combat experience – something most American divisions lacked, and it showed. The commander of the untried American 29th Infantry Division, Charles H. Gerhardt, said: 'Those Germans are the best damned soldiers I ever saw. They're smart and they don't know what 'fear' means. They come in and they keep coming until they get their job done or you kill 'em.'[6]

One of those men was Richard Onderka. Still only nineteen in the summer of 1944, he had volunteered for Germany's famous *Fallschirmjäger* after the invasion of Crete, and had ended up spending two winters in the Russian snow before making an unopposed parachute jump onto the island of Elba after Fascist Italy's capitulation the previous year; 'We were only there a day, our navy picked us up that night, but I don't remember much about it because we were all roaring drunk.' Based near the Breton port of Saint-Malo, Onderka was just glad to have survived the East. 'The second winter in Russia was the worst. We were all issued a knife which was meant to be used to cut ourselves free from our parachute if necessary – which I never had to – but I did use that knife to cut off one of my comrade's legs which was hanging by a thread. We started that winter with 120 men in my company, and by the time spring came there were just thirteen of us left alive.'[7]

In the east, the Anglo-Canadians faced a mass of German armoured divisions, many of them from the feared and detested Waffen-SS – not so the Americans in the west. The men who stormed onto Omaha and Utah would find themselves confronted by a mish-mash of transportless static divisions full of convalescents, old men and *Osttruppen*, a single SS Panzergrenadier division without a panzer to its name, and a handful of parachute units whose ranks were an odd mix of tough veterans like Onderka and fresh-faced youths drafted in to make up the numbers. Those veterans were in no mood to make it easy for their enemy, as Onderka explained:

Russia taught us to be tough. You never turned your back on 'dead' Russians – to do so could be fatal. We always sprayed them with bullets to make sure they wouldn't get up and attack us, as they used to try and trick us. When they attacked they often sent in cannon-fodder first, you know, boys and old men who had been in uniform a week at most – it was slaughter – they didn't care... We were treated as an élite, our role was to be 'firemen', sent to help whenever things were looking desperate, and that's what we did in Normandy.

A compatriot and fellow Russian front veteran from *17. SS-Panzergrenadier-Division 'Götz von Berlichingen'*, *Unterscharführer* Kübel, was looking forward to the coming battle as he and his unit travelled the two hundred miles from their base south of the Loire River to the front: 'The mood was good – among the young lads who weren't battle-hardened it was tense. They wanted to know a lot from us *alte Hasen*. The weather was wonderful, the ride a pleasure.'[8]

Kübel felt like this despite his division having no panzers or armoured half-tracks for its grenadiers, and with three thousand of his comrades being just 17 years old. But his anticipation began to pall as the SS men entered the realm of the *jabo*. 'Then the French train crew pulled the emergency brake, jumped off while we were still moving and disappeared into a forest. I was furious, but not for long... In an instant our vehicle crews realised what was happening. They fired at the aircraft with their machine-guns without a thought for their own safety. Everyone else jumped off the train and ran into the forest – we ran for our lives.'

One of Kübel's officers had the same wake-up call as he drove north:

Everyone was in a good mood and eager to see action again... Our motorised columns were rolling along the road towards the invasion beaches, then something happened that left us in a daze. Spurts of fire flicked along the column and splashes of dust staccatoed along the road. Everyone was piling out of the vehicles and scuttling for the neighbouring fields. Several vehicles were already in flames. The attack stopped as suddenly as it had started some fifteen minutes before. The men started drifting back to the column again, pale and shaky and wondering how they had survived the fiery rain of bullets ... an hour later it started all over again, only much worse. When that attack was over the whole length of the road was strewn with splintered anti-tank guns, burning vehicles and the charred implements of war. The march was called off and all remaining vehicles were hidden in nearby bushes or barns. No-one dared show themselves out in the open any more... This was different from what we thought it would be like, it had been our first experience with our new foe – the American.[9]

The SS men joined their comrades from the air-landing and infantry divisions who were already getting used to this new way of waging war – the American way. 'As soon as we fired our guns, we had to run again, and look for a good place to hide. We were hunted. Always afraid. If you couldn't run, it was over for you. Like eagles and rabbits.'

Günter Behr wasn't alone in his view on what he saw as an unequal battle, as one of his officers confirmed to his American interrogators after being captured:

I didn't see a single German reconnaisance aircraft in the air between 6 and 16 June, and the *Amis* had complete mastery of the air. We can bring out whole armies, and they'll smash them completely with their air forces within a week. Above all we have no petrol left at all. We can no longer move any troops by means that require petrol, only by rail or marching on foot.[10]

It wasn't just rankers and junior officers who suffered. Erich Marcks, the *Korps* commander and the man who had accompanied Josef Rauch's grenadiers on D-Day, was in his staff car less than a week later, trying to find out what was going on at the front, when a *jabo* struck. Impeded by his wooden leg he wasn't quick enough in abandoning his car and reaching cover in a nearby ditch – he was shot to pieces and died in the road. Before setting out he had been warned of the danger but had dismissed it; 'You people are always worried about your little piece of life.'

The town Marcks had been heading for – Carentan – was an old river port of a few thousand people at the head of the Douvre estuary, and the scene of the first major clash between the opposing armies once the landings were established. Taking the town would enable the Americans to link up Utah and Omaha beaches securely and give them a launching pad to cut off the Cotentin, liberate Cherbourg, and strike south towards Saint-Lô. If the Germans could keep Carentan, all that would be in jeopardy – but how could the *landsers* hold when there were so few of them, and they lacked everything, above all transport and armour?

The Germans had four separate formations in the area, none of which were in great shape; the backbone of the defence was formed from the second and third battalions of Friedrich von der Heydte's *Fallschirmjäger-Regiment 6* (II. & III./FJR. 6) – his first battalion had already been destroyed. Von der Heydte could also call on a battalion of *Grenadier-Regiment 1058* (III./GR.1058) from *91. Luftlande-Infanterie-Division*, and a few companies of Ernst Heyna's *GR.914* that had been bundled west after the Omaha fighting (II./914). Last and, in von der Heydte's eyes, least, was *Ost-bataillon 439.*, composed of Cossacks who had fought hard on D-Day as part of Kraiss's *352. ID*, and who were now detached to the paras. Lined up against them would be some of the very best and most aggressive soldiers the Americans possessed: the paratroopers of the 101st Airborne with support from the 2nd Armoured Division. Eugen Griesser remembers the uneven struggle:

Our group lay on the northern edge of Carentan, in the first floor of a house… To the left and right American soldiers were working their way forward... When our machine-gun opened fire, they scattered into cover. A short time later, American *jabos* appeared and fired on the houses ... their artillery opened-up to shoot the way clear for them. Everything you can imagine came at us; mortars, artillery, even naval gunfire.[11]

Oberleutnant Martin Pöppel had been leading his men against the Americans since the first airborne landings, and was exhausted: 'The men brace themselves one more time, and advance again, but are always driven back ... the Americans continue to advance.' Soon enough, the beleaguered defenders began running out of ammunition. 'I only had a little ammunition left for my submachine-gun; two full magazines on my belt and one on the weapon itself. I had little more than my 08 pistol, my bayonet, my spade and a few hand-grenades. The war couldn't be won with this meagre arsenal!'[12]

Von der Heydte knew the game was up and sent the following signal to his superiors on the late afternoon of 12 June: 'All leaders of *jäger* companies have fallen or been wounded... The last of the ammunition has been fired; at 1800hrs we will vacate Carentan... The new line can only be held if ammunition and provisions arrive.' Under relentless pressure, the paras were beginning to crack:

> The *Hauptmann* [*Hauptmann* Otto Hermann of *Nr. 5 Kompanie*] called; 'I am in command, so I will go first!' He rose from cover and dashed forward in a crouch. He had barely covered fifty metres when the *Amis* opened fire on him from all sides. He fell to the ground, badly wounded... An old *gefreiter* pushed the medic forward. 'You're the *Sani* [slang for medic, *Sanitäter*], now it's your turn!' But the *Sani* stubbornly refused to leave his position. The *grefreiter* pulled out his pistol and shot him; 'Is there another coward who wants to leave the *Hauptmann* out there to rot?' We gave covering fire while he and a few other volunteers recovered the *Hauptmann*.[13]

Hermann died a short time later. This was rough stuff at the real sharp end of combat – a junior NCO shooting a combat medic from his own unit for cowardice under fire – any worse than this and anarchy prevails.

Von der Heydte's planned withdrawal coincided with the long-awaited arrival of the 17th SS, but after the mauling they had received on their journey, their commander *SS-Brigadeführer*

Werner Ostendorff had no intention of charging blindly into battle. As the panzer-grenadiers loitered outside the town, the exhausted paras withdrew to the south. *Obergefreiter* Gerd Schwetling wasn't impressed by what he saw of the new division: 'The 17th SS was one of the new divisions that had been put together in the spring and summer, and basically had no combat experience, maybe that's the reason they were the way they were, they hadn't had any experience with *fallschirmjäger* yet either.'

Schwetling wasn't the only man underwhelmed by the 17th SS. *GR. 914's* Karl Wegner remembered their arrival in the line:

> Kalb told us that the new troops were from the *'Götz von Berlichingen'* Division, and that they would soon teach us how to fight the war. They 'paraded' by our holes in the ground; young, fit, and full of nerve wearing their splendid camouflage uniforms. The looks cast on us were ... contemptuous. I suppose we didn't look so glorious. We filthy, tired and hungry grenadiers couldn't get cheers on the parade ground, but we had seen more of the war than they had so far. Kalb just glared back at them... He stood so these young warriors could see his medal-laden chest; the Iron Cross First Class, Infantry assault badge, Silver Wound Medal, ribbons for the Iron Cross Second Class and the Eastern Front Medal. He was never one to shout about the tin on his chest, but he knew these young 'heroes' were bare-chested and would look away. Most of them did.[14]

Most of the *FJR. 6* rankers now began to refer to the SS men as the 'Kiss My Arse Division'. Uneasily, the green SS troopers and the veteran *fallschirmjäger* counter-attacked on the 13th to try and recapture the town, although Martin Pöppel wasn't hopeful about the result: 'The SS think they can do it easily – they've arrived with enormous idealism, but they'll get the surprise of their lives!' Pöppel was right. American artillery and airpower, coupled with the determined defence of the US 2nd Armored Division, first blunted the assault, and then threw it back – an *Ost-batallion* was one of the first to run. 'It ran away, leaderless, when its German commander was killed ... the enemy was able to cross the hill unopposed.'[15] The Americans were less than complimentary about the new arrivals, with one American engineer standing guard over some newly captured SS prisoners describing them as 'Lousy and undersized, scurvy and dirty, with greasy hair, flat mouths and short necks'.[16]

With Carentan liberated, the Americans were free to cut the Cotentin off and drive north for Cherbourg and its deep-water port and extensive docking facilities – if they could take it more or less intact then the logistics of the landings would become a whole lot easier, and the vast supply chain that extended all the way from the US industrial and agricultural heartlands could push straight into France and fuel the Anglo-American armies as they drove for the Reich – and winning the battle of supply was the cornerstone of Allied strategy, as Heinrich Eberbach's Chief of Staff, Alfred Gause, acknowledged. 'The enemy has a seemingly unlimited supply of ammunition. He fires twenty times more than we can. Against 80,000 rounds of artillery today we were able to reply with just 4,500.' He then put his finger on the Westheer's central dilemma in the campaign: 'The morale of our troops is good, but they cannot cope with courage alone against the enemy's use of *matériel*.' His next line, however, was ill-judged: 'The enemy substitutes artillery and bombs for courage and a lack of morale.' This simply wasn't true. But in written and verbal accounts of the Normandy fighting – many of them from senior German officers – one hears the same over and over. The *Lehr*'s Fritz Bayerlein was a prime example: 'The fighting morale of the British infantry is not very high – the enemy is extraordinarily nervous of close combat. He strives to occupy ground rather than to fight over it.' His subordinate, Helmut Ritgen, said of his American foes: 'Normally the Americans were very aggressive in the morning, but at night they were tired and stopped fighting. From 7pm till morning there was absolute peace.'[17] This sentiment, that man for man the German *landser* was superior to his Anglo-American enemy, and that if the battle had been fought on a level playing-field the Germans would have won, has become central to the German Normandy legend. Except war isn't like that, it isn't about giving the other guy a 'fair shout' – ask the Poles in the autumn of 1939, and the Belgians, Dutch, Danes and Norwegians in 1940 – it is about creating an overwhelming advantage and exploiting it ruthlessly to crush your enemy; the military professionals of the Wehrmacht understood that more than most yet squealed about it when that playing-field wasn't in their favour.

The Westheer, like so many armies before it, when faced with an enemy with a crushing advantage, had fallen back on the oldest delusion of all – the triumph of the will; the myth that fighting spirit, dash, *élan,* whatever the generals and Nazi Party bigwigs wanted to call it, was the magical key to *Endsieg* – the final victory. Hitler was its

arch-proponent and he delved back into the annals of military history
to try and find parallels that suited his narrative. Gneisenau's defence
of Kolberg in 1807 was one, Frederick of Prussia's miracle of survival
in the Seven Years' War another – but there are many others that
were, perhaps, more apt, and more relevant for the Reich, such as the
Confederacy of the American Civil War. The use of language may have
been different but reading the words of many in the Confederacy at the
time is, in some respects, to hold a mirror up to the pronouncements
of much of the German leadership during the Normandy campaign.
'We are proud of the morale of our men compared with theirs. Of the
superiority of Southern courage and skill we need not speak, after the
testimony of such witnesses as the battles we have fought we all know
it to be true.'[18]

Compare that to this regimental order circulated within 2. *SS-Panzer-
Division Das Reich* during the bitter fighting: 'We shall exploit the
inferior quality of the enemy soldier as a fighting man.'

The case of Ernst Barkmann typified the argument. A senior
NCO in *Das Reich*, Barkmann had served with distinction in Russia
before accompanying his division to Normandy. Like so many other
panzer commanders of the time, on arrival in France he found his
Panther and its superb high-velocity 7.5cm main gun far superior
to the Shermans that comprised the bulk of the American armoured
units, and very shortly he and his crew had chalked up a score of
four Shermans destroyed. However, it was on 27 July that he and his
crew achieved an almost Wittmann-like feat on the main Saint-Lô-
Countances road. There, parked under a large oak tree, he ambushed
an advancing column of fourteen Shermans and several support
vehicles, including a fuel tanker. Coolly picking them off, Barkmann
managed to brew up nine enemy tanks and even though his Panther
was then damaged by a *jabo* attack, he still managed to get it and
his crew back to safety. The Nazi propaganda machine went into its
customary overdrive, with the location renamed 'Barkmann Corner',
and the young twenty-four-year-old lauded in the press and awarded
the Knight's Cross.

Whether or not the story was entirely true – and there is some dispute
as to its accuracy[19] – the important thing from the perspective of the
Normandy campaign was what it represented. As with Wittman's
Villers-Bocage engagement – and a dozen more from the time –
Barkmann Corner fitted into the Nazis' portrayal of the war; that in
the end, final victory could and would be achieved by superiority at
an individual level – despite the mountain of evidence to the contrary

and the enemy's endless advantages. This was the central theme of the Westheer's defence of France in 1944; the superiority of the German as a fighting man. It had been prevalent throughout the war, from its very first days, but had been married back then to an advanced martial machine, equipped with the very latest weaponry and operating within an operational doctrine at the cutting edge of military thinking – this was not the case in the summer of 1944, where Germany's leaders fell back on telling the *landsers* – 'just be like Barkmann, and we'll win in the end.'

One month before Barkmann Corner, the Americans faced their old foes from Utah Beach, *Generalleutnant* Karl-Wilhelm von Schlieben and the men of his *709. ID*, as they sought to liberate Cherbourg. Von Schlieben's division was a mirror of Richter's *716. ID;* formed back in May 1941 for occupation duties from the medically unfit, the over-aged, and 'border Poles', it had sat in France ever since. Its better men had been carted off to Russia, with an entire battalion of its *Grenadier-Regiment 739* sent East in October 1943 and replaced by the Russians of *Ost-Bataillon 639*, raising the average age of the unit to thirty-six on D-Day. There were some veterans sprinkled in, Utah Beach's Knight's Cross holder Arthur Jahnke being one of course, but these men were very much the exception, with the majority of the division having no combat experience at all. As for their weaponry, it was a who's-who of the Wehrmacht's earlier conquests, with the three battalions of *Oberst* Robert Reiter's *Artillerie-Regiment 1709* being an example; his first battalion had eight Czech and eight French guns, his second sixteen French, and his third had twelve Russian – and all of them were '*ratsch-booms*', anti-tank guns rather than artillery, nicknamed as such by the *landsers* on account of the noise they made when fired. Von Schlieben's armoured support was from *Leutnant* Ogroske's nine *StuG 40* assault-guns, as well as a nearby training unit; the Château de Francquetot-headquartered *100. Panzer-Bataillon*, and its kaleidoscope of armoured misfits, including seventeen *Panzerjäger 35R* Alfred Becker-specials,[20] ten former French 1940-era tanks and a solitary German-made PzKpfw III. Originally tasked with guarding a coastline stretching a mammoth 240 kilometres, the arrival in May 1944 of *243. ID* had reduced this down to *only* a hundred – still clearly an impossible job – although the addition of *Oberstleutnant* Günther Keil's *Grenadier-Regiment 919* from *242. ID* did make things at least a little easier, without solving the basic problem of defending too long a front with not enough men or weapons.

As for von Schlieben himself, the 49-year-old *Generalleutnant* was something of a conundrum. A decorated veteran of the First World War, he had been an early convert to the *panzerwaffe*, serving as a regimental commander with *1. Panzerdivision* during the Battle of France in 1940, before going on to serve with *4. Panzer* in Russia and his subsequent elevation to divisional command with *208. ID*. In the spring of 1943 he then received his crowning glory – command of one of the Reich's élite formations; *18. Panzer*. He led the division as part of Walter Model's *9. Armee* during the decisive Kursk battle, where it suffered so many casualties that following the German defeat it was plagued with discontent and desertion. The problems within its depleted ranks were so great that after further action in Ukraine, the radical decision was taken to disband it and transfer its remaining men to the newly-forming *18. Artillerie-Division*. As for von Schlieben, there was clearly a black mark against his name now, and after two-and-a-half years of continuous command, steady promotions and awards, including the German Cross in Gold and the Knight's Cross, he was ignominiously bundled off to France and the backwater of *709. ID*. On arrival he found himself astonished by the difference between active service in Russia and the petty bureaucracy of garrison duty in the West:

> For someone who had served only in the East, the flood of orders, directives, and regulations which continually showered the troops was a novelty for me. This paper flood impressed me more than the tide along the Atlantic coast. Higher headquarters concerned themselves with trivial affairs of subordinate commanders. For example, we had a problem when it was decided that a machine-gun position needed to be moved twenty metres to the right or left... The senior commander wanted to have an old ramshackle hut demolished to create a better field of fire for the gun, so a written application had to be completed and filed with the appropriate area HQ accompanied by a sketch!

Flabbergasted by the tedium of it all, von Schlieben – like Sperrle, Feuchtinger, and so many others – consoled himself with the delights occupied France had to offer. A few days before the landings, a dinner was held in his honour in Cherbourg, with a printed menu for guests announcing that the starter of *pâté de foie gras*, would be followed by a fish course of local lobster with a hollandaise sauce, then roast lamb, and fresh local peaches to finish – all washed down with some excellent champagne. The menu would be found in the pocket of his greatcoat when he surrendered several weeks later.

For all that, von Schlieben was no fool, and understood all too well the nigh-on impossible nature of the task his belly division had been given. Yes, his formation was bigger than Wilhelm Richter's – with over twelve thousand men on D-Day – but a full third of those were *Ost-bataillone*; with 639 standing alongside their fellow Russians of 635, and two battalions of Georgians from the Caucasus – *Hauptmann* Stiller's *Ost-Bataillon 795* and *Hauptmann* Peter Massberg's *Ost-Bataillon 797* – both missing a company. In fact, this preponderance of Hiwis, pressed-men, and former POWs was one of the many reasons the Allied planners had opted for Normandy as the landing area in the first place, with a British report stating that these static divisions would be 'indifferent and full of foreigners – and so they have proved'. The most-often quoted comment on the use of *Ost-bataillone* in France has been attributed to almost every German senior officer serving in-country in 1944, but was almost certainly uttered by von Schlieben himself: 'We are asking rather a lot if we expect Russians to fight in France for Germany against Americans.' Succinctly put.

If von Schlieben's two Russian battalions were motivated at all it was by anti-communism and a desire to rid their country of Stalin, while the Georgians wanted independence from the Soviet Union – neither outcome was at stake on the Cotentin that summer, as even Hitler recognised in a rare moment of insight: 'If one gets them when their homeland lies in enemy territory, why should they be expected to fight?'[21]

Some – at least – of the *Osttruppen* acquitted themselves well, with *Ost-Bataillon 635* especially reported as having 'fought well despite poor armament'. This good showing was not replicated in 639, of whom *Oberst* Walter Köhn – regimental CO of *Grenadier-Regiment 739* – said, 'They fell to pieces completely. They held out for quite a while, but when things became critical, they took to their heels.'

As it was, the surprise was far less about how quickly the American landing forces overcame the defenders, and rather more about how the defenders held out for quite so long, especially once the Cotentin was cut off and supplies were stopped. When the bespectacled Manton S. Eddy's US 9th Division had achieved that feat on 18 June, it was only a matter of time before Cherbourg fell. The only way for it to remain unliberated would have been through indefinite naval resupply, which the Germans attempted by means of U-boat of all things. This act of total desperation was an abject failure by their own commander's admission: 'The U-boat is a complicated and highly developed instrument of war, wholly unsuited to transport purposes. My decision to employ them on this task is made easier by the fact that we are completely ignorant of the operational possibilities in the landing area.' Four boats were sent to sea from their bases at Brest and La Pallice between 20–22 June, loaded with eight thousand anti-tank shells and 350,000 rounds of machine-gun ammunition. They were all recalled on the 23rd when it was discovered that the harbour at Cherbourg was already blocked.

Needless to say, with a militarily hopeless situation, Berlin opted for self-delusion, and the usual order came out demanding the peninsula and port city be defended 'to the last man and the last bullet' – although as there was no hope of any resupply the last bullet demand wasn't such a big ask.

> Holding Cherbourg at all costs is of the greatest importance. Every day is a gain for the overall conduct of the war. The enemy must be worn down by a fighting withdrawal. There is no question of giving up. I regard it as a matter of honour for every soldier from the general down to the lowest ranks to hold Fortress Cherbourg.

Von Schlieben, newly designated as that general, could have been forgiven for asking the question; *with what?* 'What' was approximately 21,000 German uniformed personnel in what Hitler now termed *Festung Cherbourg*, although a large percentage of these men were non-combatants: *Organisation Todt* construction workers, unemployed naval staff, railway teams and so on. This left a core of 'fighting men' based primarily on *709. ID*, the remnants of *91. Luftlande-Infanterie- Division* and those men of *243. ID* and *77. ID* who had been unable to escape prior to the American breakthrough – and whose commanders, *Generalleutnants* Heinz Hellmich and Rudolf Stegmann, had both been killed in separate *jabo* attacks on 16 and 18 June respectively. One *landser* from *77. ID* who had been able to escape south was Helmut Hörner. Along with several hundred comrades he had managed to fight his way out, and wrote about it in his diary: 'My comrade collapses next to me, his eyes still wide open ... a grenade splinter pierced his steel helmet and tore a fist-sized hole in the back of his head... My eyes witness the usual picture of devastation as we breach the enemy line.' Hörner was one of the lucky ones, although he was wounded by a mine the next day.

Scrabbling as they always did, the Cotentin's defenders managed to cobble together a line to face the advancing Americans. The mainstay was *KG König* led by the *Luftlande's* Eugen König, a successor to Wilhelm Falley after his death in action on D-Day. König's battlegroup was a hotch-potch even by Wehrmacht standards. The core were four thousand men from his own division – all that were left of the original 7,500 – some fourteen hundred men from 265. *ID*, and another twelve hundred from Hellmich's 243. *ID* that had been trapped north of Eddy's thrust to the sea. König also had a handful of *Ost-bataillone*; the 600-man strong 627., the 635. detached from 709. *ID*, and two hundred men from *Ost-Bataillon Huber* – although the Volga Tatars of 627 were ordered withdrawn, disbanded and disarmed after one of their number tried to kill a German officer. So bad was the manpower situation that the order was disregarded and the Tatars stayed in the line. With the Americans able to bring their armoured units to bear, heavy weapons would be at a premium for the defence, and König could call on a small number of assault-guns, namely StuG IIIs and Marder IIIs, and three former French Army light tanks. His supporting guns were almost entirely captured Soviet stock, with several dozen of the ubiquitous *ratsch-booms*. His own division had been equipped for some reason with the mountain warfare variant of the Wehrmacht's standard 10.5cm gun, which inexplicably couldn't use the same ammunition as the non-mountain version, so after a few hours the guns were out of shells and abandoned as just so much scrap metal. *KG König* wasn't going to hold for long.

In a few days the Americans had burst through, advanced north and found themselves fighting in Cherbourg itself. The few days the defenders bought allowed the most comprehensive demolition of a major port facility yet seen in the war, with docks, quays, warehouses, loading/unloading, storage and repair sites either blown to pieces or burnt to the ground. Von Schlieben himself had gone to ground in a warren of tunnels cut into a rock quarry just to the west of *Fort du Roule*, the fortifications built back in the nineteenth century to repel the English. There, Berlin exhorted him to carry on the fight, but his heart had never been in the struggle, as he confessed to an aide: 'Cherbourg isn't a fortress … the defenders are all old men who have done nothing but stare at the Atlantic Ocean for three years, none of them are soldiers.' He thought his men were '*verbunkert*' – bunker-happy – the same attitude that afflicted the Maginot Line defenders four years previously. No wonder that one of Hitler's multiple military adjutants; Rudolf Schmundt – only a few days before he was fatally injured in the assassination attempt on his boss – confided to friends, 'I'm worried about Schlieben. I don't get the impression that he's an iron personality. The honour and reputation of the entire German officer corps rests on how long we hang on to Cherbourg.'

The Americans soon sniffed the Cherbourg commander out and began to blast the tunnels one by one with explosives. Exhausted and unwilling to carry on, von Schlieben saw the writing on the wall. 'There were signs of cracking up – you could no longer risk sending the men out alone, because it looked like they were going to make a run for it.' He sent his last radio message to 7. *Armee* headquarters at three o'clock in the afternoon on 26 June; 'Documents burned, codes destroyed'.

He still wouldn't surrender though – his sense of personal honour dictated that he would only do so when a tank was physically brought to bear against him – and the Americans were duly told of this requirement. So, in a bizarre twist that could only ever occur in war, the Americans obliged. A tank drove forward and fired point-blank into the tunnel network, whereupon, with honour satisfied, von Schlieben walked out with an aide waving a white flag made from a bedsheet, followed by almost eight hundred of his men, many of whom were wounded, and pretty much all of whom were relieved to have survived.

Allied propaganda sought to maximise the impact of the capture of the city and von Schlieben himself, with photos of the general splashed over the front pages. When questioned at the 9th Division's command post after his surrender, the tall general, looking pallid and careworn, still wearing his dust-speckled greatcoat, took umbrage at a hovering Robert Capa who seemed to snap pictures of him from all angles; 'I am tired of all this picture-taking!' he announced – Capa took not the slightest notice.

In Berlin, von Schlieben's surrender was lambasted as weakness and failure. In an attempt to salvage something from the wreckage, senior Nazis latched onto the still-resisting Günther Keil and the few surviving members of his *Grenadier-Regiment 919*. Keil had already made his mark on the Cotentin back in the autumn of 1943:

> I ordered the plains north of the Carentan Canal flooded, but by the end of May inundations had been only partially achieved and the water was not deep enough. The remaining plains had been partially

The reality of *Festung Europa – Beutepanzer*; obsolete ex-French Army Somua 35s captured back in 1940, repainted and renamed *Panzerkampfwagen* 35-S 739(*f*)s, prepare to face the Allied landings. (Courtesy of Bundesarchiv Bild 101l-300-1858-33A)

Right: Major Hans von Luck, commander of *Panzergrenadier-Regiment 125* on D-Day. The aristocratic von Luck was an ex-member of Rommel's *Afrika Korps* staff and knew him well. (Author's collection)

Below: Erwin Rommel inspects *21. Panzerdivision* on 8 May 1944. From left to right: unknown, *Major* Alfred Becker, Erwin Rommel 'the Desert Fox', and the commander of *21. Panzerdivision*, Edgar Feuchtinger. While Becker laboured away building a fleet of recycled armoured vehicles, Feuchtinger was far more interested in Parisian nightlife. (Author's collection)

Above left: Oberst Hermann von Oppeln-Bronikowski on the steps of the *Château de Canteloup*, southeast of Caen, headquarters of *schwere Panzerabteilung 503* in early June 1944. Winner of an equestrian Olympic gold medal in 1936, and commander of *Panzer-Regiment 22* on D-Day, von Oppeln-Bronikowski's bad luck helped doom the German 6. *Armee* at Stalingrad, and 7. *Armee* in Normandy. (Courtesy of Bundesarchiv Bild 101l-721-0376-06A)

Above right: Oberstleutnant Josef Rauch, commander of *Panzergrenadier-Regiment 192*, came closest to frustrating D-Day when he led his men in a counter-attack that took them all the way to the sea, only for poor leadership among his superiors to force their withdrawal that same night. The Germans would never reach the invasion coast again. (Courtesy of Bundesarchiv Bild 140-2008-0142)

Above left: Oberleutnant Hans Höller in 1944, an Austrian veteran of Rommel's *Afrika Korps*, and company commander in 21. *Panzerdivision*. He and his men would fail to dislodge the British paras at Pegasus Bridge. (Author's collection)

Above right: Obergefreiter Werner Kortenhaus of 21. *Panzerdivision*. Normandy would be Kortenhaus's baptism of fire. The teenager would survive the war and write a combat history of the division. (Author's collection)

Above left: *Panzer-Lehr's* Fritz Bayerlein – second from left – confers with Sepp Dietrich of *1. SS-Panzerkorps*, second from right. Between them is Bayerlein's chief operations officer, Kurt Kauffmann, who thought his boss 'worn out' even before the landings. (Author's collection)

Above right: The *Panzer-Lehr's* Helmut Ritgen described his division's approach march to the landing beaches as a 'nightmare'. The best-equipped and manned Army panzer division in the West in 1944, the *Lehr* was effectively destroyed in Normandy. (Author's collection)

Above left: An armoured Sd. Kfz.251 half-track of the *Panzer-Lehr* noses its way forward in Normandy under the guidance of a scout who is out in front on foot. The *Panzer-Lehr* had double the usual number of these vehicles which gave its hard-pressed panzergrenadiers a degree of protection from Allied firepower. (Author's collection)

Above right: The commander of *352. Infanterie-Division*, Dietrich Kraiss, whose decision on D-Day to try and maintain a solid front rather than counter-attack towards Omaha with everything he had was apparently militarily correct, but the wrong decision for the Germans. (Author's collection)

Above left: *Grenadier* Heinrich 'Hein' Severloh, pictured on his return from Russia in 1943. Posted to Kraiss's *352. Infanterie-Division*, he would wreak havoc among the American assault troops on Omaha from his machine-gun post on *WN62*, before being captured shortly afterwards. (Author's collection)

Above right: *Gefreiter* Peter Simeth of *352. Infanterie-Division* while undergoing training at the depot in Schlan in 1943 – now Slaný in the Czech Republic. This photo was originally sent to his brother who was subsequently killed in Russia. Simeth would be captured in Normandy and survive the war. (Courtesy of Peter Simeth)

Above left: The 23-year-old commander of *WN5* covering Utah beach, *Leutnant* Arthur Jahnke of *709. Infanterie-Division*. The Knight's Cross was won in Russia. He would stoutly defend his post, but the strongpoint was quickly overrun. (Author's collection)

Above right: *Oberst* Ludwig Krug, of Wilhelm Richter's *716. Infanterie-Division*, held strongpoint *WN17* – codenamed *Hillman* by the British – long enough to allow von Oppeln-Bronikowski's counter-attack to be launched on D-Day. When he surrendered the following morning, the surprised Suffolks were delighted to find his personal champagne cache intact. (Author's collection)

Above left: The 17-year-old *grenadier* Franz Gockel of *716. Infanterie-Division* in 1943. He would be just eighteen when he fought alongside Hein Severloh and Peter Simeth to defend *WN62* against the Americans at Omaha beach. After the war he went back to his profession as a roofer. (Author's collection)

Above right: The highly decorated German *fallschirmjäger* officer, Friedrich *Freiherr* von der Heydte. Von der Heydte commanded *FJR 6.* – soon dubbed the 'lions of Carentan' for their stubborn defence of the town. Escaping Normandy, the regiment mustered forty men from its original 4,600. (Courtesy of Bundesarchiv Bild 183-H26044)

German infantry inspect a crashed Allied glider just after the D-Day landings. (Courtesy of Bundesarchiv Bild 146-2004-0176)

Above left: Heinrich Hoffmann, a Kriegsmarine *Korvettenkapitän* commanding the fast torpedo-boat *T28*, would earn himself a Knight's Cross for his actions on D-Day – but the depleted German Navy never seriously challenged Allied naval supremacy. (Author's collection)

Above right: Gustav Wilke, commander of 5. *Fallschirmjäger-Division*. Still forming when the Allies landed, Wilke's inexperienced unit was decimated in the Normandy fighting. (Author's collection)

British soldiers escort captured German troopers – almost certainly from *716. Infanterie-Division* – down to a collection point on the beach. The Germans look dejected, but relieved to be alive and out of it.

Come to us! The *12. SS-Panzerdivision Hitlerjugend* would in some ways come to define German military tenacity in Normandy. This recruiting poster from 1943 is clearly aimed at encouraging teenaged applicants for its ranks. (Author's collection)

Above left: *You Too!* This 1943 poster exhorts teenaged members of the *Hitlerjugend* to volunteer for the Waffen-SS. (Author's collection)

Above right: The *Hitlerjugend's* first commander, Fritz Witt – with his ever-present cigar – in a sidecar about to be driven to the front on a reconnaissance by one of his regimental commanders – and soon-to-be-successor – Kurt '*Panzer*' Meyer. One of the division's medical officers is on pillion. (Author's collection)

Above left: The *Hitlerjugend's* Hubert Meyer – a senior staff officer transferred to the *HJ* from the *Leibstandarte*, Meyer would write a combat history of the *HJ* after the war and become the last president of the Waffen-SS comrades association and lobby-group – *HIAG* – before it dissolved itself in 1992. (Author's collection)

Above right: Rudolf von Ribbentrop, *Leibstandarte* officer and son of Nazi Germany's Foreign Minister, Joachim von Ribbentrop, after he was awarded the Knight's Cross of the Iron Cross for bravery in Russia. (Courtesy of Jimmy McLeod)

When Joachim von Ribbentrop was appointed Germany's Ambassador to the Court of St James in 1936, his 15-year-old son Rudolf went with him and spent a year at Westminster School. Young Rudolf is shown here in the school's required uniform of top hat and morning coat. He remembers the school's dreadful food and unheated rooms, as well as the 'innate fairness' of the British. (Courtesy of Rudolf von Ribbentrop)

The *HJ*'s panzer commander, a slightly wounded Max Wünsche, drives an also wounded Rudolf von Ribbentrop – now one of his company leaders – on a visit to the survivors of *III. Zug, 15. Kompanie, Panzergrenadier-Regiment 25* at Rots near Caen on 9 June. This was von Ribbentrop's fourth war wound. Wünsche would be captured by British soldiers as he escaped from the Falaise Pocket. (Courtesy of Rudolf von Ribbentrop)

Above: A teenaged *HJ* MG42 gunner wearing the Waffen-SS's distinctive camouflaged uniform and festooned with ammunition bandoliers. (Courtesy of Bundesarchiv Bild 146-1983-109-14a)

Right: *SS-Sturmmann* Karl-Heinz Decker of the *HJ*'s *Panzergrenadier-Regiment 25*. Decker remembers that during his NCO training he and other *HJ* candidates were given chocolates and sweets rather than beer and cigarettes like the other, older, trainees. (Author's collection)

Above left: SS-Sch*ü*tze Erhard Kinscher of the *HJ*'s *Panzergrenadier-Regiment 25*. Kinscher was soon considered for promotion due to his background as a *Hitlerjugend* leader, and having completed his *RAD* service. (Author's collection)

Above middle: A pose all *landsers* soon grew used to in Normandy – looking upward scanning for the dreaded *jabos*. These Waffen-SS troopers look pretty relaxed about it all though and none are wearing helmets or taking cover, suggesting they believe they're in a safe area. (Courtesy of Rich Deveau-Maxwell)

Above right: This is what the *landsers* feared – an RAF Typhoon fires a barrage of rockets at German troops. (Author's collection)

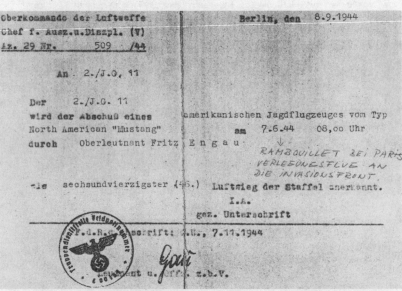

Contrary to the beliefs of many Landsers in Normandy, the Luftwaffe was there. This is a copy of an official confirmation certificate (*Abschussbestätigung*) for a victory claim by *Oberleutnant* Fritz Engau, *Staffelkapitän* 2/JG 11, achieved on 7 June 1944 during the transfer flight of I/JG 11 to the invasion front. (Courtesy of Fritz Engau and Patrick G. Eriksson, author of *Alarmstart South*)

Above: *Oberleutnant zur See* Hans Märtens's *U243* had been ordered to steam with all speed to engage the Allied invasion fleet when it was attacked and sunk by a Sunderland flying boat of No. 10 Squadron RAAF in the Bay of Biscay on 8 July 1944. Eleven sailors were killed and there were 38 survivors. (Courtesy of Imperial War Museum)

Below left: A Tiger I of *Schwere SS-Panzerabteilung 101* knocked out by British infantrymen of 1/7 Queens Regiment in Villers-Bocage on 13 June 1944. (Author's collection)

Below right: Theodor Weissenberger was one of the host of *Experten* sent west to help try and combat Allied air supremacy. Arriving on the Normandy front in his Bf 109 he downed five Mustangs on 7 June, two more the following day and another three on 12 June. He ended the war with 208 kills. (Author's collection)

Above: Karl-Wilhelm von Schlieben, commander of 709. *Infanterie-Division* and *Festung Cherbourg*, surrenders to the Americans on 26 June 1944. He is the helmeted figure to the left of the German officer with the peaked cap. (Author's collection)

Left: A German *kettenhund* (literally 'chaindog', a nickname for a military policeman), helps a dispatch rider with directions amidst the rubble of another Norman town. (Courtesy of Rich Deveau-Maxwell)

Above left: This is how von Schlieben's surrender, and Cherbourg's liberation, was reported in the Allied press for consumption by the French. (Author's collection)

Above right: Michael Wittmann receiving the *Eichenlauben* (Oakleaves) to his Knight's Cross from Adolf Hitler at the Wolf's Lair, Hitler's headquarters in Rastenburg, on 2 February 1944. He would receive the *Schwerter* (Swords) on 22 June. (Courtesy of Bundesarchiv Bild 146-1987-074-33)

Above left: Michael Wittmann (on left) and his gunner for most of the war, fellow Knight's Cross winner Bobby '*Balthasar*' Woll. Woll was wounded in Normandy and so wasn't with Wittmann when he and the rest of his crew were killed on 8 August. (Author's collection)

Above right: Michael Wittmann (centre) shortly after his demolition of the British offensive at Villers-Bocage. On the left is Sepp Dietrich, and on the right is Dietrich's adjutant, *SS-Hauptsturmführer* Hermann 'Bibl' Weiser. (Author's collection)

Above left: Ernst Barkmann – one of the famed panzer aces – after the award of the Knight's Cross for his actions at Barkmann Corner on 27 July 1944, whilst a member of *2. SS-Panzerdivision Das Reich*. Barkmann later headed up the fire department of his home city of Kisdorf. (Author's collection)

Above right: An *HJ* Sd. Kfz. 222 armoured car sits among the ruins of Caen. (Courtesy of Rich Deveau-Maxwell)

Above left: The Baltic German aristocrat and panzer ace, *Leutnant* Richard Wilfred Harry Erich *Freiherr* von Rosen, a 21-year-old company commander in *schwere Panzerabteilung 503* in Normandy in 1944. (Author's collection)

Above right: SS-Sturmmann Ewald Krassmann, a signalman in 9. *SS-Panzerdivision Hohenstaufen's Nachrichten Abteilung 9*. Krassmann and his comrades were transferred west from Russia to try and hold the line in Normandy. (Author's collection)

Richard *Freiherr* von Rosen's 57-ton Tiger I panzer blown upside down by Allied bombing at the start of the Goodwood offensive. (Author's collection)

Above left: Manfred Thorn, the driver of number 734 Mark IV panzer in the *Leibstandarte's 7. Kompanie,* was only 19 years old in Normandy, but already considered one of the 'old men' of his unit. (Author's collection)

Above right: An aide holds up Adolf Hitler's trousers, ripped and burnt by the 20 July bomb. Having survived the blast, Hitler effectively broke the German officer corps. (Courtesy of Bundesarchiv Bild 146-1972-025-64)

A captured Canadian tank crew being interrogated by Heinz Harmel (right), the commander of *10. SS-Panzerdivision Frundsberg,* and Heinz Brinkmann, one of his battalion commanders. Unsurprisingly, given the reputation of the Waffen-SS among Allied soldiers, the Canadians look terrified. (Courtesy of Rich Deveau-Maxwell)

The slaughter of Falaise. A fleeing German column lies wrecked on Mont Ormel after having been destroyed by the Polish 1st Armoured Division and 9th Infantry Battalion on 18 August 1944. A knocked-out Polish Sherman sits top right, and a Panther lies bottom left. The road is strewn with the carcasses of German horses killed in their traces. (Courtesy of the Polish Institute and Sikorksi Museum)

Above left: British troops sift through what Dwight Eisenhower said was 'unquestionably one of the greatest killing fields of any of the war' at Falaise. Miles and miles of roads, lanes and tracks were filled with the smouldering remains of an entire German field army – France was lost to the Wehrmacht. (Author's collection)

Above right: In 2019, Rudolf von Ribbentrop was 97 years old and living quietly in Germany. His father was executed by hanging after the Nuremburg war crimes trial. His last words on the gallows were 'I wish peace to the world.' (Courtesy of Rudolf von Ribbentrop) secured with barbed wire and stakes. Good progress had been made in the installation of stakes on the meadows. I had the two newly organized anti-tank platoons employed on the roads leading through the inundated area and assigned one rifle group to each as protection. Especially dangerous points were covered by one heavy and one medium anti-tank gun. The roads were also blocked with anti-tank mines. By order of Rommel, heavy anti-tank guns were to be brought up to the coast at the beginning of June and some of them installed along the sea wall in an open firing position... Several positions were equipped with remote control *Liliput panzers* [Goliath midget tanks] filled with explosives to fight advancing tanks ... each position, as well as the reserve units, was to have at least one machine-gun as air defence.

Keil had now retreated to the *Cap de la Hague* – the most northerly point of the Cotentin – where he and his men carried on the fight in the absence of a general surrender order from von Schlieben; much to the delight of the Reich's Propaganda Minister, Joseph Goebbels: 'Keil has earned himself immortality. He has been the true soul of resistance. Had von Schlieben been a man of the same calibre, then perhaps things in Cherbourg might have gone differently.'[22]

As usual though, Goebbels words rang hollow. Two days later the Americans – having sobered up from their liberation celebrations – marched out of Cherbourg and attacked Keil. The struggle ended quickly, and by midnight on 30 June the fighting was over and six thousand Germans went into the bag.

Amongst them were hundreds of *Osttruppen* – at the time the British were reporting that one in five prisoners they were taking over in the east were non-Germans. Alongside the *Ost-bataillone* attached to *709. ID* and *KG König* were at least another four: *281, 561, 600, and 649* – all disappeared in the maelstrom and were officially classed as 'destroyed'. Many of their members were killed in the fighting on nameless lanes or unknown fields, as the German military policeman (unpopularly known as *kettenhunde* – chaindogs), Niklaus Lange, gruesomely observed:

I was looking out of the ditch when a squad of Russians came running down the road, shouting and yelling... I think they were mostly Ukrainians and they were very anti-Stalin and anti-Polish in their views. I saw some of them in training before the invasion and they were big fellows, but this bombing had panicked them completely, they were charging down the road throwing away their guns and arguing about what to do next, some of them were wounded and were hobbling or limping along … another plane came over and bombed them and most of those fellows were cut to pieces in front of me. One moment they were there and the next there were only bits of clothing and bits of men with smoke coming from the pieces, it was like a butcher's slab that road.[23]

For those that survived and went into Allied captivity, the future was very uncertain indeed, as *Gefreiter* Gustav Winter of *716. ID* recounted:

There were thousands and thousands of these Russians and eastern Europeans in the *Wehrmacht* along the *Atlantikwall* beaches… I felt sorry for them because they were miserable men who had no real heart for fighting alongside us at all, but there they were, in the middle of it all … and we German prisoners often wondered what the devil became of them after the invasion. They must have surrendered in big numbers because they had no stomach for the fighting in France – why should they? But there were none of them in the POW camps that was for sure… Anyway, an English doctor I worked with in England after I was transported there, told me one night after a few drinks that when the Allies invaded Normandy there were representatives from the Soviet Union among them … commissars from the Red Army, who were there specifically to search for these Russian defector troops, and when they were taken prisoner they were immediately separated from us Germans and handed over to the commissars right there on the beaches. They were put on ships and sent back to Russia via the Baltic, back to the Soviet Union, and when they got back, they were all immediately shot as traitors. There was no Geneva Convention for them.[24]

There is no concrete evidence to substantiate the claim of Red Army commissars accompanying the landings, but Winter's view of the fate of his erstwhile comrades was widely held within the Wehrmacht. Rudolf von Ribbentrop – 'It's true that a lot of *Hiwis* surrendered in France, but I'm not sure what happened to them after they went into captivity – they must have gone somewhere for sure – but I know they were treated very badly by their own people, and I think they were probably all shot immediately!'[25]

The pitiable huddles of ex-*Osttruppen* being herded who knows where weren't the only casualties of the German loss of Cherbourg; with the port went an army commander no less –7. *Armee*'s Friedrich Dollmann. His leadership of what was by the end of June one of the largest field-armies in the Wehrmacht had been less than inspiring. A Hannibal, Wellington or Manstein he was not. Dollmann was a career German army officer from Würzburg in northern Bavaria who had served his country and lived to see his only son killed in action in the Nazi invasion of Poland in 1939. He was never meant to be in the crucible of history, and it was no surprise that when he was confronted with momentous events he left no discernible mark, except perhaps on the ranks of the ill-starred *Panzer-Lehr* that he had ordered to travel during daylight *jabo*-time on 6–7 June.

The loss of Cherbourg was the final straw, and he and his boss von Rundstedt were summoned like naughty schoolboys to Berchtesgaden in the hushed, safe forests of the Bavarian mountains, where both were berated for their failures in Normandy. Hitler demanded Dollmann's court-martial – von Rundstedt refused. Hitler then demanded Rommel dismiss him, Rommel refused – and at that point the facts become disputed. What is *not* disputed is that Friedrich Dollmann then died – the *how* is disputed. Most accounts say he had a heart attack from the unendurable stress, and that was his end, while a few others say he committed suicide by taking poison to avoid disgrace – at this distance the truth is unknowable. But with Dollmann dead, Rommel stepped in to command both the army group and 7. *Armee*.

With Carentan, Cherbourg and the Cotentin liberated by the beginning of July, the Americans finally had some space to concentrate their forces, but to effect a break-out they still needed to capture Saint-Lô. To do that the GIs would have to fight their way through the *bocage* hedge by hedge – it wasn't a fight the Americans were looking forward to, as one of their tank crewman recalled:

> The only real advantage we had was the Mustangs and Thunderbolts with their rockets. The flyboys could blast them out when we found them a target. But in the end some poor joe with a rifle would still have to put his life on the line and charge up and over the hedgerow to clear out the enemy.

That process of clearing one hedgerow, then the next, was hellish for the Americans assigned to the task, as one officer explained:

The Germans would knock off the first one or two guys, cause the others to duck down behind the bank, and then call for his own mortar support. The German mortars were very, very efficient. By the time our men were ready to go after him, the German, his men and his guns had obligingly retired to the next stop. If our men had rushed him instead of ducking behind the bank his machine-gun or machine-pistol would knock a number off ... in baseball parlance it was a fielder's choice... Back in the dugout [that is among the staff officers] I often heard the remark in tones of contempt and anger, 'Why don't they just get up and go?'

One of those same mortarmen – the veteran German para Wolfgang Langer – was happy with the captured Red Army 8cm mortars his company now used:

It had a weaker barrel thickness than our 8cm equivalent – that was the *GrW 34* with a range of 2400m – but it was longer and could shoot four to five hundred metres farther than our own pieces. We had Russian ammunition for these mortars, but the shells were no good: misfires and drop-shorts were common, so we used German ammunition... These Russian weapons were especially suited for hitting point targets. They always achieved a bullseye after the third or fourth shot.

For the American infantrymen, if Langer's mortars didn't get you, a sniper might, and a medic from the US 30th Infantry Division described exactly what that meant:

The sniper's finger presses the trigger, and the bullet passes through the helmet, scalp, skull, small blood vessels, membrane and into the soft sponginess of the brain substance in the occipital lobe of the cerebral hemisphere. Then you're either paralysed, or you're blind, or you can't smell anything, or your memory is gone, or you can't talk or you're bleeding ... but if the bullet rips through your medulla region in the back of your head, or if it tears through a big blood vessel in your brain – then you're dead.

Things were no better for the Germans, as one para's letter home detailed: 'Every moment I expected deadly shrapnel ... when one hears for hours the whining, whistling and bursting of the shells, and the moaning and groaning of the wounded, one doesn't feel too well.

I almost lost my mind. I chewed up a cigarette, bit into the ground. The others acted just like me, it was hell.' The letter never arrived – it was found, unfinished and unposted, on his dead body.

Soon enough, American commanders started to see the same caution and passivity amongst their own men that was beginning to manifest itself to the east amongst the British and Canadians. It became so severe that the Army began to address the men about it directly. An article from the *Yank* magazine was entitled 'The Enemy and You'. It asked every GI the question: 'The German's slogan is "*Ich oder du!*", "Me or you!" "My life or yours!" There he stands. What are you going to do about it?' The point was hammered home on the front page of the Army's weekly newspaper, the *Stars and Stripes,* when it proclaimed the bloodthirsty headline 'Have You Killed Your German Today?' But more and more of the men being asked that question weren't listening. In the First World War an American infantryman spent an average of ten days in the trenches and was then relieved for a period to rest and recuperate before going back up the line. This had worked well for the relatively short time the US Army was deployed in France. However, come the Second, once the decision had been made to commit forces to the landings in France, senior command in Washington had revised that ten-day limit upwards to two hundred. The Army monitored the impact of its new policy and was disturbed to find that the average soldiers combat skills showed a significant decline after only a single month of fighting, and that many frontline soldiers appeared 'close to a vegetative state' at the 40- to 50-day mark. The same reports concluded that if a man survived to reach the 200-day target, he would be permanently worn out and unfit for further service.

Unsurprisingly, there was no rush to publicise these findings. The problem was made far worse by the fact that the real trauma of battle tended to be concentrated in a relatively small number of men – those the German Army referred to as the 'bayonet strength' of a unit. For example, a typical infantry division might contain 14,000 men, with the same number or more supporting it in ancillary units, but there would only be around 5-6,000 riflemen – the unit's cutting edge – and it was amongst those men where casualties were concentrated. It wouldn't take long before a formation became relatively combat-ineffective, or at the very least damaged, with thousands of signalmen, drivers and supply staff – those whom the *landsers* derogatorily nicknamed '*etappenhengsten*'– rear-area stallions – all relatively untouched, while the infantry companies were bled out.

The Germans soon realised that the nature of the *bocage* fighting – *Buschkrieg* as they christened it – gave them a way of evening up the odds with their more numerous opponents, as one grenadier remembered: 'When we got into a long firefight, the *Amis* would fall back and within minutes we would be pounded by *jabos* or *Arifeuer*. So, we began to fall back about ten or twenty metres when we saw the *Amis* pull out, letting them hit where we used to be. Then it was something of a race to see who could get back to their positions first, us or them.' More often than not it was the *landsers* who won the race. 'We had confidence because every time we met the *Amis* without their support fire, we beat them back. I'm not saying we were élite or anything like that, we just had more experienced leaders.' But the Germans weren't winning – they were just holding – as one of their officers understood all too well:

> There was really no forward thrust, no attacking movement in these chessboard tactics; all they amounted to was the constant small occupation of one small square, previously softened up by gunfire. Even more than the First World War, everything depended on the mechanics of ground fighting, on sledgehammer tactics. Equipment and sweat were more important in the long run than courage and blood.

Whose blood was it? In the Westheer's case against the Americans, it was primarily infantry *landsers* and *fallschirmjäger* – the majority of the panzers being over in the east facing the Anglo-Canadians. For the *landsers* this would just be another of the many hundreds of battles they fought in the war, but for Germany's 'green-devils' the *bocage* of June/July 1944 would become a landmark chapter in their brief history. Formed in the shadow of the Soviet Union's pioneering airborne forces, the German equivalent had been at the forefront of the astonishing successes of the 1940 *blitzkrieg*; Witzig's subjugation of Eben-Emael being just the most spectacular of their early achievements. Carried away by hubris, the invasion of Crete the following year had eviscerated them – thousands of highly-trained volunteer paras lay dead in their harnesses on the Mediterranean island. Since then they had never jumped into action again *en masse*, instead becoming the prototype for all airborne forces ever since – well-trained, super-aggressive, light infantry. In that role they had performed outstandingly well in the Russian meatgrinder and in the scorching deserts of North

Africa. As was typical of Nazi Germany's approach to its élite forces, they preferred mass; Great Britain had two airborne divisions during the war, the 1st and the 6th; the Germans had ten. Admittedly, four of those were created in the military hyperbole of the end of 1944 and early 1945, and were pretty much *fallschirmjäger* divisions in name only, but Normandy would see veterans of the Netherlands, Crete and Russia fight alongside unblooded youngsters in Eugen Meindl's *II Fallschirmkorps* (2nd Parachute Corps). Created in 1943, the *Korps* comprised three divisions: *Division Meindl*, formed from the remnants of paras who had fought in Russia over the last two years and whose main combat formation in Normandy was von der Heydte's *FJR. 6*, and two new divisions; the *3.* and *5. Fallschirmjäger-Divisionen*. Berlin's intent was to replicate earlier successes in forming premier formations, but with the *1.* and *4. Fallschirmjäger-Divisionen* fighting to the death in Italy at Anzio and the green-devil epic of Monte Cassino, there were precious few cadres to spare for France and its new divisions. The results were formations of whom too much was expected. *5. Fallschirmjäger-Division* was in especially poor shape with barely a veteran in its ranks. Only one of its regiments; *15. Fallschirmjäger-Regiment*, was deployable during the Normandy fighting. As for *3. Fallschirmjäger-Division* the usual German imbalances were applied; automatic weapons that increased firepower proliferated – each section had two MG 42s and no fewer than five submachine-guns, so the division as a whole had almost a thousand of 'Hitler's buzz-saws' spread amongst its 16,000 or so officers and soldiers. In contrast, the US 29th Infantry had just one Browning automatic rifle (BAR) per section and no machine-guns – they were outnumbered in mortars by three to one as well. What the paras didn't have though was any armour, heavy artillery or transport. The *jäger* commanders, Eugen Meindl, Richard Schimpf and Gustav Wilke – and von der Heydte of course – were all highly-decorated officers, but their formations were limited in what they could achieve in Normandy. Von der Heydte's *FJR. 6* in particular acquitted itself well in the early fighting, its members dubbed 'the lions of Carentan' due to their tenacious defence of the town. Schimpf's *3. Fallschirmjäger-Division* lost two-thirds of its strength in just five weeks of combat. The odds were always stacked against the *jäger*, as Richard Onderka testified:

We were cut off by the Americans – the whole landscape was an inferno, fires everywhere. Eventually our officer realised we had had enough and told us we were going to surrender – it was a huge relief to most of us, but not all, some wanted to carry on fighting – for me I felt glad my military service was finished – I was only nineteen, but I felt so much older.[26]

With the likes of Onderka and his comrades going into captivity, the *fallschirmjäger* were desperate for replacements, but when over eight hundred youngsters arrived to plug the gaps in *FJR. 6*, von der Heydte was less than impressed: 'About a third of them didn't even have a steel helmet, over half had ripped footgear, their training and morale was even worse than it had been with the original regiment.'

One of his junior NCOs, *Obergefreiter* Franz Hüttich, felt much the same as his boss:

Among the replacements were many young boys around 17 or 18 years old, with absolutely no combat experience, and who had been brought into the military directly from their school benches... There was no evidence in their behaviour of training or jump school, we had to teach the boys everything, and because we were constantly in combat they had to learn very quickly if they weren't going to fall in battle. Other replacements came from the practice of *Heldenklau* ['hero-stealing'] ... these men were ground personnel who hadn't held a weapon in years. They had volunteered for the *fallschirmjäger* after hearing the persuasive talks of the recruiters ... some had also been threatened with deployment to the Waffen-SS, because the ranks of the fighting troops urgently needed filling.[27]

Things were no better for the *landsers*, the mainstay of whom was Dietrich Kraiss's *GI-bane 325. ID* – still fighting, but battered and worn out:

All of us were tired, dirty and hungry. Many of the men's feet were sore and bloody from marching in worn-out boots. When I entered the village, I saw Oberst Goth standing in the door of his command post ... the look on his face told me of the concern he had for the men. When we halted, several men just collapsed to the ground where they stood. Warnings of air attacks and orders to get under cover proved useless, they were just too tired to care.[28]

Von Kluge and Rommel had both come to the same conclusion – albeit reluctantly – the current front couldn't be held, and reinforcements were desperately needed. The two field marshals reached down into the barrel once more, and as their fingers scraped the bottom, they came up with Fritz Bayerlein's *Panzer-Lehr*. Taken out of the line around Caen a few short days before into army reserve to rest and refit, the division was in no state to go back into action, but needs must.

The resultant counter-attack on 11 July, did not go well. Attacking in two *kampfgruppen*, *Bataillon-Philips*, with 250 men from *I./Pz.Gren. Rgt. 901* and ten Panthers from *1./Pz.Rgt.6*, was initially the most successful, its grenadiers riding on the Panther hulls as they slammed into the Americans near the village of Le Désert. However, they were unfamiliar with the terrain in the pre-dawn dark so US tank destroyers were at an advantage and shot the German column to pieces. Only thirty grenadiers escaped – all the Panthers were left burning.

The following day, as the Americans renewed their advance, Karl Wegner saw something extraordinary:

> We had got very used to the way the *Amis* would fight. First would come the *arifeuer*, and when it shifted to the rear, we knew the infantry would come, usually with tanks.. Of course, the *jabos* were somewhere above hitting whatever they could see. We would fool them by putting out captured marker flags; they wouldn't shoot thinking it was their own men... We waited for the infantry to arrive... There were many tanks in this one, of course, none we saw were ours. Some looked odd this time, like great monsters with large horns sticking out in front – a new tactic from the *Amis*. These ones would charge a hedgerow and plough through it! If this didn't work the *Amis* would put explosives in the hole it had made and try to blow a path through...Eventually the *arifeuer* and *jabos* would compel us to fall back.[29]

This was advent of the Rhino tank, and it was a game-changer in *Buschkrieg*. With their usual genius for improvisation, the Americans had hit upon a solution to their *bocage* horror; to retro-fit their tanks with a sort of ram-like construction that would allow the tank to bust through a hedgerow at speed and go on to engage the German defenders before they had time to react. As with so many radical ideas, its genesis is open to conjecture, with the credit mostly going to a sergeant in the 2nd Armoured Division's reconnaissance battalion – Curtis G. Culin; although Culin himself always tried to ensure another soldier received a fair share of the praise. Whatever the truth of the matter, the idea was simple and effective – to cut up the now-useless German beach obstacles into sections, and then weld them onto the front of their tanks as forks or prongs, sometimes with explosives attached on the points to blast through the more stubborn barriers. In no time at all, some five hundred of these 'Culin Rhino devices', or 'Culin hedgerow-cutters' as they were known, were put together and fitted to three-quarters of the 2nd Armored. With the invention of the Rhino tank, much of the defenders' previous advantages disappeared in a welter of smashed hedgerows and field-banks. Just as Alfred Becker's mechanical innovations had provided 21. *Panzerdivision* with a real edge, so Curtis Culin's did for the 2nd. The *bocage* was running out – soon the Germans would be in Saint-Lô itself, without a hedgerow to be seen.

By 15 July 7. *Armee* was sending the Saint-Lô defenders the detested 'hold out to the last man and the last round' orders. A fresh-faced *Kanonier*, Thomas Förster, was caught up in the last-ditch struggle with his 8.8cm guns:

> I was just 17-years-old and in the *Luftwaffe flak* arm. I came up to the front on 14 July as a replacement... My job was to run back and forth bringing shells for the gun ... those 8.8cm shells were pretty heavy too... The day after I arrived the *Amis* came forward to attack. Within seconds we were in action...Once I saw a large dark shape moving against the smoke; it turned out to be a tank. Our Number 1 gunner looked through the sights and adjusted the gun – a deafening crack followed, I saw the tank explode, popping all the hatches, shooting flame and smoke. Several men around me threw up their arms, indicating they had seen the 'kill', I did too... I pushed out of my mind the thoughts of the young men who had been inside the tank. It was something one had to do to get though the war.[30]

A couple of days later Förster himself had a lucky escape;

> We heard the *jabos* but were confident they hadn't seen us ... we weren't really concerned. I was on my way back for more shells with this other lad, he was from Hamburg, well, we heard a whistle and he knew that sound from back home. He pushed me into a ditch, before we hit the ground a huge explosion ripped apart the gun and all those behind us. My God I had never felt anything like it before or since. The shockwaves hit us, and the air was ripped from our lungs. I knew we had lost consciousness since it was a while before

we got up... The only thing left of the others was a few cracked and broken helmets, an unforgettable sight. We couldn't stay there any longer. We found two useable rifles and headed off towards Saint-Lô. We felt we would find someone in charge in the way.[31]

As 16 July came to a close, the end was in sight for the German defence of the city, as *GR. 916*'s *Leutnant* Heinze knew all too well.

Our lines were thinning out, the dead and wounded grew in number. My men fell back in good order to wherever the next position was, a field or a hedgerow. Remarkably, many of the wounded opted to stay and fight, and perhaps die with their *kameraden*... We would launch small counter-attacks to stem the enemy advance, but very soon all of us that were left were exhausted. Then we were up against tanks, I asked for volunteers. A man from the *panzerjäger* came forward, his feet were a bloody mess, but he knew how to knock out tanks. All of his friends joined him ... we held up the *Amis* as long as we could.

That night, Dietrich Kraiss requested permission to withdraw his remaining troops south of the city towards the Vire River – the request was denied, the city must be held.

By now the defenders were mainly men of *352. ID* and Schimpf's 3. *Fallschirmjäger-Division*. In the former, the veteran *Obergefreiter* Paul Kalb spoke to his younger comrade Karl Wegner: 'Karl, any fool can see that we're beaten. There is no hope of holding this lousy French ruin. If those fools with the oak leaves and crimson on their collars had any sense they would let us keep going until we got to the other side of the river, or even better they'd end the war before we're all dead.'

Wegner felt very much the same, 'but didn't have the courage to speak out like him. Any more losses and there wouldn't be anyone left from our company ... we began to dig in once more, work was very slow, everyone was very dispirited. You could see that most just didn't give a damn anymore.'

The American pressure was relentless and the final act was coming to a close, witnessed by the likes of Thomas Förster, Hans Heinze and Karl Wegner:

After a night of trying to dig into the hard earth, the *Amis* came at us in large numbers. I fired several wild and un-aimed shots at them, it did no good. Within minutes our ad hoc company was broken... I was scared and afraid to move, the lad from Hamburg ran off with the others. A wounded man tumbled into my poor excuse for a foxhole, he was a truck driver but also a *gefreiter*, so I asked him what to do. He asked me for something white ... then we just waited for the *Amis* to get to us. I felt like a hundred rifles were pointed at me when we peered up over the dirt. With my arms straight up in the air as far as I could get them, I climbed out, shaking with fear... They searched us quickly and pushed us towards the rear of their lines... I was one of the lucky ones.

In the rubble of the city itself, Hans Heinze was fighting on with his few surviving men. Some US tanks drove down the street towards him and his troops. Grabbing a *panzerfaust,* the young officer ran out in front of the lead tank: 'The next thing I knew I was lying on the ground. I tried to move and discovered that my right arm and side were hurt. In the momentary lapse between consciousness and blacking-out my first thought was that I'd never play tennis again!'

Heinze vainly waved his handkerchief to try and avoid being crushed by the oncoming tanks, only to stare amazed as the lead commander stopped his tank, got out and asked Heinze what he wanted – he then allowed the wounded German to be pulled out of the road by two of his grenadiers, who took the now-unconscious officer to a command post for treatment.

At this point Kraiss began to disregard the orders from both Meindl and 7. *Armee* and started to withdraw his men south of the city before it was too late. But for Karl Wegner's best friend Willi Schuster, it already was:

I watched Kalb drag Willi back around the corner by his boots... Willi's cries of pain sent shivers down my spine... I went to Willi and Kalb, whose bloody hands were placing a second bandage on Willi's chest. The wounds were bad, through the lung and stomach. My God how Kalb tried to save him, like he was his own brother... Kalb looked at me and shook his head, Willi was going to die. His face became sunken and lost its colour, he knew he was finished. He stopped shrieking in pain and began to cry, softly. He looked at me with eyes one cannot describe and said his last words, I will never forget them: 'Karl, through all this to just die in the rubble, it makes no sense.' I held him until he died... Kalb stepped over the wall with his arms held high. I looked at Willi's lifeless body one more time as it lay there in the rubble, then scrambled out into captivity – thank God it was finally over.[32]

Willi Schuster was 18 years old. Saint-Lô fell on 19 July.

The Americans had now captured a major port – admittedly a wrecked one, but still a port – they were finally out of the *bocage,* and now they controlled the road network into Brittany and the French interior. They also had possession of enough of the French hinterland to manoeuvre within. The conditions were being set for the end game.

***

The following day – even as the Americans began mopping-up stragglers and the odd die-hard sniper – a 39-year-old German, Heinrich Berger, was pulled out of a bombed-out building by his best friend, Heinz Buchholz. Berger had lost both his legs in the blast and bled to death in minutes. Three other men; Günther Korten, Rudolf Schmundt, and Heinz Brandt, were badly injured in the same explosion, and died from their wounds over the next few days. Just another four casualties to add to the ever-lengthening list of the fallen; except these men didn't die in Normandy, or indeed on any front, and they weren't killed by the Soviets or western Allies, but by their fellow Germans – they died in the failed bomb plot to assassinate Adolf Hitler. At last, after years of acquiescence and collaboration with the Nazi regime, a few members of Germany's military and civilian leadership had decided to take action to end the dictatorship that had murdered millions and set their country and much of the rest of the world on a path to destruction.

The attempt failed, and with it went any possibility – however remote – of Germany ending the war with a negotiated peace. There were two immediate outcomes from the failure. The first was a bloody witch-hunt, led by the *Gestapo* and SS, to sniff out the conspirators and punish them with show trials and brutal executions – almost five thousand men and women would be killed as a result. The second – and one that was immediately relevant for the campaign in Normandy – was that the last remaining vestiges of independence the Wehrmacht had from Hitler and his Nazi apparatus were swept away. Heinz Guderian – the father of the *panzerwaffe,* architect of *blitzkrieg* – and for many the epitome of the no-nonsense general prepared to stand up to the follies of politicians, having already been sacked by Hitler once following the defeat in front of Moscow back in late 1941; broadcast to the German nation on 23 July:

A few officers lost courage and preferred the path of disgrace to the only path befitting an honest soldier – the path of duty and honour.

The people and the Army stand firmly united behind the *Führer*...
'Loyalty is the mark of honour'. Long live Germany and our *Führer*
Adolf Hitler, and now, nation to arms![33]

Six days later, *Schneller Heinz* (Guderian's nickname 'Fast Heinz')
went even further in offering succour to Hitler and Nazism:

Every General Staff officer must be a National Socialist Leadership
Officer, namely he must demonstrate that he is one of the 'best of
the best' not merely in the realms of strategy and tactics, but also
in the political realm through his exemplary attitude and active
guidance and instruction of younger comrades in the *Führer*'s ideas.
I expect every General Staff officer to accept and convert to my views
immediately – and to do so publicly. Anyone who cannot do so
should ask to leave the General Staff.[34]

In a few short sentences, Guderian sold the Army down the river – and
along with it, his soul. Not that the ever-smiling general was alone in
his calumny, the now ex-OB West, Gerd von Rundstedt, was wheeled
out of his forced retirement and sat alongside Guderian, 'Lakeitel' and
two other senior officers in the laughingly entitled *Ehrenhof* (Court
of Honour) set up in the wake of the assassination attempt to begin
the quasi-judicial slaughter of anyone implicated in the plot. The
accused weren't allowed to appear, no defence was permitted, and the
only evidence submitted was from the *Gestapo*. The high-priests of
the Army's blackened honour expelled a host of their fellow officers,
condemning them to Roland Freisler's equally-appalling People's
Court, and their conviction and execution for treason; many being
hung on meathooks with piano-wire and filmed slowly strangling to
death for Hitler's delectation. As the well-known British historian
and biographer, Sir John Wheeler-Bennett wrote in 1967 of von
Rundstedt's part in the charade: 'To such a nadir of supine degradation
had come the child of Scharnhorst, Gneisenau and Moltke.'

From now on no 'fortress' order, no 'no withdrawal at any cost'
command, or 'hold to the last man and the last bullet' instruction
was Hitler's responsibility alone – they would all be indelibly marked
with the moral cowardice of the entire German professional military
leadership.

Not that this was unexpected. The saying that 'the road to hell is
paved with good intentions' should be amended regarding Guderian
and his colleagues to read 'paved with gold'. From his accession to

the Chancellor's office in 1933, Hitler had instituted a massive and all-encompassing system of bribery, designed to buy the loyalty of the Reich's senior military cadre. Run by Hans Lammers, chief of the Chancellory office, the 'Konto 5' slush fund distributed cash, property, cars and expensive presents to generals and admirals alike. Soon the system became even more creative, exempting recipients from the payment of federal and state taxes (the top rate of income tax in Germany in 1939 was 65%), paying for any and all improvements made to their properties and then distributing landed estates stolen from their owners following conquests in the East. *Schneller Heinz* was given a two-thousand acre estate at Deipenhof (now Głębokie) in the annexed *Warthegau* area of occupied Poland. When asked by Manstein how he came by his new home, Guderian told him that he had been given 'a list of fine Polish properties which he had viewed over a few days before deciding on the most suitable'. He also told Manstein he had no idea what had happened to the former owners, but after the war, in a fit of guilt, Guderian changed the dates and circumstances of the theft in his memoirs to try and present the seizure as a legitimate retirement gift.[35]

Not that this was the only compensation the *Führer* handed out to his commanders. Known officially as *Aufwandsentschädigungen* ('compensation for expenses'), the basis of the corruption system was monthly, tax-free payments of 4,000 *Reichsmarks* (RMs) for *generalfeldmarschalle* and *großadmiralen*, and 2,000 RMs for all other senior officers, with a bonus of 400 or 300 RMs per month respectively from the end of 1939 onwards to compensate for the increased cost of wartime living – a hugely significant amount of money considering the annual salary of a general or admiral was twenty-four thousand. In addition, recipients could expect extra cash to help pay for houses, clothes, food, medical care etc. Birthdays were especially lucrative, with a cheque for a quarter of a million RMs hitting the doormat of a general's or admiral's home. Guderian and his ilk couldn't even claim that the payments were above board either, as before they received a *pfennig* they had to meet with Lammers who told them in no uncertain terms that the money was not only dependent on their loyalty to Hitler and his regime, but should never be referred to in public, and that no records should be kept about it – all the men knew it was bribery, pure and simple. At the same time a lowly *landser* employed in mine-clearing at the front, could expect a daily danger money bonus of one *Reichsmark* – subject to tax.

As for von Rundstedt, he too was part of the web of corruption, but following his dismissal in July he refused to cash the quarter-million birthday cheque sent to him by Hitler. When this began to arouse suspicion as to his loyalty, he paid the money into an account for his daughter-in-law, where it sat, untouched, until his death in 1953. His replacement as OB West, Günther von Kluge, had no such qualms, cashing his 60th birthday cheque for a cool half-million RMs back in October 1942 – it was a *special* birthday after all.

7

The Dam Bursts

The dictator's trousers and jacket had been shredded in the 20 July bomb blast – as had his ear-drums – but his determination to control every single aspect of the war, with as little input, advice, or interference from his military professionals was not only intact but strengthened. From now on, his way was the only way, and in both Belarus and Normandy it would spell disaster for the Wehrmacht. In the East, the *Ostheer* was ordered to stand its ground in the face of the continuing Soviet *Bagration* offensive, and lost a full quarter of its entire manpower as a result, in the West the arch-gambler would bet the house on a single card, only to turn a two of clubs and not an ace of spades.

With the fall of Saint-Lô, the western Allies had turned a corner in the Normandy campaign – just how sunlit the new vista would be was yet to be determined. By liberating the city, the Americans had positioned themselves to escape the hedgerow claustrophobia of *Basse-Normandie*, and break out into the more open, tank-friendly country towards Avranches, and the *départements* of *Orne*, *Sarthe*, and *Eure-et-Loir*. They all led to the gates of Paris.

The Germans had a choice to make; where would the greatest blow land next, in the west with the Americans, or in the east with the Anglo-Canadians? The decision would dictate where the weight of the Westheer's combat power would go; those self-same panzer divisions that had held Caen and its environs for so long and paid the blood price for doing so. Should they jump left or jump right? Once again, as with just about every single major decision the Germans had to make about the Normandy campaign, they got it wrong. They jumped right. The panzers would stay facing the Anglo-Canadians around Caen, protecting what they saw as the better tank-country and shorter route to the Rhine and Germany. The *Das Reich* and *Panzer-Lehr* divisions alone would stay in the west, with the *Lehr* now graded by its own *Korps* as having a combat value of '3'; meaning it was assessed as incapable of offensive action. Its losses had been severe; 3,407 men, as well as fifty panzers, eighty-two armoured half-tracks and over two hundred other vehicles.[1] Sepp Dietrich demanded of higher command; 'We need *panzergrenadiers* in particular, the *Panzer-Lehr* has virtually none left.' Bayerlein's division, lauded a few short weeks previously as the most-experienced and best-equipped formation in the entire Westheer, reported a combat strength of just over three thousand, of whom a third were non-*Lehr* attachments or washed-up remnants from other units. Kurt Kauffmann, the *Lehr's* operations officer, doubted its ability to withstand an attack: 'I realised the situation was hopeless, with more then forty per cent of our infantry gone and the tremendous Allied shelling and air activity.'

Das Reich was also in trouble, its hugely delayed and atrocity-strewn march from its pre-D-Day bases in the Toulouse area had been a disaster for both it and the civilian areas it crossed. Constant disruption to the railways and a lack of fuel and spare parts had left significant portions of the division more or less stranded. By mid-July two battalions of its panzergrenadiers – one each from the *Deutschland* and *Der Führer* regiments – the artillery's third battalion, two companies from the reconnaissance and *pioniere* battalions, and all the divisional troops, still hadn't reached Normandy. It was on its second divisional commander, Heinz Lammerding having been wounded on 24 July, his place taken by *SS-Obersturmbannführer* Christian Tychsen, the facially-disfigured and controversial commander of *Das Reich's* panzer regiment.

That left the mass of Heinrich Eberbach's armoured muscle still grouped around Caen with the 2., 21. and *Graf* von Schwerin's newly-formed 116. *Panzer-Divisionen*, the *LSSAH*, the *HJ* and the *Hohenstaufen* and *Frundsberg*. They faced an Anglo-Canadian army that was beginning to cannibalise frontline regiments and comb out rear-area support services in an attempt to keep its infantry force up to strength. Meanwhile in the west, the navy convoys kept on bringing in fresh doughboys to add to the ranks of GI olive-drab.

Indeed, so many fresh American units were reaching the battlefront – unhindered by either the Kriegsmarine or Luftwaffe – that Omar Bradley's next offensive blow; Operation *Cobra*, was ready to be launched the day Saint-Lô fell. As it turned out, poor weather proved a greater obstacle than the Germans, and the offensive was delayed until the morning of 25 July to capitalise on clear skies for the mandatory pre-offensive pulverising from the air. The forward units of the *Lehr* got a whiff of what was about to happen when they saw movement in the American lines and reported it back to headquarters: 'American infantry in front of our trenches are abandoning their positions. They are withdrawing everywhere.'

Then the next messages came in to Bayerlein: 'Bombs being dropped in front of our lines ... bombing attacks by endless waves of aircraft. Jabo attacks on bridges and artillery positions.'

It wasn't just *jabos* either. As Montgomery had done for *Goodwood*, so Bradley did for *Cobra* – he had managed to persuade high command to assign him something special; no fewer than fifteen hundred Boeing B-17 Flying Fortresses, each carrying eight thousand pounds of high-explosive,[2] flying through the sunny blue sky in wave after uninterrupted wave. The noise of thousands of engines filled the air as the *landsers* stared, entranced, at the approaching thunderclap. Minutes later the bomb-bays opened, and death and mayhem came to the German lines on a massive scale. The division that bore the brunt of the attack was *Panzer-Lehr*, as its commanding officer described: 'Back and forth the bomb carpets were laid, artillery positions were wiped out, panzers overturned and buried, infantry positions flattened, and all roads and tracks destroyed ... after an hour I had no communication with anyone, even by radio.'

Bayerlein went forward to see the situation for himself, and what he saw shocked him to the core:

My front lines looked like the surface of the moon, with the bomb craters touching rim to rim... All signal communications had been cut and no command was possible. The shock effect on the troops was indescribable. Several of my men went mad and half-crazed soldiers jumped out of craters and rushed around in the open or ran in circles until they were cut down by splinters...everything was burnt or blasted.

A young officer from *Oberst* von Hausser's *Panzergrenadier-Lehr-Regiment 901* reported to Bayerlein, 'I can't find a single strongpoint that is intact. The *HKL* [*Hauptkampflinie*; main line of resistance] has vanished. Where it used to be is now a zone of death.'[3] Once the heavies were finished, the artillery took up the pummelling, with over five hundred guns saturating the German lines with high-explosive. Bayerlein:

> Simultaneously with the storm from the air, innumerable guns of the American artillery poured drumfire into our field positions...at least seventy per cent of my troops were out of action – dead, wounded, crazed or numb. All my forward panzers were knocked-out, and the roads were practically impassable. [There was] a feeling of helplessness, weakness and inferiority.

The bombing and subsequent artillery barrage were indeed overwhelming and had a far more devastating effect than over to the east in *Goodwood*. *Lehr* especially was decimated. It took a thousand casualties it couldn't afford, particularly in its panzergrenadier companies, and lost two dozen panzers and assault-guns written off – although Bayerlein, in a fit of despondency that characterised much of his command, initially estimated his losses to be double that figure. However, as they had done for the past seven weeks, the Germans somehow managed to hold on, *landsers*, *fallschirmjäger* and panzergrenadiers clinging on stubbornly to every foxhole, every sunken lane and half-piece of cover, frustrating the Americans as they tried to fight their way forward. One of those *landsers* was *Gefreiter* Peter Simeth of *352. ID*, one of only two survivors in his platoon left from D-Day:

> Early on the morning of the 26th I was put in the forward machine-gun position with three other men; all were Marines from coastal artillery units. We had heard that the *Amis* had attacked all along a wide front. I left the position to go and relieve myself... I was preparing to squat when a shot went by my head. I let out a shout and got down... I went back to the position to find all the Marines dead, lying in pools of their own blood.

Peter Simeth was captured later that same day.

In desperation, von Kluge threw the rest of Gustav Wilke's *5. Fallschirmjäger-Division* into the fight, despite only *FJR. 15* being anywhere near combat-worthy, and with Friedrich von der Heydte's scathing assessment of it ringing in his ears:

The 5. *Fallschirmjäger-Division* was of little combat value. Less than ten per cent of the men had jump training, and barely twenty per cent of the officers had any infantry training or experience. Armament and equipment were incomplete; only fifty per cent of the authorised machine-guns, one regiment was without helmets, there were no heavy anti-tank weapons, no motorisation.

This was going to stop the American armoured advance? The division's own members didn't think so either, as *Unteroffizier* Walter Klein – a divisional medical orderly – pointed out; 'The view of my comrades was: "The next attack will be our end." We no longer had any heavy weapons. We still had rifles, but only six rounds of ammunition each.' One of the wounded Klein was treating – a decorated veteran of the Russian front - said to him; 'Don't you know *Sani* that it's no longer a battle here in Normandy? The enemy is superior to us in men and equipment, we're like lambs to the slaughter. Our supreme command has left us in the lurch – no airplanes, not even enough ammunition!'[4] Another said; 'I'm beyond caring. Two of my brothers were sacrificed in Stalingrad, and it was quite useless, and here we have the same.'[5]

Wilke's inexperienced division fell apart under the American assault. Von der Heydte's *FJR. 6* tried to hold the line, to no avail:

Suddenly I looked ahead and cried out 'Turn around! There are Sherman tanks and *Amis* ahead!' Wern turned the car around and headed to the right. In the curve, a shell struck directly above Günter Friebe. The car ran into a roadside ditch next to an apartment building... When I came to, Friebe was no longer there. On the seat in front of me there was only unrecognizable flesh and blood to be seen. Wern had lost his right arm and been hit heavily by shell splinters. My hands, face and legs were bleeding... I took off my helmet and noticed that shrapnel had pierced it.

Amazingly, *Obergefreiter* Hermann Wübbold managed to rejoin his unit and carry on the fight, Hermann Wern did not.[6]

Cobra was proving to be a different kettle of fish to the likes of *Epsom* and *Goodwood*. With so little armour and heavy weaponry, the German defence on the western side of the Allied lodgement was beginning to crack as more and more American formations were fed in. Desperate resistance without adequate reinforcement and resupply just wasn't enough, and even von Kluge knew it – but he still refused to shift his panzers west, and instead sent one of his staff officers to impress on Bayerlein personally the gravity of the situation. Arriving at the *Lehr*'s headquarters near the village of Dangy in the late afternoon of the 26th, the immaculately turned-out *Oberstleutnant* relayed his master's orders: 'You've got to hold out ... not a single man is to leave his position.'

Tired and disillusioned, *alte Fritz* finally snapped. 'Out in front everyone is holding out, everyone; my grenadiers and my *pioniere* and my panzer crews, they're all holding their ground. Not a single man is leaving his post. Not one. They're lying in their foxholes mute and silent, because they're dead. Dead.'

Von Kluge's man stood open-mouthed at the panzer general's outburst – this simply wasn't what German officers did, but Bayerlein hadn't finished. 'You may report to the *feldmarschall* that the *Panzer-Lehr* is destroyed. Only the dead can now hold the line. But I shall stay here if those are my orders.' It is surprising that Bayerlein wasn't relieved of his command immediately, as it was clear he was close to a breakdown.

A tipping point had now been reached. For the first time in the campaign the *landsers* were panicking, as the SS NCO Helmut Gunther recognised: 'I had seen the first retreat from Moscow, which was terrible enough, but at least units were still intact. Here, we had become a cluster of individuals. We weren't battle-worthy anymore. All that we had going for us was that we knew each other very well.'[7]

For the Westheer, the parallel with Moscow was truly frightening. Germany's *Heeresgruppe Mitte* (Army Group Centre), the very fulcrum of its invasion of the Soviet Union back in 1941, had almost been annihilated in that disaster, and the Ostheer had never recovered from it.

Finally, after weeks of fighting and sacrifice, Allied pressure overcame the stubborn boy's fingers, and the dyke gave way in a mighty rush. The German front in western Normandy collapsed.

A former member of the 17th SS recalled his own unit's struggle as half-a-dozen German divisions disintegrated around them. 'As we had almost no vehicles, we had to use oxen to pull the guns across the river. The *Amis* were advancing steadily, and, together with a Wehrmacht battalion we moved – using requisitioned civilian vehicles – through Tours. The whole time we had no communications with Division.' That same division was a busted flush; hastily formed, under-equipped, lacking in qualified officers and NCOs and fleshed-out with thousands of 17-year-olds, the *Götz von Berlichingen* was rudely shoved aside, as one of its NCOs, Hans Stöber, realised:

We found that *Ami* units in company strength had bypassed us. There was no choice but to order us to withdraw ... we knew that the vital thing was to stick together, but we could see that the *Amis* had learnt how to break through, ignoring their flanks and pushing on to occupy crossroads and set up blocking positions so our vehicles and heavy weapons couldn't get through. We lost vast quantities of equipment.[8]

The only German formation remotely capable of slowing the growing offensive and giving von Kluge time to stitch a new front together was 2. *SS-Panzerdivision 'Das Reich'*. The first, and arguably the finest division the Waffen-SS fielded in the war, the *Reich*'s roll of battle honours read like a history of the Wehrmacht's greatest victories. Already destroyed and rebuilt twice, it had somehow retained a hard core of veterans who resembled in many ways the formidable *Experten* of the eastern *Jagdwaffe*. But – just as the *Experten* were blown out of the skies above them – the grenadiers and panzer crews of the *Reich*, found themselves being slaughtered by the burgeoning power of the Allied war machine. Their commander of just two days, Christian Tychsen, urged them on: 'I am a veteran panzer commander. If the enemy succeeds with this breakthrough then for us the war in France is over.' That same day he was killed in a firefight near his headquarters and Otto Baum took over, the division's third commander in a week.

A counter-attack by the *Reich* and some roped-together elements of the *Götz von Berlichingen* dissipated in a hail of fire, and all of a sudden the Sherman crews found themselves trundling along the roads of Normandy with barely a German in sight.

Still the Germans tried to fight on, as the *Reich*'s Otto Weidinger made clear: 'Could we allow anyone to say that we were only willing to fight abroad, that we would not fight on in defence of our own country? The English would have done the same.'[9] Another *Reich* officer determined to fight on was *SS-Obersturmführer* Fritz Langanke. A miner's son turned Panther commander, Langanke had celebrated his twenty-fifth birthday on 15 July by shooting-up five Shermans as he defended his position near St Denis; 'A thing like that puts you on an unbelieveable emotional level. You feel like Siegfried, and that you can dare to do anything!' So, when ordered to rendevous with an Army unit at a crossroads and hold until ordered otherwise, he complied without hesitation. Attacked on arrival by American Shermans, he and a second Panther accounted for four before he noticed the *landsers* running towards the Americans with their hands held high: 'They had taken the chance to finish their war.' Hit by several tank rounds, Langanke's driver shouted; 'I can't see! The periscope's gone!' Abandoning their stricken panzer, they hot-footed it down the road until a *jabo* swooped, killing one of the crew and enraging the rest. 'If we had had the chance to get that man, there would have been another war crime!'

Even among the ranks of the SS a sense of hopelessness was setting in, as *SS-Obersturmbannführer* Karl Kreutz acknowledged when he was told he had been awarded the coveted Knight's Cross as he watched yet another massive American bombardment deluge his forward units; 'Pleased? How could I be pleased? For the first time I knew we had lost.'

Fallschirmjäger Albert Sturm and the other nine men of his platoon were fast coming to the same conclusion, as they tried to avoid being encircled by the advancing Americans:

> We received the order to mount panzers ... the 7. *Kompanie* sat on the first three panzers, Klaus Klapprat and I on the third, the command panzer... Around 0330hrs the panzer commander said to us, 'Boys, it looks like we've made it, we've just come out of the encircled area!' We were thrilled to have escaped. As soon as the first panzer disappeared around the next curve and the second one followed it, the peaceful daybreak was over. The *Ami* anti-tank weapon gave a short, dry roar ... the force of the explosion had sent the comrades who had been riding on the panzer flying away... The first panzer was burning up, and around it lay a few lifeless *fallschirmjäger* ... a mortar landed directly next to Klaus, it must have hit him hard because he jumped up, screaming like an animal and ran towards the back. I ran right after him, but before I could reach him, two medics grabbed him and laid him on a stretcher...he had multiple splinters in his chest... The machine-gunner next to me suffered a mental breakdown... In front of us was a Sherman tank, firing with all its guns. With our small-arms we could do nothing against it; we were nailed to the spot ... we stayed under cover and learned that the whole attempt to break through had failed. On the street our panzers had ground to a halt and were fighting for mere survival... Then the order came to disengage from the enemy, 7. *Kompanie* was supposed to cover the withdrawal, ha! What a joke, how many of us were left? But an order is an order... It was every man for himself.[10]

Not that far away from Sturm and his comrades another *fallschirmjäger* was receiving the same treatment as his fellow general officer Fritz Bayerlein. This time it was Eugen Meindl's turn to be reminded of his orders from 7. *Armee* – dictated to him by none other than von Kluge's own son, an *Oberstleutnant* on the staff, and 'what his father called a "front traveller", but what we in our own manner called a spy, to collect his impressions for the old man'. The irascible paratrooper reacted in exactly the same way as *Lehr*'s commander had, and poured out his anger at what he saw as the stupidity of higher command:

> Kindly convey to your father exactly what I am going to say to you – the time has come when Normandy can no longer be held. It cannot be held because the troops are exhausted. This is mainly the fault of being given orders to hold out in hopeless situations, and we are still being ordered to hold out even now. The enemy will break through to the west of us and outflank us. What's going to happen then? All that's left for the grenadiers to do is lie down and sacrifice their lives, it's heartbreaking to have to stand by and watch!

By now, von Kluge senior had realised that the American threat was not only very real, but would require a huge shift in armour to the west from the east of the front, if there was to be any hope of stopping its onward march. He ordered 2. and 116. *Panzer-Divisionen* to move west, only for Montgomery to launch Operation *Bluecoat* on the 30th, which did just enough to tie down von Kluge's panzers in the Caen sector. Hans von Luck and his men of 21. *Panzerdivision* were thrown into the fighting: 'We all hoped for a few days' peace to lick our wounds...The men were tired, our losses heavy. We had been in action now for eight weeks without a break, longer, therefore, than any other division. But in spite of that, morale was high. The men fought until they dropped.'[11] The western end of the Westheer's front was left to its own devices.

On 31 July, the coastal city of Avranches was liberated; from their tanks, armoured personnel-carriers and trucks, American soldiers gazed at the ethereal beauty of Mont Saint-Michel a few miles away out in the bay as they motored out of Normandy and into Brittany, as did *Gefreiter* Spiekerkörter of 256. *ID* in his war-booty Russian truck: 'The Americans were already in Avranches, and wanted to prevent us from breaking out. How we got through and over the bridge I still don't know. I only remember that two officers with drawn pistols tried to seize our truck from us!'[12] At noon the next day, things got even worse for the Westheer when Bradley okay'd the activation of the US Third Army to lead the ongoing offensive. The man he put in charge of the Third was the wealthiest officer in the entire United States Army, and someone whose ego – and talent – matched his personal fortune. George Smith Patton Jnr., a master of armoured warfare, in the mode of Rommel or Guderian, was the proverbial kid in the candy store, in command of one of the most mechanised military formations in the world, with nothing in front of him except miles of excellent roads and the odd garrison of second-rate reservists. When asked by his subordinates about the danger to his flanks from German counter-attacks, he would inevitably growl: 'Leave the flanks to me, you worry about your objectives!' The pistol-wielding, silver-haired self-publicist was as good as his word, and Patton's leadership of the Third Army would become a massive nail in the Westheer's coffin. In his first seventy-two hours of command, he drove 100,000 men and 15,000 vehicles along a single road and over a 500-year-old bridge at Pontaubault just south of Avranches – the tiger was loose in 7. *Armee*'s rear.

What price now for Hans von Salmuth's 15. *Armee* sitting north of the Seine,[13] or the 300,000 men and 1,600 guns of Johannes Blaskowitz's *Heeresgruppe G* twiddling their collective thumbs south of the Loire? Static units as many of them were, they would still have been invaluable to man the line and release Eberbach's armour to parry Patton – and as for Wend von Wietersheim's 11. *Panzerdivision*, who knows? But those men and all their equipment and heavy weaponry were hundreds of miles from the steel hook that was now ripping through the rear of 7. *Armee* and threatening its very existence.

Von Kluge now tried to get Hitler to accept his predecessor's plan to save the Wehrmacht's position in France; to use the panzer divisions to mask a withdrawal north of the Seine by 7. *Armee*, set up a new defensive line, while also pulling back north *Heeresgruppe G*. Most of France would be abandoned to the enemy, but the bulk of the Westheer and its equipment would be saved for another day, and the subsequent fighting would still be mainly on French soil. The one-eyed SS general Paul Hausser – now 7. *Armee*'s commander having succeeded von Kluge – saw the writing on the wall: 'A large proportion of the divisions which had been fighting continuously since the invasion began, just disintegrated into small groups as a result of the enemy armoured break-in on the Army's left flank ... most of these groups were without officers or NCOs and roamed at random through the countryside.' An *Unteroffizier* in one such group wrote: 'For five days we had nothing to eat but unripe fruit and the iron rations we took from our dead comrades ... we had to leave 178 of our wounded behind.'[14]

Once again, Hitler dismissed withdrawal out of hand, and instead relied on his own genius and gambler's instinct to fix on a plan to bring victory – *Unternehmen Lüttich* (Operation *Liège*). The neck of land Patton was pushing his army through at such an extraordinary pace was just sixteen kilometres wide at its narrowest – cut the link and Third Army would wither and die in days as supplies swiftly ran out. A single US armoured division needed 25,000 gallons of fuel per day just to keep moving, let alone fighting, and even an infantry division needed 6,500 gallons. As Hitler pored over the map in his situation room, the opportunity was clear as day; a daring thrust by the *panzerwaffe* from Mortain would cut through those few kilometres to Avranches in a day – two at most – and isolate Third Army. In a single stroke the Wehrmacht would have snatched back the inititiave it hadn't held since before D-Day, and dump a hundred thousand GIs into German POW cages. The Germans could then mass for another assault that would take them to the Normandy beaches and finally see off the Allied landings. Hitler's faith in *Festung Europa* would be vindicated, and, as he told his generals; 'Once defeated, the enemy will never try to invade again... We shall then transfer our forces to the Eastern front to revolutionise the situation there.'

German victory was just sixteen kilometres away – a *landser* on foot could easily cover that distance in a day. Back in the 1940 French campaign, Rommel's panzers had advanced that far in a morning! But a map on a table in a wooden hut hundreds of miles away in the quiet of an East Prussian pine forest did not represent what the Westheer was facing in Normandy in 1944, as 2. *Panzerdivisions junker* commander, Heinrich *Freiherr* von Lüttwitz, knew only too well; 'The Allies have total air supremacy. They bomb and shoot at anything that moves, even single vehicles or men... The feeling of being powerless against the enemy's aircraft has a paralysing effect.' But providence had saved the *Führer* three weeks earlier, and there was no way a piffling thing like an accurate sitrep was going to get in the way of his finest hour in Normandy – the Holy Grail of a *Vernichtungsgedanke* (the 'extermination battle' every German staff officer was trained to try and achieve as the zenith of the military art). Bent over the same map he was using to pinpoint *Lüttich*'s scope and direction of attack, Hitler waved his right hand (not his left as it shook too much) and corralled a massive force of eight panzer divisions from across the Norman front to his counter-offensive – eight panzer divisions, four entire *Korps*, half of whom were from his beloved Waffen-SS – an armoured fist like this hadn't been assembled on such a narrow front since Kursk the previous summer – not the best of comparisons perhaps. The question Hitler wouldn't and couldn't answer was how this miracle was to occur in the face of Allied air power, beyond resorting to the tired old '1,000 new fighters' line, although just where the *Jagdwaffe* was meant to conjure them from now was anyone's guess. In any case, even if by some miracle the Luftwaffe could put a thousand fighters up over *Lüttich* they would still be outnumbered by three or four to one and shot out of the sky. Regardless, von Kluge attempted the impossible, while pleading with his *Führer* to allow him to start the attack immediately and not wait for the illusory 'eight-division alignment', but even this decision was taken out of the *feldmarschall*'s hands – one wonders what he *was* allowed to decide at this point! His Chief-of-Staff Blumentritt was scathing on that score: 'All the planning had been done in Berlin with large-scale maps, and the advice of the generals in France was not asked for, nor was it encouraged.' Blumentritt was a member of the anti-Hitler resistance by this point, and so unlikely to comment positively on the *Führer*'s orders, but even so it is difficult to see *Lüttich* as anything other than an armchair commander's delusion.

All this time Patton dug his cavalryman's spurs into his Army's flanks and drove them on – they would reach Le Mans (7. *Armee*'s old headquarters) in three days having covered 120 kilometres, causing chaos, as Eugen Griesser remembered:

Every battalion assigned a few platoons to secure the flanks and a rearguard for the retreat out of the encircled area... Events played out as they had to. Our platoon ran aground in a sunken road against a company of Sherman tanks with accompanying infantry in half-tracks. We managed to take out the first two tanks with limpet mines and explosives before the column could respond ... we took advantage of the confusion to work our way into the bushes and split up... We marched through the night and the next morning we came upon the baggage train of some army unit. A military police motorcycle and sidecar stood at the gate of a farmyard... The *Feldwebel* demanded our papers and our marching orders... The policeman refused to understand we had been separated from our unit and therefore had no written marching orders, although we were already on our way back to our regiment. He began to ramble on about desertion, so a couple of us offered to polish his face for him. Then he wished us a good day and waved us through.

Griesser and his comrades escaped the pocket and rejoined the remnants of *FJR. 6*, only to get in hot water for the same reason: 'It's strange how well the bureaucracy functioned while all around us whole divisions were being annihilated.'[15]

Finally, after several days of delay, von Kluge managed to concentrate elements of four – not eight – panzer divisions in some sort of rough assembly area; the Army's *2.* and *116.*, and the *LSSAH* and *Das Reich* (and a scrounged *KG* from the *17. Götz*) from the armed SS, and launch them into the American flank on the night of 6/7 August. A mailed fist that should have comprised over a thousand panzers and assault-guns didn't amount to a fifth of that number. The thousand Luftwaffe fighters that Hitler had demanded turned out to be just three hundred, and were no match for the Allied fighter umbrella, as the Luftwaffe's *Oberst* von Scholz reported to Hausser at *7. Armee* headquarters: '...our fighters were hard-pressed by enemy fighters from the moment they took to the air. They could not reach the target area. They hope, however, that their aerial engagements helped just the same.' With the disdain that the Army was now openly showing the Luftwaffe, the *7. Armee* staff officer replied, 'There was no noticeable relief.' It was a reply that would have enraged Adolf Galland – *General der Jagdflieger*, Luftwaffe *Experte* and promoter of the jet-engined Messerschmitt Me 262 (Galland memorably described flying the aircraft, 'It was as though angels were pushing'). Almost helpless as his beloved fighter-arm was torn to pieces, he visited the frontline units in France at the time of the attack towards Avranches, and was shocked by what he found:

My impressions were shattering. In addition to the appalling conditions, there was a far-reaching decline in morale. This feeling of irrevocable inferiority, the heavy losses, the hopelessness of the fighting, the reproaches from above, the disrepute into which the Luftwaffe had fallen among the other arms of the Wehrmacht from no fault of the individual ... were the most severe test ever experienced by the Luftwaffe.[16]

The failure of the Luftwaffe to provide effective aerial support for *Lüttich* was never a question of a lack of courage on behalf of the pilots and their crews, it was simply a matter of arithmetic. On one day in mid-August, 2. *Jagdkorps* – the main German fighter force in France at the time – could declare only one fighter operationally ready.[17]

The 7th of August became known not as 'The Day the Luftwaffe Struck Back', but as 'The Day of the Typhoon'. Harry Broadhurst's Second Tactical Air Force flew no fewer than 271 sorties over the Mortain area alone.[18] The effects on the German *KG*s was devastating; the Germans simply couldn't move a metre on the battlefield without having to dive for cover from the *jabos* that endlessly circled above them, pouncing on them again and again, breaking up their columns, forcing them to take cover, and grinding down morale, as 2. *Panzerdivision* reported: 'The assembly of troops is spotted immediately by enemy reconnaissance aircraft and smashed by bombs and artillery directed from the air... The feeling of helplessness against enemy aircraft operating without hindrance has a paralysing effect... The effect on the inexperienced men is literally soul-shattering.' The *Leibstandarte*'s Werner Josupeit saw it at first-hand:

> The *jabos* circled our panzers several times. Then, one broke out of the circle, sought its target and fired. As the first pulled back into the circle of about twenty planes, a second pulled out and fired. And so they continued until they had all fired. Then they left the terrible scene. A new swarm appeared in their place and fired all their rockets... Finally the Typhoons couldn't find any more panzers so they bore down on us and chased us mercilessly. Their shells fell with a terrible howl. One fell right next to a comrade of mine, but he wasn't hurt. These rockets burst into just a few big pieces of shrapnel, and a man had a chance of not being hit.[19]

American resistance too was stubborn (a foretaste of what was to come in the Ardennes that winter) and led to a total lack of forward momentum. *Das Reich* recaptured Mortain, and von Lüttwitz's 2. *Panzer* doggedly fought its way forward almost twelve of those precious sixteen kilometres – but no further. As their baronial general admitted, 'We could do nothing against Allied airpower, and make no further progress.' The days of *blitzkrieg* were over for the Germans. Now, that masterful innovation of war lay in the hands of their opponents in the east and the west, as the *Reich*'s Fritz Langanke lamented: 'By this stage the whole German Army was deteriorating. We no longer had a chance to do anything big. We could only play foxes – do this or that in a small way. *Heim ins Reich* – home to Germany – was the principal thought in many people's minds.'[20] Paul Hausser's Order of the Day on launching the offensive was entirely prophetic: 'The success of this operation will determine the outcome of the war in the West.' Indeed it would.

Lüttich spluttered on but to no useful purpose. The armour that might – and only *might* – have fended off Patton's rampaging Third Army, was now either out on a limb in the west being bypassed, or pinned in the east by the First Canadian Army's Operation *Totalize*, launched on 8 August. That same day, Hans von Salmuth was sacked as commander *15. Armee*, and replaced by Gustav-Adolf von Zangen – although what change Hitler thought this move would bring about is unclear. Elsewhere, the fighting was going from bad to worse for the Germans. The Canadians were attacking the village of Cintheaux held by Heinrich's *89. ID* – a unit recently formed in occupied Norway and with no prior frontline experience – when Kurt Meyer came across a sight he would never forget, and famously wrote of in his book, *Grenadiers*:

> I am seeing German soldiers running away for the first time during these long, gruesome, murderous years. They are unresponsive, they have been through hell-fire and stumble past us with fear-filled eyes … my uniform sticks to my body, the fear of responsibility making me break out in a sweat… I jump out of the car and stand alone in the middle of the road, talking to my fleeing comrades. They are startled and stop. They look at me incredulously, wondering how I can stand in the road armed only with a carbine … they recognise me, turn around, and wave to their comrades to go back and organise the defence.

One of Meyer's own officers, *SS-Obersturmführer* Meitzel, was captured in the same fighting and taken to the Canadian position on point 140, when the *HJ* counter-attacked: 'One Canadian tank after another was knocked out and ended up in smoke and flame.' Some Canadians surrendered to their prisoner. 'I arrived at our command post again in the late afternoon, with twenty-three Canadians and a broken arm.'[21] Less than a week later, Meitzel was again taken prisoner, this time for good.

The day did not go so well for Michael Wittmann. The hero of Villers-Bocage led an attack that afternoon to try and recapture some high ground to the northeast of Cintheaux, only to come under fire from British and American Shermans near the village of Saint-Aignan-de-Cramesnil. Ordinarily, the massive armour-plating on Wittmann's Tiger would have saved him and his crew, but some of his foes were in the upgunned Sherman Fireflies, and their powerful 17-pounders pierced the Tiger's hull and ignited its ammunition. *SS-Hauptscharführer* Hans Höflinger was commanding one of the Tigers following Wittmann when he and his men were forced to abandon their own panzer after it was hit by the enfilading Allied fire: 'The turret of Michael's panzer was displaced to the right and tilted down to the front somewhat. None of his crew had gotten out.' Fire then broke out in the stricken giant and the ensuing explosion blew off the turret – Michael Wittmann was dead. He was fêted again by Goebbels and his propaganda machine, this time posthumously.

Normandy was lost, and it didn't need a highly-trained staff officer to spell out what the Allied plan was now: the Anglo-Canadians advancing south from Caen would meet up with the Americans speeding east and form a huge sack, in which would be all of 7. *Armee*. It would be a defeat for the Wehrmacht on the scale of Tunis or the Crimea, and would mean losing France. The Germans only hope was to run for their lives to escape the forming-pocket. 7. *Armee's* Chief of Staff, Rudolf-Christoph *Freiherr* von Gersdorff didn't have much of a strategic masterplan: 'We'll manage somehow.'

8

Falaise – the Westheer's Stalingrad

A young panzergrenadier from Berlin was in the back of a half-track rolling forward into yet another counter-attack, as a fleet of Allied bombers flew towards them prior to dropping their payloads. Seeing his divisional commander by the roadside, he pointed at the approaching aerial armada and shouted over to him; 'What an honour! Churchill is sending one bomber for each of us!'[1]

Less than a fortnight later that same divisional commander – still the youngest in the Wehrmacht – would find himself stumbling along a road in northern France having escaped the greatest German military disaster in the West since the Imperial Army's 'Black Day' twenty-six years earlier, 'my knees trembling, the sweat pouring down my face, my clothes soaked in perspiration'. This was how *Panzermeyer* described himself after he became separated from his division and then managed to scrabble his way out of what had become the Falaise Pocket. Behind him were perhaps sixty thousand of the best troops the Westheer had – now lying dead or wounded on roads, in ditches, and across miles of countryside, or with their hands up, stumbling exhausted into captivity. In their midst was almost an entire Army's equipment roster; hundreds of panzers, assault-guns, artillery pieces, anti-tank and anti-aircraft guns, mortars, trucks, cars, motorcycles, and just about every type of horse-drawn vehicle imaginable – many with their dead or maimed draught animals still in their traces –all burnt-out, wrecked or simply abandoned. In the heat of a French August, even men who were used to carnage gagged at the stench. This was the death of *7. Armee*. This was Falaise.

The Allied plan to destroy Hausser's army was simple; the British and the American First Army would hold the western end of an enormous sack with the ancient city of Falaise in its centre. This would leave Patton's Third and Harry Crerar's First Canadian free to drive north and south respectively and meet around the town of Chambois on the River Dives, closing the eastern end of the bag. Germany would have lost France and the Allies would be able to advance right into the heart of the Reich itself – the war would be over by Christmas.

Too late – far, far too late – von Kluge finally got Hitler to agree to call off *Lüttich* and authorise a retreat east and out of the forming pocket. Bitterly angry at the *feldmarschall* for his perceived failure, and intensely suspicious that he was attempting to broker a separate peace with the Anglo-Americans, Hitler sacked him and appointed Walter Model in his stead. Model's first order was to confirm von Kluge's last; Normandy was lost, 7. *Armee* was to retreat *en masse* to the far side of the Seine as quickly as possible. No fewer than fifteen German divisions were in danger of being trapped; along with thousands of rear-area and support personnel. Their only hope of escape was that the jaws of the Allied pincers could be held open long enough for them to get out on the few roads available. That job would overwhelmingly fall to the already-battered panzer divisions, in particular those of the Waffen-SS. For everyone else in 7. *Armee* and 5. *Panzerarmee*[2] it was *sauve qui peut*.

As for von Kluge, he was recalled to Berlin to face Hitler's wrath, but died *en route* in mysterious circumstances. Accounts differ as to his demise. Officially, the cause of death was suicide by poison, but the SS officer sent to *escort* him back to the *Führer* – Jürgen Stroop, who infamously suppressed the Warsaw Ghetto uprising with incredible barbarity – openly boasted than when he offered von Kluge the same way out as Rommel, he refused to kill himself, so Stroop shot him in the head. Whatever the truth, von Kluge had failed to stop the impending disaster in France – as Rommel and von Rundstedt had before him – and now command was in the hands of one of Hitler's favourites; Walter Model.

The next day brought a furious bombardment intended to finish us off. It began at 0400hrs with thousands of shells hitting us all at once. P-38 Lightning *jabos* joined in the attack. No-one who took part in that battle will ever forget it. The one remaining wall of the house, behind which we were sheltering, collapsed on top of our panzer, and we had to dig it out. One of the panzers from 4. *Zug* [platoon] was badly hit. Some of the armour-plating landed on the driver's lap, slicing off both his legs – he begged his comrades to put him out of his misery. All around us were craters so big they could hold a panzer, we really thought our end had come. It was amazing that no more than fifteen of our panzers were hit. We sat in them in the deafening noise, each man with his own thoughts, watching intensely the area where we thought the enemy would come from – we knew they would advance as soon as the barrage ended. Would this be the battle we'd lose? However we were still alive, and we were still fighting the next day. Up to this point I had only fought on the Eastern front. Nothing … could have prepared me for what happened … the tactic of unbroken artillery barrages lasting hours was gruesome mental and physical torture.[3]

This was how the panzer driver Manfred Thorn saw the fighting as he and his comrades from the *Leibstandarte* tried to hold open the northern side of the escape corridor. A few miles to the south it fell to the likes of men like Rudi Splinter and Egon Schulze of the *Frundsberg* to try and do the same. Splinter:

…we were enjoying some captured English rations, with luxuries such as chocolate, white bread, gold-flake cigarettes, and even toilet paper … we were helping to hold open the jaws of the Allied pincer at Falaise in Normandy to allow other units to escape.[4]

Schulze:

…we were trapped and encircled in the vicinity of Falaise and things became terribly confused. On 18 August we received orders to take our panzers and rescue some of our comrades who were encircled by the *Amis*… When we reached our destination about sixty-per cent of the place was already in enemy hands, and unfortunately all our ammo was located there. Undaunted we blew up the ammo to deprive the Allies of it, but by then the enemy had closed off the whole area. It was total chaos, with artillery duels going on, *jabos* in the sky and panzer battles raging all over. The area we held got smaller and smaller. We tried to reach our own unit with our panzers, but it no longer existed, it was every man for himself![5]

Inside the forming pocket, chaos reigned as a mass of men, horses and machines desperately tried to escape east. From the maelstrom a story emerged of an *HJ* platoon from *SS-Panzergrenadier-Regiment 25* that supposedly barricaded itself into the local *École supérieure* in Falaise, and fought to the death to try and hold off the assaulting Canadians.

Since then, this tale has been glorified by some historians and fellow-travellers to highlight the fanaticism or courage – take your pick – of the armed SS, but as the 18-year-old Karl-Heinz Decker of the *HJ* related, it is not perhaps the full story:

> ...during the night of 16/17 August we arrived in Falaise and immediately came under heavy machine-gun fire, with tracer flying at us through the darkness. We took cover among the houses and occupied one of the buildings. It was the *École supérieure*. From this building we had a good view of the crossroads where Canadian columns were passing through. We opened fire on them. They sent in a tank against us, but we disabled it with a panzerfaust and it was towed away. An assault group of Canadian infantry also made little headway against us.

In an all-too rare act of humanity, both sides then agreed a short truce to allow a wounded Canadian prisoner to be taken back to his own side to receive medical treatment. With that done, the fighting resumed.

> ...our situation was hopeless, so a break-out was planned. On the evening of 17 August we left our positions and made our way through the nearby orchard ... we said goodbye to our wounded and the *Sani* who had volunteered to stay behind with them. As soon as we went into the street we drew heavy fire ... under cover of a German air attack – a real rarity! – we managed to slip past the enemy.⁶

With Decker and the remains of his platoon gone, the Canadians took Falaise by the end of that same day. That night, the *Leibstandarte*'s *SS-Untersturmführer*, Gerhard Stiller, tried to get his panzer company out of the trap: 'I warned my panzer commanders and driver to "run the motors on the lowest rpm possible, we don't want the *Amis* to notice a thing"....the grenadiers stuck to the panzers like burrs...it was already getting light as we began our move across the bridge... that bridge could become a living hell at any moment.'⁷

Decker's fellow *HJ* grenadier, Erhard Kinscher:

> By 19 August there were only twenty men left in our kompanie; one officer, one NCO and eighteen men. Just before midday we were ordered to move our two remaining half-tracks to another village

... a VW went racing by, hit a pothole, and as it bounced a pack of cigarettes fell from it – they were quickly shared out amongst us and we took the opportunity to have a smoke... Only eight hundred metres from our start point we came under heavy fire and both half-tracks were hit and disabled. I moved back into the village on my motorcycle and our officer told us 'I think they have us trapped.' We finally decided to try another direction in the hope of finding our command post, but by the time we reached it there were only two of us left from the *kompanie*... I heard from another comrade that both half-tracks had been terribly burned, and that the dead lay all around, charred and shrunken by the heat ... so died *Kompanie 14*.

Kinscher managed to get to a village where an Allied tank was stopping anyone getting through. He somehow found an anti-tank gun and then some ammo, and knocked it out: 'The *Leutnant* pinned his own Iron Cross 1st Class on to my tunic, shortly afterwards he was kneeling on the wall of a ruined house explaining his plan for the break-out... A shot rang out and he fell dead, half his neck blown away by an explosive bullet.' Kinscher was then wounded: 'I was hit by a pistol bullet ... the shot hadn't passed cleanly through my body, I pushed my fist against the bullet hole to try and stem the blood which was pumping out. I quickly realised I had a lung wound.'[8]

Egon Schulze had a bit more luck, but not much:

During the evening of 19 August we managed to assemble a few detachments from various units to attempt a breakout, but it was pointless ... the nightime journey was eerie, we had no destination and had lost contact with command. The ground was littered with dead *Amis* and Germans, burnt-out vehicles and panzers ... suddenly firing broke out ... there was an almighty jolt and we slewed across an intersection, one of the tracks had been ripped off by a shell ... there were three of us left and we decided to blow up our panzer and try to escape on foot. As soon as we left the vehicle though we came under machine-gun fire from both sides of the road, my two comrades were killed. I was alone.

It wasn't just the SS who were fighting for their lives; Hans von Luck:

Rauch's *KG*; with Regiment 192, the Reconnaisance Battalion, and our last eight panzers, fell into the pocket... I received orders to set up a defensive blocking position to the west to prevent any further advance by the Canadian and Polish divisions... From now on Allied bombers swooped down without a break on our retreating divisions. The excellent American artillery covered all roads and routes with heavy fire day and night. Worse off were the infantry divisions, which, with their horse-drawn units, struggled east on foot and blocked all the roads.

7. *Armee* was now caught in an enormous *cuvette*, as the French would say; a wide-open valley of fields, pastures and orchards, with precious little cover and roads that were a magnet for Allied air and artillery fire. Shooting fish in a barrel is the term that springs to mind, as one British artillery observer himself vividly remembered: 'The floor of the valley was alive ... it was a gunners paradise and everybody took advantage of it ... away on our left was the famous killing ground, and all day the roar of Typhoons went on.' This mass slaughter by firepower – somewhat akin to the first Gulf War's Basra highway – is what Falaise would become known for as a battle, as von Luck recounted: 'Appalling scenes took place; the panzers and motorised units ruthlessly forced their way through to the east. On and beside every road and track leading east shot-up vehicles had broken down, and the cadavers of horses lay around. Even ambulances, packed with wounded, stood burning by the side of the road. Valiant officers tried to bring a little order into the chaos, but usually without success.' *Hauptfeldwebel* Erich Braun of von Lüttwitz's 2. *Panzerdivision* was a little more florid than the urbane von Luck:

The never-ending detonations, soldiers waving at us, begging for help – the dead, their faces still screwed up in agony, huddle everywhere in trenches and shelters – the officers and men who had lost their nerve, burning vehicles from which piercing screams could be heard and men, driven crazy; crying, shouting, laughing hysterically – and horses, still harnessed to their shafts, screaming terribly, trying to escape the slaughter on the stumps of their hind legs.[9]

German units outside the pocket counter-attacked in desperation to try and hold open an escape route a little while longer. *Das Reich* was one such unit:

Heavy enemy artillery and small-arms fire threaten to break up the attack. *Hauptsturmführer* Werner decides to outflank the enemy on the right and goes over to where *Nr. 10 Kompanie* is positioned ... we see ten Shermans with their guns firing westwards into the pocket ... our own panzers are still in Champosoult... I jog-trot back about two kilometres to the CP [command post], outside which stands a Panther which has just been repaired. I order the platoon commander to bring it forward to where it is urgently needed. This he refuses to do as he is awaiting orders from Regiment. I insist he complies with my order but he still refuses, and at last l draw my pistol and tell him that I am the one issuing orders here. He agrees. I clamber on the back and direct him forward. The *Obersturmführer* and I go forward on foot and I show him the Shermans ... within a minute three enemy tanks had been knocked out. He continues firing until he has knocked out five Shermans and inflicted damage upon several others... The destruction of the five Shermans has led to other tanks being pulled back from Point 262, thus creating a new gap in the pocket. Through this gap streams a succession of units despite the heavy barrage which continues to fall in the area... So far the number has reached four thousand men.[10]

With the escape corridor down to just a couple of miles, order broke down, as *Kesselfieber* (pocket/cauldron fever) set in among the usually-disciplined *landsers*. The *Frundsberg*'s Ewald Klapdor was caught up in the panic:

The questions 'what will happen?', 'where is there still a front?', 'is it still possible to escape to the east?' grow louder ... they are close to breaking. Thousands try to escape again. No-one wants to be subjected to authority anymore. The law of the jungle rules on the road. Eastwards! Eastwards![11]

21. Panzer's Hans Höller remembered his own flight:

We received orders to abandon our positions during the night of 19/20 August and break through in the direction of Trun... The closer we got to the breakout point the ghastlier the scene that met our eyes. The roads were blocked by two or three shot-up, burnt-out vehicles standing alongside each other, ammunition was exploding, panzers were burning, and horses lay struggling on their backs until they were finally released. In the fields far and wide was the same chaos. The enemy artillery fired into the turmoil from all sides, everything was pressing east... Panthers and Tigers from the

SS divisions took the lead... Two generals, whose infantry divisions had been wiped out, just shook their heads at our reckless attempt to break-out – they marched with us... While the panzers held the gap open, more and more groups – some quite small – filtered through the hole to the east. We set a course by compass and headed off; we had escaped the inferno once again.

The two infantry generals marching with Hans Höller weren't the only senior officers caught up in the *mêlée*. *2. Panzerdivision*'s Heinrich von Lüttwitz arrived at Saint-Lambert-sur-Dives already slightly wounded, and now tried to get his remaining men across the river to safety:

From the church in the town I directed the evacuation of my men. The crossing of the bridge over the Dives was a particularly ghastly affair. Men, horses, vehicles and other equipment that had been shot-up while making the crossing had crashed from the bridge into the deep ravine of the river and lay jumbled together in gruesome heaps... I formed separate small groups of my men, placed them under energetic officers and ordered them to march northeast. At nine in the evening on 20 August I broke out myself, but by this time enemy infantry had entered the town and the Falaise gap was closed.[12]

Richard Schimpf of *3. Fallschirmjäger-Division* was badly wounded, but carried out of the pocket by his ever-loyal troopers, as was his boss, Eugen Meindl. As for the army commander himself – Paul Hausser – his luck was little better than Schimpf's: 'We had to await the onset of darkness, when we succeeded in organising a small panzer *KG*, which was supplied with fuel collected from abandoned vehicles... I was then wounded by artillery fire.' Having already lost an eye in Russia, Hausser now had shrapnel through the jaw and had to be taken out on the rear-deck of a panzer.

Those last days and nights were chaotic, as *21. Panzer's*, *Gefreiter* Korfleur, recounted; 'On 19 August came the order – "every man for himself!" – with a second Panzer IV we set out on our way to the east. At the sight of naked, half-burned panzermen we promised that we wouldn't let ourselves be finished off in the pocket ... we had to abandon our panzers and continue on foot. During the night we slipped past the enemy, some of whom looked at us in bewilderment.'

The best guess was that 100,000 German soldiers had been cut-off in the Falaise Pocket; Höller, Stiller and Korfleur were amongst the

50,000 or so who managed to get out before it was closed for good on 21 August, leaving ten thousand dead behind them, and a mass of prisoners, including the *HJ*'s Karl-Heinz Decker: 'We followed the sounds of gunfire to try and find our own positions, but without success. By now there were only eighteen of us left. We marched for hours, we had nothing to eat and were exhausted, so we went to a farm and asked for some food and the chance to rest, however within an hour we were prisoners, the farmer had betrayed us to the enemy.'[13]

The *Frundsberg*'s Egon Schulze returned to his disabled panzer after his two comrades were killed and sat there all night and into the next afternoon. Some ambulances driven by German POWs arrived, but wouldn't take him with them as he wasn't wounded. Night fell, and he set off walking. 'As I was walking, I came upon a forester's lodge full of Waffen-SS comrades and *fallschirmjäger*, they were organising another break-out and I joined them. However, we were fired on by British tanks, resistance was useless, we had hardly any weapons and were surrounded, so we surrendered on 21 August.'[14]

Rudi Splinter was another new prisoner, but he thought himself lucky to be alive after being injured by a mortar blast and then waking up in a makeshift dressing-station. Taken prisoner by the British, he was still in the dressing-station when he had a close shave with some Polish soldiers who appeared out of nowhere and began shouting out: '"Are there are any SS troops here?"... I answered him in his own language, he was taken aback and asked how I could speak Polish, I told him I was from Pomorze [Pomerania] and that one of my parents was a Pole and the other a German, he rushed over and shook my hands like a long lost brother ... he was very friendly and gave me some cigarettes.' Splinter was lucky, the Poles then went into the next-door room and saw two badly wounded panzer crewmen, 'one had a leg blown off and the other had been wounded in the groin. They were in a real mess. The Poles took one look at their black uniforms with the traditional panzer death's head collar tabs, assumed they were SS, and emptied their Sten gun magazines into them, slaughtering them as they lay there helpless.'[15] Konrad, a Berliner and thrice-wounded *panzergrenadier* platoon leader in *Das Reich*'s *Der Führer* Regiment, got separated from his men and ended up surrendering to a British medic, despite his misgivings: 'In Russia the Red Cross armband was not respected and I thought there was a strong chance I would be shot anyway.' Kept under guard, with a Sten gun pointed at his head, Konrad was surprised to be given a mug of hot tea with milk and sugar – a real treat! He would return home in 1948 to discover his mother had been deported east to a Soviet *gulag* as punishment for having a son in the Waffen-SS – she died there.[16] As for Erhard Kinscher, his lung wound was so bad that after he was taken captive he was given the last rites twice – he survived.

Ike said of the Pocket:

> The battlefield at Falaise was unquestionably one of the greatest 'killing fields' of any of the war areas. Forty-eight hours after the closing of the gap I was conducted through it on foot, to encounter scenes that could be described only by Dante. It was literally possible to walk for hundreds of yards at a time, stepping on nothing but dead and decaying flesh.

A lot of that flesh belonged to members of the *HJ*, as Wilhelm Fecht knew: 'We came out of Falaise with just twenty men from our battery, all the others had been killed or captured.'[17]

The German field army in France died at Falaise – already ground down by a bloody battle of attrition which it could never hope to win – the success of Operation *Cobra* and Patton's drive behind the German rear to meet the Poles and Canadians at Chambois finished it off. After Falaise, the Westheer was still *occupying* large tracts of France, but wasn't in *control* of them.

9

The South Falls

Remarkably, even as *Heeresgruppe B* literally fought for its existence in Normandy, down south life went on pretty much as before for the 300,000 occupation troops of *Heeresgruppe G*. The summer brought its usual blast of sun and heat, and the majority of men thanked their lucky stars as they tucked into some of the finest food and drink southern France could produce. Attacks by the *maquis* were becoming more frequent as the *résistants* became emboldened, but as long as your average *landser* took sensible precautions and kept his wits about him, he'd be pretty safe. There were fewer Germans now of course, with many of the fitter and more experienced men sent north, but there were still two entire armies down south; the Avignon-based *19. Armee* of Friedrich Wiese, and Kurt von der Chevallerie's *1. Armee* over in Bordeaux. Both men were *General der Infanterie*, which was handy as the only armoured formation in the whole army group was Wend von Wietersheim's *11. Panzerdivision*.

Appearances were deceiving though. Yes, there were still two armies in position, but they had been hollowed out by the transfers north; *1. Armee* comprised just 88,000 men at the beginning of August, and *19. Armee* had lost four of its nine divisions; *271* and *272* in late July, *277* a month earlier, and even the belly *338* in the first days of August. That meant divisional frontages on the coastline of 155 miles on average – an impossibility that saw tokenism reach new heights among the dispirited regiments.

What were they still doing there? Weak militarily they were, but sitting in southern France they were achieving nothing except occupying space. The war was being won and lost in the north, and it was there that every man, every gun, every vehicle, every artillery shell counted – not on the Côte d'Azur or in Gascony. What could von Rundstedt, Rommel or even von Kluge have done with over a quarter of a million more men and hundreds more guns? In all likelihood it wouldn't have been enough to drive the Allies back into the sea, but it might have been enough to wear them down and contain them in their lodgement into the winter.

On the morning of Tuesday 15 August, the first waves of Alexander Patch's Seventh US Army began to land on sixteen beaches along a 45-mile section of the French Riviera. The naval bombardments and bombing raids that helped cover them in were nowhere near as heavy as on D-Day, but they had no need to be. Patch noted that 'resistance by German units has been weak at most points,' the landing troops often having difficulty even finding any defences to overcome, with quite a few of the bunkers and strongpoints they assaulted being nothing more than dummy positions fitted out with telegraph poles painted to look like gun-barrels – so-called 'Quaker guns'. That first day set the tone for the rest of Operation *Dragoon*, as the landings in the south were codenamed. By nightfall there were 66,000 US troops ashore, and casualties had been a meagre four hundred. Going the other way were over two thousand POWs, many of them *Osttruppen*.

Local counter-attacks were launched over the next couple of days to try and stymie the landings but they were easily contained, and by the 18th the Germans had to admit that retreat was inevitable. Having told his own generals two months earlier that abandoning France south of the Loire was 'impossible', Hitler now decided that it was actually possible, and in a rare moment of military logic directed Johannes Blaskowitz to withdraw his army group north, join up with *Heeresgruppe B* as it retreated from Falaise and form a new defensive line on the far side of the Seine – two months after his generals recommended much the same course of action. Blaskowitz sighed with relief, but still had some hard decisions to make: firstly, what to do with his only armoured reserve, *11. Panzer*. Should he use it as a mobile rearguard to try and save the bulk of his largely immobile formation, or should he keep it intact and sacrifice the greater part of his forces? Back in '42, Rommel had chosen the latter and let his Italian allies take the fall after the El Alamein defeat, while he fled west with his mainly German mobile troops. Blaskowitz chose a different path. With all the bridges on the lower Rhône blown up by Allied air attack, he ordered ferries and river boats to bring von Wietersheim's panzers across, an undertaking that took a week. In the meantime, the majority of his divisions were sent marching north up the Rhône valley to try and escape back to the German border.

His second decision was to what to do about Toulon and Marseilles. If they fell intact into Allied hands, the flow of men and equipment from the sea would sky-rocket – Blaskowitz ordered the occupying 242. and 244. IDs to stay where they were, destroy the ports and their facilities, and fight it out. Any vehicles the two divisions possessed were handed over to other units and the grenadiers began to dig in. In another moment of sound military thinking, Hitler didn't even insist on intoning his usual 'fighting withdrawal' mantra, *Heeresgruppe G* was simply ordered to move as fast as possible.

A relieved von der Chevallerie, with no Allied landing to worry about, led his men out of Bordeaux, Bayonne and Poitiers and headed northeast towards the Loire in three separate columns. There was something almost medieval about the withdrawal of *1. Armee*, as thousands of them weren't combat troops but were instead uniformed members of paramilitary and civilian organisations like the *Organization Todt*, the *Reichsarbeitdienst*, the *NSKK*, the *Reichsbahn* and so on, mixed in with camp-followers and collaborators, desperate to escape the revenge they feared was coming. Weapons were few and far between, most of the men were armed with little more than a rifle or a pistol. Vehicles too were scarce, so the retreat was mainly on foot. There wasn't much heavy equipment to be salvaged, and with the Allies concentrating their *jabos* in the north the straggling convoys were harried from the air rather than savaged.

Somewhat miraculously, only one of the three columns met with disaster; Botho Henning Elster's 'Foot March Group South' was bringing up the rear, but after two weeks of slogging along it lost contact with the column ahead and found itself more or less cut-off between Issoudun and Châteauroux. Under attack from *résistants*, the Germans handed over eight million francs in cash to the local authorities to try and buy safe passage, but Elster thought his men's position was doomed regardless, and so to prevent further bloodshed he decided to surrender to the nearest Allied units. Helped by the *maquis*, Elster managed to contact the Americans and negotiate terms, including keeping his arms to safeguard his men from further French attacks. After a final march north lasting several days, he surrendered his 19,604 officers and men to US General Robert C. Macon of the 83rd Infantry Division on 16 September on the Loire Bridge at Beaugency, southwest of the city of Orléans. Meanwhile, von der Chevallerie had been replaced as army commander by the Berliner

Otto von Knobelsdorff, who managed to lead his remaining 60,000 men to still-German Lorraine later on that same month.

Back down south, the Allies landed Jean de Lattre de Tassigny's *Armée B* as part of the 200,000 men put ashore by the end of August. This was the largest French force on the Continent and would eventually comprise a quarter of a million men, half of whom were colonial troops from north or sub-Saharan Africa. With American support, their first major task was the liberation of Toulon and Marseilles. Toulon was the biggest French naval port in the country and was defended by three fortresses that ringed the harbour, one of which had two huge gun turrets built into it, both armed with twin 34cm guns salvaged from the scuttled French battleship, the *Provence*. Nicknamed 'Big Willie' by the Allies, the fortress was bombarded from the sea daily until finally silenced on 23 August. Beginning their assault five days earlier, the French soon pushed the defending troops of *Generalleutnant* Johannes Bäßler's 242. ID back into the city itself. Bäßler was a tough Russian front veteran, but his men lacked transport and heavy weapons and were seriously outmatched, and once he himself was wounded, resistance collapsed. Eighteen thousand German defenders went into captivity, including Bäßler – he would die of his wounds before the year was out.

The great Mediterranean port city of Marseilles was attacked at the same time by additional French units, and with much the same result. *Generalmajor* Schaeffer's outgunned 244. ID held out for a week in the old St Nicholas fort before their exhausted commander sent a final message to his army headquarters; 'It would be purposeless to continue a battle which could only lead to the total annihilation of my remaining troops.' He then surrendered the garrison and his remaining 11,000 men. Schaeffer was found by French troops at dawn on 28 August, eating a plate of gruyère cheese in an underground bunker equipped with little more than two telephones and a desk. Pale and haggard, he signed the official capitulation document with a borrowed pen.

As for the bulk of 19. *Armee*, even as Toulon and Marseilles were liberated, the race was on as to whether it or the Allies would reach the vital road junction at Montélimar on the Germans' direct route north. The Americans won. Desperate, the Germans counter-attacked, and for the best part of three days Friedrich Wiese held the road open and kept the Americans at bay. Finally, on 29 August the bulk of the army had escaped the potential trap and 8,000 exhausted Germans surrendered to John Dahlquist's 36th US Infantry Division; only half were combatants, the rest little more than civilians in uniform.

A search of the wreckage on the escape road and in the town itself found another two thousand dead and wounded scattered among fifteen hundred dead horses and 4,000 burnt-out vehicles, including half of *11. Panzer*'s armour and a quarter of its artillery. Von Wietersheim only kept his men moving by requisitioning every civilian vehicle his men could lay their hands on.

It was another 84 miles to Lyon, and then another 200 after that to the Rhine, but remarkably, by 18 September, Blaskowitz and Wiese had shepherded most of their men to safety and formed them into a new defensive line from the Belfort Gap in the east to Chaumont in the west, where they were joined by von Knobelsdorff and the remaining 60,000 men of *1. Armee*. Blaskowitz reported to Berlin that *Heeresgruppe G* was 'still able to fight, although weakened'. He had lost just under 160,000 men killed, wounded or captured (the vast majority becoming prisoners), the best part of fifteen hundred guns, and almost all his panzers; but with no air cover, little if any resupply, and a formation largely on foot or horse-borne, the pugnacious Prussian had somehow saved 140,000 men, two dozen panzers and 165 guns to continue the defence of the Reich. In recognition of this achievement, Hitler sacked him two days later, whereupon his relieved wife told her friends: 'Hans is now at home and planting cabbages.'

10

La Belle France Abandoned

With typical hyperbole, Fritz Bayerlein said that no campaign in history 'can approach the battle of annihilation in France in 1944 in the magnitude of planning, the logic of execution, the collaboration of sea, air and ground forces, the bulk of the booty, or the hordes of prisoners'.

There are many grounds on which this bold statement could reasonably be challenged – although the point on 'collaboration of sea, air and ground forces' has perhaps the most veracity – but there can be no denying that the Falaise disaster and the retreat from the south were dreadful defeats for the Wehrmacht. In the Reich though, they didn't resonate in the public consciousness nearly as much as Stalingrad. Back then, State radio had broadcast Beethoven's *Eroica* and Bruckner's *Symphony No. 7* pretty much non-stop, and three days of national mourning were declared as the newspapers published seemingly endless casualty lists, and a torrent of death notices landed on German doormats bearing the dreaded legend; '*gefallen für Führer, Volk und Vaterland*'. That outpouring of communal grief was understandable. Twenty divisions had been lost, one in fifteen men in the Army. Since then, the German public had not become inured to losses, but had definitely got more used to them. The surrender of the Reich's African toehold in Tunis had seen 125,000 more men march into captivity – but they were still alive at least. The fifty to sixty thousand Falaise casualties were indeed bad, but at roughly the same time as the pocket was being closed the Red Army was immolating five times that number of *landsers* in central Russia and Belarus. The issue for the German people was not the numbers but the long-term implications, what the French calamity revealed about the state of the

Nazi war effort: how could Final Victory be achieved now that France had been lost?

Rudi von Ribbentrop, not yet recovered from his *jabo* injuries, and then hospitalised with jaundice before the Falaise disaster, knew the answer to that particular question:

> I handed over my men to one of the remaining officers, and was admitted to hospital, so I was lucky enough not to be involved in the Falaise battle. I was already having treatment by then ... my illness was equivalent to a wound and I hoped at the time to be able to return to my regiment, which was the case.... I thought the war may be lost when the Allied forces broke out of Normandy, we lost France, and they then advanced towards our frontier.[1]

The Wehrmacht was nevertheless still in France. Paris, and the country east of the Seine, remained in German hands; shaken and bloody hands, but still there. Hitler – in one of his usual grandiose, proclamations – insisted that 'when Paris fell, then France fell with it'; hardly revelatory, and in the summer of '44 the issue had already been decided before Paris was liberated. As it happened, only two days after Eisenhower's grisly tour round the Falaise charnel house, Paris was finally freed, and Parisians mobbed French soldiers wearing American uniforms, carrying American weapons and driving American vehicles. Just before its liberation, a small *kampfgruppe* from the *Panzer-Lehr* was ordered to help defend the city from both the advancing Allies and local *résistants*, as their medical doctor Hans Hermann detailed: 'One would hear a round whistle through the air and not know from where it had come.'[2] For the Germans, the surrender of the French capital was a bit of an anti-climax. *Generalleutnant* Dietrich von Choltitz, the rather podgy, monocled commander of the city garrison, assembled his staff for a last lunch on the day of the capitulation in his headquarters at the Hôtel Meurice. *Leutnant Graf* von Arnim remembered it vividly: 'Silent from the effort of showing no emotions, we gathered as usual... But apart from that, it was the same setting, the same waiter, and the same food.'[3]

However, with the fortitude that often characterised their wartime performance, the German Army and Waffen-SS didn't fall apart after Falaise and Paris; there were no wholesale surrenders, no mass capitulations, the Westheer didn't disintegrate. *Landsers*, SS men, *fallschirmjäger*, panzer-crews and artillerymen, all collectively decided not to give up but instead to find a route east and rejoin the units being conjured up by the men Hans Höller described as 'the best weapons we had; our old corporals, sergeants and the other NCOs.'

He meant men like Heinrich Fugmann – a lowly *Oberjäger* from *FJR. 6* – who was put in command of a platoon set to guard the regiment's baggage during the run-up to Operation *Cobra*. After the break-out, Fugmann and his men got left behind in the ensuing chaos. They were alone, miles from their own lines, with no heavy weaponry, no hope of resupply, and surrounded by enemies. In the circumstances, surrender would be both honourable and the only practical option – instead Fugmann led them east.

> With twenty-five to thirty men travelling mostly on foot and hitching rides, we arrived near Paris. On a country road we were stopped by a technical officer ... he asked us how the situation at the front was. He took us to a *Soldatenheim* ['soldiers' home', a German rest and recreation centre akin to a NAAFI] where we got something to eat and could bathe after months in the field. From a clothing warehouse that was about to be blown up he got us new uniforms and, most importantly, new underwear, as ours was filthy and lice-ridden.

The next day the platoon hitched a ride with a small convoy of *Nachrichtenhelferinnen* (female communications personnel). 'Several times on the trip we were forced to abandon the buses because of low-level *jabo* attacks ... some of the women took cover in nearby road ditches and canal pipes, and after the attacks they crawled out of hiding shaking and screaming ... it was a hellish trip and we were truly delighted to reach Nancy.'[4]

Nachrichtenhelferin Hanna Rösch was in a similar convoy to Fugmann and his charges: 'By day we were attacked by *jabos* and by night by partisans... During *jabo* attacks we scrambled from the lorries and flung ourselves down in neighbouring fields.'

At Nancy, Fugmann and his men joined up with the remnants of their regiment as it began to be rebuilt. When first ordered to reform in Lorraine's former capital city, von der Heydte could muster just 40 men from his original 4,600: 'At least I no longer had to worry about securing transportation.' On his way there, the veteran para officer had a run-in with some rear-area staff.

> We arrived in a small town and passed by an inn with the sign 'German Officers Home'; loud, jarring music was coming from the inn.

We weren't really in the mood for loud music, we were just hungry and thirsty and I ordered my men to stop... I found a few drunken officers from the rear-area who were with some not-so-sober-French prostitutes. That was it! The German officers ... wanted to refuse me entry to their 'officers' mess'... I called a few of my soldiers into the inn and ordered them to arrest them, strip them of their shoulder straps and decide what cout-martial should be applied to them. I'll never forget their dumbstruck faces when they saw my rank ... and they saw that we were *fallschirmjäger.*[5]

In a few weeks, von der Heydte's forty men had grown to over a thousand.

HJ signals officer Walter Kruger was wounded by shrapnel at Falaise but nevertheless remained determined to escape capture. He bandaged his wounds as best he could and set off on foot. After walking for three days he arrived near Breteuil in Oise, where he found other survivors, collected them together, and headed east again. His fellow Waffen-SS officer, Fritz Langanke of *Das Reich*, found himself in the same situation after blowing up his damaged Panther and heading east cross-country: 'We just kept on going along with the rest of the German Army.' Finally reaching the Seine at Elbeuf – with *résistants* everywhere – he and his crew had to chance the river even though his gunner and loader couldn't swim. They both drowned. Langanke clung to the carcass of a dead cow that was floating in the water, got across and rejoined his division. Hans Stöber of the *Götz von Berlichingen* was matter-of-fact about his escape from Falaise: 'The Poles never closed that pocket for anybody who really wanted to get through.' Two weeks later he was back in action in a scratch *kampfgruppe* of *116. Panzerdivision* in the Saar.

It wasn't just members of the Westheer élite like *fallschirmjäger* and Waffen-SS troopers either. *Gefreiter* Adolf Hohenstein, a 22-year-old bespectacled former engineering student, had spent most of his war building bridges with a labour unit in Russia before being transferred west to the Bayonne-based *276. ID*. Younger than most of the division, which had been filled with older men conscripted from Germany's many coal mines, Hohenstein described his new unit as 'pretty weak, we spent too much time doing old Prussian exercises rather than field training.' Dispatched to Normandy in mid-June, young Adolf had watched helpless as his best friend Heinz Alles bled to death from a severed artery in his leg, without hope of medical aid.

'A man was lucky if he could get an injection, the doctors could only try to do something for those with a chance of life.' He soon realised that those considered as lightly wounded; lost a finger or toe, a clean bullet or sharpnel wound through a leg or arm that hadn't broken a bone – were bandaged up and sent back to the front after a five day rest. Nevertheless, on then being surrounded at Falaise, *Gefreiter* Hohenstein hadn't panicked – 'in Russia we had been surrounded again and again.' This time he led his men east and came to a small village called Le Sap near Vimoutiers, where the locals had, in anticipation of their imminent liberation, laid out tables of food and drink for the advancing Allies. Hohenstein said to them: 'Me and my men just want to get through here in one piece. In a few hours you'll have a chance to find out if the other army treats you better than ours.' The exhausted *landsers* grabbed some food and drink and carried on marching, reaching the same crossing over the Seine at Elbeuf as Fritz Langanke had. The infantrymen had better luck than the panzer commander and managed to get across unhindered. Hohenstein was far from elated though. 'After Normandy we had no illusions any more. We knew that we stood with our backs to the wall.'[6]

Hohenstein's divisional commander – *Generalleutnant* Curt Badinski – was marching too, but only into captivity. Captured in the pocket he joined the twenty-five other general officers lost in the Normandy fighting; including one *Heeresgruppe* commander, two *Armee* commanders, three *Korps* commanders and twenty divisional officers. One of the latter, alongside Badinski, was the man who came closest on D-Day to achieving the nigh-on impossible and pushing an Allied landing force back into the sea – Dietrich Kraiss. His *352. ID* had been the surprise package that day, and it had then fought to extinction to try and hold the line – even as that line kept on being pushed further from the surf. Officially, it was announced that Kraiss died on 2 August from wounds received two days earlier near Saint-Lô, although he may well have been killed at the end of July on the Saint-Denis to Lengronen road, where American armour and artillery shot a German column to pieces. As the infantry sifted through the aftermath a staff car was found with a dead general inside, but as it was already stripped by souvenir hunters, no positive identification could be made. Whatever the circumstances, Kraiss was dead, and his command fell to *Oberstleutnant* Ernst Heyna of *GR. 914*. Heyna and the remnants of *352. ID* were finally withdrawn to Holland to refit in early September. Resting in Arnhem, they were as shocked as anyone when British paratroopers started falling almost on top of their positions. Immediately ordered to join the nearby *Frundsberg*, Heyna reported he had 200 men ready for action – 200 from the 10,000-plus on D-Day, never mind the thousands that had gone through its ranks during the Normandy battles. By the time Operation Market Garden had been defeated, the winged-horse division was reduced to a handful of survivors.

But it was still fighting – somehow. It joined the other forty-nine infantry and twelve panzer and panzergrenadier divisions still in France after Falaise, of which seven were bottled up in the Atlantic ports Hitler had declared as *Festungen*. Most of the rest washed up on the east bank of the Seine, although to call them divisions was a misnomer. They were wreckage. All together they mustered one hundred and twenty panzers – an average of ten per division (*Lehr*, 2. and 9. *Panzerdivisionen* didn't even have that). As for the infantry units, they were so depleted that eight were disbanded and their few remaining men distributed to the others. Annoying as it must have been for Hitler, it was *Heeresgruppe G's* divisions that were in the best shape; Blaskowitz having worked minor miracles in keeping them relatively intact and cohesive. Perhaps that played a part in his recall to command that December.

The Normandy divisions hadn't fared as well as their southern compatriots though. 'When we entrained for Normandy we were a proud fighting division – a force to be reckoned with – complete with all our vehicles, panzers and artillery, we were eighteen-thousand men strong.' The *Hohenstaufen's SS-Hauptsturmführer* Wilfried Schwarz might have also added that those vehicles consisted of no fewer than 191 panzers and self-propelled guns, 287 half-tracks, and just under 4,000 soft-skinned vehicles. A few weeks later, *SS-Rottenführer* Wolfgang Dombrowski described the condition of the same formation: 'The division was virtually burnt out in the Normandy fighting.' Dombrowski himself had survived by tagging along with a fleeing Army unit.[7] Hans Stöber's *Götz von Berlichingen* was in much the same condition; from its June strength of just under 20,000 (including a thousand Hiwis), it had been whittled down to 8,500 by the end of July, having lost over half its officers and NCOs. Only one in every six men in Helmut Gunther's 120-strong company were left as he thought to himself: 'What a poor pig I am, fighting here with my back to the wall,' before he was wounded by shrapnel and evacuated for treatment just in time to avoid Falaise. Nonetheless, in a few weeks he was recovered, and the division was back up to a strength of 10,000 as it withdrew to the Saar to face Patton's oncoming Third Army.[8]

Men like him, Hans Stöber and Wolfgang Dombrowski needed to get back to their units. The Seine couldn't be held; its big, meandering bends presented any defender with a nightmare. Hans von Luck met up with his divisional commander to be given a set of orders he never thought he'd receive:

> We are now threatened with a new pocket south and west of the Seine, and all the bridges over it appear to have been destroyed... I am authorised to bring Rauch's *KG* and the reconnaissance battalion over the Seine at once and move it to an area northeast of Paris... Divisional HQ will move even further east, probably to the region west of the Vosges... You Luck will take over all elements of the division that are still operational... I don't give much for your chances of still being able to cross the Seine.

Then Feuchtinger delivered another bombshell to his shocked subordinate: 'From now on you are on your own. I can't tell you where you will get fuel, ammunition or food. Help yourself. As to the route of your march to the east and its destination ... you will receive further orders. All the best, Luck. Bring me back lots of men from our division.'[9] Almost in spite of his absentee commander, von Luck got his men to the Seine and began to ferry them across with the help of some SS troopers:

> When we had chosen our crossing-point we let no-one else through... While the engineers were constructing a pontoon ferry, every possibility was considered and tried for getting over the 400-metre wide river. *Hauptmann* Krieger, my adjutant at the time, told me a few days later that he and his men had taken doors off their hinges in the neighbouring villages and made them buoyant with empty fuel cans. Each of these 'mini-ferries' was able to convey about eight men.

Fritz Bayerlein, as gloomy as ever, said of the crossing: 'Ferry points for the Seine crossing were prepared and allotted to divisions... This allocation wasn't observed, and everyone crossed the river wherever they felt like it. Most of the ferries were confiscated by the SS, who generally didn't allow members of other units to use them.' This was a view disputed by von Luck: 'Our collaboration with the SS panzer people went well. I assured them that they would be carried over on our pontoon ferry last of all.' Von Luck himself decided to try his luck getting across in his VW jeep, which was meant to be amphibious, but which he had never tested before. Loaded down with von Luck, a driver, an observer, and Helmut Liebeskind – and decked out in enough foliage to make it look like a floating bush – all were pleasantly surprised when it floated, although a brush with a *jabo* meant a 15-kilometre detour down river: 'An hour later we were back with the *kampfgruppe*, which by then had almost given us up for lost.' The calm order von Luck imposed on his *KG's* crossing-point wasn't universally imposed, as the *Hohenstaufen's* Herbert Fürbringer acknowledged: 'Things looked awful on the Seine! Columns, in some cases disintegrating, streamed en masse towards the Seine ... the decision by supreme command to change banks came too late. In particular it jammed roads and side-roads with bombed or shot-up columns, which...formed an almost inextricable mess...Where was the once-so-famous iron discipline of the German soldier? This mass was a great target for the enemy's *jabos*.'[10] Herbert Fürbringer and von Luck's *KG* were some of the 300,000 men and 25,000 vehicles ferried over the river in the space of five nights, according to Allied estimates. Not that the far side of the Seine was a safe-haven for the bedraggled survivors of *Heersgruppe B*; far from it, as the *Hohenstaufen's SS-Hauptsturmführer* Hans Möller recalled:

> The situation could change by the hour. Every second was vital and called for quick decisions ... we had lost radio contact, had we been struck off as lost already? The weather was favourable for a while, it had rained and low-cloud hindered enemy *jabos*... Not wanting to lose any more vehicles we ... waited in good cover for dusk... I kept my thoughts to myself, but I knew all the sleeping forms – exhausted and wrapped in blankets and tents – were thinking the same thing – we were all absolutely worn out.

One man who wasn't involved was Werner Kortenhaus. Injured by his own panzer track, he was recovering in hospital. Playing chess with a young *landser* in the ward, his opponent remarked on the assassination attempt on Hitler: 'He'd be better dead.' A nearby wounded SS NCO overhead the flippant comment, leaped up and slapped him hard round the head, demanding the soldier take back what he'd said. Reflecting on the incident, Kortenhaus said, 'We reckoned the whole game was up.'

With the Seine indefensible, Model swiftly ordered a further retreat to the Somme. That couldn't be held either, and once again the dishevelled remnants of *Heeresgruppe B* struggled northeast. Weary, hungry, with supplies only getting through sporadically, the Wehrmacht's famed cohesion and discipline seemed to be crumbling, as *5. Panzerarmee*'s Heinrich Eberbach believed: 'For the first time, not just Poles or Alsatians were deserting to the enemy, but even Germans ... the fighting morale of German troops had cracked.' Eberbach himself would never see if his dire prediction came true. On 31 August while out on a reconnaissance patrol he was captured near the city of Amiens.[11]

It wasn't just the German Army that was quitting France, it was the Luftwaffe and Kriegsmarine too. The U-boat offensive to interdict the Anglo-American cross-Channel convoys was lying on the sea-bed, along with over 750 German sailors – as Dönitz wrote later: 'In the end I could no longer match the moral fortitude displayed by the U-boat crews... To continue U-boat operations would be an irresponsible act.' Several of the U-boat pens on the French Atlantic coast – built at massive cost in labour and treasure – were still in German hands, their garrisons surrounded and besieged, but the remaining submarines were ordered to quietly slip anchor and try and make it back to German ports. They were needed in the Baltic to combat the growing power of the Soviet Navy.

The Luftwaffe – that most-maligned service of all – was also abandoning France. Helmut Benneman's *JG 53* – the *Pik As* ('Ace of Spades') of Battle of Britain and Stalingrad fame – left their base at Catillon near Amiens in the nick of time as American tanks advanced towards it, as *Leutnant* Alfred Hammer remembered:

> Some soldiers stationed nearby reassured us by telling us that the Americans 'stopped fighting' every night at 6pm precisely, and only resumed the following morning having shaved with hot water... We were then gravely alarmed to see them continue through the night and thus threaten our departure the following morning.

In truth, Hammer was lucky to be alive and to have an aircraft to fly; in just one month of operations during the campaign the *Gruppe* reported forty-two of its Bf 109 fighters shot down, eighteen lost to accidents, twenty abandoned as unserviceable, and a further twenty lost through 'other causes' – two hundred per cent of its operational strength. Willi Heilmann watched the *Jagdwaffe* leave Villacoublay airfield, south of Paris: 'Boxes and trunks were packed and loaded onto lorries ... any machines that couldn't be flown had to be scuttled.

In sections, the pathetic remains ... made their way eastward.' The remnants of Gerhard Michalski's *JG 4* were in much the same condition and were withdrawn from France at the same time. One of Michalski's pilots – Hermann Weber – took off in his Focke-Wulf 190 on the morning of 29 August and climbed east through the morning fog; 'I immediately headed off in the direction of the Franco-Belgian border at top speed.' Heilmann summed up his comrades' mood. 'We had all flown in vain.'[12]

Surely now it was only a matter of weeks if not days before the Anglo-Americans thrust into Germany and ended the war – except they didn't. The why is not the subject of this book, but suffice to say the Allies missed a golden opportunity, their advance petered out, and the Germans outran them. Erich Heller:

> On 1 September 1944 I found myself on the Rue de Paris, about ten kilometres outside Hirson on the French border with Belgium, along with a disorganised crowd of other soldiers. We had marched all night, the last remnants of *Das Reich*. Not many of us were left after the escape from Falaise. We were joined by some stragglers from the *fallschirmjäger*, some *panzergrenadiers* from *2. Panzerdivision*, and a Mk IV panzer from the *Panzer-Lehr*... There was barely enough fuel left to start the vehicles, but the Panzer IV still had two anti-tank and some high-explosive rounds... I assembled the group leaders and asked for their opinions on what we should do; it was unanimous, disable the Mark IV and the guns and strike out on foot.

Silently moving past advance American units, the group managed to avoid contact, swim the River Meuse, and eventually reach Germany near Losheim on 11 September. 'The Americans were no longer following ... there was no artillery fire, no *jabos*, and no tanks... It gave me great personal satisfaction to bring back almost fifty men alive.' Erich Heller was proud of what he had achieved; 'Looking back, I think that was my greatest achievement of the whole war. Above all, though, it was chiefly down to the NCOs and men, whose conduct during the journey made my task easier, and allowed us all to win our freedom again.'[13]

A full week before Heller and his men reached the Reich, Brussels was liberated after an Allied advance of 110 miles in just two days. The very next day, Hitler performed a *volte face* and reinstated Gerd von Rundstedt as OB West, moving Model to *Heeresgruppe B*. He also ordered that all Tigers and *Jagdpanther* self-propelled guns rolling off the production lines in Germany were to be prioritised for the West, while the East would get all the Panthers and Mark IVs. Albert Speer's efforts in armaments manufacture were still delivering incredible results. In fact, German armour and aircraft numbers wouldn't peak until two to three months later in November and December – although as the Soviet Red Army had captured the Reich's major source of gasoline, the Ploieşti oil fields, at the end of August, the Wehrmacht's fuel tanks would start running dry very soon. As for manpower, the *Ersatzheer* – the Wehrmacht's replacement system – cut every corner it could and more, and increased its flow to the Army to well over the 60,000 men a month mark it was achieving back in the summer.

So began the miracle of autumn '44 for German arms in the West, when despite losing over two thousand panzers and assault guns, well over two thousand aircraft – so much for a 'non-existent Luftwaffe' – and suffering around three-quarters of a million casualties, the Westheer managed somehow to hold on, defeat Bernard Montgomery's audacious parachute landings at Arnhem, and keep the Allies from entering Germany itself. Indeed, so transformational was the autumn miracle, that before the year was out the Germans would – to the complete surprise of the Anglo-Americans – go on the offensive one more time in the Ardennes, and many of the men who had been chased out of France and Belgium a couple of months previously would once more be advancing. They would do so without Werner Kortenhaus: 'After my recovery I went back to the fighting, this time on the Eastern Front, and at the end of the war I was captured by the Russians in Czechoslovakia.' The young NCO went into captivity with the rest of *21. Panzerdivision*, including Hans von Luck and Josef Rauch. Von Luck was released in 1950 and returned to what was then West Germany. The unfortunate Rauch spent another five years behind the wire before gaining his freedom. Their former peer, Hermann von Oppeln-Bronikowski, went on to become *Generalmajor* von Oppeln-Bronikowski, the 142nd winner of the *Schwerten* (Swords) to his Knight's Cross of the Iron Cross, and commanding officer of *20. Panzerdivision* until the war's end – von Schlieben's old command as it happened. He eventually surrendered to American forces, as did Ernst Goth, formerly of *916. Grenadier Regiment*.

As winter set in, Johannes Blaskowitz's *Heeresgruppe G* still stood on French territory – or rather territory that the French and Germans had been contesting on and off for decades – even as their comrades in *Heeresgruppe B* were chased off it farther north. *General der Infanterie* Hans von Obstfelder had succeeded Otto von Knobelsdorff as commander *1. Armee*, and now attempted to both stop the US Third Army from taking Metz and hold the northern Vosges Mountains against the American Seventh – a tall order he was never going to accomplish. Friedrich Wiese's *19. Armee* was rebuilt and tasked with holding Strasbourg against its nemesis from the retreat up the Rhône, *Armée B,* now renamed the 'French First Army'. It would be destroyed twice more before the war ended. Another unit brought back to life – Wend von Wietersheim's *11. Panzerdivision* – had one more crack at the Americans in the battle of Arracourt in late September, only to lose most of its panzers and grenadiers in four days of heavy fighting against elements of the US 4th Armored Division. Even Fritz Bayerlein's *Panzer-Lehr* didn't breathe its last in France. Reconstituted back in the Reich, it continued the fight until surrendering in the Ruhr Pocket in the spring of 1945. By then Bayerlein was no longer in command; he would survive the war and go on to become a technical consultant on the 1961 film, *The Guns of Navarone*. His fellow panzer leader – Edgar Feuchtinger – somehow avoided the sack after his dreadful performance in France and continued in command of *21. Panzer*. Clearly bored with his service, Feuchtinger set up house in a farm near the German town of Celle with his mistress and three fellow officers, whom he shielded from frontline duty with his rank. He indulged in black-marketeering and was also under suspicion of perpetrating a large-scale insurance fraud to line his own pockets. Finally arrested in January 1945 and charged with a shopping list of crimes, he was tried, found guilty, reduced to the rank of *Kanonier* (the lowest in the artillery world), stripped of all his awards and decorations, imprisoned in the notorious Torgau military prison, and sentenced to death. With every man who could hold a rifle needed at the front however, Hitler himself pardoned him and ordered him sent to Georg Scholze's *20. Panzergrenadier-Division* as a replacement – ironically, Scholze had commanded one of the *Lehr*'s panzergrenadier regiments in Normandy. Unsurprisingly, Feuchtinger declined the option of martyrdom and promptly deserted. He managed to avoid detection and gave himself up to the British after Germany's surrender. Sent to the special detention centre at Trent Park designed for senior Nazi officers, his notoriety went before him and many of his fellow detainees protested his presence there. Ever the charmer, Feuchtinger persuaded his captors he was a victim of Nazi injustice and received an early release in 1946. He would go on to pass military secrets to the KGB for almost a decade before his death in 1960.

As for the *fallschirmjäger,* August von der Heydte fought in the Ardennes that winter, survived the war and became a parliamentarian and university professor of political science. His fellow para officer, Richard Schimpf, returned to service after his injury at Falaise and eventually retired from the West German air force in 1962 as a *generalmajor.* Hein Severloh's testimony of events at Omaha on D-Day was used by Paul Carrell in his 1960 book on the landings; *Sie kommen! Die Invasion der Amerikaner und Briten in der Normandie 1944,* and by Severloh himself when Helmut Konrad von Keusgen ghostwrote his memoirs – *WN 62 – A German Soldier's Memories of the Defence of Omaha Beach Normandy, June 6th 1944,* in 2000. The self-proclaimed Beast of Omaha died six years later at home in Lachendorf. Many of his former comrades of *352. ID* are buried in the German war cemetery at La Cambe in Normandy. Today, museums and memorials dot the landing beaches and battlefields of Normandy, among them Wilhelm Richter's former divisional headquarters, and that of Hans von Salmuth's *15. Armee* at Tourcoing, just north of Lille. The whole region is as quiet, lush and enchanting as it has always been.

11

Looking Back

How did the Wehrmacht lose France? Ever since the war's end, the accepted narrative has been that the German defeat in Normandy reflected overwhelming Allied material superiority, total Allied air supremacy, and ruinous interference in military decision making by Hitler and his favourite generals at the highest level. In particular, Allied dominance in the air has consistently been highlighted as a decisive – if not *the* decisive – factor. This assessment was primarily a German perspective, and propogated partly by accounts of the campaign from some of the same German generals who lost it and lived, and reinforced by a host of writers; not least the former *General-SS* officer and propagandist Paul Carrell (real name Paul Schmidt). Since this thesis gained currency in the 1950s and 1960s it has become more nuanced. Revelations about Allied codebreaking, especially Ultra, and the effectiveness of Allied deception plans such as Operation *Fortitude* have added to the picture, as has a greater appreciation of the Red Army's immense contribution on the Eastern front, particularly the huge success of Operation *Bagration*, which was shredding the Ostheer as the Normandy fighting was doing the same to the Westheer.

But these answers probably fit the question of *why* the Wehrmacht lost France, far better than the question of *how*. This book is about that *how*, and, specifically that how through the eyes of the German soldiers, sailors and airmen who fought in France and were defeated.

That *how* originated in Hitler's *Führer* directive No. 40 of 23 March 1942, which instructed the Army, Kriegsmarine and Luftwaffe to work together to protect the Third Reich's Continental empire. Followed up at a conference six months later, the Nazi supremo outlined his strategy for defending mainland Europe against the anticipated Allied Second Front. That strategy was to build a wall – a wall that would run from the Spanish/French border in the foothills of the Pyrenees in the south, to near enough the Arctic Circle in northern Norway. Along its length there would be 15,000 strongpoints of varying sizes, and it would be completed in five to six months. In choosing this approach Hitler and his acquiescent senior officers tried to turn the clock back to a pre-gunpowder age. In that era, the most successful fortifications in history – the walls the Byzantine Emperor Theodosius built in the fifth century to protect Constantinople – stood unbreached for a thousand years, until Ottoman Turkish cannon and tunnelling brought them crashing down. Hitler didn't even have to look back very far to see the age of the wall in the art of war was over – less than four years earlier his own Wehrmacht had overcome France's vaunted Maginot Line with ridiculous ease. Regardless, a flawed strategy was then paired with flawed delivery.

A huge construction programme was initiated, with a workforce comprising fourteen fortress engineer construction battalions, four regular engineer construction battalions, five Rock Drilling Companies and two minelaying companies working in France alone. Hundreds of thousands of workers were involved – many of them forced labour – and only ten per cent of them Germans. At full pitch this host were pouring 769,000 cubic metres of reinforced concrete a month, and in total they laid a staggering 13,134,500 cubic metres, in between being detailed to go and repair damage to the rail network caused by Allied bombing – but it wasn't enough, it would *never* be enough. As the para *Oberstleutnant* Fritz Fullriede wrote in his diary afterwards: 'What a big mouth we had about the *Atlantikwall*.'

With typical German *in*efficiency each service arm did its own thing as to the construction, so there were no fewer than seven hundred different strongpoint designs in what was meant to be a standard system of defence. The Army – naturally – was responsible for the lion's share, and, taking its cue from its supreme commander, chose to fight the war of 1944 with the tools of the past; in its case, war-booty and horseflesh. Having dismantled the Czech Army in '39, trounced the French Army the following year, and then taken the Red Army to the brink of disaster another year later, Germany's generals proceeded to arm a half-built wall with the weapons of the defeated; there were one hundred and thirty-two medium or heavy artillery guns covering the landing beaches on D-Day (not including the forty *Nebelwerfers* and lighter pieces covering the surf itself), of which forty-six were

French, twenty-four were Czech, and twenty Soviet – requiring eleven different types of ammunition for nineteen different gun types, many of which dated from the First World War. Some guns didn't even fit the embrasures built for them. Of the two thousand French tanks captured in 1940, a few hundred were sent to rear-area units in the Balkans or elsewhere, but many had their chassis scrapped and their turrets used as gun-ports in the Wall, much like Gustav Winter's *betonpanzer* or the multitude of so-called *Tobruk* gun-positions.

It was all a charade, but so many letters, diaries and personal accounts from *landsers* paint a different picture – they actually *believed* in the defences, and trusted in them – men like the 17-year-old grenadier Helmut Voigt: 'I felt quite confident that we could hold back enemy armour for long enough to allow the inland panzer reserves to come up and counter-attack.' This was despite Voigt's position being 'an earth mound with a hollow concrete block inside it ... and on top of the block was a tank turret. The turret was very, very old; I think it came from a pre-war Italian tank.' How great then the shock when they were completely overwhelmed on the day itself by a naval and airborne armada for which they were total unprepared.

> Some of these impacts were enormous. That turret rang almost like a bell ... the gunner was silent and tense, and he began praying in between the blasts. Just as he finished a prayer we suffered a direct hit... Pieces of concrete fell on me... I looked up to see if the gunner was alright, and to my amazement the whole turret was gone. The complete steel structure had been blown off the concrete... Outside I saw the turret upside down about twenty metres away, and the body of the gunner near it. He was horribly shattered ... broken like a doll.[1]

With a wall of sand, the Wehrmacht needed to do one of two things to succeed in France; pack that Wall with so many men that wherever the Allies landed they would be met with overwhelming combat power, or make the right choice as to where the landings would be and concentrate there – they did neither. The focus of Hitler's aggression was always in the East. That was where the mass of German military might was concentrated from 22 June 1941 right up to the end of the war. The Western theatre was always secondary. Hitler's plan for the *Atlantikwall* envisaged a third of a million men manning it, but spread out along 2,400 miles, that meant not much more than a hundred men per mile, and even though the Westheer exceeded that total number, it also had to garrison five occupied countries. Hence the belly army and the *Ostruppen*. Tens of thousands of these men manned the frontline defences, and were no match for a modern fighting force, despite some being willing: 'Some men aged forty and over, and some of the Eastern men, were also positive, so it wasn't a simple distinction of "all the older and Eastern men had no appetite for combat".'[2]

> In our company there was this Russian called Ivan... One day I saw him crying and I asked him what was wrong. He said he was sad because he felt he would die here so far from home and family... Well, shortly after that I met a *Feldwebel* from one of our other companies, he told me that they were having quite a bit of trouble with their Russians... I sent Ivan over to him to be put in charge of his Russians. A few days later I received a box of cigars with a note from that *Feldwebel*. It told of the wonders worked by Ivan getting these men to fight better than they ever had.[3]

The proverbial sacrificial lambs, under-equipped, often indifferently-led, they couldn't even move, being dependent like so much of the Westheer on the horse for transport, much like an army from the Middle Ages. Whereas the Allies had the same ratio as the Wehrmacht had when it invaded the Soviet Union in 1941: one motor vehicle per five men. By '44 the Westheer had one *horse* per five men. The Allies appreciated this fact, and specifically intended to make their landing against this type of opposition; hence the Normandy beaches garrisoned by *709.* and *716. IDs* – and why the appearance of Dietrich Kraiss's *352. ID* on Omaha was such a surprise.

The concentration of force that could have made all the difference to the Wehrmacht was partly denied to them by the success of their earlier defence against the Canadian raid on Dieppe back in 1942. Both sides drew a whole host of lessons from that battle; the problem for the Wehrmacht was that it took the very opposite view from the enemy. The Allies decided it was pointless to try and take a major port by direct assault, whereas Berlin believed that was exactly what the Allies planned – they completely underestimated the Allied ability to land masses of supplies directly onto the beaches or via the innovation of the floating Mulberry artifical harbours – 3,098,529 tons and 2,052,299 men by the end of August. Freed from the need to secure a man-made harbour on day one of the landings, the Allies could make the same appraisal as the legendary Viking leader, Rollo, and appreciate the anchorage afforded by the Bay of the Seine and the

Normandy coast. The fact that it was a longer haul from the English south coast ports to Normandy than it was across the straits of Dover was irrelevant for a global sea-power like Great Britain, something a First World War infantryman like Hitler could never appreciate.

The other sphere of modern war in 1944 that the Wehrmacht failed to get to grips with was the battle in the sky. This was not a charge that could be levelled at SHAEF. Airpower was key to the Allied plan to win the war at an acceptable human cost. Thousands of pilots and aircraft were effectively 'stockpiled' for the landings, and no fewer than one hundred and sixty-three new air bases built in southern England to support the armada. The impact of Allied air domination runs through every German account of the campaign, from the humble *landser* all the way up to OB West. The generals on the losing side were clear: 'It was only thanks to the superiority of the enemy air force that our own well-prepared attack was checked.' This was Paul Hausser's post-war view on the failure of the Mortain counter-offensive, and it was echoed by 7. *Armee*'s *Oberst* (later *Generalmajor*) von Gersdorff, 'The attack was stopped from the air.' Air Marshal Coningham, the commander of Second Tactical Air Force (2nd TAF), agreed with Hausser and von Gersdorff about the Day of the Typhoons, declaring that his rocket-firing, bomb-dropping fighter-bombers had been 'a decisive battle winning factor' claiming a grand total of eighty-nine panzers and assault-guns 'definitely destroyed', another fifty-six tracked vehicles 'probably destroyed', one hundred and four motor vehicles 'set on fire', and another forty-seven 'possibles'. And yet...

When the Allied 21st Army's own Operational Research Section spent eight days meticulously surveying the Mortain battlefield immediately following the German retreat, they only found forty-three panzers, three assault-guns, and a mere thirty trucks. Nineteen of the panzers had definitely been destroyed by ground fire, seven had been abandoned intact, four had been blown up by their crews, three were classed as having been put out of action by 'unknown causes', and just seven showed signs of being hit by aerial rockets. Two others had been disabled by aerial bombing. The researchers' findings at Falaise were even worse for the airmen. There, the analysts spent three weeks combing the carnage around Pierrefitte-Argentan-Chambois-Vimoutiers-Trun – an area known with typical military black humour as 'The Shambles'. They examined one-hundred-and-seventy-one armoured fighting vehicles, and found only eleven had been hit by bombs or rockets, with the vast majority blown up or abandoned by their own crews. Air attack had fared better against soft-skinned vehicles, trucks, cars, bowsers and so on, the evidence suggested that strafing had accounted for a third of all those losses.

None of this should have been a huge surprise. In the run up to D-Day, Typhoon pilots were recorded as being able to hit a viaduct five hundred yards long and eight yards wide once in fifteen attempts with rockets, while the chance of hitting it with a bomb was one in every eighty-two dropped – a Mark V Panther was approximately half the width of said viaduct, and just six yards long.[4] It would seem that the effect of Allied air power was more psychological than physical in terms of defeating the Germans.

The absence of the Luftwaffe was undoubtedly a crushing blow to the morale of the *landsers* and panzer-crews, as *landser* Helmut Hesse attested to: 'The *Jabos* were a burden on our souls... *Ja*, I saw the Luftwaffe. Seven of them, 7,000 *Jabos*.' Soldiers like Hesse had been conditioned by three years of savage warfare on the Eastern front where, according to *General der Panzertruppe* Erhard Raus's postwar treatise for the Americans, 'The Russian Air Force was often no factor at all in ground warfare. Sometimes it played a secondary role.'[5]

In truth, Normandy wasn't the first time the Luftwaffe was found wanting; it had had its problems right the way back to the failure over Dunkirk and the Battle of Britain. By the time the landing craft hit the Normandy beaches it was in a death-spiral with nowhere near enough pilots being sent forward to replace the losses, which led to less training of the new boys, who consequently became casualties faster than they could be replaced; as two members of the *Jagdwaffe* discussed when secretly recorded in captivity: 'All we have now is young pilots with no experience.' And 'What sort of training have the newcomers had? It's pitiful and appalling.'

One of their commanders, and 176-kill *Experte* himself, Johannes 'Macky' Steinhoff agreed: 'We were assigned young pilots who were timid, inexperienced and scared ... it was hard enough leading and keeping together a large combat formation of experienced pilots, with youngsters it was hopeless.'

The figures speak for themselves. Of the one-hundred-and-seven *Jagdwaffe Experten* who scored over a hundred kills, only eight joined their units after mid-1942.[6] The only way the Luftwaffe could hope to achieve anything like even local parity by the summer of 1944 was by shifting their hard core of *Experten* to wherever it was needed. These men, the virtual flying war machines from the Eastern front, went up day after day over France with their inexperienced *kameraden*, and were bled white, despite their courage, as even Paul Hausser acknowledged. 'The promised support of our own fighters never materialised; they were met and dealt with above the fields by the enemy.'

The Luftwaffe's woes cut no ice with Hitler though, and in late August he sacked the jowly Hugo Sperrle in disgust. Lionel Ellis, decorated army officer, military historian and author of three volumes of the official *History of the Second World War* said of him:

> The commander of the 3rd Air Fleet, Field Marshal Hugo Sperrle, had held that appointment during the whole German occupation of France, "living soft" in Paris. He does not seem to have had any lively reaction when the Allies landed, and none of his subordinates is distinguishable in the air fighting in Normandy. The War Diaries of the Army commands in the West have few references to the Luftwaffe that aren't critical, and they give no indication that Sperrle had any voice in shaping the conduct of operations.

Much the same could be said of all the senior German commanders in France during the campaign, even the much-vaunted Erwin Rommel. Bernard Montgomery's own pre-D-Day estimate on facing his old desert adversary was:

> ...an energetic and determined commander; he has made a world of difference since he took over... He will do his best to 'Dunkirk' us – not to fight the armoured battle on ground of his own choosing, but to avoid it all together by using his tanks well forward... It is now clear that his intention is to deny us any penetration; Overlord is to be defeated on the beaches.

Monty's assessment was remarkably accurate, though this accuracy was perhaps somewhat underpinned by the Ultra decrypts supplied to Allied high command by the codebreakers at Bletchley Park. But Rommel failed to achieve his goal of defeating the landings in the surf, and no senior German general managed to impose his will on the battlefield, with von Rundstedt, von Kluge, von Schweppenburg and Eberbach stumbling from one patch-up operation to the next. From D-Day onwards, German senior generalship is summed up by Günther Blumentritt's words: 'There was no plan any longer. We were merely trying, without hope.'[7]

Perhaps this was only to be expected in a Reich where one man had made himself the spider at the centre of every web; military, political and economic. This was another hugely important facet of the 'why we lost' narrative expounded by Germany's generals after the war. Their argument went that Hitler overruled or forbade every sensible decision they tried to make, and if he had left it to them then things might well have been different. The 'it was Hitler's fault' proponents highlight the dispersal of effort that saw masses of scarce resources waiting for landings all the way from Norway to the French Mediterranean coast – and they have a point. But it's worth remembering a few counter-arguments. By the summer of 1944 the Mediterranean was an 'Allied sea', where they had successfully conducted three landing operations already, had air supremacy and an army *in situ*. Hitler also guessed correctly that it was Churchill's preferred option – the British PM was never an enthusiastic fan of *Overlord* – and the Allies did indeed actually land there in mid-August. As for a possible assault on Norway, that was a little harder to see – but again, the Anglo-French had landed there in 1940, and the British had been conducting large-scale commando raids on it ever since. Hitler also tended to see the war in economic terms as much as military, and therefore an attack that would cut off the war-critical flow of Swedish iron ore to German factories was a possibility; after all, the Allies had proven they would focus huge resources to destroy the Reich's economy – witness the heavy-bomber campaign and its concentrated attacks on the key German ball-bearing and synthetic fuel industries. Hitler also made a few decisions that went against orthodox military opinion at the time and turned out to be correct, as *General der Artillerie* Wilhelm Fahrmacher acknowledged when he wrote of Hitler's decision not to release *11. Panzerdivision* from *Heeresgruupe G* for the Normandy fighting: 'Hitler ... refused any weakening of the German *19. Armee* in southeastern France by withdrawing *11. Panzerdivision;* it was the only armoured unit which this Army had at its disposal... Subsequently the presence of *11. Panzer* proved to be the lifesaver for *19. Armee* ... this armoured unit kept the Rhône valley free to the north.'[8]

The fact remains though, that in war there is almost always opportunity – perhaps only fleeting and slim at best, but opportunity nonetheless, and given massive Allied superiority, as soon as the Germans realised their plans were mirages, they needed to think and act radically to give the *landsers* a chance, and this is where Hitler failed – he had put himself at the apex of command and then had nothing to offer except a battle of attrition the Westheer could only lose.

While elements of senior German leadership decry their defeat and point to its inevitability given the odds stacked against them, there has been an equally vocal chorus from the Allied side lauding the magnificence of German arms. Writers point to the incredible feats of endurance and skill shown by the likes of the *HJ*, and marvel at how a green, inexperienced division could achieve as much as it did with an average age of just eighteen-and-a-half, and short at the outset of the campaign by over two thousand NCOs and one hundred and forty-four officers. Fingers point to George Patton's account to Omar Bradley of an interrogation by his own G-2 intelligence staff of a captured German general when he was asked why he had fought on when the situation was hopeless, and he had replied: 'I am a professional, and I obey my orders.' Others highlight *Gefreiter* Adolf Hohenstein's words when asked the same question: 'If for the rest of my life I was to chop wood in Canada or Siberia, then I'd sooner die in Normandy.'[9] Paul Carrell's narrative of the battle for France encapsulates this judgement perfectly, continually lambasting Hitler while praising the prowess of German soldiers. It concludes by quoting an official Canadian history of the campaign:

> The German soldier and field commander showed themselves, as so often before, to be excellent practitioners of their trade. The German fighting soldier was courageous, tenacious, and skilful. He was sometimes a fanatic, occasionally a brutal thug, but he was almost always a formidable fighting man who gave a good account of himself, even under conditions as adverse as those in Normandy certainly were. German commanders and staff officers were in general highly competent. Man for man and unit for unit it cannot be said that it was by tactical superiority that we won the battle of Normandy.

A line often repeated by historians and veterans of the campaign alike is that Normandy wasn't fought by generals but by lieutenants and corporals – *leutnants* and *gefreiters* – and that the latter were manifestly better than the former; the Germans are lauded for their often superior equipment, their tactical *nous*, their operational expertise, and the sheer resilience and tenacity of their fighting men – and there is some truth in this. Take the equipment point – the German MG 34 and 42 machine-guns were more effective than the British Bren gun, but then they took one hundred and fifty and seventy-five man-hours respectively to manufacture – the Bren took fifty. The Mark V Panther was markedly superior to the Allied M4 Sherman tank, but only 6,000 were built, against almost 50,000 Shermans – and only fifteen hundred Tiger Is were made versus 80,000 Soviet T34s. What effect then a German kill ratio of six to one?

The incontrovertible fact of the 1944 French campaign is that the Germans were beaten by an enemy better than them – they lost, and they lost because they did not wage war as well as their opponents. This should be no surprise. For all its vaunted military expertise and professionalism, the fact remains that Germany has never learnt how to win a war – after all it hasn't won one since becoming a country. A German infantry officer serving in France – *Hauptmann* von Steinacker – wrote in his diary: 'The enemy artillery was firing brilliantly, directed from the air of course. German aircraft were nowhere to be seen.' Nothing extraordinary about that, except Steinacker wasn't serving in Normandy in 1944, but on the Somme in 1916.

The Tommy, the GI, the Canuck arguably may not have been a match for the *landser*; his machine-gun wasn't either, or his tank – but that is only a fragment of the picture. The men from Mansfield, Boston and Winnipeg may not have been as good at soldiering as those from Duisburg or Stuttgart, but they kept on going, and the art of war is not about winning the first battle, or the third, or the tenth, it is about winning the last. The US War Department's 1942 booklet distributed to all American service personnel sent to serve in the UK makes the following comment on the British character: 'Don't be misled by the British tendency to be soft-spoken and polite, the English language didn't spread across the oceans and over the mountains, jungles and swamps of the world because these people were panty-waists ... you won't be able to tell the British much about taking it... 60,000 British civilians – men, women, children – have died under bombs, and yet the morale of the British is unbreakable and high ... they are not particularly interested in taking it any more ... they are far more interested in starting to dish it out to Hitler.'

Waffen-SS, German Army and comparable British Army Ranks

Waffen-SS	German Army	British Army
SS-Schütze	Schütze/ Grenadier	Private
SS-Oberschütze	Oberschütze	Private
SS-Sturmmann	Gefreiter	Lance corporal
SS-Rottenführer	Obergefreiter	Corporal
SS-Unterscharführer	Unteroffizier	Lance Sergeant (only used in the British Brigade of Guards)
SS-Scharführer	Unterfeldwebel	Sergeant
SS-Oberscharführer	Feldwebel	Colour/staff Sergeant
SS-Hauptscharführer	Oberfeldwebel	Sergeant-Major - Warrant Officer Class 2
SS-Sturmscharführer	Hauptfeldwebel	Sergeant-Major - Warrant Officer Class 1
SS-Untersturmführer	Leutnant	Second-Lieutenant
SS-Obersturmführer	Oberleutnant	Lieutenant
SS-Hauptsturmführer	Hauptmann	Captain
SS-Sturmbannführer	Major	Major
SS-Obersturmbannführer	Oberstleutnant	Lieutenant-Colonel
SS-Standartenführer	Oberst	Colonel
SS-Brigadeführer	Generalmajor	Brigadier
SS-Gruppenführer	Generalleutnant	Major-General
SS-Obergruppenführer	General	Lieutenant-General
SS-Oberstgruppenführer	Generaloberst	General
	Generalfeldmarschall	Field-Marshal

Bibliography

Atkinson, Rick, *The Guns at Last Light, The War in Western Europe, 1944–1945*, Abacus 2013

Bartmann, Erwin (translated by Derik Hammond), *Für Volk and Führer*, Helion 2013

Beevor, Antony, *Arnhem*, Viking 2018

Beevor, Antony, *D-Day: The Battle for Normandy*, Viking 2009

Bishop, Chris, *SS: Hell on the Western Front*, Spellmount 2003

Boyd, Julia, *Travellers in the Third Reich*, Elliot & Thompson 2017

Carrell, Paul (translated by Ewald Osers), *Invasion: They're Coming!* Bantam 1964

Carruthers, Bob, *Voices from the Luftwaffe*, Pen & Sword 2012

Hessler, Günther (ed. Bob Carruthers), *The U-Boat War in the Atlantic volume III: 1944–1945*, Pen & Sword 2013

Cawthorne, Nigel, *Fighting them on the Beaches: The D-Day landings June 6, 1944*, Capella 2007

Cooper, Matthew & Lucas, James, *Panzer – The armoured force of the Third Reich*, Book Club 1979

Eckhertz, Holger, *D-Day through German Eyes – Book One and Two*, DTZ 2015

Evans, Richard, J., *The Third Reich At War*, Allen Lane 2008

Fischer, Wolfgang (edited & translated by John Weal), *Luftwaffe Fighter Pilot – Defending the Reich*, Grub Street 2010

Fürbringer, Herbert, *La Hohenstaufen: 9.SS Panzer Division 1944: Normandy, Tarnapol-Arnhem*, Heimdal 2002

Galland, Adolf, *The First and the Last*, Buccaneer Books 1990

Gersdorff, Rudolf *Freiherr* von, Hausser, Paul, Fahrmacher, Wilhelm, Eberbach, Heinrich, and Lüttwitz, Heinrich Freiherr von (ed. David

C. Isby), *Fighting the Break-out – The German Army in Normandy from Cobra to the Falaise Gap* – Greenhill 2004

Griesser, Volker (translated by Mara Taylor), *The Lions of Carentan: Fallschirmjäger Regiment 6, 1943–1945*, Casemate 2011

Hargreaves, Richard, *The Germans in Normandy*, Pen & Sword 2006

Hastings, Max, *Das Reich: The March of the 2nd SS Panzer Division through France June 1944*, Pan 1983

Hastings, Max, *Overlord: D-Day and the Battle for Normandy 1944*, Pan 2015

Holmes, Richard, *The World at War*, Ebury 2007

Ed. Holmes, Tony, *Dogfight – the Greatest Air Duels of World War II*, Osprey 2011

Hooton, E.R., *Eagle in Flames – The Fall of the Luftwaffe*, Arms & Armour 1997

Jost, Bertrand Jost, *This too shall come to pass, Les Malgre Nous*, Createspace 2013

Keegan, John, *Six Armies in Normandy*, Penguin 1983

Kershaw, Robert J., *It Never Snows in September*, Ian Allan 1994

Klapdor, Ewald, *Die Entscheidung: Invasion 1944*, self-published 1984

Lucas, James, *Storming Eagles – German airborne forces in World War II*, Cassell 1988

Lucas, James, *Das Reich*, Cassell, 1991

Luck, Hans von, *Panzer Commander: The memoirs of Colonel Hans von Luck*, Cassell 1989

McNab, Chris, *The Luftwaffe 1933–45, Hitler's Eagles*, Osprey 2012

Milano, Vince and Bruce Conner, *Normandiefront*, The History Press 2011

Miller, Russell, *Nothing Less than Victory – The Oral History of D-Day*, Michael Joseph 1993

Mitcham, Samuel W. Jr, *Eagles of the Third Reich*, Stackpole 1988

Mitcham, Samuel W., *Hitler's Legions: German Army Order of Battle World War II*, Leo Cooper 1985

Munoz, Antonio, *Iron Fist: A Combat history of the 17th SS Panzergrenadier Götz von Berlichingen*, Axis Europa 1999

Murray, Williamson, *Strategy for Defeat – The Luftwaffe – 1933–1945*, Chartwell 1986

Neitzel, Sönke and Welzer, Harald, *Soldaten*, Simon & Schuster 2012

Perrett, Bryan, *Knights of the Black Cross*, Robert Hale 1986

Reynolds, Michael, *Steel Inferno: 1 SS Panzer Corps in Normandy*, Spellmount 1997

Reynolds, Michael, *Sons of the Reich: II SS Panzer Corps*, Spellmount 2002

Ritgen, Helmut (translated by Joseph G. Welsh), *The Western Front, 1944: Memoirs of a Panzer Lehr Officer*, Fedorowicz (J.J.) 1996

Schneid, Sadi, *SS-Beutedeutscher. Weg und Wandlung eines Elsässers*, Lindhorst, Askania 1979

Thorn, Manfred, *Von der Leibstandarte zum Sündenbock und Prügelknaben*, Nation & Wissen Verlag 2016

Trigg, Jonathan, *The Defeat of the Luftwaffe – A Strategy for Disaster*, Amberley 2016

U.S. War Department, Washington D.C., *Instructions for American Servicemen in Britain 1942*

Werner, Herbert, *Iron Coffins*, Da Capo Press 2002

Whiting, Charles, '44 – *In Combat on the Western Front from Normandy to the Ardennes*, Century Publishing 1984

Williamson, Gordon, *Loyalty is my Honor*, Motorbooks 1997

Zaloga, Steven J., *Saint-Lô 1944 – The Battle of the Hedgerows*, Osprey 2017

Zaloga, Steven J., *D-Day Fortifications in Normandy*, Osprey 2005

Notes

Introduction
1. Cawthorne, Nigel, *Fighting them on the Beaches*, p87.
2. Showalter, Dennis, *Instrument of War*, p7.

1. Festung Europa – 'Fortress Europe'
1. *Statistisches Jahrbuch für die Bundesrepublik Deutschland 1960*, p78.
2. Eckhertz, Holger, *D-Day through German Eyes*, p93, interview with Cornelius Tauber, 716. *ID, 736. Grenadier-Regiment.* Doubts have been raised in some quarters as to the veracity of some of the information in this book. In the author's opinion – with some exceptions, notably the contribution of a 'specialist weapons officer' describing an experimental fuel/air explosive system – these interviews ring true.
3. Ibid – p5, interview with *Gefreiter* Stefan Heinevez of 709. *ID, 919. Grenadier-Regiment.*
4. Ibid – p64, interview with Marten Eineg of 716. *ID, 726. Grenadier-Regiment.*
5. Atkin, Ronald, *Dieppe 1942: The Jubilee Disaster*, London: Book Club Associates.
6. Tucker, Spencer C., *A Global Chronology of Conflict: From the Ancient World to the Modern Middle East*, p1885.
7. McNab, Chris, *Hitler's Armies*, p197. Horses in the German Army were divided into four categories; heaviest breed draft horses, heavy breed draft horses, saddle and light draft horses and light horses. Each category had a different ration scale with the heaviest type getting the most at 5640 grams of oats, 5300 grams

of hay, and 5750 grams of straw including 1500 grams for bedding straw.

8. *Untermensch* – derogatory Nazi racial slur meaning 'sub-human' and used to describe all races seen by the Nazis as inferior to their own Aryan master race, the *herrenvolk*.

9. Hiwis – short for *Hilfswillige*, literally 'willing helpers'. These were mostly captured ex-Red Army men who volunteered to switch sides and work for the Germans. When the phenomenon first started to appear in the summer of 1941 during Operation *Barbarossa*, these Hiwis were employed in menial tasks like digging latrines and carrying rations, and then over time as casualties mounted amongst the invaders they often graduated to carrying ammunition and then finally manning the guns they were servicing.

10. In 1941 the Nazis invaded the Soviet Union with a force of 153 divisions, leaving the Army's remaining fifty-five divisions split across Europe and North Africa; two in Libya, seven in the Balkans, eight in Norway and Denmark, and thirty-eight in France, Belgium and the Netherlands. A total of 208 divisions in all. By the spring of 1944 the Army had grown to 298 divisions, with 193 in the East, twenty-eight in Italy, fifty-nine in France and the Low Countries, and an astonishing eighteen in Norway and Denmark.

11. The British launched twelve commando raids in Norway during the War; the first being Operation *Claymore* in March 1941 aimed at the Lofoten Islands in the north of the country. The islands were an important centre for the production of fish oil and glycerine, both used in the German war economy. The landings destroyed local fish oil factories and some 3,500 long tons of oil and glycerine. The British and Norwegian units also returned with 228 German prisoners, 314 pro-Allied Norwegian volunteers and a number of Quisling regime supporters. Naval gunfire and demolition parties sank some 18,000 tons of enemy shipping. Further raids followed with the islands being attacked again in December that year in *Operation Anklet*.

12. Canaris was implicated in the 20 July 1944 bomb plot to assassinate Hitler, arrested and imprisoned. As the war came to an end, in a typically Nazi act of last-ditch cruelty and macabre humiliation he was hanged on 9 April 1945 at Flossenbürg concentration camp after being led to the gallows stark naked. In a small gesture of consolation, his widow was awarded a pension for life by Franco's fascist government for her late husband's

advice to the Spanish dictator to keep his country out of the war – advice Franco took and was ever grateful for.

13. Miller, Russell, *Nothing less than Victory*, p94, interview with *Gefreiter* Heinz Herbst, *H. Kompanie*, 613 Long Range Reconnaisance Unit.

14. Mazower, Mark, *Hitler's Empire*, p141.

15. My personal favourite of Frederick's many attributed quotes is 'a crown is merely a hat that lets the rain in.'

16. A Jewish eyewitness to this atrocity described it thus: 'On the way to the station, Jews were forced to make a detour through an extremely muddy area. Germans called this area Rotes Moor. They [military policemen] stood on both sides [of the road]. Jews were told to run through the mud and sing, while a hail of whips was falling on their heads. The mud was so thick that shoes got stuck in it... People's heads, especially men's, were bleeding. They threw away their bundles, so that they could run in the mud... Finally, they reached the station... A new ordeal started. Body searching. They looked everywhere. Those who looked better were told to undress and naked women were carefully examined... Those who had something to hide had to roll naked in the mud – in December! Those who had undergone the search were packed onto railway cars... The journey took 36 hours.' Grynberg, Michał, Żydzi w rejencji ciechanowskiej *1939–1942*, p94.

17. Eckhertz, Holger, *D-Day through German Eyes*, p150, interview with Gustav Winter, *716. ID, 726. Grenadier-Regiment.*

18. Ibid - p109, interview with Cornelius Tauber.

19. Ibid – p64, interview with Martin Eineg.

20. Ibid – p227, interview with Helmut Voigt *716. ID, 736. Grenadier-Regiment.*

21. Miller, Russell, *Nothing less than Victory*, p389, interview with *Gefreiter* Joseph Häger, *4. Kompanie, I/736. Grenadier-Regiment, 716. ID.*

22. Ibid – p81, interview with *Gefreiter* Werner Beibst.

23. Ibid – p92, interview with *Feldwebel* Rainer Hartmetz, *77. ID.*

24. Eckhertz, Holger, *D-Day through German Eyes*, p153, interview with Gustav Winter.

25. Remarks made by Adolf Hitler at the Angerburg Conference on 16 July 1941 to Hermann Goering, Alfred Rosenberg, Martin Bormann and Wilhelm Keitel.

26. Author interview with *SS-Schütze* Asbjørn Narmo.

27. On 14 July 1942 the German Army instituted the *Tapferkeits – und Verdienst-Ausziechnung für der Ostvölker* – 'Decoration for Bravery and Merit for the Eastern Peoples', in five grades.

28. Littlejohn, David, *Foreign Legions of the Third Reich volume 4*, p330.

29. Mazower, Mark, *Hitler's Empire*, p163.

30. Ibid – p153.

31. Ibid – p458.

32. Littlejohn, David, *Foreign Legions of the Third Reich volume 4*, p331. *General der Kavallerie* Ernst-August Köstring, in his role as *General der Osttruppen*, reported to Himmler at the beginning of June 1944 that there were approximately 100,000 *Osttruppen* in the Luftwaffe and Kriegsmarine, and an astonishing 800,000 in the Army.

33. Eckhertz, Holger, *D-Day through German Eyes*, p189, interview with Heinrich Runder 709. *ID*, stationed on the Cotentin near Utah Beach.

34. Mazower, Mark, *Hitler's Empire*, p40.

35. Ibid – p197.

36. Cawthorne, Nigel, *Fighting them on the Beaches*, p218.

37. McNab, Chris, *Hitler's Armies*, p262.

38. Interview with Rudolf von Ribbentrop.

39. Guderian was never coy about the debt he owed the British for his ideas on armoured warfare: 'It was principally the books and articles of the Englishmen; Fuller, Liddell Hart and Martel, that excited my interest and gave me food for thought.'

2. Throw Them Back into the Sea!

1. There is no evidence that *21. Panzer* actually went into combat with the Allies in their ancient Panzer Somua 35(f)'s. It would seem that their crews were sent to the rear first to be re-equipped with new PzKpfw IV's before going into action.

2. See Trigg, Jonathan, *Death on the Don*.

3. Eckhertz, Holger, *D-Day Through German Eyes*, p271, interview with Paul Breslau.

4. Miller, Russell, *Nothing less than Victory*, p88, interview with *Oberleutnant* Helmut Liebeskind, *125. Panzergrenadier Regiment, 21. Panzerdivision*.

5. Ibid – p86, interview with *Obergefreiter* Werner Kortenhaus.

6. Eckhertz, Holger, *D-Day through German Eyes*, p171, interview with *Leutnant* Thomas Beike.

7. Murray, Williamson, *Strategy for Defeat: The Luftwaffe 1939–1945*, p207.

8. Hessler, Günther, edited by Bob Carruthers, *The U-boat War in the Atlantic volume III: 1944–1945*, p163.

9. Miller, Russell, *Nothing less than Victory*, p234, interview with Klaus Herrig

10. Milano, Vince & Conner, Bruce, *Normandiefront*, p260.

11. Miller, Russell, *Nothing less than Victory*, p96, interview with *Gefreiter* Aloysius Damski, *352. ID.*

12. Milano, Vince & Conner, Bruce, *Normandiefront*, p67.

13. Mazower, Mark, *Hitler's Empire*, p456.

14. Mayo, Jonathan, *D-Day: Minute by minute*, p103.

15. Eckhertz, Holger, *D-Day through German Eyes*, p204, interview with *Grenadier* Heinrich Runder. Runder was wounded later that same day manning an MG 34, and then captured.

16. Ibid – p29, interview with *Gefreiter* Stefan Heinevez. The *Sturmgeschütz III*, or StuG III was a 7.5cm anti-tank gun mounted on an old turret-less Panzer III chassis.

17. Ibid – p50, interview with *Unteroffizier* Henrik Naube.

18. Milano, Vince & Conner, Bruce, *Normandiefront*, p30.

19. Miller, Russell, *Nothing less than Victory*, p395.

20. Mayo, Jonathan, *D-Day: Minute by minute*, p231.

21. The *Svenner*, sunk off Sword Beach, was the only Allied ship lost on D-Day to German naval action.

22. The British had used well-known British car manufacturers names as codenames for German positions near Sword; hence Morris, Hillman, Humber, Daimler etc.

23. The actual number of panzers and assault guns von Oppeln-Bronikowski had for his counter-attack on 6 June is a matter of debate. Carrell states it was ninety-eight, and that was what von Oppeln-Bronikowski himself believed and recounted to him, while Cawthorne says it was ninety-four in his book *Fighting them on the Beaches*. Samuel W. Mitcham Jr in his *The Desert Fox in Normandy* has sixty panzers of *I. Bataillon's 1–3. Kompanien* as the 4th was detached to von Luck at the time. Carrell says that Vierzig and his *II. Bataillon* arrived and pulled their panzers up to the left of von Gottberg's before the two officers conversed prior to the attack – then no further mention is made of Vierzig or his battalion. Mitcham also states that the division lost some fifty panzers on its way through Caen to its counter-attack, although this is very hard to believe. Any disparity in total panzer numbers

almost certainly comes with the confusion of the day itself, with losses incurred on the move through Caen earlier, and the usual issues that face all armoured formations such as breakdown and mechanical failure. I have opted for Mitcham's figure of sixty as it is more likely that such a number could be repulsed by the British force it faced – although I intend no disrespect whatsoever to those brave men who sat atop the ridge that day and knocked the panzers for six!

24. Miller, Russell, *Nothing less than Victory*, p398.

25. Mayo, Jonathan, *D-Day: Minute by minute*, p259.

26. Schulman, Milton, *Defeat in the West*, pp102–3.

27. *WN14* was the only one of the 'upper' four strongpoints near Sword Beach not named after a British car manufacturer, it was given the name of a fish (of course!), as was *WN20*; 'Cod', and *WN21* 'Trout', both were on the beaches themselves, the latter being at Lion-sur-Mer and so very close to where Rauch's panzer-grenadiers managed to reach the sea that evening.

28. The *Ia* was the divisional operational chief of staff, a post held by an officer who had been selected and trained as a *Generalstaboffizier* – general staff officer – to represent the German General Staff Corps in both command and staff functions. They ranked from *Hauptmann im Generalstab* (Captain) through to *Oberst i.G.*(Colonel).

29. Cawthorne, Nigel, *Fighting them on the Beaches*, p127.

30. Miller, Russell, *Nothing less than Victory*, p79.

31. Ibid, p431.

32. Ibid, p429.

33. Cawthorne, Nigel, *Fighting them on the Beaches*, p183

34. Eckhertz, Holger, *D-Day through German Eyes*, p90, interview with *Soldat* Martin Eineg.

35. Ibid, interview with *Gefreiter* Gustav Winter. Winter lost the end of his nose, the little finger of each hand, and some of his toes to frostbite whilst on the Russian front. In Normandy he manned a *betonpanzer* on D-Day.

36. Milano, Vince & Conner, Bruce, *Normandiefront*, p138.

37. Mayo, Jonathan, *D-Day: Minute by minute*, p221.

3. Hold the Line!

1. On D-Day the *HJ* was recorded as having 79 Panthers and 96 Pz IVs, while *Panzer-Lehr* had 86 Panthers, 97 Pz IVs and an additional 60 other panzers and assault-guns.

2. Normandy covers 30,627 square kilometres (11,825 square miles), roughly 5 per cent of the territory of metropolitan France. The Operation Bagration battlefield in the East was fought over an area of roughly 207,600 square kilometres (80,200 square miles).

3. The one-armed head of the *Hitlerjugend* in 1943, Artur Axmann, has been credited with proposing the idea of the *HJ* division, as has *SS-Gruppenführer* Gottlob Berger.

4. Author interview with Rudolf von Ribbentrop.

5. At one point, Schmierer hid in a loft on a farm where the SS had a headquarters on the ground floor. Staying hidden, it was a couple of days before he could move on safely. After several weeks of travel, he was stopped by the Russians at a checkpoint, whereupon they discovered his SS blood-type tattoo. He was arrested and sent to Siberia, and only released in 1956. Author interview with Hans Dall – Schmierer's nephew.

6. Hargreaves, Richard, *The Germans in Normandy*, p17.

7. Meyer, Hubert, *The History of the 12.SS-Panzerdivision Hitlerjugend*, p19.

8. Meyer, Kurt, *Grenadiere*.

9. Messenger, Charles, *The Last Prussian*, p169.

10. Eckhertz, Holger, *D-Day through German Eyes*, p299.

11. Milano, Vince & Conner, Bruce, *Normandiefront*, p136.

12. Instituted after the launch of Operation Barbarossa, the Honour Roll was intended as an award for bravery for those who had already earned the Iron Cross in both classes, and then had again distinguished themselves. Awarded at the discretion of the high command, it was seen as a very prestigious decoration, and only 4,556 individuals earned it during the war.

13. An example of a 'near-static' division was *243. ID*, which had six infantry battalions organized in two regiments. For transport, two battalions had bicycles, two had horses, and only two had any motor vehicles – and not many of those.

14. Milano, Vince & Conner, Bruce, *Normandiefront*, p203.

4. Planes, Ships and Rolling Stock

1. During the same ceremony, as a sop to the vain Göring, already a *Generalfeldmarschall* since 1938, the head of the Luftwaffe was promoted to the new-rank of *Reichsmarschall*, created especially for him.

2. The twelve new *generalfeldmarschalle* of the 1940 ceremony would experience mixed fortunes in the years following;

Walther von Brauchitsch, Wilhelm von Leeb and von Rundstedt
would all be sacked by Hitler (von Rundstedt several times of
course), Fedor von Bock would first be sacked and then killed
alongside his wife and daughter in an RAF attack. Walther
von Reichenau would also die, in an air-crash after suffering a
heart attack. Erwin von Witzleben would be executed by the
Nazis for his part in the 20 July Plot, while Günther von Kluge
would commit suicide for his role in the same affair. Albert
Kesselring and the two Wilhelms, List and Keitel, would all be
tried for war crimes; Kesselring and List would be imprisoned
and Keitel hanged. As for Erhard Milch, he surendered to
the British commando, Brigadier Derek Mills-Roberts, on the
Baltic coast on 4 May 1945. Mills-Roberts was so incensed by
what he had seen of Nazi atrocities at the liberation of Bergen-
Belsen concentration camp, that he firstly broke Milch's own
marshal's baton over his head before beating him with a
champagne bottle, resulting in Milch suffering a fractured skull
among other injuries.

3. Mitcham Jr, Samuel W., *Eagles of the Third Reich*, p213.

4. General Guiseppe Valle was Chief of Staff of the Italian fascist air
   force, the *Regia Aeronautica*, in 1939. He was forced to resign
   in disgrace following an investigation which found that only
   thirty per cent of the three thousand aircraft claimed to be in the
   Italian air force were modern airframes, the rest being hopelessly
   obsolete, hulks or unserviceable wrecks – Valle had lied to secure
   an ever-increasing share of the military budget.

5. *JG 26's* honorific title of *Schlageter* was from '*Albert Leo
   Schlageter*', a German *Freikorps* member executed by the French
   in 1923 for attempting to destroy railroad tracks taking coal
   from the Rhineland back to France as part of the war reparations
   imposed on Germany in the Treaty of Versailles.

6. As a demonstration of just how important the Luftwaffe's ground
   radar capability was to them in 1944, almost one in five men in
   Luftflotte 3 worked in the radar screen.

7. Due to the risk, the Luftwaffe had suspended daylight
   reconnaissance flights over the UK as far back as August 1943.
   But just before D-Day, one of Wolff's Bf 109s did manage to
   photograph Portsmouth harbour during daylight. The British
   were ready and Squadron Leader Eric Holmes – the RAF's area
   controller for No. 11 Group – had a Free French Spitfire waiting
   to ambush the German as he came in to land at Cherbourg.

8. Hooton, E.R., *Eagle in Flames*, p282.

9. Carruthers, Bob, *Voices from the Luftwaffe*, p118.

10. Fischer, Wolfgang, *Luftwaffe Fighter Pilot – Defending the Reich*, preface.

11. Mitcham Jr, Samuel W., *Eagles of the Third Reich*, p215.

12. Hessler, Günther, edited by Carruthers, Bob, *The U-boat War in the Atlantic volume III: 1944–1945*, p172.

13. After the capture of Le Havre, the RAF sent Flight Lieutenant R.F. Delderfield to the port to compile a report on the effect of the several bombing raids made on it since D-Day. One of the witnesses Delderfield interviewed was an expatriate Englishman called Roger Loiseau who ran a hotel in the city. He stated that the attack on the night of 14 June 'killed 3,200 Germans and sank 41 U-Boats and E-Boats in the pens. 800 Germans were shot by their officers because they mutinied. Most of these men were sailors.' This seems rather unlikely and is not confirmed by German sources.

14. Cawthorne, Nigel, *Fighting them on the Beaches*, p190.

15. Interview with Helmut Schmökel in Hamburg, Germany, conducted by Stephen Ames.

5. The Battle for Caen

1. By 1945, Bill Slim's ostensibly 'British' Fourteenth Army facing the Japanese was the largest army formation in the world, with about a million men under command. The majority of its men weren't British – of its thirteen divisions only two, the 2nd and 36th Infantry, were from the home islands, but there were also tens of thousands of Britons in the army's support services, along with detached regiments and battalions salted into majority non-British units.

2. The Canadian War Crimes Commission (CWCC) spent a year from August 1944 to August 1945 investigating the war crime (and others), with Kurt Meyer the chief suspect as having given the order. He was tried in December 1945, found guilty of inciting his troops to commit murder and of being responsible as a commander for the killings. Sentenced to death on 28 December 1945; his sentence was commuted to life imprisonment in 1946. He was released in 1954. The men murdered on 7 June were North Nova Scotia Highlanders Corporal Joseph MacIntyre, and privates Ivan Crowe, Charles Doucette, Reginald Keeping and James Moss. The Sherbrooke Fusiliers were Lieutenant Thomas Windsor, and troopers James Bolt, George Gill, Thomas Henry, Roger Lockhead and Harold Philip.

3. Hastings, Max, *Overlord*, p145.

4. Ibid – p67.

5. Milano, Vince & Conner, Bruce, *Normandiefront*, p210.

6. Author interview with Andreas Fleischer.

7. Milano, Vince & Conner, Bruce, *Normandiefront*, p111.

8. Hastings, Max, *Overlord*, p66.

9. Jost, Bertrand, *This too shall come to pass*. Letter from his grandfather.

10. Milano, Vince & Conner, Bruce, *Normandiefront*, p17.

11. Villani, Gerry, *Voices of the Waffen-SS*, p146.

12. Schneid, Sadi, *SS-Beutedeutscher. Weg und Wandlung eines Elsässers*.

13. Von Luck, Hans, *Panzer Commander*, p187.

14. Hargreaves, Richard, *The Germans in Normandy*, p86.

15. Williamson, Gordon, *Loyalty is my Honour*, p86.

16. Tieke, Wilhelm, *In the Firestorm of the Last Year of the War*, p103.

17. Williamson, Gordon, *Loyalty is my Honour*, p88.

18. Ibid – p89.

19. Interview with the author.

20. Cawthorne, Nigel, *Fighting them on the Beaches*, p133.

21. One of HMS *Robert*'s monster guns can be seen today mounted outside the front of the Imperial War Museum in London.

22. Keegan, John, *Six Armies in Normandy*, p201, excerpt from Werner Kortenhaus.

23. After the war, von Rosen would go on to become a major-general in the German *Bundeswehr*, write a memoir entitled *Panzer Ace: The Memoirs of an Iron Cross Panzer Commander from Barbarossa to Normandy*, and co-write a combat history of the 503rd Heavy Panzer Battalion.

24. Williamson, Gordon, *Loyalty is my Honour*, p92.

25. Miller, Russell, *Nothing Less than Victory*, p15.

26. Cawthorne, Nigel, *Fighting them on the Beaches*, p208.

27. Hastings, Max, *Armageddon*, p93.

28. German Army intelligence report dated November 1944.

29. NAPOLA: National Political Institutes of Education. *Nationalpolitische Erziehungsanstalten*; officially abbreviated NPEA, commonly abbreviated Napola for *Nationalpolitische Lehranstalt*, meaning National Political Institution of Teaching, secondary boarding schools established to educate the future Nazi élite.

30. Villani, Gerry, interview with *HJ* soldier.
31. Interview with Erwin Bartmann.
32. Whiting, Charles, '*44*, p76.
33. Klapdor, Ewald, *Die Entscheidung: Invasion 1944.*
34. Atkinson, Rick, *The Guns at Last Light*, p97.

6. *The Battle for Saint-Lô*
 1. Cawthorne, Nigel, *Fighting them on the Beaches*, p87.
 2. Interview with Richard Onderka.
 3. Lucas, James, *Das Reich*, p135.
 4. Interview with Richard Onderka.
 5. Milano, Vince & Conner, Bruce, *Normandiefront*, p196.
 6. Whiting, Charles, '*44*, p81.
 7. Interview with Richard Onderka.
 8. Whiting, Charles, '*44*, p56.
 9. Ibid – p57.
10. Milano, Vince & Conner, Bruce, *Normandiefront*, p141.
11. Griesser, Volker, *The Lions of Carentan*, p108.
12. Ibid – p114.
13. Whiting, Charles, '*44*, p73.
14. Milano, Vince & Conner, Bruce, *Normandiefront*, p210.
15. Hargreaves, Richard, *The Germans in Normandy*, p79.
16. Atkinson, Rick, *The Guns at Last Light*, p101.
17. Ritgen, Helmut, *The Western Front, 1944: Memoirs of a Panzer Lehr Officer*, p105.
18. *Richmond Daily Dispatch*, 2 September 1861.
19. The historian Steven Zaloga stated in his 2015 work *Armored Champion: The Top Tanks of World War II*, p313, that he had analysed Allied combat reports and was unable to locate the losses claimed by Barkmann.
20. Improvised tank destroyers comprising a French Renault R-35 chassis with a Czech 4.7cm anti-tank gun.
21. Mazower, Mark, *Hitler's Empire*, p460.
22. Hargreaves, Richard, *The Germans in Normandy*, p101.
23. Eckhertz, Holger, *D-Day through German Eyes*, p221.
24. Ibid – p167.
25. Interview with Rudolf von Ribbentrop.
26. Interview with Richard Onderka. Onderka was sent to England as a POW and ended up staying in the country until he died in his 80s at home in Leicester. He never returned to Germany.
27. Griesser, Volker, *Lions of Carentan*, p126.

28. Milano, Vince & Conner, Bruce, *Normandiefront*, p209.
29. Ibid – p222.
30. Ibid – p228.
31. Ibid – p231.
32. Ibid – p246.
33. Guderian, Heinz, *Tagesbefehl* 23/07/1944.
34. Ibid – *Tagesbefehl* 29/07/1944.
35. Mazower, Mark, *Hitler's Empire*, p192.

7. *The Dam Bursts*
   1. Zaloga, Steven, *Saint-Lô 1944*, p61.
   2. For missions of under 400 miles the B17 could carry 8,000lbs instead of its more usual 4,500lbs for longer missions.
   3. Hargreaves, Richard, *The Germans in Normandy*, p167.
   4. *Ibid* – p167.
   5. Beevor, Antony, *D-Day*, p353.
   6. Griesser, Volker, *The Lions of Carentan*, p142.
   7. Hargreaves, Richard, *The Germans in Normandy*, p170.
   8. Hastings, Max, *Overlord*, p331.
   9. Hastings, Max, *Das Reich*, p237.
   10. Griesser, Volker, *The Lions of Carentan*, p149.
   11. Luck, Hans von, *Panzer Commander*, p203.
   12. Beevor, Antony, *D-Day*, p371.
   13. Finally, at the end of July, two IDs; 326. and 363. moved across the Seine but it was too little too late.
   14. Beevor, Antony, *D-Day*, p357.
   15. Griesser, Volker, *The Lions of Carentan*, p151.
   16. Galland, Adolf, *The First and the Last*, p290.
   17. Hargreaves, Richard, *The Germans in Normandy*, p201.
   18. Reynolds, Michael, *Steel Inferno: I SS Panzer Corps in Normandy*, p 218.
   19. Ibid – p220.
   20. Hastings, Max, *Overlord*, p360.
   21. Reynolds, Michael, *Steel Inferno: I SS Panzer Corps in Normandy*, p240.

8. *Falaise – the Westheer's Stalingrad*
   1. Beevor, Antony, *D-Day*, p427.
   2. *Panzergruppe West* had been renamed as 5. *Panzerarmee* in August.

3. Thorn, Manfred, *Von der Leibstandarte.*
4. Williamson, Gordon, *Loyalty is my Honour*, p96.
5. Ibid – p84.
6. Ibid – p87.
7. Reynolds, Michael, *Steel Inferno: The I SS Panzer Corps in Normandy*, p264.
8. Williamson, Gordon, *Loyalty is my Honour*, p91.
9. Reynolds, Michael, *Steel Inferno: The I SS Panzer Corps in Normandy*, p84
10. Lucas, James, *Das Reich*, p147.
11. Klapdor, Ewald, *Die Entscheidung*, p379.
12. Whiting, Charles, *'44*, p90.
13. Williamson, Gordon, *Loyalty is my Honour*, p87.
14. Ibid – p84.
15. Ibid – p96.
16. Villani, Gerry, *Voices of the Waffen-SS*, p141.
17. Williamsom, Gordon, *Loyalty is my Honour*, p89.

10. La Belle France Abandoned
1. Interview with the author.
2. Ritgen, Helmut, *The Western Front, 1944: Memoirs of a Panzer Lehr Officer*, p119.
3. Beevor, Antony, *D-Day*, p508.
4. Griesser, Volker, *The Lions of Carentan*, p154.
5. Ibid – p152.
6. Hastings, Max, *Overlord*, p406.
7. Kershaw, Robert, *It Never Snows in September*, p20.
8. Munoz, Antonio, *Iron Fist; A Combat History of the 17 SS Panzergrenadier Division "Götz von Berlichingen"*, p82.
9. Luck, Hans von, *Panzer Commander*, p207.
10. Fürbringer, Herbert, *La Hohenstaufen: 9.SS Panzer Division 1944: Normandy, Tarnapol-Arnhem*, p393.
11. According to Antony Beevor in his book *Arnhem*, Eberbach was captured in his bed and taken to Major General Pip Roberts.
12. Hargreaves, Richard, *The Germans in Normandy*, p241.
13. Williamson, Gordon, *Loyalty is my Honour*, p97.

11. Looking Back
1. Eckhertz, Holger, *D-Day through German Eyes*, p234.
2. Ibid – p109.

3. Milano, Vince & Conner, Bruce, *Normandiefront*, p164.
4. Copp, Terry (1994) *"Operation Research and 21 Army Group,"*
   Canadian Military History: Vol. 3: Iss. 1, Article 9.
5. Raus, Erhard, The *German Ordeal on the Eastern front*, *p110.*
6. Spick, Mike, *Aces of the Reich – The Making of a Luftwaffe*
   Fighter Pilot, Greenhill.
7. Cooper, Matthew & Lucas, James, *Panzer*, p77.
8. Isby, David C., ed, *Fighting the Breakount*, p75.
9. Hastings, Max, *Overlord*, pp232–3.

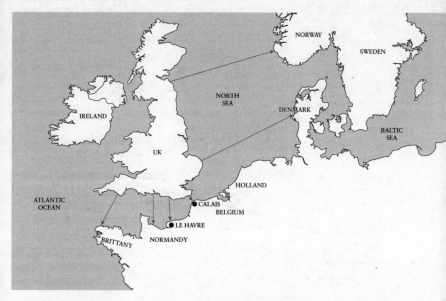

The choices for the Allies – and the reason why German forces were spread so thin.

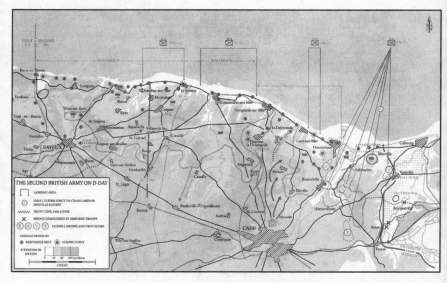

Second British Army: Gold, Juno and Sword Beaches.

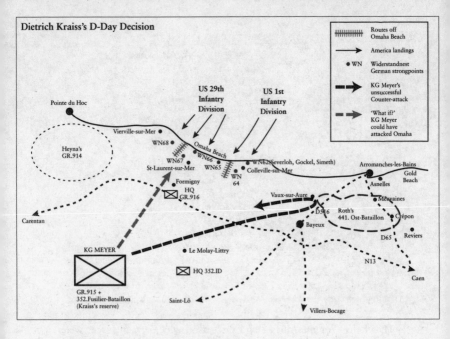

Dietrich Kraiss's D-Day Decision

Throw them back into the sea! Chapter 2.

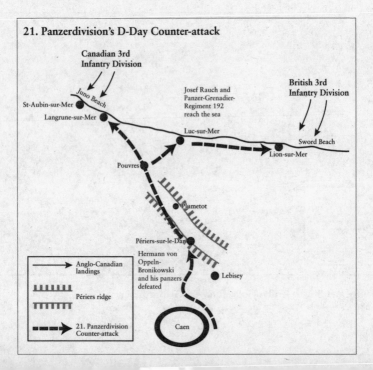

21. Panzerdivision's D-Day Counter-attack

Index